INFERNO

The Fiery Destruction of Hamburg, 1943

KEITH LOWE

Scribner

New York   London   Toronto   Sydney

SCRIBNER
1230 Avenue of the Americas
New York, NY 10020

SCRIBNER and design are trademarks of
Macmillan Library Reference USA, Inc., used under license
by Simon & Schuster, the publisher of this work.

For information about special discounts for bulk purchases,
please contact Simon & Schuster Special Sales:
1-800-456-6798 or business@simonandschuster.com

Designed by Kyoko Watanabe
Text set in Minion

Manufactured in the United States of America

1   3   5   7   9   10   8   6   4   2

Library of Congress Cataloging-in-Publication Data

Lowe, Keith, date.
Inferno : the fiery destruction of Hamburg, 1943 / Keith Lowe.
p.   cm.
Includes bibliographical references and index.
1. Hamburg (Germany)—History—Bombardment, 1940–1945. I. Title.

D757.9.H3L69 2007
940.54'2135—dc22   2006051272

ISBN-13: 978-0-7432-6901-8

The author gratefully acknowledges permission from the following source to
reprint material in their control: Faber and Faber, Inc., for an excerpt from "Give Us"
from Collected Poems by Primo Levi, translated by Ruth Feldman and Brian Swann.
English translation copyright © 1988 by Ruth Feldman and Brian Swann. Reprinted by
permission of Faber and Faber, Inc., an affiliate of Farrar, Straus and Giroux, LLC.

CONTENTS

Part III

THE AFTERMATH

Appendixes

LIST OF MAPS

INTRODUCTION

*He who fights with monsters should look to it that he himself
does not become a monster. And when you gaze long into
an abyss the abyss also gazes into you.*

—Friedrich Nietzsche[1]

In his eyewitness account of the Hamburg firestorm and its aftermath, Hans Erich Nossack admitted to feeling a mixture of awe and elation whenever he saw the fleets of British bombers flying over the city. Despite his natural fear during an air raid, he often found himself willing the bombers on, almost hoping for the opportunity to witness a truly catastrophic event. Rather than going to the shelter he would stand spellbound on his balcony watching the explosions rising above the city. He did not blame the British and American airmen for the havoc they were wreaking, but saw it rather as the inevitable expression of man's urge to destroy—an urge that was mirrored in his own morbid fascination. The fact that this fascination was accompanied by a simultaneous revulsion, both at what was happening before him and at his own emotions, did not lessen the power of his darkest cravings.[2]

There is a sense in which the whole of the Second World War can be seen as a battle between these dark cravings—the human urge to destroy and the desire to keep such instincts in check. From the victors' point of view the war has often been portrayed as an almost mythical struggle by the "free" world to rein in the destructive urges of Hitler's regime. And yet the Allies were just as destructive toward their enemies as the Axis powers ever were—necessarily so, since destruction is the very business of war. The tragedy of this particular conflict was that both sides should so completely abandon all restraint, until there was no way out of the war but by the total devastation of one side or the other.

Nowhere is this more apparent than in the bomber war. Each side began bombing with relative caution—especially the British, who promised early on that all bombing would be confined to strictly military objectives. Each side gradually descended into varying degrees of what the Germans called *Schrecklichkeit* ("frightfulness")—the deliberate terrorizing of civilian populations. And each side accompanied its bomber raids not only with increasingly bloodthirsty calls for the utter destruction of its enemy, but with jubilation whenever that destruction was partially achieved. The uncomfortable elation experienced by Nossack at the bombing of his own city was merely a token of what was happening across the whole of Europe.

At the end of the war, when things had returned to "normality," both sides tried to distance themselves from these events. This denial of the past has been most pronounced in Germany, where it seemed that the only way the population could cope with the horrors they had witnessed was to pretend they had never happened. In 1946, the Swedish journalist Stig Dagerman described traveling through the moonscape of Hamburg on a train: Despite the massive expanse of ruins not a single other passenger looked out of the window. Dagerman was immediately identified as a foreigner precisely *because* he looked out. The story is an apt metaphor for the way Germans have collectively avoided looking at the ordeal they experienced. Until recently, there have been very few German authors willing to engage emotionally with the subject, because to do so would open too many wounds. The peculiar mix of collective guilt for being a part of a nation that unleashed war upon the world, and anger at the heartlessness of their own treatment—so that they were simultaneously both perpetrators and victims of atrocity—has made it much easier simply to turn away and pretend that life continued as normal.[3]

In Britain and America there has been a corresponding avoidance of the consequences of our bombing war. We know all about what it was like for our airmen, and the bravery they displayed in the face of formidable German flak and fighter defenses is a strong part of our collective folklore. Triumphant films have been made about it, such as *The Dambusters*, or Hollywood's *Memphis Belle*. There are countless books about the airmen's experience—about the stress of waiting at dispersal, the nerves of the long flight into battle, the terror of flying through flak, or even of being shot down by fighters. This is as it should be—these are the things we did, and it is important that we remember them. But after the bombs have been dropped, and the surviving bombers have returned home, that's where the story tends to end. What happened on the ground, to the cities full of people beneath those falling bombs, is rarely talked about; even when it *is* discussed, it is usually only in terms of the buildings and factories destroyed, with only a cursory mention of civilian casualties. We, too, like to pretend that nothing terrible actually came of those bombs. (I am talking here about our *collective* consciousness. The airmen themselves are among the few of us who actually do seem to have thought about it, understood what it was they were doing, and either come to terms with it or made a conscious decision not to try to square the impossible—there was a war on, and they know what we don't, that war is a terrible thing out of which *no one* comes out looking good.)

The one exception to this rule is, of course, Dresden. The disproportional amount of attention Dresden gets is our one act of contrition for the destruction we rained down on the cities of Germany. There are various reasons why this particular city has become the emblem for our guilt—it was a truly beautiful city, the scale of its destruction within just a few days was awe-inspiring, and since it occurred toward the end of the war many people have wondered with hindsight whether it was not an unnecessary tragedy. All this is worthy of discussion, but it does not excuse our forgetfulness about other cities in Germany. What about Wuppertal, Düsseldorf, and Berlin? Berlin suffered more bombing destruction in terms of area than any other city in the war: almost four times as much as Dresden.[4] And what about Hamburg? Just as many people died in Hamburg as in Dresden, if not more, and in ways that were every bit as horrific.

In Continental Europe the destruction of Hamburg is regarded as a defining moment in the Second World War. It happened eighteen months before Dresden, at a time when much of Germany was still confident of final victory. It was a far greater shock to the system than Dresden was, unleashing almost a million refugees across a nation that had still not quite accepted the consequences of bombing. These refugees brought with them tales of unimaginable horror: fires hot enough to melt glass, a firestorm strong enough to uproot trees and hurl them into the flames, and rumors of 200,000 people killed within the space of just a few days and nights (although in fact the total was more like 45,000).

I have been consistently surprised by the general ignorance of these facts among my own countrymen. In the course of the two years of writing this book I have come across very few people outside the world of military historians who knew that Hamburg was ever bombed at all, let alone the sheer scale of the destruction that took place. On the Continent the bombing of Hamburg is a byword for horror, and yet in Britain few people know it even happened. In North America, too, there is widespread ignorance of the basic facts, although to some extent America's geographical and emotional distance from Hamburg excuses this. Even those who have heard of the Hamburg firestorm are generally unaware of its ghastly human consequences.

The main purpose of this book is to put this right. My intention is to convey the events as they appeared at the time, not only to the British and American airmen who fought their way across the skies of Europe, but to the people of Hamburg who became the victims of their bombs. Hamburg was a handsome and prosperous city before it was destroyed, and I will explain some of the city's history in Part I, and try to re-create the atmosphere in this *Hansestadt* in the years leading up to 1943. The logic is that it is only by knowing what was there before the bombing that we can truly appreciate what was lost—both physically and psychologically. I have devoted several chapters to the immediate and long-term aftermath of the firestorm because this has never adequately been described before, in Germany or abroad. The effect of the catastrophe on the German people, and on Germany itself, was extremely far-reaching, and continues to cause controversy today.

The second purpose of this book is to try to correct the erroneous belief that war is somehow a glorious or heroic undertaking. During the course of my research I have interviewed dozens of bomber veterans, and they are unanimous on this point: There is nothing glorious about sitting in a Lancaster or a B-17 bomber for upward of five hours, in the freezing temperatures of the upper atmosphere, waiting to see if you will live to return home safely. At best it is dull, at its worst it can be utterly terrifying: The rare moments of exhilaration are insignificant compared to this.

There is nothing glorious about being bombed, either, as the British learned during the Blitz when over 40,000 British civilians were killed. The most infamous German raid was on the city of Coventry, where local industries, civilian houses, and historic buildings in the center of the city were completely devastated. In their collective imagination this is what British people believe it must have been like for the Germans—a little like Coventry, or perhaps slightly worse. This is a false impression. What happened in Essen, Bochum, Düsseldorf, and the other cities around the river Ruhr was like two years of Coventrys, night after night after night. Coventry suffered only a single major bombing raid—Essen was bombed on a much larger scale, twenty-eight times. Hamburg is on another level altogether. What happened in Hamburg is more accurately compared to Hiroshima or Nagasaki.[5]

Until recently America did not really know what it was like to be bombed at all. Geographically remote from any hostile neighbors, the United States has always enjoyed almost total immunity from air attack,[6] and until a few years ago it had never been seriously threatened. The shock was therefore all the greater when a group of Al Qaeda terrorists flew two commercial airliners into the World Trade Center on September 11, 2001. The sheer horror of this action still consumes Americans with righteous indignation—and so it should—but tragic as this event was, it was essentially only the destruction of a handful of buildings. True, almost 3,000 people perished, but imagine the sense of awe, of shock, if it had been the whole of Lower Manhattan that had been destroyed. Imagine an area from the tip of the island all the way up to Madison Square entirely consumed by a *single* fire, and the rest of the city as far as Central Park reduced to rubble. What would have been America's reaction if the death toll had not been 2,800, but ten times that number, fifteen times? Imagine eight square miles of the city without a single building left standing—mountains of rubble literally as far as the eye can see, corpses littering the streets, the smell of decay pervading everything. This is what happened in Hamburg in the summer of 1943.

This book would not have been possible without the help of scores of former Allied airmen and German civilians who consented to be interviewed. Their willingness to share their diaries and to rake over painful memories from more than sixty years ago has been quite humbling, and I can only thank them for the patience with which they answered my questions. I am aware that there is something distasteful about some of the questions I was obliged to ask, especially in the specific details I demanded. Indeed, when interviewing people who lived through the firestorm I often found myself experiencing a mixture of emotions similar to that described by Nossack as he watched the bombers fly over his city—excitement at the prospect of gathering good material, a perverse hope that their descriptions would become even more graphic, and a faint sense of shame at the inappropriateness of my enthusiasm. Writing about catastrophe (or, for that matter, reading about it) is not the same as experiencing it, and there is inevitably something voyeuristic about examining someone else's misery in this sort of detail. I hope, therefore, that this book will convey not merely my own uncomfortable fascination at the terrifying stories these people told me, but also the lingering feeling of revulsion they have communicated to me at the human cost of war.

There is no space here to list the scores of people and institutions on both sides of the Atlantic who have helped me over the past few years. Some of them are named in an Acknowledgments section at the end of this book, but this cannot do justice to the enormous contribution these people have made, or to their selfless enthusiasm for my project. There are, however, a handful of people who deserve special mention. First and foremost I am deeply indebted to Mirko Hohmann and Malte Thießen for sharing their knowledge of the German sources, and for looking after me on my various trips to Hamburg. Paul Wolf was a huge help in gathering elusive American material, and Sonia Stammwitz helped with the translation of some of the denser German documents, as did Jenny Piening and Sylvia Goulding. Ion Trewin and Ian Drury both took time out of their busy schedules to read early drafts of the manuscript, and their comments were extremely useful. I am tremendously grateful to my agents Simon Trewin, Claire Scott, Nicki Kennedy, and Dan Mandel, and to my editors Eleo Gordon and Lisa Drew: Without their support this book would never even have been started.

Last I must thank Liza and Gabriel for giving me a reason to leave my study each evening, and lock away the terrible stories and photographs that have been my companions by day. Several years of research into some of the most frightening events of the twentieth century have taught me not to take their presence for granted.

Keith Lowe, 2007

AUTHOR'S NOTE

According to the old adage, Britain and America are two nations divided by a common tongue, and nowhere was this more apparent than in the different terminology that the two air forces employed to describe the same things. To avoid confusion I have used British terminology to describe the British "operations," and American terminology to describe their "missions." For a comparison of different terms, please see Appendix D.

On the whole I have used German sources to describe the German experience, but on one or two occasions I have turned to existing English translations out of necessity. For those who are interested in further study, there is a substantial Notes section at the back of this book—but this should not be necessary for the general reader.

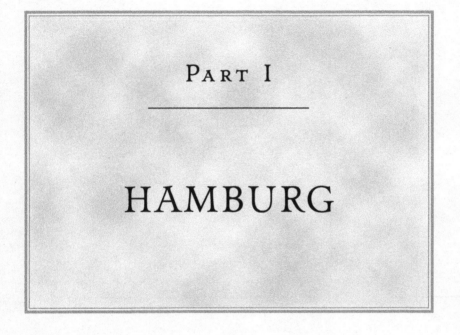

PART I

HAMBURG

Chapter 1

CITY ON THE RIVER

Wherever there's trade, there tread Hamburgers.

—HAMBURG SAYING,
MID-NINETEENTH CENTURY[1]

The city of Hamburg lies on the banks of the river Elbe in northern Germany, about sixty miles from the coast of the North Sea. In truth, it is not a very hospitable place to found a city. Situated on a fluvial plain, most of the ground is little better than a marsh, and it is prone to flooding. Ever since the area was first settled the city fathers have fought a constant battle against the storms and tides that regularly cause the waters of the river to rise and break their banks. The threat extends far beyond the city boundaries. For mile after mile the earth lies flat, perhaps rises a little, and then is flat again, providing scant protection from the whims of the river. In times of flood the entire area becomes submerged: farmland, docklands, parks, city streets, and houses—all are ruined. When eventually the water subsides it leaves behind it a blanket of silt covering the city and countryside alike, reducing everything to a dull, muddy uniformity.

There is nothing to protect the city from the weather either. No mountains infringe on the curve of the horizon, or provide a break to the prevailing winds rolling in from the North Sea. The moist sea air produces huge banks of cloud, which smother the region for most of the year, bringing frequent rain and occasionally sleet and snow. In winter, if the wind changes direction and blows in from the Baltic, temperatures plummet, and drift ice begins to appear on the river. Even in summer the nights can be cold and wet, and the temperature rarely reaches the highs that other parts of Europe experience.

The element that most dominates the city is water. The river Elbe is its life blood, linking it to the North Sea and trade routes across the globe. At

3

the city's core is a second river, the Alster, which, since it was dammed in 1235, has formed two large lakes right in the city center. To the east, elaborate networks of canals creep like tentacles into the city's warehouse and workers' districts. To the south, in the midst of the Elbe itself, lie a series of islands that have been linked together over the centuries into a vast complex of docks and waterways: this is Hamburg's harbor, one of the largest ports in the world, and the watery foundation of all the city's considerable prosperity.

Apart from its harbor, Hamburg is an unremarkable place. Unlike Dresden, which lies a couple of hundred miles upstream, it has never been considered a jewel, and its architecture is generally functional rather than ornate. Its handful of city churches have none of the scale and grandeur of other German cathedrals, like that at Cologne. There are no palaces or castles here like those in Berlin, or Potsdam, or Munich; in fact, the grandest houses the city has to offer are the upper-middle-class villas along the Elbe Chaussee. The city boasts more bridges than Venice, but that is where the comparison ends, and not even its most enthusiastic citizens would pretend otherwise. Few pleasure boats travel the city's many canals, hardly any of the buildings are more than sixty years old, and the sound of voices and footfalls is drowned by the noise of traffic flowing down the six-lane highways that scar the city in all directions.

Even before the Second World War, Hamburg was never really considered a destination for sightseers. Even then, the historic center of the city was not particularly historic, since most of it had been destroyed by fire less than a century before, and the few tourists who came to this part of Germany generally preferred the picturesque town center of nearby Lübeck. Neither is it particularly considered a city of culture. Hamburg did not have a university until after the First World War, and while the Musikhalle and the Hamburg Opera are much admired by the middle classes, the city has always been better-known for the more low-brow pleasures to be found on the Reeperbahn in the St. Pauli district.

To their credit, the people of Hamburg have never much cared about the lack of superlatives connected to their city: They are proud of what they do have, and unconcerned about what they do not. They are a tough, practical people, accustomed to dealing with challenges and to making the best of any situation that fate might throw at them. Over the past two centuries they have seen their city ravaged in turn by epidemics of cholera, by famine, by economic recession and unemployment, and of course by flooding. The town center has been destroyed by fire not once but four times—despite the huge quantities of water that seem to dominate the city's open spaces.[2] In the face of such a history it is little wonder that there are so few ancient architectural gems here.

However, the lack of grand monuments in the city cannot be blamed entirely on natural disasters: It is also the result of an inherent reserve that has deep roots in the city's mentality. For more than eight hundred years Hamburg has been a place of merchants, and the centuries have carved it into a middle-class rather than an aristocratic city. The town center is dominated by the towers of that most bourgeois of German buildings, the Rathaus (or town hall). It sits before a large piazza, where Adolf Hitler once addressed a crowd of over 20,000 people, overlooking the great Alster lakes. The streets around the Rathaus are filled with exactly the kind of buildings one would expect in a city of merchants: shops, office buildings, and, a little farther south, the warehouse district of the Speicherstadt. The only towers to break the skyline, apart from those of the Rathaus, are the spires of the city's five main churches.

As for the rest of Hamburg, it is generally a green, pleasant place to live. To the west of the city are the tree-lined boulevards of Eimsbüttel, Eppendorf, and Harvestehude, with their tall, elegant apartment buildings and rows of flower-filled balconies. To the north, the leafy suburbs of Winterhude, Barmbek, and Alsterdorf cluster round the huge Stadtpark. Farther north still, in Ohlsdorf, the greenery conceals the largest cemetery in Europe: four square miles of gravestones among well-tended gardens.

The working-class districts have traditionally been confined to the east of the city, in suburbs like Hammerbrook, Hamm, Rothenburgsort, and Billbrook. Here low-rise apartment blocks have always crammed high concentrations of people within easy commuting distance of the docks and warehouses. There is nothing here—not a building, not a tree, not a lamppost, not even a street sign—that is more than sixty years old. In some areas even the people have moved away. In Hammerbrook, for example, there are few apartments, only offices and warehouses, garages and depots. After office hours, the only human beings that walk along Süderstrasse are the prostitutes trying to attract the attention of one of the occasional passing cars. In the smaller streets even these signs of life are missing, and the whole area lies silent.

While the historic center of the city might lie on the north shore of the Elbe, it is the harbor that is its true heart. The industrial landscape here is vast and impressive, and has a savage beauty unparalleled by any other place in Germany. Formations of cranes stretch as far as the eye can see, towering above the warehouses and the dry docks of Hamburg's shipbuilding companies like the silent regiments of some huge mechanical army. The many-colored blocks of transport containers rise in mountains from the quayside, dwarfing the trucks and railway trains that come from all over Europe to collect them. Their reflection stains the gray waters of the Elbe with every color of the rainbow.

When the population of Hamburg gathers each May at the Landungsbrücken to celebrate the official birthday of the harbor, they are not merely giving thanks for the wealth that floods in through its gates. The harbor is more than just a source of jobs and economic prosperity: It has provided Hamburg with its very identity as a city of trade. Because of it, Hamburg has been known for centuries as Germany's gateway to the world.

According to tradition, the harbor was founded over 800 years ago, in 1189, when the emperor Frederick Barbarossa granted Hamburgers the right to duty-free trade all along the Lower Elbe as far as the sea. With such an advantage over their neighbors, the city's merchants soon managed to build Hamburg into a major trading center. By 1242 the city was powerful enough to draw up an agreement with nearby Lübeck, thus forming the template for the Hanseatic League. This alliance brought them major trading partners right across the region—not only in Germany, but also in Bruges, Amsterdam, London, and even as far away as Novgorod—making this marshy, watery city one of the wealthiest in Europe.[3]

By the sixteenth century Hamburg was nothing short of a huge, city-wide storehouse, holding vast quantities of goods for resale throughout Europe. Tall warehouses stacked with grain, oil, salt, and beer rose out of the narrow canals and waterways that carried the tide of commodities right into the heart of the city. The more expensive goods, such as honey, fine wines, and amber, were stored on the higher floors to keep them safe from the floodwaters of the Elbe, while the lower floors were reserved for cheaper goods such as fish or lumber. With the discovery of the New World, local merchants who had made themselves rich by trading in cloth or foodstuffs soon began to trade in precious gems and metals, saltpeter, coffee, tea, tobacco, and exotic spices. One of the most lucrative cargoes was peppercorns, which Hamburg's spice traders brought back in sackloads from the Orient. Even today, the wealthier citizens of Hamburg are still occasionally called *Pfeffersäcke* ("peppersacks")—a derogatory nickname for fat-cat businessmen.

The city's residents lived in similarly tall houses, rising above the squalid streets like warehouses of humanity, storing workers for use in the busy port. In such cramped conditions hygiene was impossible, disease was rife, and life expectancy short. Despite the ubiquitous waterways, fire was a very real danger. In 1284 the entire city had been completely destroyed by a huge fire that, according to tradition, left only a single building standing. In 1684, after a series of smaller fires, a second conflagration destroyed 214 houses. Nearby Altona also suffered a major fire in 1711, followed by the deliberate burning of two-thirds of the city by Swedish troops two years later.[4] After each catastrophe, the city was rebuilt with houses even taller and more densely occupied than before.

In among this jumble of homes and warehouses were also small islands of industry—tanneries, weaving houses, potteries, breweries, and shipbuilders. Some of the most important industries for the city were brought here by outsiders. Hamburgers first learned the art of sugar refining from the Dutch, and by the early 1600s Hamburg was one of the biggest exporters of refined sugar in the world. Dutch immigrants also brought the velvet and silk trades to the city. The French brought new baking techniques, and *Franzbrötchen* are still something of a city specialty. Greenlanders brought their skill in extracting oil from whale blubber and set up a whole district of workshops in Hamburger Berg (now St. Pauli): The glut of train oil they produced meant that the citizens of Hamburg could afford to put lanterns along the major streets, making this one of the first cities ever to have street lighting.[5]

As a maritime power, Hamburg has always teemed with such foreigners, and the face of the city seems to have changed with every new influx of immigrants. It was not only the sailors and adventurers who settled here, drawn to Hamburg along the world's trade routes in search of a better life; refugees also came. While the rest of Europe was persecuting its religious minorities, Protestant Hamburg tended to extend a cautious welcome to anyone who brought in new money or new trades. In the sixteenth century Jews from Spain and Portugal settled here after being expelled from their own countries and built one of the largest Jewish communities in Europe. Dutch Calvinists found safety here from the Catholic armies of Philip II, and came to dominate the city's foreign trade. Later, Huguenots would flee here after the purges in France, as would aristocrats after the French Revolution. Hamburg fast became one of the most cosmopolitan places in Europe, a Renaissance Babel where English gentlemen and French princes knocked shoulders with Finnish sailors, Brazilian rubber merchants, and the countless migrants from Mecklenburg and Schleswig-Holstein who flocked here to try to take a tiny share of the city's considerable fortune.

Hamburg has always been like this: hardworking, multifarious, and quick to embrace new ideas. Throughout its history, the only constant has been change. Buildings rise, are demolished by fire or flood, and are rebuilt: Whole suburbs are regularly created and destroyed. The population comes and goes from all over the world, creating distinct communities that flourish for a few generations before dispersing once more as they are integrated into the whole. This is natural to Hamburgers, and continues to this day.

Even the river is not constant. Before the Second World War, parts of it often became so silted up that it caused problems for the ever-larger ships that traveled in and out of the harbor with the tides, and specialist pilots had to be used to guide foreign ships to the safety of their berths. Sometimes whole islands of silt would form in the center of the river; for months, or even years, they would give the illusion of solidity, before the waters rose once more and they were swept away toward the sea.

Chapter 2

THE ANGLOPHILE CITY

I am the enemy you killed, my friend.

—WILFRED OWEN[1]

Through its trade links, Hamburg has developed associations with many countries over the centuries, but there are two relationships that are particularly interesting, especially when considering the events of the Second World War. Hamburg's connections with Britain and America go beyond that of mere trading partners: Somehow these two English-speaking nations seem to have found their way beneath Hamburg's skin. This is particularly the case with the British—or, more specifically, the English. Even during the height of the war Hamburg still thought of itself as an anglophile city, and it was not until the dreadful events of July 1943 that Hitler's propaganda minister was able to note with wry satisfaction that the city was at last learning to hate its English cousins.[2]

Hamburg's ties to England were extremely deep-rooted and remain close to this day. As part of the Hanseatic League, the city has been trading with London ever since the thirteenth century. The first English company to set up a permanent office in the city was the Merchant Adventurers Company in the sixteenth century. It was followed by other English merchants, trading wool and fine English cloth for Continental wine, linen, and timber, and by 1600 Britain had established itself as a significant trading partner.

As Britain's power grew, it became increasingly important for the city to maintain a good relationship with its neighbors across the North Sea. This was not always easy. For example, when Dutch men-of-war attacked British merchant ships in the Elbe in 1666 the British blamed Hamburg for allowing the warships passage, and insisted on compensation. The lawsuit between them continued for four years, but when Britain eventually

9

threatened reprisals against the city there was nothing the burghers could do but resort to the centuries-old tradition of buying their way out of trouble. There was no question of Hamburg standing its ground: The city had only two warships at the time, which it used for escorting convoys, while the British navy consisted of 173 ships, equipped with 6,930 guns.[3]

Hamburg's precarious relationship with Britain blundered on, with various minor mishaps along the way, until the end of the eighteenth century. Then, in the 1790s, the city unwittingly found itself embroiled in a dispute between France and England, and its relationship with both countries rapidly degenerated. The dispute centered on Napper Tandy, the leader of the ill-fated Irish revolt against the British, who had fled to Hamburg in 1798 with three of his comrades. The British legation demanded that Hamburg hand the rebels over, but the French envoy objected, arguing that to do so would be a violation both of Hamburg's neutrality and of international law. France was at war with virtually the whole of Europe at the time, including Britain, and would not tolerate any action that could be considered pro-British.

After a month of negotiations over the prisoners, Britain finally threatened military action. To emphasize the point, she seized several ships sailing under the Hamburg flag and stationed a blockade at the mouth of the Elbe. Left with no choice, in 1799 the Hamburg authorities handed over the prisoners. The French, under Napoleon, were furious at what they saw as a betrayal of Hamburg's neutral status, and immediately set up a complete embargo of goods traded from the city. In the end Hamburg was allowed to buy its way out of trouble once again, by paying the French Republic a huge four million livres in compensation. But Napoleon remained angry, and vowed to bring the city of Hamburg to heel.[4]

Finding itself on the wrong side of Napoleon turned out to be one of the biggest mistakes in the city's history. Ever since the fourteenth century its policy of strict neutrality had, by and large, been respected by the other nations of Europe. As a consequence, Hamburg had managed to avoid the many wars that had repeatedly devastated other cities in the region over the past four hundred years. But Napoleon was determined to build an empire and had no intention of allowing this city-state to continue trading with his enemies, regardless of whether they did so under a neutral banner or not.

The first stage of Hamburg's downfall occurred in 1801, when the Danes, who had allied themselves to the French, finally accomplished what they had been threatening for centuries: They occupied the city. Their intention was only to disrupt British trade, and they only stayed for two months, but it emphasized Hamburg's powerlessness in the face of a sizable army. It also showed what the French and Danes thought of the "neutrality" of Hamburg's relationship with the British.

Five years later, in October 1806, Napoleon's army finally defeated the Prussians at Jena and Auerstadt. With the removal of the main power-brokers on the continent, there was nothing to stop Napoleon marching all the way to the Baltic. A month later, on November 19, 3,000 French troops entered Hamburg.

In truth, Napoleon was not much interested in Hamburg: It was merely a pawn in a much larger game with the British, his other major enemy. Almost the first thing the French did after invading the city was to confiscate all British property, and to burn British wares in a huge bonfire on the island of Grasbrook. City merchants were told to declare all profits made by trading with Britain, and all correspondence with France's enemy was immediately banned. The British responded by blockading the entire European continent, cutting off Hamburg from all foreign trade. It was disastrous for the city: within a short time its economy was wrecked, and its people left virtually destitute. Four years later, on December 10, 1810, the French completed the process by disbanding the Hamburg city guard and officially annexing Hamburg into the French empire.

The city was to remain in French hands until May 1814, when Marshal Davout finally surrendered to the British/Prussian allies. By this time Hamburg was ruined: Its once hugely profitable trading houses lay bankrupt, its banks out of business, its industries destroyed, and its population on the brink of starvation. Hamburg's ancient talent for rebuilding and reinventing itself out of every disaster had been stifled, and for a while it seemed as though the city would be unable to recover. But help was on its way, and from an unlikely source. After contributing to the city's downfall, it was Britain that came to Hamburg's rescue. In the following years dozens of British firms opened up branches in Hamburg, providing much-needed jobs for the residents. Penniless Hamburg merchants became commissioning and transport agents for the British, and within a short time the port was trading once more. The city was grateful. It was this era, more than any other in Hamburg's history, that would lay the foundations for the city's love affair with Britain that continues to this day.

The following decades reflected the new balance of control in the city, as trades opened up with British markets in mind. The first steamship to drop anchor in Hamburg's harbor was a British one, and by 1825 there was a regular passenger service to Britain. This was followed by trade services to several British colonies and protectorates, such as Sierra Leone and Zanzibar, and in 1851 Godeffroy & Woermann began the city's first-ever trade service to Australia. The world was once again unfurling before Hamburg, but it was a world in which Britain was the undisputed superpower.

While trade increased exponentially in the decades after the Napoleonic Wars, the vast majority of the ships that anchored in the harbor were British. In 1835 only 14 percent of them flew the flag of Hamburg.[5] This did not change until after 1850 when Hamburg became a major center of shipbuilding in its own right, and giant German shipyards such as Blohm & Voss and Howaldtswerke began to transform the south shores of the Elbe into a center of industry. New freight companies were also founded, such as Ferdinand Laeisz's Flying P Line and the Hamburg-Amerikanische Packetfahrt-Actien-Gesellschaft (HAPAG), which was soon to become the biggest shipping company in the world.

Despite this renaissance of German trade and industry there remained a distinctly British atmosphere about Hamburg right up until the Second World War. Hamburg's relationship with Britain was not merely economic, it was personal. After centuries of trading with one another, wealthy patricians from Hamburg often sent their sons to England to spend half a year or so among the English, and there were many personal friendships that stretched across the North Sea. These were not confined to the rich city merchants—tradesmen, students, and even dock workers had close relationships with their counterparts in Britain.[6] There were links with the English at all levels of Hamburg society, and by the middle of the twentieth century Hamburg was universally known in Germany as "the anglophile city"—a fact that would appear painfully ironic after the events of 1943.

Hamburg's relationship with America was of a very different nature from that with Britain. If Britain had treated the city rather paternally in the years after the Napoleonic Wars, America would treat it more like an equal partner: Right from the start, each side saw the other as an unmissable opportunity to get rich quick. While Hamburg's relationship with Britain had taken centuries to mature, that with America was virtually love at first sight. Within just ten years of opening formal relations, America had overtaken the Mediterranean as a trade destination; within fifty years it had overtaken most of Hamburg's traditional partners. From now on, the city would increasingly turn away from its European brothers and sisters, and devote much more effort to its new relationship across the Atlantic.

Like most other countries, Hamburg did not have any kind of association with the American states before 1783, for the simple reason that they were a British monopoly, so trade with them was effectively closed. After America won its independence, however, the city of Hamburg was among the first to send the fledgling nation its best wishes, and to propose a trading relationship. Within a very short time, Hamburg merchants like Voght & Sieveking were sending ships across the Atlantic with their holds full of Westphalian and Silesian textiles, and returning with all those commodities that had proved so lucrative for British traders over the preceding decades: rice, sugar, cocoa, coffee, cotton, and, of course, tobacco.

The links between Hamburg and America were based on the huge volume of trade that passed between them, but over time a much more personal side to the relationship evolved. In the second half of the nineteenth century one of the city's biggest exports to the United States was not ceramics or textiles or glassware, but people. America was opening up as a land of opportunity, and thousands of Germans were emigrating there each year in search of a better life—many of them Hamburgers.

Despite the great wealth of certain sections of the community on the Elbe, poverty was common,[7] and for many in Hamburg's slum districts the temptation to start afresh on the other side of the Atlantic proved irresistible. It was not a decision that was made lightly. Traveling to America was a desperate business, and conditions during the long sea voyage were comparable to those in eighteenth-century slave ships. Travelers would be crammed into a dark hold with barely anything to eat and only half a pint of water to drink each day. There was little sanitation, no doctors, and after seventy days at sea it was not uncommon for diseases like typhoid or cholera to have claimed up to a fifth of the passengers. For those who survived, conditions on the other side of the Atlantic were often only marginally better than those they had left at home, but a large proportion did find a better life, and the letters they sent back were enough to inspire yet more people to make the journey.

By 1866 there were more than 14,000 people traveling from Hamburg to America each year. They came from all over northern Europe—even from as far away as Russia—but many also came from Hamburg itself. A faster, more reliable steam service now navigated the route, and companies like HAPAG were growing rich on the hopes and dreams of this constant stream of emigrants to the United States.[8] Later on, even members of the middle and upper classes were making the journey across the Atlantic, this time on luxury cruise liners. At the turn of the century, the biggest passenger ships could make the crossing in under six days. There was even talk of flying Zeppelins across the ocean, and Hamburg was a major center of Germany's growing aircraft industry.[9]

By the early 1900s there was not a single community in northern Germany that was untouched by emigration to the United States. The emigrants' presence was felt in North America, too. At the outbreak of war in 1914, the German population of the United States was so large that the Canadians were induced to take precautions against the possibility of cross-border attacks.[10] In Hamburg almost everyone had friends or relations in America—after all, the majority of emigrants to the United States had embarked on their journeys from this very port.

Chapter 3

CITY OF REBELLION

*All that is solid melts into air, all that is holy is profaned, and
man is at last compelled to face with sober senses, his real
conditions of life, and his relations with his kind.*

—KARL MARX[1]

At the outbreak of the First World War Hamburg was no longer recognizable as the small city that had been invaded by Napoleon just a hundred years before. The Industrial Revolution had transformed it into a metropolis for the region: It was now the second-biggest manufacturing center in Germany after Berlin, and the third-largest port in the world after London and New York. The constant influx of immigrants had brought the population over the one million mark and forced the city to expand well beyond its medieval city walls. Whole new suburbs had been built to house the city's workers—while others had been demolished to make way for a brand-new warehouse district, the Speicherstadt. It was home to a whole variety of heavy industries—not just shipbuilding, but engineering and electrical companies, oil refineries, asbestos factories, as well as coffee-roasting and rice mills—and one of the most prosperous places in the whole German Reich.

After four years of fighting, however, virtually all of this had been ruined. Not only had the city sacrificed 40,000 of its young men to the trenches, but the rest of the population was now starving. The British blockade of the German coastline had caused shortages across the country, but in Hamburg this was compounded by the effect it had on the city's economy. Trade was the oil that kept Hamburg working, and once starved of trade the whole city began to fall apart: Industries failed, food and fuel became desperately scarce, and the people became increasingly angry at the military regime that was responsible for their hardship. The atmosphere of Hanseatic

15

conservatism that had characterized the city for hundreds of years was rapidly being replaced by radicalism, and strikes and protests were erupting all along the lower reaches of the Elbe.

Things finally came to a head in November 1918, shortly before the Armistice was signed, when Admiral Hipper ordered his ships out on one final desperate attack on the British Grand Fleet. The sailors at the naval bases of Kiel and Wilhelmshaven saw this as a pointless suicide mission, and promptly mutinied. The uprising quickly spread across northern Germany, and on November 5 workers at several of Hamburg's shipyards voted to strike in sympathy with the sailors. At first the city council managed to pacify them, but that evening 10,000 workers attended a meeting of the radical Independent Social Democratic Party (USDP) and agreed to hold a general strike throughout the city. During the night groups of sailors occupied key strategic positions in the city—the Elbetunnel, the main station, the union buildings, and the city barracks—and even boarded torpedo boats in the harbor to disarm them. The following morning a crowd of some 40,000 workers and soldiers marched on the General Command in Altona, and effectively seized power over the whole of the Hamburg area.[2]

By the time Germany accepted the Allies' armistice terms on November 11, Hamburg, along with many other cities, was already in the hands of revolutionaries. The consequences of this fact were enormous. In later years, when relative order had once more been restored, many Germans would come to remember the end of the war not as a time of defeat at the hands of the Allies—after all, the Allied armies had never even reached German soil—but as a period when their country had collapsed from within. With the passing of time, the Germans began to believe that they had not actually lost the war at all, but had merely been betrayed by their own people. As the General Paul von Hindenburg himself said, his army had not been defeated, but "stabbed in the back."[3]

In reality, the November revolution had little or no effect on the outcome of the war, which had already been lost on the battlefield. Nor was it a particularly violent revolution. The transfer of power from the old elite to the new republic was relatively peaceful—it was not until well after the war was over that the real problems began. During the winter of 1918–19 the well-ordered society that Germans thought they knew seemed to vanish. In the face of drastic shortages of food and fuel, crime levels began to soar.

Violence became increasingly common, inflation spiraled out of control, and transport difficulties made Germans' lives thoroughly miserable.

In Hamburg there was a complete breakdown of the social order. Gangs roamed the city, and there were frequent gun battles in the streets after dark. Communist riots under a man named Spartacus had broken out in the city. One British observer witnessed a particularly brutal scene at around this time. Leslie Hollis was a Royal Marine stationed in Hamburg as part of a force brought in to oversee German war reparations in the city, when he found himself caught up in the chaos.

The weak German Government was powerless to restore order. Disgraceful scenes were witnessed. People suspected of being war profiteers were paraded naked round the city in tumbrils, the womenfolk being allowed the dignity of girdles of dead rats. I remember a deplorable scene by the beautiful Alster Lake in the centre of the city. The Spartacists had captured some of their political opponents. They were thrown into the lake and told to swim for it. As soon as they had reached a distance of imagined safety they were shot from the shore. We were powerless to act because this was a domestic affair. Retribution for the Spartacists was very swift.[4]

By April 1919 food was so hard to come by that people began breaking into shops and storehouses to feed themselves. On one occasion some 2,000 men tried to storm a warehouse on Markusstrasse and had to be fought back by policemen under the cover of machine-gun fire. Police stations themselves came under attack from gangs trying to obtain firearms. On June 23, after learning that one of the city's factories had been manufacturing products out of meat that had gone bad, thousands rioted in the streets, looted shops, and even tried to storm the town hall. The whole of Hamburg was living in a virtual state of siege, and relative order was not properly restored until General Lettow-Vorbeck's *Freikorps* finally occupied the city in July and imposed martial law.[5]

In such an atmosphere, it is not surprising that political extremism gained a strong foothold in the city. When so much of the city was going hungry, groups from the far left felt they had a perfect right to plunder stockpiles of food and fuel in the city's warehouses. Conversely, groups on the far right were in favor of extreme measures to bring the looters under control. The *Freikorps*, for example, had no compunction about suppressing real or supposed threats to the government in an extremely brutal and bloody manner. Originally set up to bolster the police, the *Freikorps* was a volunteer military organization that was often little better than a coalition of vigilante groups. It was a magnet for disaffected youth and bitter ex-soldiers alike, and served as a training ground for many of those who would reappear as Nazis in the following years.[6]

However, the extremist group with by far the largest following in Hamburg was the Communists. Political groups from the far left had a long history in the city. While the union movement had been fighting for important labor reforms in the second half of the nineteenth century, there were always more radical wings of the movement that believed the only way for workers to win a fair deal was to seize power for themselves. With the revolution of November 1918 they finally got their way, and ruled the city for several months as the Workers' and Soldiers' Council. After the election of March 16, 1919, they handed power back to the city parliament, but there were always radical groups who wanted to seize it again, and it was not long before they tried. On October 23, 1923, at around five o'clock in the morning, hundreds of Communists attacked Hamburg police stations in a desperate attempt to gain control of the city by force. Led by the Communist leader Ernst Thälmann, the uprising centered on the workers' suburbs of Eimsbüttel, Barmbek, Schiffbek, and Bergedorf. In the end they failed, but not without much loss of life on both sides: seventeen policemen and sixty-one Communists were killed in the fighting, and a further 321 people were wounded. In the aftermath of the rebellion almost a thousand people were arrested.[7]

In the following years the atmosphere in Hamburg began at last to calm down. Although Ernst Thälmann retained his seat in the Hamburg parliament, the Communists never managed to come close to ousting the more moderate Social Democratic Party (SPD), and the traditional conservatism of the Hanseatic temperament began gradually to reassert itself. Slowly but surely, prosperity returned to the city. Despite the severe restrictions of the Treaty of Versailles,[8] Hamburg's good links with Britain and America gave it access to capital on favorable terms, and the city was able to recover much more quickly than the rest of Germany. By the end of the 1920s company business was flourishing once more, and the average worker was back to earning his prewar wages. While a current of radicalism still flowed beneath the surface, an air of relative contentment had returned to the city.

Unfortunately, this period of relative stability came to an end during the winter of 1929–30, when the whole world was plunged into an economic slump. As global prices went into free fall, and exports shrank to almost nothing, Hamburg's fragile economy began once more to collapse. Within two years unemployment levels had reached almost 40 percent, and political radicalism returned. The only difference was that this time it was not the Communists who attracted the protest vote. Radicalism in the 1930s would wear an altogether different face.

Chapter 4

THE RISE OF THE NAZIS

Clear the streets for the brown battalions,
clear the streets for the Storm Trooper . . .

—1930S NAZI PARTY SONG[1]

In the summer of 1930 an event took place in Hamburg that would soon become a local legend. On August 19 about 200 people gathered at the Am Stadtpark beer hall in Winterhude to attend an election meeting of the Nazi Party. It was an impressive turnout for a minority party. Ever since the recession had taken hold, the Nazis had been enjoying increasing support in Hamburg, and there were people here from all different sections of society. They were expecting speeches—the usual anti-Semitic, anti-Marxist, antiliberal invective—followed by a debating session, and then perhaps a drink in the adjoining pub before returning home to bed. Tonight, however, there had been rumors that the local Communist Party was planning to disrupt the meeting. As a consequence the arriving audience was greeted by bands of Nazi storm troopers, who had been called in to "protect" the meeting in case of a fracas. As the audience took their seats there was a distinct sense of unease in the air.

The meeting started without any disturbance, and for a while it looked as though the rumors were unfounded. But at 9:00 P.M. the door of the beer hall flew open and a large man entered, claiming to be a member of the "Red Front"—a militant wing of the Communist Party. He was followed by a long chain of others: "Tall chaps; fists of iron; splendid men. The best of the Hamburg Communist Party."[2] Fifty or so of these "Red Marines" took their seats in the audience, and a similar number went to stand in a corner at the back of the room, beside an open window.

At first their presence did little to disrupt the meeting, and the speeches went ahead as normal. The trouble did not begin until the question-and-

20

answer session, when the meeting chairman finally challenged the visitors to announce whether their presence was peaceful or not. He was answered by a flying beer glass, which smashed on the wall behind him. Within moments a storm broke loose across the room. Communists and Nazis attacked one another with whatever weapons came to hand: knives, glasses, bottles, even chairs. In panic, most of the audience fled for the door, but some stayed to join the storm troopers in a desperate battle. One of them was an old man, who used his cane to strike repeatedly at the Red Marines. When his cane broke he picked up a chair leg and used that instead. His white beard was soon flecked with blood.

The Communists outnumbered the Nazis almost two to one, and they also had a large mob outside who were trying to break down the door. Despite this, the Nazis managed to force their attackers into a corner, and one by one the Red Marines began to fall. Of the hundred or so men who had interrupted the meeting, at least eighty were battered to the floor, and the remaining Communists were eventually forced to escape through the open window at the back of the beer hall.

At last the police arrived, along with emergency medics, and cleared everyone out of the room. While the crowd outside was being dispersed, the victorious Nazis regrouped on the banks of a nearby river and congratulated themselves on a job well done—they were convinced that they had won the fight because they had the stronger ideology, and therefore the stronger will, the greater strength, the wilder courage. They eventually marched, singing and celebrating long into the night. The battle they had just fought would soon pass into Nazi legend as a vital stepping stone in the party's long struggle to win power in the city.

While this beer hall brawl actually had little or no significance in the Nazis' rise to power in Hamburg, the episode does say a great deal about the way the Nazis saw themselves. From the very beginning, the National Socialist German Workers' Party (NSDAP) was imbued with a sense of struggle against a hostile world. They saw the Communists as a particular threat, because they were one of the few groups that actively fought against them, but they could also see other more subtle dangers. Religious Christians exercised an insidious control over the minds of the German people by worshipping the passive virtues of humbleness and forgiveness. Foreign immigrants polluted German blood, just as Communists polluted German minds, and the Jews threatened to enslave the ordinary German worker in a perpetual bondage to capitalism. All of this was not only tolerated but encouraged by corrupt and spineless politicians, who themselves were little more than puppets to foreign governments and a sinister conspiracy of world Jewry. The Nazis believed themselves besieged on all sides, much as they were that night in the Am Stadtpark pub, and that the only way to save themselves, and Germany, was through violence.

The beer hall battle was one of the most common images in Nazi propaganda. It was a microcosm of what they believed was necessary throughout the whole of Germany: a violent bloodletting both to beat away the myriad enemies of the people and to purge the nation of weaklings. The fact that the Nazis are almost always outnumbered in such stories is an important part of the myth, and reflects a fundamental flaw that would eventually lead to their downfall. In the years to come senior Nazis began to believe that they would *always* triumph, no matter what the odds against them, provided they maintained a fanatical belief in the strength of their cause.

At the beginning of the 1930s the NSDAP had already done far better than most people ever thought possible. For over a decade they had been a minority party, with little appeal to anyone outside their core, fanatical audience. But with Germany reeling in the aftermath of the Wall Street Crash, the Nazis suddenly began to appeal to a much wider spectrum of people. The country now had over six million unemployed workers—121,000 of them in Hamburg alone[3]—and an increasingly desperate electorate was casting about for someone to blame. The Nazi Party was there to provide the answer. Their long list of scapegoats began with the party's enemies inside the country—Communists, Jews, liberals—and ended with the international community that had crushed Germany beneath the heel of the Versailles Treaty at the end of the First World War. Hitler's invective against all these groups, which had seemed petulant when the country was in recovery, now began to have enormous popular appeal.

The success of the party in Hamburg was perhaps the most surprising of all. For decades the city had been a stronghold of *left*-wing politics, with the most serious challenge to the moderate Social Democrats (SPD) coming from the German Communist Party (KPD). In fact, in 1928 Hitler's National Socialists had just three seats on the city council, representing only a tiny proportion of the vote. But Hamburg was hit particularly badly by the stock market crash. The city had borrowed heavily from America during the 1920s, and when American banks started to call in their debts a whole host of companies was forced into bankruptcy. Those that survived suffered terribly at the sudden fall in international trade. With unemployment, the city's expenditure on welfare also began to spiral out of control.

A disillusioned electorate rapidly began to turn away from anyone associated with the administration that had gotten them into this mess. The party they turned to was the Nazis, whose three seats on the city council grew to forty-three in under three years. By 1932 they already had fifty-one seats, making them the strongest voice on the council.[4] What was happening all over Germany was also happening here—a switch in the balance of power that was so rapid it was breathtaking. As Victor Klemperer, a university professor in another doomed city on the river Elbe, wrote in 1933:

> It's astounding how easily everything collapses.... Day after day commissioners appointed, provincial governments trampled underfoot, flags raised, buildings taken over, people shot, newspapers banned, etc. etc.... And all opposing forces as if vanished from the face of the earth. It is this utter collapse of a power only recently present—no, its complete disappearance (just as in 1918)—which I find so staggering.[5]

There is a strong view that Hamburg never truly supported the Nazis, despite their victory. The Nazi vote here was always several points below the national average, and the other main parties remained very strong right until the bitter end.[6] However, if general voters did not take to Hitler in quite the same way as they did elsewhere, those who did support the Nazis turned out to be particularly zealous. Actual membership of the Nazi Party was much higher here than the national average,[7] and brawls like those in the Winterhude beer hall were relatively common events. It was as if the very strength of the opposition here only served to increase the Nazi Party's siege mentality.

As Hitler's power grew, Hamburg began to win something of a reputation for fanaticism, especially when it came to persecuting other political parties. Even before the Nazis had come to power, storm troopers had already murdered one of the KPD councillors—Ernst Robert Henning, who was shot in 1931. When civil liberties were suspended in February

1933, Hamburg was one of the first authorities to round up Communist Party functionaries and throw them in prison. This was soon followed by the arrest of Social Democrats, trade unionists, and other opponents of National Socialism, many of whom were later either executed or sent to concentration camps. In the coming years 1,417 men, women, and teenagers from Hamburg would be executed for political reasons—twenty of them former members of the city parliament.[8] Even members of the Nazi Party itself were not safe. In June 1934, during the "night of the long knives," dozens of Hitler's political opponents within the local Nazi Party were murdered as part of a huge, nationwide purge. The violence of the Hamburg beer hall had at last expanded to a concerted campaign of brutal control on a national level.

Hitler gained overall control of the national parliament after the elections of March 5, 1933, when the National Socialist Party seized 44 percent of the vote. He was quick to consolidate power. With many of his opponents already under arrest, less than three weeks after his election victory he managed to bully the Reichstag into passing the "Enabling Act." This infamous piece of legislation, officially entitled the "Law for the Lifting of Misery from the People and Reich,"[9] gave him the right to bring in emergency legislation whenever he felt it necessary, without having to refer to parliament. This effectively granted Hitler absolute power.

Over the next four months he systematically dismantled all opposition to Nazi rule. All other political parties were dissolved, and a law was passed making their reformation illegal. Trade unions associated with the SPD were banned in May. Newspapers and radio stations that did not agree with the Nazi position were also banned, and replaced with Nazi propaganda organs. In Hamburg, which had more newspapers than any other city in Germany, this had a substantial effect: On April 29, the *Hamburger Echo* was put out of business, quickly followed by the *Hamburger Nachrichten* and the *Hamburgische Correspondent*. Even though the Hamburg City Council had complied enthusiastically with almost everything the national government had asked of it, the Bürgerschaft itself was finally dissolved on October 14. From that day until the end of the war, absolute power over the whole city passed to the hands of the Nazi gauleiter and Reich Governor Karl Kaufmann.

Over the following months and years the tendrils of Nazi control began to reach into every area of life in Hamburg. Books that displeased the Nazis were burned on the Kaiser-Friedrich-Ufer, and works by ostracized artists like Ernst Barlach were removed from Hamburg's public collections. People in positions of power or influence were gradually removed from office and replaced with Nazi sympathizers: not only in the city parliament but in police stations, hospitals, schools, and even private businesses. During the course of 1933, 10 percent of commissioned police officers were dismissed for political reasons.[10]

To ensure that the Nazi message was spread as widely as possible, organizations were set up to cover every area of German life. To replace the banned trade unions, the Nazis set up their own equivalent, the *Deutsche Arbeitsfront*. Weekend holidays and acceptable cultural activities were organized for the people by *Kraft durch Freude* ("Strength through Joy"). Boys were encouraged to join the Hitler Youth, and girls to join the *Bund deutscher Mädel* ("League of German Girls"). While these organizations were supposedly voluntary, they effectively became compulsory as the years went on.

The brave new world of Nazism was perhaps felt most keenly in schools and colleges. Wiebke Stammers, who was a schoolgirl in Hamburg at the time, remembers vividly the changes that took place:

> We no longer had religious lessons. They disappeared from the timetable. . . . And we had instead what was laughingly called *Lebenskunde*, which was all about the Party and the history of the Nazi Party, the life story of Hitler, all the people in the Party, where they came from, what they'd done. It was terribly boring.[11]

Gradually her schoolbooks were replaced with new editions that complied with Nazi ideology. History books propagated the "stab in the back" myth of the First World War, geography textbooks described Germany's need for *Lebensraum* by expanding her borders, and biology textbooks emphasized the ideas of racial purity, struggle for survival, and self-sacrifice for the good of the race.[12] When Wiebke's headmistress refused to join the Nazi Party, she was sacked and replaced with somebody more compliant to the regime. Likewise, two of her teachers were fired after being denounced by pupils for making anti-Nazi comments in class. Two of her classmates were also expelled from school, because they did not join in with the denunciation. What happened to all these people in later years is unknown, but it is certain that at the very least they would have been watched carefully by the authorities.

Underlying all these actions was an unspoken threat of violence against anyone who did not agree with Nazi ideology. Those who did not fit into the standard Aryan mold—committed Christians, handicapped people, Gypsies, homosexuals, foreigners—were in particular danger. In a cosmopolitan city like Hamburg there were seemingly endless targets for persecution. Even teenage jazz enthusiasts found themselves on the wrong side of the authorities. When American phonograph records were finally banned early on in the war, scores of swing fans in Hamburg were rounded up and sent to the youth concentration camp at Moringen. Their crimes? Sexual promiscuity, dancing "like wild creatures" to "negro music," and deliberately speaking in English, a language that was also banned at the beginning of the war.[13]

The people who suffered most, however, were undoubtedly the city's Jews. Shortly after the Nazis came to power a national boycott of Jewish businesses was declared. Despite intimidation from the SA (*Sturmabteilungen*, or storm troopers), many Hamburgers defied the boycott—but the message was clear nevertheless. Six days later, on April 7, 1933, a law was passed banning Jews from the civil service. This was soon followed by similar laws prohibiting Jews from working in the medical profession, the media, the performing arts, the legal profession, and the army. In 1935 the infamous Nuremberg Race Laws were passed, depriving all Jews of citizenship and forbidding marriage between Aryan Germans and Jews.[14] Once again, the background to this anti-Semitism was one of constant low-level violence. Random acts of brutality against Jews in and around Hamburg accumulated, and there were incidents of policemen standing by while Jewish shopkeepers were assaulted. The net result was a general culture of fear and helplessness in much of the city, but particularly among Hamburg's Jewish community. They could sense what was coming: Those Jews who could afford it, and who were able to gain visas, fled to other countries. Within two years of the Nazi's coming to power a quarter of the city's Jews had emigrated.

For those who stayed behind the final proof of their helplessness was not long in coming. On the night of November 7, 1938, in response to the murder of a German diplomat by an expatriate Jew, Joseph Goebbels orchestrated the nationwide pogrom that would come to be known as

Kristallnacht. During the course of just twenty-four hours, over a thousand synagogues across the country were either vandalized or burned to the ground. Jewish cemeteries like that at Altona were vandalized, Jewish homes were set alight, thousands of Jewish shops were looted and their windows smashed, and nearly 100 people were murdered. Approximately 30,000 Jewish men were rounded up and sent to concentration camps. Afterward, in a final absurd insult, Germany's Jews were ordered to pay a collective bill of one billion Reichsmarks to the government—to cover the cost of the damage to their own property.[15]

While most Germans were shocked by the pogrom, there were very few who dared to speak out against it. Hamburg, to its credit, was one of the few places where such vandalism was openly condemned. In its "Reports on Germany," the exiled Social Democrats claimed that:

> The broad mass of people has not condoned the destruction, but we should nevertheless not overlook the fact that there are people among the working class who do not defend the Jews.... If there has been any speaking out in the Reich against the Jewish pogroms, the excesses of arson and looting, it has been in Hamburg and the neighboring Elbe district.[16]

Those who spoke out against the *Kristallnacht* pogrom were taking their lives in their hands: The judicial authorities in Hamburg were notoriously harsh when judging political dissidents.[17] However, while Hamburgers might have been unusually vocal about the atrocities they had seen, few people translated their outrage into action. As one Hamburg woman wrote in her diary shortly afterward, while the persecution of the Jews had "inflamed all decent people with anger," there was depressingly little that any of them did about it:

> For me nothing was more devastating than the fact that nobody, not even those who opposed the régime most vehemently, stood up against this, but remained passive and weak. I cannot stress these facts too strongly. It was as if we were caught in a stranglehold. And, worst of all, one even gets used to being half throttled; what at first appeared to be unbearable pressure becomes a habit, becomes easier to tolerate; hate and desperation are diluted with time.[18]

∗   ∗   ∗

Once the battle against the enemy within was under way, Hitler turned his attention to the enemy without. The Treaty of Versailles at the end of the First World War had considerably reduced Germany's power and imposed severe restrictions on its armed forces, and limited rights to defend its borders. As the main architects of the treaty, Britain and France were considered responsible for Germany's humiliating status, although the whole of the League of Nations was implicated. One of Hitler's first actions on the international stage, therefore, was to pull out of the Geneva Peace Conference in October 1933 and withdraw from the League of Nations.

In direct violation of the Versailles Treaty, Germany now embarked on an expansion of its armed forces. In March 1935 the German government shocked the world by revealing the existence of the Luftwaffe, a branch of the Wehrmacht that had hitherto been banned. A year later Hitler broke the terms of the Versailles Treaty once again, by marching his troops into the Rhineland on the border of France. With his borders secure, Hitler now reintroduced the conscription of men into the army, and embarked on a huge four-year plan of rearmament. It was becoming increasingly difficult to believe that such measures were meant only for Germany's defense, and many began to suspect that Hitler was actually inviting a reaction from the rest of the world. In the words of Hermann Göring, Hitler was "preparing the German economy for total war."[19]

Given its shipping links and huge manufacturing capacity, it is unsurprising that Hamburg now became very important to the Nazi regime's plans. In 1936 military contracts suddenly began to pour into Hamburg's shipbuilding companies—so much so that HAPAG actually lodged a complaint that its military commitments were making it fall behind on orders for merchant and passenger ships. Other shipping companies also became worried that they were becoming far too dependent on the German navy for business.[20]

The upside to the story was that all this rearmament was a much-needed tonic to Hamburg's ailing industries. Until now the city had gained very little from the change of regime. While the rest of Germany had started to recover as early as 1934, unemployment in Hamburg was still extremely high. The entire Lower Elbe area had always depended on international trade, and Hitler's policy of restricting imports in favor of German-made goods had had a disastrous effect on the city's trade and shipping industries. Rearmament, however, brought a much-needed injection of jobs and money into Hamburg. New businesses were set up, all of them devoted to the preparation for war: oil refineries, engine factories, and aviation engineering works. The need for huge amounts of raw materials also increased trade, particularly with Scandinavia.

Hitler had big plans for Hamburg. For centuries it had been surrounded by satellite towns, many of which had worked in direct competition with the city, but on April 1, 1937, this was to change: Altona, Wandsbek, Harburg, and twenty-eight smaller municipalities were consolidated into a single industrial and administrative giant that would become known as Greater Hamburg.[21] With this single action the city became hugely more efficient. It also doubled in size overnight, and its population increased by 41 percent to 1.68 million.

In keeping with the city's new status, Hitler drew up grand plans for a new Kongresshalle, a 250-meter-high Gauhaus, and a huge motorway bridge spanning the Elbe.[22] The Hamburg-Lübeck autobahn was completed in 1937, and the clearance of the slums in the Neustadt was also carried out as a priority—ostensibly under a program of housing reform, but actually because the area was a hotbed of Communist resistance to the Nazi regime.

The importance of Hamburg's position in the new Reich was underscored by the fact that Hitler visited this city more than any other during his time as leader of the Nazi Party.[23] As Hamburg churned out warships and U-boats, the Reich chancellor was busy provoking the world toward conflict. In March 1938 he marched his troops into Austria to "encourage" the Austrian people to vote for an *Anschluss* (or "union") with Germany. (At the same time he transported more than 10,000 Austrian guests up to Hamburg to attend the launch of the troopship *Robert Ley*—a rare example of Hitler's use of the carrot as well as the stick.)[24] A year later, in defiance of an agreement made with Britain, Hitler's tanks rolled into Czechoslovakia. A pattern was beginning to emerge—Germany was turning on her neighbors one by one.

During his last major visit to Hamburg in February 1939, Hitler hinted that such actions were only the beginning. At the launch of battleship *Bismarck* he explained that his ultimate aim was "the future eradication of the enemies of the Reich, now and for all time."[25] The festive atmosphere of a launch was a long way from the beer hall brawls that had characterized the early years of the Nazi Party—but the themes in Hitler's speech were still the same. Several years on, and the Nazis continued to be obsessed with enemies of the Reich, which still appeared to outnumber Aryan Germans on every side.

When Germany invaded Poland on September 1, 1939, the "enemies of the Reich" finally stepped forward. Two days after Hitler's accumulated weaponry began pouring toward Warsaw, France and Britain finally picked up the gauntlet and declared war on Germany.

The violence of the beer hall had at last expanded to its logical extreme. The Treaty of Versailles was dead, extremism of all kinds was taking over Europe, and the entire continent was spiraling inexorably downward into a vast, all-encompassing war. At the center of it all were the Nazis, surrounded by enemies, outnumbered, but fanatically certain that the strength of their ideology would see them through to ultimate victory, whatever the odds against them. Like the staunch defenders of the Nazi election meeting in Winterhude in 1930, the forces of the Fatherland would carry on fighting until there was no one left to fight. For Germany this would result in six years of increasing hardship followed by the agony of defeat and disgrace. For the city of Hamburg, whose "Red Marines" had long since been battered into silence, it would result in almost total annihilation.

Chapter 5

HAMBURG PREPARES FOR WAR

Truly, I live in dark times!

—BERTOLT BRECHT[1]

Despite the eagerness with which the Nazis seemed to embrace conflict, there was actually very little enthusiasm for war among the general German population, especially in Hamburg.[2] The city had never done well out of war, and the memories of the hardships created in 1914–18 were still relatively fresh in people's minds. Mathilde Wolff-Mönckeberg summed up the feelings of many when she wrote in her diary that she and everyone she knew was in "absolute despair" at the outbreak of war. "We were convinced that immediate and total annihilation would follow."[3]

Many in the city's Nazi administration seem to have shared these fears. Throughout its history Hamburg had been vulnerable to attack from both the sea and the surrounding land. Now it faced a brand-new danger—a threat from the air. Unlike many other towns closer to the French borders, Hamburg had never suffered from bombing during 1914–18. This did not mean that it was unacquainted with the overall concept of bombing; quite the opposite, in fact—the city had been a center for German aviation even before the First World War, and many of the German Zeppelins that bombed British cities had been based in airfields around Hamburg.

To combat this new danger from the air, city officials immediately set about creating a system of civil protection unlike anything Hamburg had ever seen before. The first thing they did was to launch a program of strengthening the cellars of houses and apartment blocks throughout the city, to protect them from the possibility of blast bombs. However, it was

31

very soon realized that there were not enough cellars to go round. The soggy, waterlogged soil upon which Hamburg was built meant that whole districts were devoid of cellars—the high water table of the Elbe flood plain would simply have swamped them—so in these areas extra air raid shelters were built. Even before the war there were some eighty-eight public air raid shelters in Hamburg. By April 1940 the number had risen to 549. A year after that there were 1,700 shelters, splinter-proof buildings, and bunkers across the city, with room for over 230,000 people.[4]

The city authorities quickly recognized that the main threat from bombing was that of fire. While high-explosive bombs caused terrible damage to buildings, that damage was very localized. Fire from incendiary bombs, on the other hand, could destroy whole areas of the city. So they set about training a whole army of firemen and air raid wardens in every suburb. In theory, each block had its own fire officer. The railway authority alone had almost 1,500 firemen, and 15,000 fire watchers kept a lookout over the port area. Over 700 sandboxes were placed in public streets and squares, and measures were taken to ensure that an emergency water supply would be available if the water mains should fail. New wells were dug, water carts requisitioned, and containers built. In Blankenese the cellars of two derelict buildings were converted into huge water tanks, which could be called upon in times of emergency.[5]

Everyone in Hamburg knew how quickly a conflagration could spread if it were allowed to get out of control: They had learned about the Great Fire of 1842 at school. In the early part of the war, the entire population therefore set about removing anything flammable from the one place in their buildings that was most vulnerable to falling bombs—the roofs. People cleared their attics of anything flammable, and all superfluous woodwork, such as partitions, was removed. Businesses started fitting their buildings with incendiary-proof ceilings, and firewalls were set up, especially in the harbor area, to stop fires spreading.

Finally, in an attempt to throw any enemy bombers off-target, a city-wide program of camouflage was put in place. Stations were masked so that they would look like ordinary buildings from above; oil depots were hidden; wharves were disguised to look like normal parts of the riverbank. In an incredible effort of building, the whole of the Binnen Alster was hidden beneath a fake reconstruction of the city center, complete with imitation streets and false buildings. The idea was that British bombers

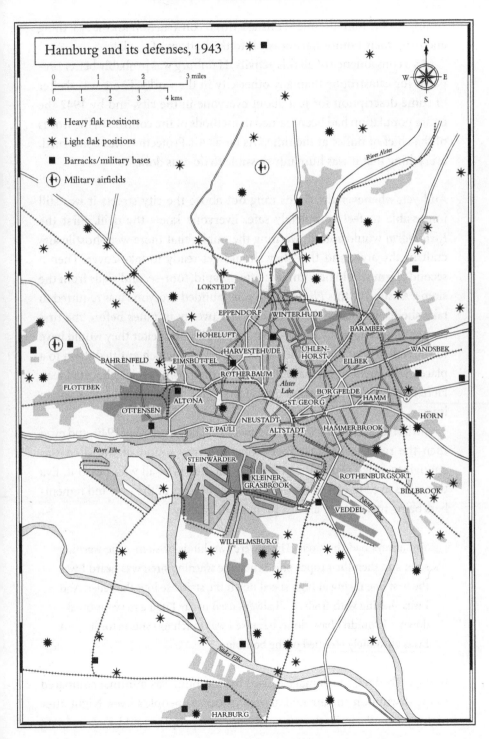

Hamburg and its defenses, 1943

0   1   2   3 miles
0   1   2   3   4 kms

* Heavy flak positions
* Light flak positions
■ Barracks/military bases
⊕ Military airfields

River Alster

LOKSTEDT
EPPENDORF   WINTERHUDE
HOHELUFT   BARMBEK
HARVESTEHUDE   UHLEN-   WANDSBEK
BAHRENFELD   EIMSBÜTTEL   HORST   EILBEK
ROTHERBAUM
Alster
Lake
FLOTTBEK   BORGFELDE   HAMM
ALTONA   ST. GEORG
OTTENSEN   HORN
NEUSTADT
ST. PAULI   ALTSTADT   HAMMERBROOK

River Elbe

STEINWÄRDER
ROTHENBURGSORT
KLEINER   BILLBROOK
GRASBROOK
VEDDEL
Norder Elbe
WILHELMSBURG

Süder Elbe

HARBURG

aiming for the Rathaus might mistake this reconstruction for the real thing and drop their bombs harmlessly into the bottom of the lake.

As a consequence of all this activity, Hamburg was probably better prepared for catastrophe than any other city in the world. There was shelter of some description for just about everyone in the city, and by 1942 the entire population had been trained in methods of fire control. In the words of the chief of police at the time, "As far as Air Protection was concerned, everything that it was humanly possible to do, was done."[6]

And yet, whenever the sirens rang out above the city streets it was still impossible to feel completely safe. Everyone knew the drill. First the *Kleinalarm* would sound, warning the public that there were hostile aircraft in the area, and that they should get ready to take cover. Then a second alarm would be sounded: fifteen rapid, four-second wails from the sirens. As soon as this *Fliegeralarm* was sounded everyone was required to take shelter immediately: They had just twenty minutes before the first bombs would start falling. On arrival at the bomb shelter they would have to show their *Platzkart* to the shelter supervisor, which entitled them to a place in the shelter, and make their way to their own special, allocated seat. Here they would wait—sometimes for several hours—until it was safe to leave.

Although Hamburg was not actually attacked until May 1940, and even then the raids were fairly ineffective, the very sound of the siren was enough to strike fear and anxiety into the hearts of all who heard it. Eva Coombes lived in Hamburg during the early years of the war, and remembers being in a state of almost permanent anxiety:

> You always had the siren. There were two kinds of siren—the warning siren and then the proper one. When the warning siren was heard I was the first one racing at high speed down the staircase into the cellar. And I was shaking with fright . . . I always used to say I had a nervous breakdown—I couldn't have done, because I was much too young for it—but I was absolutely terrified of the bombing.[7]

In the early days, the damage caused by bombing was minimal compared to the disruption the air raid alarms caused to people's lives. Night after night, particularly in the summer months, people would have to drag themselves from their beds to take shelter, before returning to their rooms to try to snatch a few more hours' sleep before daybreak. Frustratingly, most of the alarms were false ones. The bombers changed course, or flew past Hamburg to bomb Kiel or Lübeck, or some other city nearby. The British got into the habit of flying "nuisance raids" over Germany for the sole purpose of keeping the people awake during the night, and this often caused more disruption than the bombs did. In his diary, Hitler's propaganda minister recorded his regular irritation at "the absurd fact that ten nuisance planes drove fifteen to eighteen million people out of bed."[8]

By the end of 1940, Hamburg had already had more than 200 air raid warnings,[9] most of them in the middle of the night, and the authorities were having to learn strategies to cope with the chronic lack of sleep among the people. Schoolchildren were allowed to come to school late on mornings after an air raid warning, or perhaps even miss school altogether. In the end, a scheme known as the *Kinderlandverschickung* was set up to evacuate children to safer areas in the interior of the Reich, and tens of thousands of children were sent away to schools in places as far away as Bavaria. They stayed away until the following year, when a decrease in the number of raids allowed them slowly to filter back to the city.

Adults were not given nearly such special treatment. They were required to turn up to work no matter how little sleep they had had the night before, and there were severe punishments for absenteeism. With so many men away at the war there were serious labor shortages, and lack of sleep was no kind of excuse for shirking. In fact, as the war progressed, many workers were required to work even longer hours. In January 1942, for example, the standard working week for public officials was increased from forty-six to fifty-eight hours, and vacation periods all but disappeared. After much resistance, women were also conscripted into war work at the beginning of 1943.[10]

With no holidays, longer working hours, and sleep deprivation at epidemic levels, grumbling became a part of life: "the soul moving its bowels," as Goebbels charmingly called it.[11] A tired, grumpy population was much more likely to complain about all the other hardships they had to endure: rationing of food, fuel, and tobacco; clothing shortages; travel restrictions; and the ubiquitous queues that meant shopping trips always lasted for hours.

Soon the luxuries of 1939 were only a distant memory. Before the war, Wiebke Stammers would always cut away the fat from her meat.

> I remember my mother's favorite saying, "May God forbid that if war ever broke out again you would be going down on your hands and knees to eat it. And you would eat anything." And I said, "I would rather starve than eat fat." . . . It never occurred to me that it would ever come true— but she was right.[12]

In actual fact, the conditions suffered by the people of Hamburg were not nearly so bad as those endured by the British during the same period. But many people remembered the disastrous food shortages of the First World War, and they were constantly worried by the specter of famine. In desperation, large numbers turned to "hamstering"—making trips to the countryside to buy extra rations on the black market. In the words of Wiebke Stammers, "Many a diamond ring went to the country to buy food."[13]

While most people simply got on with life and tried to make the best of things, for some the constant restrictions were too much to bear, and their grumbling became increasingly subversive. Else Baker clearly remembers her father, who was a Hamburg docker, openly criticizing Hitler: Her mother was constantly asking him to lower his voice, for fear that he would be overheard.[14] Likewise, whenever twelve-year-old Hannah Kelson complained, her parents would immediately silence her, saying, "For God's sake don't let anybody hear that!"[15]

They had good cause to worry. The SD (the *Sicherheitsdienst*, or security service of the SS) had informers in all walks of life, and reports on individuals who criticized the regime went all the way to the top.[16] The authorities were becoming increasingly worried about the small pockets of resistance that were beginning to appear across the country, such as the White Rose movement in Bavaria (which also had members in Hamburg), and various Communist groups in Berlin. In Hamburg the swing movement was gaining in popularity, and there had been incidents of "swing youth" waylaying members of the Hitler Youth and beating them up.[17] Unsurprisingly, the Nazi regime could not tolerate such actions, and each of these movements was violently suppressed.

*   *   *

By the middle of 1943 there was very little good news about the war to be had in Germany. German troops had suffered their first heavy defeats in Russia, at Stalingrad and Kursk, and Rommel's troops had finally been ejected from the coast of North Africa. While the Nazis and their allies still controlled the whole of mainland Europe and huge areas of Russia, some people in Hamburg began to realize that the tide was finally turning.[18]

The relative lull in the bombing war between July 1942 and July 1943 was no consolation either.[19] With attacks increasing in other parts of Germany, the Hamburg authorities sensed that it was only a matter of time before the war would return to their doorstep. As the Hamburg chief of police would soon write in his report, in the run-up to July 1943 all the air protection services maintained the highest level of preparedness.[20] Their only mistake, if there was one, was to assume that when the great attacks came they would be similar to those that had gone before.

It appears that the general population felt much the same way. Although they feared the next attack, it seems most people believed they had done everything they could to protect their homes—they would simply deal with each raid as it came. With hindsight, their concerns seem petty. They grumbled about losing sleep because of the air raid warnings. They sent their children to the countryside, but only grudgingly, as a precaution. At night they sometimes worried that an attack might damage their roofs, or blast their windows; or if they were very unlucky a direct hit might destroy their home altogether. It never occurred to them that their entire city was at risk. The worst they could imagine was that they might themselves be killed, or perhaps someone close to them.

By day, it was easy to forget that there was a war on at all. The city had not been bombed during daylight hours since the beginning of the war—why should that change now?—and the actual fighting was still hundreds of miles away. People went about their business just as they always had done. The sun was shining—it was a glorious summer—and the streets were filled with children making the most of their summer vacation.

On the afternoon of July 20, 1943, Fredy Borck was playing in the courtyard of his apartment block in Rothenburgsort when he heard the sound of an airplane up above. Suddenly propaganda leaflets rained down out of the sky around him.

We didn't dare touch the leaflets, because it was said they might be poisoned. So we ran to the house and brought fire tongs and coal shovels, and used those to pick them up. We weren't supposed to read them either, but we did. It was an appeal to the people to leave the city immediately, because we were to be the next bombing target.[21]

A debate ensued among the family about what they should do. They had a shack in Krümmel near the coast that they could go to, but there was no guarantee of safety there either—there was a large munitions factory nearby, which could easily be an alternative target for Allied bombers. Besides, Fredy's grandmother refused to leave the city. So they decided to stay—"It would not be so bad"—and Fredy went back out into the court-yard to play. The sun shone, scorching the city for the rest of the week, and for a while the war seemed hundreds of miles away.

PART II

DARKNESS FALLS FROM THE AIR

Chapter 6

A BRIEF HISTORY OF
BOMBING

Give us something to destroy . . .
Don't despise us; we're heralds and prophets.

—PRIMO LEVI[1]

The one thing that could never be said about the horrors created by the Combined Bomber Offensive is that they were not foreseen. At the beginning of the twentieth century, while most of the world was still celebrating the advent of powered flight as a thing of wonder, there were many who worried that mankind was not yet responsible enough to wield such power peacefully. Their fears were crystallized in 1908 by H. G. Wells, whose hugely popular novel *The War in the Air* described the possibility of a world war in which aerial bombing campaigns would destroy every major city and bring about "universal social collapse."[2] His fictional descriptions of the bombing of New York make uneasy reading for anyone acquainted with the effects of British and American bombs in 1943:

> They smashed up the city as a child will shatter its cities of brick and card. Below, they left ruins and blazing conflagrations and heaped and scattered dead . . . Lower New York was soon a furnace of crimson flames, from which there was no escape. Cars, railways, ferries, all had ceased, and never a light led the way of the distracted fugitives in that dusky confusion but the light of burning.[3]

Over the next few years, such predictions became increasingly common. When Italian aviators fighting in North Africa dropped the world's first aerial bombs on Turkish troops in 1911, there was general dismay that the genie had finally been let out of the bottle. Reports in English newspapers claimed that such bombing would revolutionize warfare. A Swedish writer named Gustaf Janson described how aerial bombardment would one day see entire cities "burnt, blown to pieces in explosions, annihilated, exterminated."[4] Across Europe, the popular imagination was fired with images of a man-made Sodom and Gomorrah.[5]

At the time, however, such ideas were still mere fantasy—fairy stories with which to frighten children. Powered flight was only in its infancy, and there was not a single country capable of delivering the mass of machines necessary to produce such devastation. The few occasions before 1914 when aircraft *were* used to drop bombs only seemed to demonstrate how ineffective they were. For example, after the initial excitement over the Italian bombing of Libya died down, most of the world's press dismissed it as pointless. The German correspondent for the *Berliner Tageblatt* claimed that the results had been virtually nil, and that Italian aviators had had very little effect on the war at all. A French military observer reported that the bombs he had seen produced no casualties and no damage whatsoever. Many of them fell into the sand without exploding, and those which detonated produced only a small and harmless blast. More important, the Turks themselves did not appear in the least bit frightened by the experience.[6]

And yet the idea that aerial bombardment could be used as a devastating force still persisted, both in the popular imagination and in the minds of military theorists. The image of Sodom and Gomorrah seemed to tap something deep within human nature: not only the nightmare of being on the receiving end, but also the dream of being able to wield such irresistible power oneself. Soon, military thinkers across the world were beginning to weave their own fantasies: Most seemed to think that bombing would end up *saving* lives, by making wars shorter, more decisive affairs. Some went so far as to claim that the threat of bombing would eventually bring peace and order to the world.[7]

The outbreak of the First World War destroyed all such benign theories for good. The first bombings of the war were isolated affairs, but it was only a matter of time before these separate attacks were grouped together into full-scale bombing offensives. It was the Germans who first embraced bombing as a strategic weapon. France was attacked regularly, especially Paris, but it was Britain that received the full shock of the German air offensive. The idea was to attack British ports, stations, arsenals, factories—in fact anything that contributed to the British war effort at all—methodically and incessantly. Most of the early attacks came from Zeppelins, which were able to fly incredibly long distances without having to stop and refuel, but at the same time German manufacturers were developing the world's first effective long-range bomber airplane—the twin-engined Gotha.

The effect on the civilian population was dramatic. For centuries Britain had been an island fortress, protected from the rest of Europe by the English Channel—but in a few short years the advent of powered flight had rendered the country suddenly defenseless. When the first bombs began to fall during World War I there were scenes of panic in all the areas affected. Rates of absenteeism in factories and offices rocketed in the days after an attack, and the quality of the work done by those who did turn up was vastly reduced. Skilled workers in armaments factories made far more mistakes in precision work in the days after an air raid. In Hull, women and children fled the city at the first sound of the alarm signals, and spent night after night huddled in sodden fields outside the city. As one commentator observed, the exposure to the cold must have caused far more harm than the few bombs dropped from the Zeppelins.[8]

Worse was to come with the arrival of the Gothas, flying in broad daylight and strewing bombs as though the country had no defenses at all. On May 25, a formation of Gothas dropped a load of bombs on a crowded shopping arcade in Folkestone, killing 95 people and wounding 260. Two weeks later they attacked London, killing 162 civilians, including 16 children in an infant school in Poplar. It was the first of seventeen attacks on the city by Gothas.

By the end of the summer of 1917 it began to look as though the increased intensity of air raids was having a disastrous effect on British morale. An emergency committee, set up under the chairmanship of Jan Smuts, decided that there were only two ways to counter the German attacks. First, the air force should be made independent of both the army and the navy, so that it could respond specifically to the air threat. Second, and most important, the fight should be taken back to the Germans. According to Smuts, the way to total victory over Germany was to launch a massive air campaign on German cities; if not now, then certainly in the near future:

The day may not be far off when aerial operations, with their devastation of enemy lands and destruction of industrial and populace centres on a vast scale, may become the principal operations of war, to which the older forms of military and naval operations may become secondary and subordinate.[9]

The prime minister, David Lloyd George, backed up this prediction with a solemn promise of revenge for the damage the Germans had caused in London: "We will give it all back to them, and we will give it to them soon. We shall bomb Germany with compound interest."[10]

In accordance with the findings of the Smuts Report, the Air Ministry set about creating the world's first independent force of airplanes and airships—the Royal Air Force (RAF), which finally came into being on April 1, 1918. Five weeks later one of the most influential men in the whole history of air power, Brigadier General Sir Hugh Trenchard, was appointed to command an independent force of British bombers in France. Trenchard's brief was to attack every German railway junction, airfield, factory, and iron foundry within 150 miles of his airbase at Nancy. Since most of these targets were in heavily built-up areas, bombing them would have the added effect of undermining civilian morale.

The new commander of the independent bombing force took to his task with gusto. Trenchard was well-known in the British establishment for his tremendous efficiency and enthusiasm for air power. Known affectionately as "Boom," because of his booming voice, he was a man of strong opinions who had a talent for finding and nurturing gifted subordinates. His many disciples included both the future leader of Bomber Command in the Second World War, Arthur Harris, and the American prophet of air power, William Mitchell, who regularly sought Trenchard's help and advice in 1917 and 1918.

According to Trenchard, the airplane was almost exclusively a weapon of attack, and any use of aircraft to defend against enemy bombers was at best useless, and at worst recklessly wasteful. When in 1917 two squadrons of fighters were withdrawn from the Western Front to defend London he was greatly angered, and argued that the British were merely playing into German hands by diverting men and equipment away from the one place where they were most useful. The destruction the Germans were wreaking on British and French cities was simply something that must be borne until the RAF's own bomber attacks on Germany were able to throw them back on the defensive. Trenchard recognized the limitations of bombers in the

First World War, but also saw their potential, particularly in the breaking of enemy morale.

As Trenchard began his bombing campaign on the towns of western Germany, the traditional British restraint over the fate of noncombatants quickly became a thing of the past. There is no question that this policy was sanctioned by the British government. In September 1918 the air minister, Lord Weir, wrote to Trenchard, saying, "If I were you, I would not be too exacting as regards accuracy in bombing railway stations in the middle of towns. The German is susceptible to bloodiness, and I would not mind a few accidents due to inaccuracy." Trenchard's reply showed no squeamishness for the fate of civilians: "I do not think you need be anxious about our degree of accuracy when bombing stations in the middle of towns. The accuracy is not great at present, and all the pilots drop their eggs well into the middle of the town generally."[11] For Trenchard, the main use of bombers was in breaking the morale of the German people. As he said after the war, "The moral effect of bombing stands undoubtedly to the material effect in a proportion of twenty to one."[12]

The seeds sown by the German Zeppelins and Gothas in 1917 had grown into a full-blown policy of indiscriminate destruction: "Area bombing" had been born. The only blessing for German civilians was the fact that the policy was short-lived. On November 11, 1918, the armistice agreement was signed, and the towns of Germany were spared any further bombardment. However, the specter of strategic bombing had been released, and would return twenty years later to haunt the entire European continent for six long and devastating years.

The advent of strategic bombing marked a huge change, not only in the way wars would be waged in the future, but in the whole concept of what constituted warfare in the first place. Whereas in the past the devastating effects of war had been confined to a relatively small area—the immediate "battle zone"—now aircraft could leapfrog over armies and bring destruction to areas hundreds of miles behind the front lines. Since aircraft could go anywhere, the battlefield had grown to encompass entire nations. Moreover, the targets of these aircraft were no longer specific factories or arsenals, but "the morale of the people." Generals on both sides used these new weapons to take the fighting to the heart of their enemy's cities, and they did this for the simple reason that now, at last, they could.

It is easy to condemn the actions of people like Trenchard, or the German Zeppelin commanders who ordered the bombing of London and Paris, but the opposing sides were waging what the French quickly called "*La guerre totale*,"[13] and there was a dreadful but undeniable logic to their actions. When an entire nation's resources are backing the prosecution of a war, why should a military commander draw any distinction between the soldier at the front and the civilian in a factory who produces weapons? Shortly after the war, studies on air power began to appear across the world, and they almost all agreed on this point: There was no longer any difference between civilian and soldier. When farmers produce food for the army, miners produce their raw materials, railway workers bring them to the front, and women and children provide soldiers with comfort while they are on leave, all these people become legitimate targets. In an era of total war there can be no holding back, because any action that produces a knockout blow to the enemy will potentially save the lives of tens of thousands. This is the logic that drove the military strategy of the time.

After the dreadful waste of all the static, defensive land battles of the past four years, air power soon began to be seen as a perfect way to restore movement to warfare. It was the offensive weapon *par excellence,* striking suddenly and giving the enemy no time to parry the blow by calling up reinforcements. It was also cheap. In the face of widespread cuts in defense spending after the war, Trenchard was able to keep the fledgling RAF intact simply because it was so much cheaper to police the British Empire with a bomber force than it was to launch expeditions by the army on the ground. Trenchard's vision was to create a long-range bomber force with which Britain could maintain her empire and keep her European neighbors at bay, much as Britain had done through the use of her navy for most of the previous two hundred years.

However, as theorists like the influential Giulio Douhet pointed out, Britain did not rule the air as she did the sea. Not only that, but air power was fundamentally different from sea power—airplanes were not limited in scope or direction of movement, and now even the very heart of the British Empire itself was vulnerable. London, "the great metropolis until now rejoicing in her inviolability," could now be attacked just as easily as anywhere else. [14]

The fact was not lost on the population of London, who still remembered the panic caused by the 1917 Gotha attacks. During the 1920s and

1930s a succession of lurid novels appeared in which the bombing of London produced swarms of refugees like "human rats,"[15] or where in the postapocalyptic ruins of the city "the people lived on the rats and the rats lived on the people."[16] Films like the 1936 science fiction movie *Things to Come* showed how bombing would be used in a global war that would eventually destroy civilization throughout the world. The opinions of the professionals were no more reassuring. In 1923 J. F. C. Fuller warned that the dropping of poison gas on London might injure as many as 200,000 people in just half an hour, and "throw the whole city into panic."[17] Douhet was even more graphic in his predictions, and claimed that bombing a city like London would result in "a complete breakdown of the social structure," which would inevitably lead the people to rise up in revolution against their own government.[18]

All these various prophets of air power singled out London in their descriptions because at that time the British capital was still by far the most powerful city in Europe, and also the one most protected by natural barriers. If London were vulnerable, how much more vulnerable must every other European city be? As a consequence, fear of bombing was fairly universal throughout western Europe between the wars. Even Canada and the United States were not immune to such anxieties, despite their geographical remoteness from any enemy—as was demonstrated by the faintly absurd air raid scares in Ottawa and New York during the last year of the war, and again in 1942.[19] But it was only in Britain that such concerns reached a point of virtual hysteria. By the 1930s even the most enthusiastic champion of bombing, J. M. Spaight, was forced to admit to a widespread pessimism among his contemporaries, who foresaw "a fate comparable to that of Sodom and Gomorrah" for British cities.[20]

As the Second World War approached, the predictions became more and more gloomy. In 1937, the military theorist Sir Malcolm Campbell wrote the following account of the likely outcomes of an air raid on London:

> First would come hundreds of aeroplanes . . . each carrying up to a thousand small incendiary bombs. These would be dropped at a rate of one every five seconds, and each machine would leave a string of fires in its wake. If all the fire-fighting appliances in the country were concentrated in the one place, they would not be able to cope with a tenth of the fires

that would rage over the whole area attacked. Even if they could, hard on the heels of the fire-raisers would follow fleets of heavy bombing machines, dropping their loads of high-explosive bombs on a city already virtually fated to destruction by fire. And as if that were not enough, then would come other fleets of aircraft to drench the flaming ruins with poison gases. Unless the people could take refuge in safety below ground, the casualties in a city like London must amount to a million or even more, while the material damage would be simply incalculable. The picture is not over-drawn—it is what inevitably will happen to a country which fails to take the elementary precaution of making itself strong enough to hold what it has.[21]

When such a premonition is extended beyond just one city to ten, twenty, fifty cities, it is no longer a vision of Sodom and Gomorrah. It is a vision of Armageddon.

It must be stressed at this point that not everybody believed that such destruction was inevitable. There had been many and varied attempts to ban bombing ever since the first Hague Peace Conference in 1899, but as is so often the case with such conferences, the proposals were always rejected by too many of the countries that really mattered.[22]

In one famous instance, in March 1933, the peace conference at the League of Nations took up the question of firebombing. Poison gas had already been banned in 1926 because its uncontrollable nature threatened the lives of innocent civilians; it was argued now that incendiaries caused fires that were every bit as uncontrollable as gas when they were dropped on city targets, and so should be banned in the same way. Everyone agreed, and for a while it looked as though firebombing would indeed be banned. The conference was already working out the practical details when, in October of that year, the newly elected Adolf Hitler walked out of the conference and withdrew from the League of Nations. Without Germany, the ban came to nothing. Ironically, Hitler's action had ensured the death of hundreds of thousands of his own countrymen.[23]

Over the next few years the whole world rearmed itself and rapidly sank back into the quicksand of war. It is difficult now, even with hindsight, to see how another world war could possibly have been avoided after the Nazis took power in Germany. Repeated attempts to mollify Hitler at the negotiating table proved a waste of time: The entire doctrine of the Nazi Party was centered on preparing for war.[24] By 1937 the newly formed Luftwaffe was rehearsing its *Blitzkrieg* tactics with the bombing of Republican towns like Guernica in the Spanish Civil War. In the spring of 1938 Hitler annexed Austria. In 1939, despite frantic British attempts at appeasement, he marched into Czechoslovakia. In September he invaded Poland, followed by Denmark, Norway, Holland, Belgium, and France. In just under ten months Hitler and his allies had taken control of virtually the whole of mainland Europe.

Despite all the dire predictions of the 1930s, the war in the air had actually been fairly restrained until this point. At the outbreak of hostilities President Roosevelt had appealed to both sides to renounce the "bombardment from the air of civilian populations and unfortified cities," and both sides had hastened to agree.[25] Neither side wished to provoke the ire of the world's greatest industrial nation.

Britain in particular promised that it would "never resort to the deliberate attack on women and children and other civilians for purposes of mere terrorism,"[26] and for a long time the British kept their promise. During the six-month lull between the invasion of Poland and the invasion of Norway, the RAF took serious losses in coastal raids on the German navy, but these were completely unsuccessful because the air force was forbidden to attack ships when they were at their most vulnerable—when they were in port—because of the possibility of hitting civilians. During the battle for Norway aircrews were instructed not to use any bombs at all, but only their machine guns, in order to avoid hitting innocent bystanders.[27] For all Britain's refusal to ratify international agreements on bombing, she actually began the war with admirable, if somewhat unrealistic, restraint.

With the exception of the bombing of Warsaw in 1939, Germany exercised similar control. It made no sense to destroy the cities and industries of those countries Germany wanted to occupy, and Hitler certainly had no intention of provoking America into renouncing its neutrality. The Luftwaffe was in any case overwhelmingly a *tactical* air force—it mostly confined its activities to the battle zone, by dive-bombing and strafing opposing troops. The *strategic* bombing they carried out was generally directed at the destruction of enemy airfields and transport links, and not at civilian populations.

The change came during the invasion of the Low Countries in May

1940, when the Germans surrounded the Dutch port of Rotterdam. The general in command of the 39th Panzer Korps told the Dutch defenders that unless they capitulated immediately the city would suffer "complete destruction" by German bombers.[28] The following day, when negotiations between the two sides broke down, the Luftwaffe was dispatched to keep the general's promise. Soon a hail of bombs was falling on the heart of the old city, setting large areas on fire. It later became apparent that the Dutch garrison had actually surrendered before the air strike had taken place, but the order to recall the bombers came too late to save the city. That evening, while the houses still burned, the German army entered Rotterdam just as they had eventually entered Warsaw—unopposed.

The bombing of Rotterdam had sealed the Wehrmacht's success in Holland, but it turned out to be a propaganda disaster for Germany. Over the next few days reports appeared across the world claiming that as many as 30,000 civilians had been killed (although in reality the figure was more like 1,000).[29] Outraged, the British finally lifted some of their restrictions on bombing military targets inside Germany. On May 15, the day after Rotterdam was bombed, Churchill sent ninety-nine bombers to attack rail and oil installations east of the Rhine. A few days later thirty bombers were sent to attack the Blohm & Voss shipyards in Hamburg—the first of 213 attacks on the city. While a handful of bombs did hit the shipyards, in the darkness most of the bombs fell in residential areas around the Reeperbahn, and thirty-four people were killed. The German press immediately hailed it as a "ruthless terror attack on the civilian population."[30]

So began Britain's strategic bombing campaign against Germany: a long-term and systematic effort to destroy all German rail links, oil installations, airfields, armaments factories, metal foundries, stockpiles of raw material—in fact, anything at all of military value. Hitler responded, predictably, by ordering his air force to prepare for a full-scale air offensive against Britain, both as a reprisal for the attacks on Germany and as preparation for a cross-Channel invasion of the British Isles. The battle for mainland Europe was over—the Battle of Britain was about to begin.

Britain was the last piece in Hitler's jigsaw of western Europe, and his generals set about trying to conquer it in much the same way as they had conquered the rest of the Continent. Their first task was to achieve command of the air, which meant destroying as many Royal Air Force planes and

airfields as possible. Only when they had gained complete
would a cross-Channel invasion be possible.

When the Luftwaffe made its first bombing sorties over ~~
1940, there was still an atmosphere of relative restraint surrounding the
bombing war. Hitler explicitly forbade his air force to attack London and
other cities—partly because he had promised not to make war against
women and children, and partly because he wanted his forces to concentrate
on the targets that mattered.[31] At first the Luftwaffe attacked in daylight, but
when German losses began to mount they were forced to switch to night
attacks.

This was where both sides finally lost what was left of the mutual
restraint with which they had started the war. In the dark, the German
bombs increasingly missed their intended targets and fell on residential
areas; then, on the evening of August 24, 1940, a dozen German bombers
veered off course and accidentally dropped their bombs on central London.
In retaliation, Churchill immediately ordered his bombers to attack Berlin.
Although the raid caused little material damage it infuriated Hitler, who
told a mass rally about ten days later, "If they attack our cities, we will simply
erase theirs."[32] In reprisal for the Berlin attack, he ordered Hermann Göring
to stop attacking purely military targets and concentrate his bombers on
the city of London itself.

There has been some speculation that Churchill ordered the attack on
Berlin deliberately to provoke this response in his enemy. The RAF was
struggling to hold the Luftwaffe at the time, and it was only after the Luftwaffe switched to area bombing that it was properly able to recover. If this
was the case, then it was an expensive gamble: London suffered seventy-
one major raids during the Blitz, and 20,000 men, women, and children in
this city alone lost their lives.

Attacks on towns across the whole of Britain soon followed. In November the Luftwaffe destroyed Coventry, and Hitler was so impressed that he
invented a new verb, *coventriren*—"to coventrate." Over the next six months
the Luftwaffe attempted to "coventrate" Birmingham, Liverpool, Manchester, Sheffield, Portsmouth, Plymouth, Bristol, Swansea, Cardiff, Glasgow,
and Belfast. Britain responded by targeting places in Germany where the
centers of industry were surrounded by densely populated residential areas.
The idea was that even if the factories themselves were not destroyed, the
homes of those who worked in them would be. If this was not officially a

policy of "area bombing," in practice that was exactly what it was. The pinpoint targeting of specific installations was simply not possible: From 15,000 feet, in the dark, it was considered accurate if an aircraft bombed within five miles of its aiming point. On December 12, 1940, the British government finally gave up all pretense, when Winston Churchill ordered the bombing of Mannheim: For the first time the British had designated the city itself as the target, rather than anything specific within its limits. As the British official history of the bombing war points out, with the advent of such area bombing, "The fiction that the bombers were attacking military objectives in the towns was officially abandoned."[33]

It was almost an exact copy of what had happened in the First World War: a few piecemeal attacks, leading to a German offensive on Britain, and gradually the initial restraint exercised by both sides was whittled away to nothing. The only difference between the two wars was one of scale. On September 17, 1940, alone, the Luftwaffe unloaded more than 350 tons of bombs on London—more than the total dropped on the whole of Britain throughout the First World War. By the following April, they were able to drop over 1,000 tons of high explosives on the British capital in a single night. During the nine months of the Blitz more than 40,000 British people were killed, and a quarter of a million homes completely destroyed, leaving three quarters of a million people homeless.[34] All the terrifying prewar predictions were beginning to come true.

And yet, in one respect, the prophets of air power seemed to have got it completely wrong. Contrary to the message preached by all the theorists before the war, the morale of the British people was not broken by the ordeal they had been through. If anything, they had become more determined, and their response to the bombings was vengeful rather than fearful. Politicians began to clamor for retaliatory strikes against German cities; their speeches were echoed in the newspapers, which were filled with indignant leader columns requiring the RAF to fly to Berlin and give as good as Britain was getting.[35]

As Hitler turned his attention toward Russia, and the raids on Britain began to peter out, the leaders of the bruised and battered RAF were finally given the space they needed to plan their revenge. The air force was still too weak to take the fight to the heart of the Reich, but it was obvious that Britain was now in this war for the long run. Over the next eighteen months they would build up their strength to create the most formidable bomber force the world had yet seen. Just as they had done in the First World War, they now set their sights on a huge bombing campaign to destroy the German infrastructure. The only difference was that this time there would be no armistice to save the German people from British wrath.

To carry out this bombing campaign, the Air Ministry looked for a new commander-in-chief to lead Bomber Command. The man they finally settled upon was an experienced and determined airman named Arthur Harris. Over the next three years Harris would preside over the greatest, most systematic destruction of population centers the world has ever known, and in the process would become one of Britain's most controversial war figures. The climax of his reign, when the world began to believe that his air force might even win the war single-handedly, would be the bombing of Hamburg.

Chapter 7

THE GRAND ALLIANCE

They have sown the wind, and they shall reap the whirlwind.

—HOSEA, 8:7[1]

Air Chief Marshal Sir Arthur Harris took over the reins of Bomber Command at the end of a very low period for the RAF. For the previous six months the bombing arm had been suffering a serious crisis of confidence: Their insistence that "the bomber will always get through" had proved wrong, their accuracy when they did get through was appalling, and their losses had been heavy.[2] In two years of bombing they had not even dented the German war economy—although they did not yet know how truly ineffective they had been—and they had killed only as many Germans as they had themselves lost in aircrew. One British defense scientist of the time calculated that only a single German died for every five tons of bombs dropped—a hopeless waste of resources even if one did agree with the brutal realities of area bombing.[3] Critics of Bomber Command had begun to appear throughout the British establishment. Even Churchill himself was skeptical about bombing: "Its effects, both physical and moral, have been greatly exaggerated," he said in September 1941. "The most we can say is that it will be a heavy and I trust a seriously increasing annoyance" to the Germans.[4]

By the spring of 1942, however, all this was beginning to change. Brand-new planes were rolling off the production lines, such as the Avro Lancaster, which could carry twice the bomb load of almost any other bomber in existence, and the De Havilland Mosquito, which could fly higher and faster than even most German fighters. New radio technology was being developed to improve navigation, and new bombsights were being produced to improve the RAF's appalling accuracy record. To accompany these changes, the RAF had been on a massive recruitment drive, transferring men from the other armed forces and drafting some from previously reserved occupations in order to swell their ranks for the years to come.

So when Harris first arrived at Bomber Command's headquarters in High Wycombe many of the problems that had plagued his predecessors were already well on the way to being solved. What was needed now was a determined leader, capable of making wise use of the formidable weapon in his hands. It is easy to see why Harris was chosen for the job: While his wisdom might sometimes have been called into question, not even his fiercest critics would have accused him of lacking determination.

Arthur Harris was born in Cheltenham, England, in 1892. His father, who was a civil servant in the British Raj, always wanted him to go into the army—something that the young Arthur Harris was dead set against. After a series of arguments on the matter, he left home at the age of sixteen and traveled to Rhodesia (now Zimbabwe), where he tried his hand at farming, gold mining, and driving horse teams. It is ironic that after all this he should have joined the army anyway, but six years later, at the outbreak of the First World War, that is exactly what he did. After taking part in the fight for German West Africa, he made his way back to Britain in 1915 and joined the Royal Flying Corps—which at that time was also a part of the army—and began a lifelong relationship with airplanes. Over the next twenty years he flew everything from night fighters to flying boats. He ended the First World War as a major with the Air Force Cross, and went on to command squadrons of bombers in some of the farthest-flung outposts of the empire under Trenchard's Air Control scheme. Eventually, in 1933, he returned to England and worked his way through the ranks of the Air Ministry, finally becoming commander-in-chief of Bomber Command midway through the Second World War.[5]

By all accounts Harris was an extremely forceful man, possessed of almost boundless energy and a bluntness that verged upon rudeness. He despised the other armed services, and was fond of saying that the army would never understand the value of tanks as a replacement for the cavalry until they could be made to "eat hay and shit."[6] He had a dry, cutting sense of humor, and would not suffer fools gladly. After the bombing of Pearl Harbor he was called by a friend in New Jersey who wanted advice on how to defend his factory against incendiary bombs. Harris told him to get a long-handled shovel and throw any bomb out of the window—and then went on to say that he should wrap it up and send it to Harris, who "would eat it and every incendiary bomb that fell on America in the war."[7] His aggressive nature was reflected in the way he drove. Late one night, while racing his Bentley between London and High Wycombe, he was stopped by a policeman who reproached him: "You might have killed somebody, sir." Whereupon Harris replied, "Young man, I kill thousands of people every night!"[8]

Harris made few friends, but those he did make remained loyal to him throughout their lives. The chief of air staff, Charles Portal, had been his friend for years, as had many of his subordinates—particularly Robert Saundby and Ralph Cochrane, who had first served with him in Iraq in 1922, and Don Bennett, who had served with him in a flying boat squadron at the end of the 1920s. His plain speaking also made him friends in the American air force, especially General Ira Eaker, who shared many of the same problems as Harris when it came to dealing with the other armed services. Most important, however, he inspired a fanatical devotion among the aircrews who served under him, many of whom vociferously defend him to this day. To them he was always known as "Butcher" Harris, or "Butch" for short—a man who would always get the job done, however distasteful it might seem to others, and whose first concern was providing his men with the right equipment and resources so that they could do their job, too.

Harris was a staunch disciple of Trenchard, and firmly believed that if enough concentrated misery could be inflicted on the cities of Germany over the next eighteen months the Nazis would be compelled to surrender. One of his first actions after taking command was to appear on a newsreel where he said, in clipped tones, "There are a lot of people who say that bombing cannot win the war. My answer to that is that it has never been tried yet. We shall see."[9] He had no qualms about area bombing, and remained unapologetic about it to the end of his life. "If the Germans had gone on using the same force for several nights against London," he said after the war, "... the fire tornado they would have raised would have been worse than anything that happened later in Hamburg, and the whole of London would have gone as Hamburg went."[10]

Right from the start, Harris's aim was to attack the very heart of the Reich: Berlin, the capital city; Hamburg, the center of shipbuilding and trade; and the Ruhr valley, Germany's industrial heartland. But the RAF was not strong enough yet to make a serious impact on such heavily defended targets, so he concentrated instead on demonstrating to the world what British bombers were capable of once they were deployed in force. The aim was threefold: to quiet the critics at home, to show support for the Russians, and to demonstrate to the Germans exactly what lay in store for them if they continued the war.

The targets he picked were two medieval cities on the Baltic coast of Germany: Lübeck and Rostock. Both seem to have been chosen for their vulnerability rather than their strategic importance: Their crowded, wooden buildings were highly flammable, and would provide a perfect opportunity for Harris to test his belief that incendiaries, rather than high explosives, were the most efficient means of destroying a city. As Harris himself said, the closely packed Hanseatic town of Lübeck was built "more like a fire-lighter than a human habitation," and when 234 aircraft firebombed it on March 28, 1942, 60 percent of the old city was consumed.[11] Over a thousand people lost their lives—it was the worst single attack on a German city so far.

A month later, a whole series of similar attacks were launched on Rostock, which again destroyed about 60 percent of the city center by fire. As German propaganda minister Joseph Goebbels stated in his diary, community life in the city had come to an abrupt end: "The situation in the city is in some sections catastrophic."[12] Harris later justified the attack by pointing to the Heinkel aircraft factory on the outskirts of the town, but the real victory here was a psychological one. While the British had failed to make any real impact on major targets, like Berlin or the cities of the Ruhr, they had at least managed to prove their worth against smaller targets. Here, at last, was a demonstration to the world that the power of the RAF was on the rise.

The destruction of Lübeck and Rostock was merely a taste of things to come. On May 30 Harris launched the first 1,000-bomber raid of the war. The target was originally supposed to be Hamburg, concentrating as many bombers in one attack as the port normally saw in a whole year—but the people of Hamburg received a temporary reprieve when the weather over the German coast deteriorated, and the target was switched at the last moment to Cologne. That night 1,046 aircraft took off for the north Rhineland, and within a few hours had dropped 2,000 tons of bombs on the city. An estimated 3,300 houses were utterly destroyed in the attack, along with 36 factories, and 469 people were killed, most of them civilians.

Twelve thousand separate fires had raged through the city, the gas mains had exploded, the water mains were severed, and all transport systems were put into such disarray that the disruption was still being felt months later.[13] But most important, the RAF had achieved a major propaganda success. The magic figure of a thousand bombers was far greater than anything the Luftwaffe could achieve, and when Britain was falling behind their enemy in every other arena of the war this was an important morale boost for the British people.

A second morale boost occurred later in the summer of 1942, when the Americans finally entered the fray. America had officially joined the war shortly after the bombing of Pearl Harbor at the end of 1941, but they were by no means ready for it. Like their British allies, they had been slow to arm themselves. While Germany had been rapidly building her air force since 1935, and Japan likewise throughout the 1930s, it was not until July 10, 1940, that Roosevelt convinced Congress to spend an extra $5 billion on war production. Slowly the world's greatest industrial giant began the long process of building its air force. By the time the Axis powers declared war against America in December 1941, the United States was already producing some 26,000 military airplanes per year, compared to Britain's 20,000 and Germany's 11,000. Even so, without experienced crews to fly these aircraft it would take eighteen months before the Americans would be able to deploy in force over the skies of northern Europe.

The overall commander of the United States Army Air Force (USAAF) was Lieutenant General Henry "Hap" Arnold, the son of a Pennsylvania medical doctor. Arnold had learned to fly before the First World War when he joined the Aeronautical Division of the U.S. Army Signal Corps, and had even at one point held the world altitude record. Throughout the First World War he ran the army's aviation schools, and rose steadily through the ranks until, in 1938, he became head of the Army Air Corps (the AAC was the forerunner of the USAAF, which did not form until June 1941).

If Butch Harris was an uncompromising commander, Hap Arnold was positively severe. He drove his staff relentlessly, and is reputed to have given one officer such a dressing down that he slumped dead over Arnold's desk from a heart attack. Impatient, austere, unceasingly demanding, he would rarely tolerate any form of failure or delay, regardless of whether there was a good reason for it. However, like Harris, he was widely respected as a man who got things done, and he had many friends within the air force. And, like Harris, he proved extremely shrewd in his choice of subordinates, and surrounded himself with brilliant and energetic people like Carl Spaatz, Ira Eaker, and Fred Anderson.

By the time of the Hamburg raids, Arnold's representative in Britain was Ira Eaker, commander of the U.S. Eighth Air Force. The contrast between Arnold and Eaker was stark. While Arnold was brusque, Eaker was both thoughtful and likable, and spent many years conducting what amounted to public relations for the U.S. Army Air Force. He was also a highly educated man, and had attended Georgetown University, Columbia University, and the University of Southern California. Despite their differences in character the two men seem to have got on extremely well, to the extent that they were able to write three books on military aviation together.

Early in 1942, Eaker was dispatched to Britain to set about creating an organization capable of taking the fight to Germany. From the very beginning he and his entourage were welcomed by the British, who immediately handed over several airfields for their use. There has been some suggestion over the years that British friendliness in these early days was governed by ulterior motives, and that what they really wanted was to assimilate the fledgling USAAF into a combined air force firmly under British control. However, it seems much more likely that the British were simply glad to accept a new ally, and willing to pass on as much help and advice as was necessary to get them operational as soon as possible. And their help was considerable. The RAF immediately shared their radar and communications systems, as well as vital intelligence; British Spitfires were put at the USAAF's disposal, both for fighter escort and to carry out weather reconnaissance; fuel trucks and other equipment were donated to U.S. airbases; U.S. airmen were given places on RAF training courses; British resources were used to help build new airbases; and the list goes on.

Relationships between the two forces, especially in the upper levels of command, were remarkably harmonious. When Eaker first arrived in Britain he lived with Harris and his family, and he often brought gifts and toys from America for Harris's young daughter. He also regularly attended Harris's "morning prayers" at Bomber Command Headquarters, when Harris and his staff chose the following night's targets. To some degree, therefore, the RAF and the USAAF were working as a combined force right from the outset. But from an official point of view, the RAF and the USAAF were, and would remain, completely separate forces, each with its own priorities and methods.

Five weeks after Harris's 1,000-bomber raid on Cologne, American airmen were ready to make their first operational flight over mainland Europe. On July 4 six USAAF crews, flying in borrowed planes, accompanied a squadron of British bombers on a daylight raid against German airfields in Holland. It was a baptism of fire: Two of the six American planes were shot down by flak, and a third had its starboard engine blown to pieces and barely managed to limp home. Nevertheless, a point had been made. The Americans had arrived in Europe.

Six weeks later a dozen American bombers made their first independent attack of the war, this time flying their own planes—the formidable B-17 Flying Fortresses of 97th Bomb Group. Their target was the Rouen-Sotteville railway marshaling yards, to the west of Paris. As the formation crossed the English Channel, one of the lead planes was carrying General Eaker himself, and it is proof both of the strength of American enthusiasm and their unshakable faith in their aircraft that such a high-ranking commander was allowed to fly on this earliest of missions. Fortunately he, and all the American aircrews, returned safely late that afternoon—although two Spitfires in the British fighter escort were shot down.

The Americans had a very different philosophy from the British. While the RAF had been forced to fly by night in order to avoid casualties, just as the Luftwaffe had been earlier in the war, the Americans were absolutely determined to conduct their bombing in daylight. There were two reasons for this. First, they were morally opposed to the bombing of civilians—at least in Europe—and strongly believed that bombing in daylight, when they could see their proper targets clearly, would result in fewer unnecessary casualties.[14] And second, they were convinced that daylight bombing would be far more effective. Unlike the British, whose bombing precision had barely improved since the First World War, the Americans had developed the highly accurate Norden bombsight, which allowed them consistently to drop bombs within fifty feet of a practice target from a height of four or five miles above the earth.[15] There was a myth in the USAAF that their aviators could drop a bomb into a pickle barrel from 30,000 feet. When their accuracy was so good, it made perfect sense to pinpoint their efforts on exact targets, rather than waste their bombs over large areas by night.

To start with, Harris, Portal, and even Churchill objected to the American insistence on daylight attacks, largely because they thought the whole policy was doomed. It was one thing to hit a practice target in the clear blue skies of California, but a different thing altogether to find a specific building in the center of a German city—especially when that city might be shrouded in the thick cloud of a European winter and defended by both Luftwaffe fighters and walls of predictive flak.[16] The Americans refused to be swayed, and it took them until the second half of 1943 to come to the painful realization that, in the absence of a long-range fighter escort, their terrible losses in the skies over Germany would simply be too heavy to bear.

But all that was in the future. For now the policy of daylight bombing seemed to be successful, largely because the Americans confined their fledgling efforts to targets in western France or the Low Countries, where they could still be accompanied by fighters. By the end of 1942 the Americans had flown over 1,500 sorties in twenty-seven operations (missions), and lost only thirty-four aircraft—a loss rate of just 2 percent. American optimism was so high that in August 1942 Ira Eaker confidently predicted that he and "Butch" Harris together would be able "completely to dislocate German industry and commerce and to remove from the enemy the means for waging successful warfare" as early as the middle of 1943.[17] When the two leaders were finally to join forces in the bombing of Hamburg, his prediction would almost come true.

Right from the beginning the British and American air forces had worked closely together, and this cooperation was formally sealed when the British and American military and political leaders met in Casablanca in January 1943 to plan a combined air offensive against Germany. Since the Allies were not yet strong enough to attempt an invasion of mainland Europe it was decided that the only way to carry the fight to the Axis powers was to increase the bombing campaign. Indeed, if the Allies were ever to attempt an invasion, it was essential that they first achieve air supremacy over the Germans.

To this end, the Combined Chiefs of Staff issued a directive to Air Marshal Harris and General Eaker, ordering them to begin demolishing a whole range of German targets: submarine yards and bases, aircraft production, ball-bearing factories, oil and rubber plants, and military transport systems.

They were also required to undermine German morale, as the preamble to the directive made clear:

> Your primary aim will be the progressive destruction and dislocation of the German military, industrial and economic system, and the undermining of the morale of the German people to a point where their capacity for armed resistance is fatally weakened.[18]

The plan was to subject Germany to a round-the-clock bombing campaign on a vast scale. RAF Bomber Command would continue their campaign against the cities by night, while the U.S. Eighth Army Air Force would attack specific military targets by day.

The coming year would be very different from anything that had gone before. Attacks would be bigger, more widespread, and they would be repeated again and again until the destruction was total. Over the next six months the Americans built up their air force from eighty or so operating planes to a force of well over 300, and began to accumulate vital combat experience over targets in northern Europe. The British, meanwhile, began a relentless offensive against the industrial cities of the Ruhr. In March they hit the Krupps armament factory in Essen, causing severe damage to buildings and machinery there. In May they devastated Dortmund and then Wuppertal in quick succession, especially the latter, where a miniature firestorm consumed most of the city center. In June they attacked Düsseldorf, starting fires that raged over forty square kilometers—twenty military installations were hit, seventy-seven companies put out of business, and 140,000 people were made homeless.

Germans all over the country began to notice the increasing intensity of the bombing, and gossip began to fly from one city to the next. Wild estimates of the death tolls began to circulate: In Dortmund, they said, 15,000 people had been killed (the figure was actually around 600), in Düsseldorf 17,000 (in reality it was 1,200), and in Wuppertal 27,000 (actually 3,400).[19] Worse than the numbers being touted were rumors about the way the people had died. Tales were told about victims' being turned into living torches by the phosphorus bombs, or becoming stuck in the melted asphalt of the roads. Rumors such as these certainly reached the people of Hamburg, but few people who lived there truly believed that the same fate lay in store for their city. When British reconnaissance planes dropped leaflets claiming that Hamburg would be next, no one heeded them. Even those Germans who thought the Nazis were doomed believed that Hamburg would be left largely intact, because the British and Americans would need the town and its harbor later on.[20] Besides, propaganda leaflets had been dropped throughout the war, and few people paid much attention to them.

But Hamburg would indeed be next. Even while Dortmund and Düsseldorf were still reeling from their huge attacks, Harris issued an operations order in which he stated his intention "to destroy Hamburg":

> The "Battle of Hamburg" cannot be won in a single night. It is estimated that at least 10,000 tons of bombs will have to be dropped to complete the process of elimination. To achieve the maximum effect of air bombardment this city should be subjected to sustained attack.

Moreover, having learned that fire was the best weapon, Harris ordered that most of the bombers should carry "maximum economic incendiary loads," in order to saturate the fire services of the city.[21]

Harris expressed the hope that the Americans would join in with the bombing of Hamburg, but it was not up to him to make that decision. Until now the USAAF had never bombed a target that the British had bombed the previous night—it was deemed too dangerous—and round-the-clock bombing had been merely a theory, not a reality. But the Americans also had their eye on Hamburg. The city contained many targets that the Americans considered high priority, including aircraft parts factories and submarine builders. U.S. planes had tried to attack the city at the end of June, but had been forced back by heavy cloud. Now, weather permitting, they would be all too happy to join the RAF, and when General Eaker finally confirmed the order to attack the Blohm & Voss shipyards on the banks of the Elbe, Hamburg's fate was sealed.

It must be said that not everyone on the Allied side was happy about this new target. Shortly before it took place Sir Henry Tizard, the brilliant academic who was responsible for creating the British radar network, wrote a letter to the prime minister expressing his misgivings about the proposed series of raids. Tizard was an outspoken critic of many aspects of British bombing policy and doubted that the war could ever be won by bombing alone. He was particularly unhappy about the prospect of destroying Hamburg, a city that he believed was essential to keep intact so that it could be used to administer Germany after the invasion:

> Hamburg is anti-Russian, anti-Prussian and anti-Nazi. It may well be soon, if not already, anti-war. Apart from submarine construction and shipping generally it is not industrially important. It is a centre of commerce rather than of production. It is a very important port and might therefore be much more useful to us alive than dead.[22]

Churchill did not agree, and neither did his chief of air staff. In a strongly worded rebuttal, Sir Charles Portal pointed to the numerous industrial, chemical, transportation, and engineering targets within the port. "It seems abundantly clear that Hamburg is much more than a dormant centre of peace-time commerce," he said, "and if so I certainly do not think we should refrain from bombing it."[23]

Tizard's suggestion was rejected: The bombing of Hamburg would go ahead as planned. The final piece of the jigsaw was a code name for the series of attacks, and the one they eventually settled upon was "Operation Gomorrah." The symbolic implication of the title was clear: God's power to rain down fire and destruction upon the earth now lay in man's hands, and was being wielded in what the British establishment saw as just retribution for the damage that the Luftwaffe had caused during the Blitz.

Chapter 8

THE BRITISH PLAN

Technology is making gestures precise and brutal, and with them men. It expels from movements all hesitation, deliberation, civility.

—THEODOR W. ADORNO[1]

On the morning of July 24, 1943, Air Chief Marshal Sir Arthur Harris arrived at Bomber Command HQ in High Wycombe at his usual time of 9.00 A.M. At the base of a large grassy mound, guarded by sentries, was a doorway that led to the enormous underground Operations Room. Harris made his way into the bunker and took his seat at the desk in the midst of the room. Behind him a huge board listed the available crews and airplanes, squadron by squadron, while on either side were great wall maps of Europe and a target priority list of dozens of cities and objectives. Around the table stood a dozen or so others: Harris's deputy commander-in-chief, Sir Robert Saundby; the meteorological officer, Magnus Spence; the senior air staff officer and his deputy; naval and army liaison officers; and various representatives from Intelligence and Operations. Today, an American VIP was also present—Brigadier General Fred Anderson, the commander of the USAAF's bomber force in Britain.

The routine at Bomber Command HQ was well established. Normally there would be a brief report of the previous night's operations, followed by a weather report from Magnus Spence. Excepting Harris himself, Spence was probably the most important man at the meeting, and his reports on the movements of various weather fronts across Europe were essential when it came to choosing the following night's targets. Having listened to Spence's summary, Harris would select two or three likely targets and, with a hasty shuffling of folders and photographs among his staff, the possibilities would be laid out on the table before him. There was rarely any discussion over what the target should be—Harris ran the meeting, and the decision was unequivocally his. After examining the various folders for a few moments, he would make a final decision, and the meeting would draw rapidly to a close: Harris would return to his office nearby, and his subordinates would immediately set about putting the operation in motion.[2]

This morning, however, everyone knew what the target was likely to be—weather permitting. The attack on Hamburg had been scheduled for two days now, but had been canceled twice at the last minute because of a bank of heavy cloud moving south toward the city. Now, as Magnus Spence laid out the weather charts on the table and began to explain the conditions, it became obvious that the weather was at last good enough to go ahead. Harris studied the charts for a few moments and then gave the order to proceed as planned. Moments later he rose from the chair, leaving the other members of the HQ team to telephone his decision through to the Pathfinder Force, the bomber groups, the army, the navy, and Fighter Command. General Anderson would take the news back to his USAAF headquarters at Wycombe Abbey personally. Operation Gomorrah was now on.

The plan had been outlined in detail two days before, on the morning of July 22, when the operation was first ordered.[3] In theory it was fairly simple. Every available aircraft from bomber squadrons across the country would take off between about 10:00 and 10:30 that night. They would fly to specific points along the coast, and merge into one huge stream of bombers flying across the North Sea. About eighty miles from the German coast they would converge on a single point, where they would turn in a tight flow and fly down toward Hamburg. (The bomber stream never flew directly toward the target, for fear of giving their destination away to the German radar stations.) At exactly one o'clock on Sunday morning, the Pathfinder aircraft would drop red and yellow target marker flares over Hamburg to indicate the aiming point. Two minutes later the first crews would start dropping their bombs.

Because of the sheer number of planes taking part in the raid, they were to attack in six waves of about 100 or 120 bombers each.[4] Each wave would have an average of about eight minutes to clear the target, which meant that there would be fifteen or sixteen bombers passing over the aiming point every minute. The most important thing was to achieve as much concentration as possible, so that the whole of the area around the aiming point was saturated with bombs. This way the fire services would be overwhelmed, and would be unable to prevent massive conflagrations springing up throughout the area. To try to prevent the bombing from becoming unfocused, more Pathfinders would continue to mark the target—this time with green target indicators—after the attack had begun. If the bombers could not spot the red markers, they were to aim at the greens instead. Having released their bomb loads, they were all to return home on a roughly parallel course.

Such plans were more easily ordered than executed. Even an undefended target could be difficult to find in the darkness of night, and in the past the RAF had often bombed the wrong parts of a city, or even missed a city altogether. To try to prevent such disastrous wastefulness, British scientists had developed a whole range of electronic navigational aids. The most important of these for medium- to long-range targets like Hamburg was called H2S. This worked a little like an airborne radar device, except that instead of transmitting high-frequency pulses out into the surrounding sky it would direct them downward, at the ground. By plotting the echoes on the screen of a cathode ray tube, it was possible to get a rough picture of the ground below, even through heavy cloud. The system was still in its infancy, and the picture it gave was sometimes so fuzzy as to be useless. However, it was particularly good at picking up built-up areas surrounded by water, so Hamburg was relatively easy to identify: The wide river Elbe and the distinctive lake in the center of the city would provide an unmistakable outline.

The second major difficulty was the strength of the defenses, both on the way to Hamburg and over the city itself. The whole of the coast of Europe was guarded by squadrons of German night fighters. As soon as a formation of bombers came within a hundred miles of mainland Europe, the German long-range *Freya* radar would pick them up and the defenses would get ready for action. Once the bombers came within thirty miles or so, a second, short-range radar system called *Würzburg* would be able to direct night fighters toward the bomber stream. The *Würzburg* system was extraordinarily effective for its time. Using one radar set to pick up an individual plane, a second set could guide a night fighter to within just a few hundred yards of his quarry. The night-fighter pilot would then be able to engage his own personal *Lichtenstein* radar, and home in for the kill. The only drawback of the system was that each radar station could only direct one interception at a time. This was why the British had evolved the tactic of concentrating all their bombers into a tight stream: If they could push as many planes as possible through a single point, the German defenses would only be able to intercept a handful before the majority had gone past unscathed.

It was not only German night fighters that were directed by radar. The Reich had flak defenses that stretched all the way from the sea to Berlin and beyond, and these too were radar-controlled. As soon as RAF bombers appeared over a city like Hamburg, radar-controlled searchlights that were a slightly different color from all the others—usually an intense blueish beam—would immediately begin to hunt them down. Once this blue master beam had locked onto a British bomber, all the other searchlights would join it, creating a huge cone of lights with the hapless airplane at its apex. Thus lit up, the plane would have to dive violently to prevent the full force of German flak batteries from blowing it out of the sky.

Another problem was predictive flak. Using their radar screens, the German defenders could plot the height, speed, and direction of flight of any one of the British bombers. They could then predict exactly where the airplane would be in the time it took the flak shells to fly 20,000 feet up into the air, and direct the flak batteries accordingly. The only way for a British pilot to avoid this was to zigzag and corkscrew across the sky—which, when the sky was full of other airplanes, greatly increased the chances of a collision. When a crew was about to release their bombs even this course of evasive action was denied them—if they were to hit the target they were obliged to fly straight and level for a full minute before the bombs were released and they could think about escaping once more. Only when the photoflash had gone, marking the place they had bombed on an intelligence photograph, could they turn their tail and head away from the hail of flak shells.

Hamburg had some of the most formidable flak defenses in the whole of Germany. Not only was there a ring of batteries on the outskirts of the city, but four massive gun towers stood in the center of the city and the port. The heaviest guns were capable of firing a pair of 128-millimeter shells twice a minute, each weighing twenty-six kilograms, to a range of 45,000 feet vertically into the sky.[5] If an aircraft received a direct hit from a shell like this it would spell disaster for the crew inside—if not immediately then during the long flight over the North Sea on the way home. Even if an aircraft was not hit, the threat of all the incredible firepower exploding all around them could seriously unnerve a crew and cause them to drop their bombs early and off-target.

Given the importance of the target and the strength of Hamburg's defenses, Harris was determined to use every advantage he could to make sure the operation succeeded. By the summer of 1943 Germany's radar-controlled defenses were beginning to cause intolerable casualties, so Harris began to press the prime minister to authorize the use of a new secret weapon that would jam the German radar. This secret weapon was code-named Window, and it consisted simply of bundles of paper strips, coated with metal foil on one side. When these bundles were dropped down the flare chute during the flight over Germany they would disperse, and as the strips floated down to earth they created a false blip on the German radar screens. With thousands of these false readings it would become impossible for the German radar operators to tell where the real bombers were—at a stroke, all of their defenses would become useless.

Until now this device had never been used, because the Ministry for Home Security was terrified that Germany would copy it and use it against Britain. However, by 1943, a new Blitz by the Luftwaffe was unlikely, so on July 15 Churchill finally gave Harris the go-ahead. Ironically, the Germans already knew of the principle behind Window—their own version was called *Düppel*—but the German chief of air signals, General Martini, had prevented its use because he, too, was afraid of the consequences if the British ever copied the idea.[6] Over the coming week Martini's worst fears would come true.

Since Window only worked on the *Würzburg* and *Lichtenstein* frequencies, the bombers would also be using two other devices: Mandrel, which interfered with the German long-range *Freya* radar; and Tinsel, which was a way of jamming German radio frequencies by transmitting the sound of the aircraft engines to drown out the voices of the pilots and their radar controllers.

This then was the British plan of attack for what would become known as the Battle of Hamburg. As Harris made his way back to his office, his deputy, Air Vice Marshal Sir Robert Saundby, remained in the Operations Room bunker to organize the practicalities of the raid. First he telephoned Air Vice Marshal Don Bennett, the head of the Pathfinder Force, which would be leading the operation. After discussing the precise route to and from the target with Bennett, Saundby set about organizing all the other details of the attack: bomb loads, takeoff times, aiming points, and so on. Only after every detail was precisely laid out would he and the rest of the staff retire to their own offices across the base at High Wycombe. Over the rest of the day, department by department, the beginning of the devastation of Hamburg was carefully prepared.

Chapter 9

THE FIRST STRIKE

*I know death hath ten thousand several doors
For men to take their exits.*

—JOHN WEBSTER[1]

At airbases across the eastern half of England it was a beautiful summer's day. Clear blue skies and bright sunshine had brought most of the young men from their quarters early, and for the first few hours of the day they passed the time in whatever way suited them best: reading, sharing cigarettes quietly outside their quarters, or playing cricket on the wide open spaces of the airfield. There was an atmosphere of expectancy in the air this morning: Operations had been canceled two days in a row now, and if they were canceled again there would be the chance of a day out in one of the local market towns. They could dash for the bus to York or Nottingham, Lincoln or Cambridge, or even take a train to London. They might perhaps catch a matinee at the cinema, and then a quick meal before joining the many other servicemen at one of the pubs or Saturday night dance halls. For those with wives or girlfriends, it would be a chance to spend valuable time together; for those without it would be an opportunity to meet some of the local girls. Unlike those in the other armed services, the men in Bomber Command were not quite so restricted by the discipline of barrack duties, and when they were not on operations their time generally belonged to themselves. It was a good life for a young man—just so long as he remained on the ground.

The past two days had been frustrating for everyone: After going through all the preparations for the hazardous flight to Hamburg the operation had been scrubbed at the last minute. Thursday had been particularly bad. Many crews had taken their airplanes to the end of the runways and were about to take off when the trip had been canceled. Some had already taken caffeine pills or benzedrine, dispensed by the station medical officer to keep them awake during the long flight across the North Sea and back. It was too late to get to any of the local towns to blow off steam, so those who could had made their way to the village pubs to try to counteract the action of the drugs in their system with alcohol. Others settled down in the mess, or tried to get an early night. Even those who hadn't taken the MO's "wakey-wakey" pills often found it difficult to sleep. After gearing themselves up for action throughout the day it was difficult to let go of all the accumulated anxiety. They knew that any cancellation of operations was only a temporary reprieve: If they didn't fly on their first, or tenth, or twentieth operation tonight, then they would only have to do it tomorrow instead, or the day after that.

While most of the young airmen relaxed in the morning sunshine, a few, usually the skippers of the aircraft, would make their way over to the station office to hear the results of the morning's "Group tie-up" with Bomber Command headquarters. Others would go to the messes, where the battle order was pinned to a board whenever operations were on. When they discovered that "ops" were indeed on, there was a general sigh all round. There was no indication of what the target would be, but the fuel loads designated for each plane were the same as yesterday, so it would probably be Hamburg again. There would be no chance of a trip to Betty's Bar, or the Snakepit, or the Windmill Theater this Saturday night. Reluctantly, they headed back out onto the airfield to relay the news to their aircrews out on the grass.

Once a crew knew that ops were on, a change came over them: The frivolity of a cricket match would be replaced with an air of purpose—they had a job to prepare for. They would leave off what they had been doing and make their way out to where their planes were standing, around the perimeter of the airfield. Here, trains of bombs would already be arriving, ready to be fused by the station armorers and then loaded into the airplanes. This morning there was something else waiting for them, too: stacks and stacks of brown paper parcels, piled up on the runway beside each plane. Many of the men were used to taking propaganda leaflets on a raid, but this was something different. Unable to contain their curiosity, some of the men opened the packages up, but what they found inside only confused them further. Each package seemed to contain nothing but bundles of foil strips—about fourteen inches long and an inch wide—silver on one side and black on the other. Speculation about what they could be was rife. "We couldn't make head nor tail of it," said Harold McLean of 427 Squadron. "One chap peed on it to see if it reacted. It didn't."[2]

While the airmen were puzzling over these strange packages, the ground crew, the "erks" as they were affectionately known, were busy checking over their aircraft. After a while the airmen climbed up into the machines to join them. No matter how curious they might be about these enigmatic parcels, there was work to be done in the plane—equipment to be checked, mechanisms to be tested. This was the machinery on which their lives depended, and very few crews ever thought of neglecting their preparations for a night on ops. The gunners would oil their guns, and perhaps realign them so that they converged at the right point. The bomb aimer would check his instruments, as would the wireless operator and the navigator. Then perhaps the pilot and the flight engineer would take the machine up for a quick air test, just to make sure that it was flying smoothly, before returning to base for lunch and the long, slow wait till dusk.

That afternoon was a nervous one for many. Until briefing in the evening there was nothing to do but hang around, trying not to think of the night that lay ahead of them. They were barred from leaving the base, so there was no chance of distracting themselves with a trip to the local village. Instead they would take to their quarters and try to catch an hour's sleep, or lie on the grass in the bright summer sunshine, gazing across the airfield at the gas pumps pumping fuel into their aircraft, at the erks cycling round the perimeter track, or the WAAF drivers bringing bomb trains back to the hangars. Many airmen describe feeling strangely divorced from all the purposeful activity that surrounded them during the long hours of the afternoon, as if it had nothing whatsoever to do with them. And yet, subconsciously, they were aware that it had everything to do with them—that they, indeed, were the reason for it. It was impossible to forget that in a few hours' time they would be taking off in those huge, forbidding machines, and the peaceful English afternoon would be transformed to a nightmare of flak and fighters in the skies over Germany.

Experienced airmen would try to avoid thinking of what lay ahead, and distracted themselves with games of chess or football, or by laughing at the latest buffoonery of Pilot Officer Prune in *Tee Em* magazine. It was best not to think of all the narrow escapes of previous sorties over the cauldron of Essen and the other cities of the Ruhr valley. And yet the thought inevitably surfaced: Perhaps tonight their luck would finally run out. Bomber Command losses were running at almost 5 percent at the time—in other words, one in every twenty planes on any given night would not be coming back. A standard tour was thirty operations. It did not take a mathematician to work out that the odds of finishing their tour alive were stacked against them.

For inexperienced crews the prospects were even worse: There was always a far higher proportion of losses among those on one of their first five operations. Brand-new crews, or "sprogs" as they were known, would have felt especially nervous about what lay ahead of them. All the training in the world could not prepare a young man for the stress of combat, and many were worried about how they might react. If a pilot panicked, or if a gunner froze at the wrong moment, it could mean not only his own death but that of his crewmates. It is important to remember that many airmen were still in their teens when they began flying—the average age of a new recruit into the training schools was twenty-one—and many viewed their first operation as an important rite of passage into manhood.[3] At this stage of the war they were aware that a significant number would not pass the test without being blown out of the sky.

At last, around five o'clock, the men were called to briefing. Gradually the crews would filter into the briefing room and take their places in the rows of chairs, some of them talking and joking to take their minds off the night ahead, but the majority gazing quietly at the board at the end of the room, curious about what lay beneath the sheet that covered it. Once the door was closed behind them there would be a roll call, and then finally the officer in charge of operations—usually one of the flight commanders, but occasionally the CO—would pull down the cover to reveal the target map. Across the room men would crane forward to see where the red line of ribbon on the map led to. For the benefit of those at the back, the officer would declare in a loud, clear voice: "Your target for tonight, gentlemen, is Hamburg."

For many crews there was a sense of at least partial relief on seeing the target. After numerous flights to the Ruhr, where the defenses were second only to those at Berlin, it would make a welcome change: The flight to Hamburg was mostly over the North Sea, so there was much less chance of being caught by flak on the journeys in and out. On the other hand, in some squadrons Hamburg was just as notorious as anything the Ruhr could offer. At 57 Squadron, for example, Hamburg had a particularly bad reputation. The squadron had not attacked the city since March, when the commanding officer, Freddie Hopcroft, and his crew had almost been killed. Ever since then the CO had briefed other targets with the words, "Now, boys, the defenses are nothing like as good as Hamburg, so you should be all right." After several months of this the strengths of the Hamburg defenses had gained a near-mythical status, and to learn that they were finally flying to the city naturally filled 57 Squadron crews with a terrible sense of trepidation.[4]

After a general briefing by the CO, describing their route, their time of attack, and so on, a variety of other officers would take the stage. The met officer would give them information about what sort of weather conditions to expect, both over the target and on their journey in. The armament officer would explain details about the bomb loads, and the signals officer would brief them on what radio countermeasures they would be using. Tonight, for the first time, the ground stations would be transmitting average wind speeds (or "Zephyrs," as they were code-named) to all the crews at regular intervals, in order to help with navigation.

Eventually, the intelligence officer took the stage. The intelligence officer always commanded the men's attention far better than the other lecturers, because he was the one who told them where all the danger spots would be on the way in to the target. He also told them *why* they were going after this particular target. Hamburg, he explained, was not only a major hub of manufacturing, it was also Germany's main center of submarine production. If they could knock Hamburg out of the war it would deal a blow not only to the Germans at home, but to their effort in the Battle of the Atlantic.

Today, however, the intelligence officer had something else to tell them. Once he had finished his normal spiel, he began to explain the secret behind all the brown paper packages that the crews had seen being loaded into the aircraft earlier. The silver foil strips inside the parcels were called "Window," he said, and they were a new and simple measure designed to confuse the German radar defenses.

"You will already have been told how to drop Window," he continued; "it has been worked out as carefully as possible to give you maximum protection, but there are two points which I want to emphasize strongly. Firstly, the benefit of Window is a communal one: The Window which protects you is not so much that which you drop yourself as that which is already in the air dropped by an aircraft ahead. To obtain full advantage, it is therefore necessary to fly in a concentrated stream along the ordered route.

"Secondly, the task of discharging the packets of Window will not be an easy one. You are hampered by your oxygen tube, intercom connections, the darkness, and the general difficulties of physical effort at high altitudes. Despite these hardships, it is essential that the correct quantities of Window are discharged at the correct time intervals."

He went on to explain that Window was considered so important that the Air Ministry was already developing machines to ensure a steady flow from the aircraft. In the meantime, however, it was up to the airmen themselves to maintain a "machinelike regularity" when dropping the bundles down the flare chute.

"When good concentration is achieved," he continued, "Window can so devastate an RDF defense system that we ourselves have withheld using it until we could effect improvements in our own defenses, and until we could be sure of hitting the enemy harder than he could hit us. The time has now come when, by the aid of Window in conserving your unmatched strength, we shall hit him even harder."[5]

The intelligence officer was often a figure of fun during briefings. Whenever he claimed that an operation would be a piece of cake, or that the route out to a target would be free from flak, he would be greeted with jeers from the more cynical airmen in the room. Today, however, his speech was generally greeted by a respectful silence. While some of the old hands privately doubted that a few bundles of silver foil would protect them from the ferocity of the German defenses, most crews seemed to accept the speech at face value. The secrecy that had so far surrounded this new device had obviously impressed them: This was not merely the normal intelligence guesswork, but something that had been worked out scientifically. Most of the airmen knew enough about radar to recognize its limitations—that it could be jammed by clouds of foil strips seemed entirely plausible. Only time would tell.

Once this speech had been made, the commanding officer took the stage once more and asked if anyone had any questions—but by now they had been well briefed, and few people had anything left to ask. Then he told them to synchronize their watches and wished them all luck—and with that he left the room. The briefing was over.

As the men filtered out of the main briefing room there was no time to talk about the unusual speech they had just heard, even if it had been seemly to do so. Many of them now had to go to shorter, specialist briefings, to make sure that all the minutiae of their duties were fixed firmly in their minds. Navigators would be given the exact route to and from the target, along with details about the turning points, the winds they were likely to encounter, and so on. Wireless operators were told which German frequencies they would be jamming and reminded to listen for the *Zephyr* transmissions, while bomb aimers would be reminded about what color target indicators they would see, and which were the right ones to bomb.

It was only when all the crew members came together again for their flight meal in the mess, at around seven o'clock, that they were able to discuss the forthcoming operation. But by now most of them were tired of it, and wanted to talk about something else. The only mention of the job that faced them would come in typical RAF gallows humor: They would shake their heads at one another and run finger across their throats to imply that another crew was going to be shot down. The anxious questions of new crews would be greeted with callous replies: "Oh, I wouldn't worry about *that*, you're not going to make it tonight anyway."[6] As they collected their trays of bacon and eggs, beans, tomatoes, and even fruit juice—rare luxuries in British civilian life in 1943—some would use their sense of impending doom to flirt with the girls behind the counter and entreat them to give them extra-large helpings. After all, they'd say, this might be their last meal. It wouldn't do to die on an empty stomach: The least the kitchen staff could do was to fatten them up, like lambs for the slaughter, before they were sent out into the hellish skies over Germany.

After their meal, the men made their way out to the parachute store to pick up their parachutes and don their flying gear. They would empty their pockets of everything personal—even the stub of a cinema ticket could give away important intelligence if they were captured—and then fill them again with all the various things they might need: escape kits, foreign currency, perhaps a penknife for emergencies, and the all-important flying rations to stave off hunger on the way home. The gunners and bomb aimers began to look strangely inflated: dressed in several layers of jackets, including one electrically heated one, it was a miracle that they ever managed to fit into the confined spaces of the gun turrets.

As the crews waited for the trucks to come and take them to dispersal there was much laughing and joking—but the station staff, who had seen hundreds of aircrews fly off never to return, knew it was all just bluff. Even the most blasé airmen were exhibiting nerves, and each of the many different ways they found to fight down their fear had its own poignancy. Some of them lay on the grass, smoking pipes and gazing out into the dusk. Others flirted shamelessly with the WAAF drivers who came to pick them up, snatching a last opportunity to speak with a woman before taking off into the unknown. For the many New Zealanders, Australians, and Canadians among the crews it sometimes helped to talk about their homes, thousands of miles away on the other side of the world. Superstition was rife. Some of the men were laden with lucky charms and dolls, and when they lost or forgot one it could send them into a blind panic. Many slavishly followed a little ritual as they prepared themselves—always wishing their crew members luck with the same words, always buttoning their coats in the same order, always taking the same seat in the truck out to dispersal where their plane was waiting for them, huge and silent in the dusk by the perimeter track.

Out on the airfield, with half an hour to go before it was time to start the engines, the airmen's anxiety mounted still further. For Bill McCrea this was the worst time. Surrounded by the smell of kerosene and engine oil, the gray-blue mass of the airplane looming over him, there was nothing left to dispel his rising nerves:

> You had to hang around at dispersal, and talk to the ground crew. That was very, very bad. We'd talk about anything, anything at all. Anything apart from what you had to do—the job. Sometimes I felt physically sick. . . . It wasn't what was happening at the time that was the problem. Whenever anything happened you could fight it, you had things to do. It was the thought of what *might* happen—that was the worrying thing.[7]

At last, as the sun was sinking over the horizon, it was time to start the engines. The crew indulged their last ritual of the evening—relieving their bladders against the huge wheels of the aircraft—before climbing into their various positions inside. The pilot and flight engineer would run up the great Merlin engines in the correct order, one by one: "Starboard inner: contact." A press on the starter button, and the engine would roar into life. "Starboard outer . . ." With all four engines running, the pilot and flight engineer checked the oil pressure, tested the throttles and the magnetos for each engine. The navigator spread his maps, and the air gunners crammed themselves into the turrets that would be their cages for the next six hours. On a signal from the flight engineer, the ground crew would pull away the wooden chocks from in front of the wheels and the aircraft would start to taxi round to the dispatcher's trailer, where groups of WAAFs had gathered to wave goodbye to each plane as it headed off down the runway. A green light was flashed as the signal for takeoff—radio silence was imperative, even now, in case the Germans got wind of the impending attack—and with a roar, the first of 792 Lancasters, Stirlings, Halifaxes, and Wellingtons took off into the gathering dusk.

Kenneth Hills, a bomb aimer with 9 Squadron, remembers this moment as one of the most nerve-wracking of all:

> Taking off was always a sobering moment (bearing in mind what a tire burst would do for you when you were full of high explosive and 100-octane fuel), bumping down the runway, seeing the perimeter hurtling at you, waiting for the lift-off which seemed endless, then suddenly you are clear, no bumps, no tire burst, just a lovely sound from the Merlins, and you are on your way.[8]

The first plane to leave the ground was Sergeant P. Moseley's Stirling of 75 (New Zealand) Squadron at 9.45 P.M. He was soon overtaken by the faster Lancasters of the Pathfinder Force, who would be leading the attack. Of the hundreds of planes that headed down runways across England that evening, only one failed to take off; forty-five more would return to their bases with various technical difficulties—an average figure for this time in the war.

For those who were left on the ground, takeoff was always an impressive sight. "About twenty yards away we could just discern a vast dinosaurish shape," wrote one American observer on a similar night, as he watched the last of the stream of planes leaving the airfield:

> After a moment, as if stopping to make up its mind . . . it lumbered forward, raising its tail just as it passed us, and turning from something very heavy and clumsy into a lightly poised shape, rushing through the night like a pterodactyl. At this instant, a white light was flashed upon it and a Canadian boy from Vancouver who was standing beside me, put down its number and the moment of departure. It vanished from sight at once

and we stood staring down the field, where in a few seconds a flashing green light announced that it had left the ground. . . .

A great calm settled over the place as the last droning motors faded out in the distance and we all drove back to the control room where a staff hang onto the instruments on a long night vigil. . . . I went to sleep thinking of the . . . youngsters I had seen, all now one hundred and fifty miles away, straining their eyes through the blackness relieved only by the star-spangled vault above them.[9]

An hour later, just after 11:00 P.M., the last of the huge fleet of aircraft took to the air. The battle of Hamburg was about to begin.

Once each plane was finally airborne everybody's nerves began to subside. Each member of the crew had his job to do, and there was a sense of relief that the operation was finally under way. In the cockpit at the front the pilot held the controls in both hands, wrestling the aircraft up into the sky, while the flight engineer advanced the throttles for one side or the other, to correct any swing that had developed after takeoff. Flying a four-engined heavy bomber in 1943 was a physical business, and required brute strength, especially when taking off or landing.

Behind the pilot and the flight engineer, curtained off from the cockpit, sat the navigator, sideways on, at his table. Charts and logbooks were laid out before him, lit by a small Anglepoise lamp as he took his first reading of the night. "First course, Skipper, 032 degrees," he bellowed through the intercom. It was difficult to hear one another over the deafening noise of the aircraft engines, and the men often had to speak loudly and clearly to make themselves understood.

Just behind the navigator, separated by banks of equipment, sat the wireless operator. Unlike the other members of the crew, the W/Op often spent the flight in his shirtsleeves: The Lancaster's heating system had a hot-air outlet right beside him, and he was often the only member of the crew to stay warm throughout the trip. Beyond him was the main spar, which in the Lancaster was a waist-high wall of metal between the two wings—and beyond that were all the stacks of Window, piled up next to the Elsan chemical toilet, ready to be dropped down the flare chute. A narrow ladder led up to the turret, where the mid-upper gunner sat scanning the sky above for the possibility of intruding German night fighters.

The final two members of the crew sat in the extremities of the plane. In the nose, beneath the cockpit, the bomb aimer faced downward, with nothing but a sheet of perspex between him and a drop of thousands of feet to the ground below. At the very back sat the "tail-end Charlie"—the rear gunner—with nothing to look at but the fading glow of the sunset on the western horizon. Back here, separated from the rest of the crew, the gunner faced the prospect of a lonely night. It was cold, too. It was all too easy to mistake a smudge on the glass for an approaching night fighter, so the rear turret had a square section cut out of the perspex in front of the gunner's face, called a "clear view panel." The rear gunner was literally flying with a window open. At 20,000 feet temperatures could fall to thirty degrees below freezing and lower, and even his electrically heated suit could not always take the edge off a chill like that. Besides, some rear gunners either did not wear their heated suits or did not plug them in, because they found the warmth made them drowsy. Rear gunners were often the only members of the crew to spot an approaching night fighter, and when the long dreary night could be interrupted in a split second it was better to remain alert, even if that did mean shivering in Arctic temperatures.

There were four main types of British bombers in use at this stage of the war. The newest and most effective was the Avro Lancaster: a huge, sleek machine capable of flying to Berlin and back laden with over six tons of bombs. Its long, cigar-shaped fuselage was punctuated by five perspex blisters, through which its crew would constantly scan the skies for attackers. Four Rolls Royce Merlin engines along its wings could carry it to a height of 22,000 feet and above, and at speeds of 266 mph. The Lancaster was unquestionably the best night bomber of the Second World War.

Slightly bigger and more temperamental in the air was the Handley Page Halifax. With a ceiling of 20,000 feet, the Halifax was relatively safe from flak, but its blind spot beneath the back of the aircraft made it vulnerable to fighters coming from behind and below. Despite its impressive ceiling, and a top speed of over 275 mph, it could only carry just over half the bomb load of a Lancaster.

The Short Stirling was often described as a "gentleman's aircraft": It was easy to handle, and capable of absorbing an enormous amount of punishment before it succumbed to flak or fighter fire. Without the waist-high spars that the Lancaster had in its interior, it was also relatively easy to escape from—which was fortunate, because its lamentable ceiling of only 16,000 feet made it the first target of all the German flak batteries. There are tales of Lancaster and Halifax crews cheering when they heard that Stirlings would be accompanying them on an operation, because they drew all the German fire away from the higher-flying machines.

The last type of airplane that flew on Hamburg tonight was the twin-engined medium bomber, the Vickers Wellington. This unfortunate aircraft was virtually obsolete by this stage in the war, and seemed to combine all the worst drawbacks of all the four-engined "heavies." It was slower, smaller, and had fewer guns with which to defend itself. It flew at a similar height to the Stirling, but could carry less than half its bomb load. Seventy-three of these airplanes had taken off for Hamburg this evening, with a further twelve tasked with minelaying in the Elbe estuary and dropping propaganda leaflets over France.

For the first part of the trip, the main force would also be accompanied by a small force of light bombers: eleven De Havilland Mosquitos would follow them across the North Sea, before peeling off to attack alternative targets in Kiel, Lübeck, Bremen, and Duisburg. These additional targets were merely diversions, designed to keep the Germans guessing about the main force's true destination.

At first glance such diversionary missions looked extremely dangerous for the crews concerned: Bombers are like herd animals—safe in numbers, but extremely vulnerable whenever they venture out alone. If one considers that the Mosquito was made only of plywood, and usually had no defensive armament whatsoever, then these four diversionary raids begin to look like a suicide mission. However, Mosquitos were so fast, and were capable of flying at such extreme altitudes, that they were in fact virtually untouchable. All of them would return to England the next morning completely unscathed.

This then was the force that took off from airfields across England on July 24. Their first task was to climb as high and as quickly as possible—the higher they were, the safer they were. As they did so, they set course for their crossing points on the English coast: 4 Group and the Canadians of 6 Group headed toward Hornsea, 1 and 5 Groups made for Mablethorpe on the coast of Lincolnshire, while 3 Group and the Pathfinders of 8 Group headed for Cromer in Norfolk.

Over these seaside towns all the separate squadrons in each group

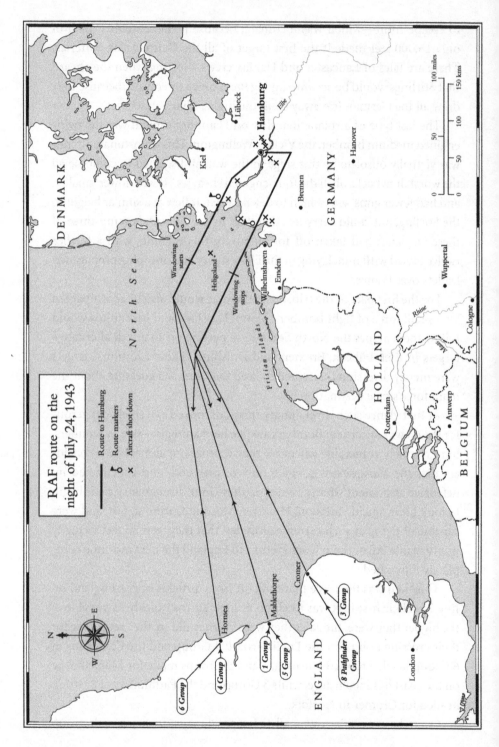

RAF route on the
night of July 24, 1943

—— Route to Hamburg
♠ ○ Route markers
✕ Aircraft shot down

would merge into a wide stream heading out to sea. For those in the vanguard it was possible to make out many of the other aircraft filling the sky around them. It was well after ten o'clock at night now, but with double summertime bringing the clocks forward two hours the sky was still fairly light, especially to the north. For those coming later it was already too dark to make out any of their fellow airplanes. Only the occasional blink of green and red navigation lights told them that they were not alone on their journey, but as they headed out to sea even these lights were extinguished, rendering almost 800 aircraft virtually invisible in the night.

As they headed toward the darkness of mainland Europe, the atmosphere inside each airplane was professional, businesslike. Each member of the crew had his own specific duties and was left to perform them in his own way. In general, strict radio silence was observed, and crews did not even speak to each other on the intercoms unless there was something important to report. The only sound was the constant drone of the aircraft engines as they continued to climb as high as they could go, but in the thin, warm air of summer many airplanes struggled to reach their operational ceilings.

Leading the bomber stream were the Pathfinders of 8 Group. Behind them, spreading back over almost 200 miles, was the rest of the force. They were heading to a point about eighty miles from the German coast—54°45N, 07°00E—where the three separate streams of bombers were to merge into one and turn toward the southeast and their target. The lead aircraft had already been in the air for two and a half hours. They turned at about twenty past midnight and headed in toward the German coast on a bearing of 103°.

Ten minutes later the flight engineer in each of the leading aircraft climbed over the main spar into the back of the plane and began dropping the first bundles of Window.[10] They had been provided with stopwatches and told to throw the bundles down the flare chute at exactly one-minute intervals. The bundles were supposed to disperse into small clouds of paper that would float harmlessly down through the air. In practice, however, the "machinelike" efficiency called for at the briefing often ended up being a little more chaotic. Sometimes the Window would blow back into the aircraft, filling the air in the back of the plane with metallized paper strips. Once or twice the bundles did not open properly and the solid packets hit other bombers, ripping off aerials or even breaking through the perspex of one of the gun turrets.[11] Even when the Window did disperse properly, it often blew up onto the mid-upper turrets of the airplanes, obscuring the mid-upper gunner's view. One side of the paper was covered with a black coating that easily rubbed off, and after fifteen minutes or so the perspex on the mid-upper turret was so smudged and blackened that the gunner there was rendered effectively blind. This black coating also came off on the man tasked with throwing it from the plane, and many bomb aimers and flight engineers soon looked like chimney sweeps, covered from head to toe in soot.

Despite the various mishaps, though, most of the crews managed to continue dropping the bundles of metal strips according to plan. As they plowed on toward the German coast they had no idea whether this new device would work. Gradually they began to feel anxious once again. In less than half an hour they would be over Hamburg, and the real test of their new tactics would begin.

By now the Germans knew the RAF was coming. A long-range *Freya* radar station near Ostend in Holland had picked up the first airplanes heading across the sea at around eleven o'clock, and the defenses had been plotting the course of the bomber stream ever since, waiting to see where it turned before committing their night fighters to action.[12] By half past midnight, shortly after the first planes in the bomber stream had turned toward Hamburg, the night fighters of several airfields were already airborne. Since Hamburg was now a possible target, at 12:33 A.M. the order was given to sound the *Fliegeralarm* sirens.[13]

In 1943, Germany had the most impressive defenses of any country in the world. Their first line of defense was the infamous Kammhuber Line— a belt of interlinked night-fighter "boxes" that stretched along the length of the European coast. Each box had its own fighters, which would patrol that box only, ensuring an evenly spread defense across the whole line. Hamburg in particular was protected by more than a dozen airfields, with their headquarters at Stade to the west of the city.[14] Closer in to the city were belts of searchlights, and dozens of batteries of heavy flak. It was a formidable setup, and the whole structure was now on high alert, waiting for the British to arrive.

As the bomber stream approached the coast, it was being watched closely by the head of the German 2nd Fighter Division, Generalleutnant

Schwabedissen, in his headquarters at Stade airfield. Housed in a giant bombproof bunker, Schwabedissen's central combat station was the nerve center of all the defenses in northwest Europe and was a true triumph of German technology. One of only five control centers in the whole country, it was nicknamed the "Battle Opera House," or the "Kammhuber Kino," because of its resemblance to a cinema. Inside, dominating the huge combat control room, was a gigantic frosted-glass screen, about fifty feet wide, inscribed with a map of Germany. Onto this glass screen were projected spots of light, which represented all the different airplanes in the sky at any one time—white spots to show the enemy planes approaching, green spots for the German night fighters, and illuminated writing to describe their height, position, and direction of flight.

Even the Luftwaffe's commander of fighters, Adolf Galland, found this feat of technology impressive:

> The whole was reminiscent of a huge aquarium lit up, with a multitude of water-fleas scuttling madly behind the glass walls. Each single dot and each change to be seen here was the result of reports and observations from radar sets, aircraft-spotters, listening posts, reconnaissance and contact planes, or from units in action. They all merged together by telephone or wireless in this centre, to be received, sorted, and within a few minutes transposed into transmittable messages. What was represented here on a giant map was a picture of the air situation ... with about one minute's delay.[15]

In front of this huge map, on rising steps like an amphitheater, fighter control officers (*Jägerleitoffiziere*) were seated in several rows, ready to direct their night fighters by radio into the hunt. Above them, on a raised balcony, Generalleutnant Schwabedissen and his staff conducted the battle against the Allied bombers in an unhealthy fog of cigarette smoke, his orders rising above a symphony of ticking teleprinters, humming ventilators, and the urgent murmur of telephone operators across the room.

Tonight everyone in the room was watching the screen just as avidly as any cinema audience. Schwabedissen had already ordered his night fighters to scramble, and scores of green T-shapes were making their way across the frosted-glass map. Ahead of them a mass of white dots was making its way toward the German coastline. But something was wrong: While the front of the bomber stream still appeared to be moving forward, the tail end remained static on the map—it was as if the RAF bomber force were expanding before their eyes.

Up on the balcony, General Schwabedissen demanded to know what was going on, but nobody was able to give him a straight answer. Across the room nervous operators were engaged in urgent telephone conversations with radar stations throughout northwest Germany. The messages they were getting back were always the same. It was impossible: There appeared to be not hundreds of bombers approaching, but *thousands*—too many for the radar screens to cope with. Some radar sets appeared to have stopped working altogether: Instead of registering single, distinct blips on their screens they showed nothing but a general fuzz, as if the bombers were approaching in a solid wall several miles wide.

In the air, the situation was just as confused. Night-fighter pilots who had been following instructions from their fighter control officers now found themselves being sent round in circles. When it became clear that something was wrong with the ground radar, they began to rely on their own airborne *Lichtenstein* sets—but these, too, were beginning to show false readings, as one German fighter pilot named Wilhelm Johnen recalled:

It was obvious that no-one knew exactly where the enemy was or what his objective would be. An early recognition of the direction was essential so that the night fighters could be introduced as early as possible into the bomber stream. But the radio reports kept contradicting themselves. Now the enemy was over Amsterdam and then suddenly west of Brussels, and a moment later they were reported far out to sea in map square 25. What was to be done? The uncertainty of the ground stations was communicated to the crews. . . . No one knew where the British were, but all the pilots were reporting pictures on their screens. I was no exception. At 15,000 ft my sparker announced the first enemy machine on his Li [airborne *Lichtenstein* radar set] . . . Facius proceeded to report three or four pictures on his screen. I hoped that I would have enough ammunition to deal with them! Then Facius suddenly shouted: "Tommy flying towards us at a great speed. Distance decreasing . . . 2,000 yards, 1,500 . . . 1,000 . . . 500 . . . He's gone." "You're crackers, Facius," I said jestingly. But I soon lost my sense of humour for this crazy performance was repeated a score of times.[16]

No matter where the pilot flew he made no contact with any bombers at all: They simply disappeared, like phantoms, as soon as he approached. Window, it seemed, was having exactly the effect that the British desired.

As the leading British Pathfinder aircraft crossed the German coast near Heide, they began dropping the first of their yellow route marker flares. The idea was to give the bomber stream, which was still spread out all over the sky, a single point to fly through—that way they would be a far more concentrated force as they arrived in Hamburg. However, it was not only the RAF bombers who saw the flares—a handful of German night fighters in the area also saw them. In the absence of anything else to help them find the bomber stream, they headed toward the light. One of them managed to shoot down a Halifax, which fell in flames and exploded over the sea. A few minutes later a second Halifax was attacked, but this time the rear gunner returned fire at once, and it was the German plane that fell, eventually crashing into the ground near Flensburg.[17]

It is easy to summarize such events with just a few words, but combats like this were desperate affairs, especially for British bomber crews. After more than two hours of utter silence, a burst of fire could appear from the darkness and kill seven men in an instant. Crews that were shot down rarely saw it coming. If they did, then sometimes a short burst from one of the gunners was enough to scare the enemy off—an alert bomber crew could be just as deadly as the night fighters themselves, as the combats over the German coast tonight demonstrated. Usually it was the rear gunner, with his clear vision panel at the back, who saw the danger first. He would broadcast a warning to the pilot across the intercom: "Fighter on the port quarter—corkscrew port!" The temptation to turn away from an attacker was strong, but the trick for survival was to turn *into* him so that he could not follow. Then, for the next thirty seconds or so, the bomber pilot would have to throw his aircraft about the sky, hoping that he had dropped out of his attacker's line of sight. As long as he kept flying in a spiral motion then at least his enemy would not be able to keep his guns trained on him for more than an instant. A minute later the bomber would be back on course again, with nothing to show for the experience but the mess of charts and instruments that had been thrown off the navigator's desk, and the faint smell of fear throughout the aircraft.

Tonight there would be very few such incidents. Most of the German night fighters remained tied to their "boxes," unable to locate the bomber stream amidst the confusion. So the bombers continued unmolested across the coast, and down to their next turning point above Kellinghusen, a few minutes north-northwest of Hamburg.

Some of the crews dropped propaganda leaflets on German towns along the way. More would drop leaflets later, either over the target or on the way home. Leafleting was an unpopular pastime in the higher levels of Bomber Command, and staff officers joked that its only effect was to supplement German civilians' rations of toilet paper. (They were only half joking: When middle-class Hamburg housewives were reduced to cutting squares of toilet paper from biscuit wrappers, this important commodity was in short supply.[18]) Tonight's leaflets showed a picture of RAF bombers flying over the burning streets of Dortmund, with the caption *Die Festung Europa hat kein Dach* ("Fortress Europe has no roof"). To press the message home, one or two of the airmen emptied the contents of their urine bottles onto the leaflets before dropping them out—a petty act of contempt to add to the injuries they were about to inflict.[19]

Eventually, after almost three hours in the air, the navigators of the leading Pathfinders began to recognize the outline of the city on their H2S sets: They had arrived. As they began their final approach into Hamburg, the crews of over 700 bombers braced themselves for the onslaught of flak and searchlights they expected to encounter above the most heavily defended target in northern Germany. But the nightmare never materialized. There were fifty-four heavy and twenty-six light flak batteries defending the city, and twenty-two searchlight batteries[20]—but all of them were reliant on the same *Würzburg* radar sets that were being disrupted so efficiently by Window. In some cases the battery commanders could hear the drone of airplanes in the sky above them, and yet when they turned to their radar operators for confirmation the response was the same as before: Instead of clear, distinct pulses showing where the aircraft were, the radar screens were a mass of flashing zigzag curves, making it impossible to distinguish anything specific at all. Some batteries began to shoot random, unaimed barrages into the sky—others remained silent. Hamburg's defenses had been completely blinded.

For some of the more experienced bomber crews, the sight that greeted them when they finally arrived over the target was a dream come true. "Under normal circumstances the searchlights kept a fairly accurate pinpoint on any aircraft," says Leonard Cooper, a flight engineer with 7 Squadron (Pathfinder Force), "but on this occasion they were just waving around all over the place."[21] Ted Edwards, a pilot from 100 Squadron, was equally impressed: "We were quite amazed to see the searchlights just weaving around the countryside over enemy territory. They hadn't got a clue where we were."[22]

For those skeptics who had doubted that Window would work, it was a moment of revelation. "They said that Window was going to upset the German radar when we went in, but we more or less said, 'Oh, *yes*?!'" remembers Leonard Bradfield, a bomb aimer with 49 Squadron. "But when we actually got there it was *happening*! We were absolutely delighted."[23] He continues:

> It was absolutely fantastic. We came up the Elbe and could see the river quite clearly. The radar-controlled blue master searchlights were standing absolutely upright and the white ones were weaving around, just searching. There were no night fighters because they were all in their boxes waiting to be given the vectors. The flak was just in a block over the target. . . . It was the only time on any bomb run I was able to have 20 seconds completely unimpeded, without being stalked by the flak.[24]

It is important to note that although the flak was being fired blindly, the sheer number of shells being fired into the air meant that several aircraft in the vanguard of the attack were still hit. Later on in the attack two planes would be shot down by flak, with no survivors.[25] Not everyone managed to escape the searchlights either. Gordon Moulton-Barrett, who was on his first operation as a "second dickie" pilot, remembers seeing a Lancaster coned by lights: He watched as the aircraft immediately dropped vertically, falling 10,000 feet in a matter of seconds, before pulling out of the dive and disappearing once more into the safety of the darkness. To the impressionable Moulton-Barrett it seemed like a brilliant, death-defying maneuver, and he had to suppress the urge to applaud.[26] For the Lancaster and its crew, however, it had simply been a matter of survival: A steep dive was the only way of escaping from a cone of searchlights.

With just a few minutes to go before Zero Hour (1:00), the Pathfinders were sizing up the dark city below them. As previously mentioned, the plan was to drop three different kinds of markers for the main force to aim at:

yellow target indicators (TIs) to start with, at Z-minus 3, along with flares to light up the city for the subsequent planes; red ones next, aimed visually, between Z-minus 2 and Zero Hour; and green ones to back up the reds for the rest of the raid in the event things did not go quite according to plan. While the marking began exactly on time, led by a Lancaster of 83 Squadron, many of the first group were eight or nine minutes late. Without their flares to light the city, many of the next group did not drop their red TIs at all. Fortunately for the city center, those that did fall were fairly spread out. There were four main groups: Some fell in the Baaken dock area south of the river, near the Grasbrook gasworks; another group fell in the east of the city, between Wandsbeker Chaussee and Hasselbrook railway station; two more salvos fell in the west, in Altona.[27]

For the few minutes before the bombs began to fall the sky over Hamburg was lit up by a spectacular firework display—a prelude to the coming bonfire—as the beautiful pyrotechnic candles cascaded out of each target marker and floated gently down to earth. The Germans called these markers *Tannenbäume*—Christmas trees—a homely term that described their beauty, but not their terrible purpose.

As the bright lights drifted downward the first Lancasters of the main force began to make their bombing runs. The aircraft were effectively in the hands of the bomb aimers now. As the target was sighted, the navigators would hand over responsibility to the bomb aimer, who would guide the pilot to the correct point directly over the red glow of the TIs. Leonard Bradfield remembers the run in clearly:

> It was a brilliant night. You could see the ground absolutely crystal clear. You could see the outline of the city, and you could also see where the markers had gone down.... To bring her up in line directly over the target took some twenty seconds straight and level. Then we let the bombs go. We had the 4,000-pounder as usual, and we had four 1,000-pounders, one of which was on a delayed action. Then we had the ninety four-pound thermite incendiary bombs. Owing to their light weight we had to drop them quite early in the sequence. But the 4,000-pounder was the master—you could really feel the "cookie" go. I'm talking in terms of under half a minute from the first to last being dropped.... We then had to fly another twenty seconds for our photo flash to fall so it could take a photograph of where our bombs landed.[28]

It was this brief period over the aiming point itself that was the most nerve-wracking for most crews. A single minute could seem like a lifetime when the crews were obliged to fly straight and level, a perfect target for the flak guns below. The bomb aimer would direct the pilot by shouting above the drone of the engines: "Left, left . . . steady . . . bombs gone!" The leap of the aircraft as the heavy 4,000-pound "cookie" fell away was echoed by a leap of nerves into their throats—as soon as the photo flash had gone the pilot would immediately veer away from the immediate danger area and head for the darkness beyond. But tonight, with the city's defenses in such disarray, even this most hazardous of times was relatively safe. As one pilot recalls:

> I remember thinking, "It's going to be great from now on, for the rest of my tour!" You could see other Lancs silhouetted against the fires all just going steadily on, whereas in the past people would have been weaving quite madly. Everyone seemed to have come to the same conclusion: From now on it was going to be easy.[29]

During the next hour, over 700 planes would pass over the west of the city, and many pilots reported seeing the sky around them filled with planes. In such circumstances the danger of collision was very real, and many crews had to endure the horror of seeing bombers flying directly above them, bomb doors open, about to drop their load. Tonight, fortunately, nobody was harmed by a fellow bomber—but one Stirling did collide with a Ju88 night fighter as he dived to avoid a searchlight. Geoff Turner and his 75 Squadron crew managed to limp home, but the night fighter was almost certainly finished. It turned on its back and fell headlong toward Hamburg, to be recorded later as a "probable" victory to the British crew.[30]

On Sunday, July 25, between one and two o'clock in the morning, 2,300 tons of bombs were dropped onto Hamburg—a new and frightening world record for a single attack. A lot of this weight was made up of huge high-explosive bombs—8,000-pound "blockbusters" and 4,000-pound "cookies"—but it was undoubtedly the incendiaries that did the most damage. The fires started by the first waves made it easier for the later waves to find their way to the target, and these in turn stoked the fires further. A total of 350,412 individual incendiary bombs fell in and around the city, starting countless fires—again, a new world record.[31]

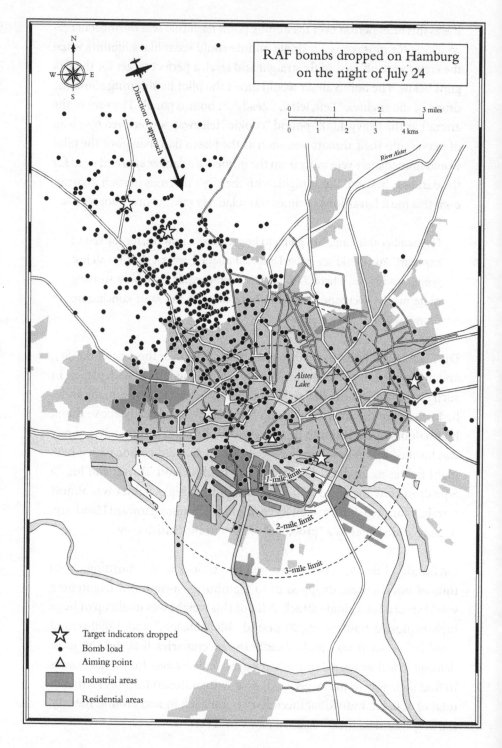

RAF bombs dropped on Hamburg
on the night of July 24

Direction of approach

River Alster

Alster
Lake

1-mile limit

2-mile limit

3-mile limit

☆ Target indicators dropped
• Bomb load
△ Aiming point

Industrial areas

Residential areas

The official British intelligence report of the time announces such figures with a certain pride, which was certainly echoed in the hearts and minds of most of the crews who took part in the attack. Once they had dropped their bombs and turned away to the south of the city, they had the opportunity to see the results of their work. The comments they noted in their log books afterward were almost always the same: "Good trip," "A very good prang," "Very nearly perfection." Scores of crews in the latter stages of the attack reported seeing very large explosions in the docks. By the time the last Halifaxes of 6 Group had dropped their bombs, the whole of the west of the city had become "a mass of raging fires with black smoke rising to 19,000 feet." Crews in the final wave reported the merging of all the separate fires into "one large conflagration spreading over the whole city." This fire was so huge it could be seen by British Mosquitos flying on dummy attacks over Duisburg, 140 miles away.[32]

It is easy to begrudge these men their feeling of pride at the destruction they were wreaking, but it is foolish to be surprised by it. Their job was to wage war, and tonight they had done their job well. For many of them it was nothing new. They had seen similar scenes over Dortmund, Wuppertal, Cologne, and Essen. They had seen the war from the other side, too, in London, Coventry, Sheffield, Plymouth, and many other cities across Britain. For most of the young men in the bombers, tonight was simply a logical extension of all that had gone before—the concept of "an eye for an eye," expanded to the scale of whole nations. And we must remember that the crews were not only British. The Polish airmen in Bomber Command had a reputation for being particularly bloodthirsty, reveling in any opportunity to avenge the rape of their homeland. Canadians, Australians, New Zealanders, and South Africans, who had never seen an attack on their home soil, were here for reasons that were more vague: a principle to be upheld, or a sense of loyalty to the British Empire and "home country." Many had joined up as volunteers simply for the excitement of flying. For them, their only thought now was to get home safely to their beds, one day closer to their next period of leave, and one operation closer to the magic total of thirty.

Mixed in with their satisfaction was a sense of relief that the main part of the job was at last over, as they headed back into the safety of the darkness. But their relief was misplaced: This was perhaps the most dangerous time of all. Silhouetted by the fires behind them, their guard down because of the natural complacency that follows such bursts of adrenaline, they were easy targets for night fighters. And now, at last, the night fighters were arriving. Once the attack on Hamburg had begun, many fighter controllers had abandoned their radar sets and told their crews to head straight for the city. Some had seen the fires and flown in on their own initiative. By half past one in the morning, the skies on the way out of Hamburg were becoming far more dangerous than they had been going in.

The more disciplined crews would not drop their vigilance for a moment. The skipper would return to zigzagging the plane and warn the gunners not to look into the fires below for fear of losing their night vision. Navigators would set course along the designated route, roughly parallel to the route in, to take advantage of the safety provided by the bomber stream. Flight engineers and bomb aimers, their job done, would return to dropping bundles of Window down the flare chute, lest they lose the advantage they had gained over the enemy radar. And the wireless operators would continue broadcasting Tinsel, the sound of their engines, on the German frequencies to block out any radio communication between their rivals in the air.

However, not all crews were quite so disciplined. Nervous and inexperienced pilots ignored the laid-down route and made a beeline straight for the coast. It was an understandable temptation, particularly for those new pilots and navigators who had never experienced flak before. Some rear gunners could not keep themselves from staring, mesmerized, into the inferno on the ground behind them, only to find that when they finally did tear their eyes away they were effectively blinded by the darkness. Some crew members lit up cigarettes, which they would puff between breaths on their oxygen masks, while others would open up their flying rations with a yawn, exhausted by anxiety.

Almost half of the Allied casualties tonight were shot down by night fighters on the journey home—and of those, most had been off-track. Without the benefit of thousands of bundles of Window to mask their movements, they had been located by the German radar and summarily dealt with. Some, like the crew of Flying Officer J. S. Cole, were lucky to escape. After being picked up by searchlights over Cuxhaven on the coast, he was attacked by a Messerschmitt Me109—a day fighter—but was able to dive away without being hit.[33] Likewise, Sergeant S. Grzeskowiak was on his first operation when his Wellington was attacked by a Ju88 night fighter. He managed to escape after being hit, but was leaking gasoline all the way home, and eventually had to crash-land at Trusthorpe in Lincolnshire. These crews lived to tell the tale, for now at least.[34] Others were not so lucky. Wallace McIntosh, a rear gunner with 207 Squadron, saw a Lancaster "blazing like hell" just 1,000 yards away as a German fighter came in repeatedly to attack it. As the plane fell out of the sky he saw five parachutes open up, but the Lancaster's rear gunner, obviously trapped inside the plane, carried on firing till the end. "I have never seen such bravery," McIntosh recalls. "The poor bugger was still sitting there firing away and the fighter went back in to have another blast at him, with the gunner still defiant, and the Lancaster blew up."[35]

For the vast majority of crews, however, the journey home was just as uneventful as the journey in. By four o'clock in the morning the first of the Pathfinders had already landed back at their bases, and the main bomber stream was crossing back over the coast into England. This was the last moment of danger for the RAF crewmen. For some of those that had been hit by flak there would be an emergency landing at an unfamiliar airfield. There was always the chance that returning planes could be attacked by German intruders. But the biggest fear was the possibility of ground fog, which could make landing extremely hazardous. Tonight, at the height of summer, the likelihood of fog was not great—but even in clear conditions it could be dangerous landing in the dark. Despite all his wealth of experience, the commanding officer of 83 Squadron, John Searby, collided with a Lancaster of 156 Squadron as the two came in to land at Warboys. Fortunately, both aircraft landed safely.

After taxiing back to their original positions on the airfield, the crews would emerge from their planes, grinning with relief. Transports would take them back to the station buildings where they would be ushered inside for debriefing. Blinking in the light, and glad of the chance for a cup of tea and a smoke, the men would sit down at a table with the intelligence officer to tell their stories. Every aspect of their trip was noted down: the effects of Window, the weather conditions over the target, how easy it had been to spot the target indicators, how extensive were the fires in the city, and so on. If they had been attacked by enemy fighters, or seen anything at all unusual, special care was taken to record the details. Only after this process was over were the men allowed to have breakfast and go to bed, exhausted by their long night in the air. For many of them the whole process would be repeated again, tomorrow night: The summer months were all too short in the war over northern Europe, and Bomber Command had to make use of every crew it could while conditions allowed.

* * *

This then was the pattern of a single night in the life of the Bomber Command crews—a typical operation made extraordinary by the introduction of a new weapon. Window had been a phenomenal success, and would continue to save the lives of RAF airmen for the next six weeks, before the Germans were finally able to counter its effects. Many crews have since thanked their luck that they were flying in the summer of 1943, because they were able, during that brief period of relative safety, to clock up enough operations to finish their tour. This simple, radar-jamming device had secured their future.

As they made their way to breakfast, however, few of the men were thinking of the future. Six hours of heightened senses and intense emotions had left them worn out, and every one of them was now ready for bed. Their reward for the night's efforts was a huge meal of bacon and eggs—as much as they could eat—but as soon as it was finished they returned to their quarters. Some were so exhausted they were unable even to undress before they fell into bed.

While they slept, the day was only just beginning for everyone else at the station. Out on the airfield the erks would already be hard at work to repair any damage to the squadrons' precious airplanes. Intelligence staff would be developing and analyzing the bomb photographs taken by each of the airplanes and collating all the information in a report for Group Headquarters. Their reports today would be very upbeat indeed. Despite a fair amount of "creepback" over the countryside to the northwest of the city—a phenomenon caused by successive crews dropping their bombs marginally early—it was plain that the bombing had been very concentrated in certain areas, and a great deal of damage had been caused.

Over the next few days reconnaissance planes would fly high over Hamburg taking daytime photographs of the damage to further enhance the intelligence reports, but even now, with what they knew already, the atmosphere at airfields across the country was extremely optimistic. Casualties had been low (only twelve planes missing out of 792), and it seemed to many that a new era in the bombing war had begun.

But few people could possibly have guessed where this new era would lead.

Chapter 10

THE DEVASTATION BEGINS

The fronts draw nearer, the nights grow longer . . . the Luftwaffe is helpless, German cities are defenseless. . . . Each night brings the threat of devastation closer. It is only a question of time.

—BRITISH PROPAGANDA LEAFLET, 1943[1]

To claim that the people of Hamburg had no inkling of what was about to befall them on this, the first night of Operation Gomorrah, would not be quite true. Most had heard of what had happened to the cities of the Ruhr over preceding months, and while German radio and newspaper reports were deliberately vague on the details, the city's anxious housewives allowed their imaginations to fill in the gaps. Rumors abounded. People told each other furtive stories about factories and houses being blown sky-high and human beings rushing frantically for the rivers like living torches. Some claimed that the British had deliberately targeted the cathedrals at Cologne and Aachen in an attempt to destroy German heritage. Others swore that when the Americans bombed Kiel and Flensburg they had dropped fountain pens and other everyday articles filled with explosives.[2]

The Allies did whatever they could to fuel such fears. BBC broadcasts to the Continent became progressively more triumphant in tone.[3] British and American planes dropped hundreds of thousands of leaflets on northern Germany, many of which fell on Hamburg. These gave a variety of lurid statistics about what had happened to other German cities, before going on to imply that the people of Hamburg would be next to feel the devastating bite of the bombs.[4]

Despite all this, however, many people refused to believe that the bombers were heading their way, for the simple reason that they did not *want* to believe it. After four long years of fighting they were sick of the war, and some even hoped that the Allies would hurry up and invade so that the whole thing could be over quickly.[5] More rumors began to circulate claiming that the Allies were being deliberately lenient toward Hamburg because they would need the city when they finally invaded.[6] Regardless of everything that had happened since 1939, Hamburg was still largely an anglophile city: Many people could not bring themselves to believe that their friends and allies of the past 150 years would ever have the will to inflict such suffering upon them.[7]

Besides, the city had not been targeted properly for four and a half months now. What few alarms there had been recently had all proved false. Despite constant warnings from the authorities to remain alert, while the skies were clear and the sun shone, it was easy to pretend that they were safe from attack.

Were it not for the war, the day before the bombers arrived would have been an idyllic one. It was a hot Saturday in July, and the whole city seemed to have come outdoors to enjoy the sunshine. Hamburg had been experiencing an unusually long spell of glorious weather, and the long, warm days reminded people of peacetime. Now that the school holidays had begun the city's many parks were thronging with children playing *"Völkerball* or *Kippel-Kappel,* and the open-air swimming baths at Aschberg and Ohlsdorf were filled with the sounds of teenagers splashing or calling to one another as they dived from the railings. Down by the Elbe, off-duty workers rolled up their trousers and strolled through the shallow water, or rested on the river's sandy banks beneath the trees. Old couples walked arm in arm along the Alster, or sunned themselves on their balconies and in their gardens. In the absence of any air raids the atmosphere in the city was fairly calm, perhaps even relaxed. A gentle breeze blew in off the river, caressing the spires of the churches, while the city streets below went about their everyday business undisturbed.[8]

Despite the shortages, there were still plenty of ways to relax in the city. At the beginning of July the famous Althoff Circus had been in Wandsbek, delighting the city's children with a combination of clowning and breathtaking acrobatics. Lovers of horse sports were looking forward to the "Preis von Deutschland" at Farmsen Racecourse, and the Hitler Youth were holding their area championships in canoeing. In the evenings there was also a wide variety of entertainment. A Hungarian dance orchestra had been playing in the Orchideen Café, and Strauss's *Die Zigeunerbaron* was showing at the Volksoper on the Reeperbahn. The cinemas played a variety of escapist films, mostly adventure movies or romances such as *Der dunkel Tag* ("The Dark Day") and *Du gehörst zu mir* ("You Belong to Me").[9]

There was "double summertime" in Germany, just as there was in Britain, so it stayed light in the evenings almost until ten o'clock. As the fleet of RAF bombers took off across the North Sea, many Hamburgers were just coming out of the cinemas and theaters. Others were still finishing their evening meals, or sitting out on their balconies to enjoy a cool drink before bedtime. Those who didn't have to get up for work on Sunday celebrated the end of the week with friends or family, perhaps even with sons or husbands on leave from the front, but toward midnight most of the city was turning in. It was a hot, sultry night, and many people had given up on the idea of struggling for sleep indoors: Instead they dragged their mattresses out into the courtyard to see if they would sleep better in the open air.[10] As they lay looking up at the bright stars above them, for a while the war seemed far away.

Awake or asleep, the whole city was brought back to reality when the quiet of the night was suddenly broken by the sound of sirens. The noise did not produce panic—in fact, in general, it was greeted with little more than weary sighs. The alarms had already gone off once tonight, at around 9:30, but they had been canceled again just ten minutes later. Now, at around half past midnight, people fully expected a repeat performance, and many people merely rolled over and went back to sleep. Hamburgers were used to the sound of sirens: In the previous three years they had endured no fewer than 318 air raid warnings, the vast majority of them false alarms. Even the actual attacks they had experienced—137 in total—were mostly fairly minor, especially in the past twelve months.[11] Familiarity had bred complacency throughout the city.

In Lokstedt, in the northeast of the city, Wanda Chantler was struggling to wake a room full of women and convince them to come to the air raid shelter. Wanda was a twenty-year-old Polish woman who worked in a forced labor camp packing cans of fish for soldiers at the front. As first-aid officer for her barracks she was obliged to go to the shelter, but no matter how she tried, few of the others would come and join her.

First of all there was a great big howl of sirens. And the girls all said, "Oh, it's like this every night—nothing will happen." They went off so often, those sirens: We sometimes got them twice a night. We all got so fed up, particularly those that were on the day shift, because they had no sleep—the planes never came in the daytime, they always came in the night. But these girls said, "We're not getting up. Nothing will happen."[12]

Reluctantly, she and five other women trudged down to the makeshift underground shelter on the other side of the compound—a move that most probably saved her life.

Elsewhere, many Hamburgers were showing similar reluctance to go to the shelters. Hannah Kelson was fourteen years old, and had a typical teenager's response to any suggestion that she should leave her bed just because the RAF might be coming: "Let them come, I don't care."[13] For others it was the conditions in the bunkers themselves which kept them away. Martha Bührich, a fifty-seven-year-old teacher who lived in Barmbek, preferred to sit on a stool in the doorway of her bathroom rather than go to the "community bedlam" of the air raid bunkers.[14] Conditions in some of the shelters could be extremely uncomfortable, as some people invariably brought as much as they could carry "just in case"—not only jewelry and important papers, but whole suitcases filled with clothes, pet dogs and cats, and even chickens.[15] In such conditions it is not surprising that many wanted to avoid going to the shelter unless it was completely necessary.

There were also, however, more voyeuristic reasons to stay aboveground. A raid on the city could be a spectacular event, and many Hamburgers admit that they often stood in their doorways or on their balconies during an attack to watch the progress of the bombs. The novelist Hans Erich Nossack never went to his shelter when the sirens sounded, because he was too curious to see what would happen. Nor was he the only one: He records watching some women on the roof of a neighbor's house applauding as a British plane that was caught in searchlights got shot down.[16] Civilians have always turned out to watch battles from a supposedly safe distance—however, as Nossack makes clear, the true reason they watched was not to see the battle in the sky, but the unfolding destruction of their own city. "I had one unequivocal wish," he says: "Let it get really bad!"[17]

Tonight Nossack was not on his balcony to witness events: He was on holiday in the countryside, just to the south of the city. Like many others he was unmoved by the sound of the sirens. It was the noise of the airplanes humming overhead that snapped him out of his complacency.

I jumped out of bed and ran barefoot out of the house into this sound that hovered like an oppressive weight between the clear constellations and the dark earth, not here and not there but everywhere in space. . . . One didn't dare take a breath for fear of inhaling it. It was the sound of eighteen hundred airplanes approaching Hamburg from the south at an unimaginable height. We had already experienced two hundred or even more air raids, some of them very heavy, but this was something completely new. And yet there was an immediate recognition: this was what everyone had been waiting for, what had hung for months like a shadow over everything we did, making us weary. It was the end.[18]

In the center of town many others were also beginning to realize that this was the full-scale raid they had been dreading. Staatssekretär Georg Ahrens was now broadcasting a warning over the radio on all channels: "Go immediately to your air raid shelters! Enemy bombs may drop within the next three minutes!"[19] As people finished dressing and grabbed a few things to take with them, the streets became busy with people making their way to the public shelters. There was still plenty of time, but they ran anyway, out of both a desire to get a good place in the bunker and a genuine fear for their lives.

For those who were late, further confirmation came of what lay in store for them. Cascades of bright red and yellow marker bombs, and later green ones, too, began to fall over the city, filling the night with a miraculous glow. For one woman at least, on fire duty at one of the city's department stores, these *Tannenbäume* were a sight she would never forget: "I stood there looking out of the hatch at the wonderful sky. This was something one would otherwise never see. . . . The whole sky above Hamburg alight— prettier, much prettier than a firework display."[20]

Sixteen-year-old Gotthold Soltwedel, who was serving as a flak helper on the huge flak tower in the center of town, also saw this display:

I can still remember the first "Christmas trees" exactly. Dazzling colored flames hung over us on little parachutes; and likewise on the ground, in the middle of the Heiligengeistfeld, colorful incendiaries lay as markers for the bombers. I can also still hear the first bomb howling down. It was very near. As if on command we charged away from the guns and into the entrance of the bunker, knocking our *Leutnant* to the floor in the process. He screamed at us dreadfully and called us cowards.[21]

By now there were very few people out in the open—even the majority of fire wardens had taken cover, coming out intermittently to conduct quick patrols of the buildings. Earlier in the year, Goebbels had discussed with Hitler the idea that fire wardens should be stationed on the roofs of houses during air raids so that they could combat incendiary bombs as soon as they fell, but he soon realized that this would cause too many casualties.[22] In general, only official observers and those manning flak batteries were around to see the sheer mass of marker bombs, incendiaries, and the spectacular explosions of the 4,000-pound "cookies" and 8,000-pound "blockbusters."

From his flak battery in the northeast of the city, Rudolf Schurig had a panoramic view of the unfolding situation.

> We soon saw anti-aircraft fire at eight o'clock, and then they were there: direction Eimsbüttel, Altona. The first *Tannenbäume* fell there, a glowing green hail of fire, which was to mark the target for the following aircraft. And suddenly the sky above that district was as light as day. A large number of bright parachute flares, which ignite very low down and slowly drop, lit up the district as if it were an enormous freight depot, lit by many flood lamps. Here the first anti-aircraft shells were fired, the first of our new artillery. How it thundered! . . . At each volley we had a feeling of security. We would show the Tommies what it meant to attack Hamburg, our Hamburg![23]

Things started to go wrong when the effects of the RAF's new radar-jamming device, Window, took hold. As Rudolf Schurig was soon to discover, his earlier sense of security had been misplaced.

> Everything seemed to be going well, as we had practiced in exercises and battle hundreds of times. But suddenly our radar apparatus stopped working. This happened regularly to this highly sensitive machinery, and would quickly be fixed; in the meantime we would switch to the neighboring battery. But they were unable to give us any information, as their radar was also broken. . . . It was then confirmed that none of the radar

in Hamburg was functioning; we did not yet know why. . . . A paralyzing terror began to creep over us. We felt like someone who has been given a rifle to defend himself, but who is blindfolded at the same time.[24]

For Johann Johannsen, who was manning a flak battery in Altona, things were even worse. Altona was directly beneath the RAF marker flares, and was about to receive the full force of the bombs.

High above us we could hear the drone of the enemy machines. Suddenly countless flares were above us, so that the whole city was lit up in a magically bright light. . . . With incredible swiftness the disaster was suddenly upon us. Before and behind our battery heavy chunks of metal were striking. Howling and hissing, fire and iron were falling from the sky. The whole city was lit up in a sea of flames! With dogged fury we remained at our guns, exposed to the raging force of the attack. Everyone looked for something to hold on to, so as not to be hurled down by the pressure of the exploding bombs. Every now and then I cast another look over toward my house. I skipped a breath—a column of fire shot up high—everything was in flames![25]

Johannsen was in the unenviable position of being able to see his house from the flak position. Bound by duty to remain at his post, he was powerless to react when he saw his home on fire: The best he could do was to pray that his family had not been killed and continue firing at the enemy. In any case, with bombs raining down around him there was plenty to occupy him here. Moments later he was startled by a terrible howling above him, and an incendiary bomb came hurtling down exactly between their two flak guns: It crashed through the roof of the building and set fire to the fourth floor below. Despite injuries to his hands and face from exploding shards of glass, Johannsen was still not given permission to leave his post and check on his family—the flak battery needed all the men it could get. Despite physical pain and mounting anxiety he remained at the guns until after the All Clear was sounded.

For some of those who were sheltering in bunkers and cellars, things were almost as terrifying as they were for those outside. The difference was that while the flak gunners at least had a role to play, those in the shelters could do nothing but sit and wait. The tension and uncertainty that built up over several hours became almost unbearable.

Hiltgunt Zassenhaus had been studying for her university exams at home when the alarms went off. She lived in the northwest of the city, so the bunker where she and her family took shelter was beneath the flight path of the bombers as they approached. At the beginning of the attack the shelter was virtually empty, and there was space to relax and reread a letter from her brother Björn.

> Then came a sudden flicker of the lamps, a roar, an explosion. Was it inside or outside? The light went out. My pocket torch fell to the ground. The pram rolled toward me, set in movement by the shaking of the bunker. I jumped up. The light flickered a couple of times—then another explosion—and all was dark. I fell on my knees, my head in my hands.[26]

The sound of the bombs was terrifying, but it was perhaps even more frightening when the bomb was so close that it was no longer audible. As another woman who lived through this series of raids explains, the bombs became truly terrifying when one stopped hearing them and started to *feel* them.

> Whenever a person hears a "singing" or "whistling," it doesn't matter if he is in a cellar or in a living room, the impact of the bomb is some distance away. But woe betide you if you can feel the air pressure blast on your ears (very unpleasant); then the bombs are falling directly in the vicinity. One hears no booming, nothing, only this terrible blast of air pressure.[27]

In Hiltgunt Zassenhaus's bunker one such wave of pressure blew the internal cover off the ventilation shaft, and the iron doors of the bunker actively groaned under the strain. The girl cowering inside was paralyzed with fear.

Once it became obvious that this was a full-scale attack and not simply one of the frequent false alarms, scores of other people began to arrive, desperate to escape the nightmare outside in the streets. Within a short time the bunker was overflowing with shocked and frightened people.

One explosion followed another. Suddenly from outside a despairing hammering on the bunker door—wild screams tore the night. Someone opened the door, and the crowd fell in like the possessed; they screamed to one another and struggled for breath, and the block walls echoed with the howling of children and the wailing of women. Over all droned the voice of Herr Braun [the bunker warden]: "Calm down! We have space for everyone!"[28]

Beneath the seemingly endless explosions the young woman lost all sense of time, and in the pitch darkness she lost all sense of space. All she was aware of was the heaving mass of humanity around her. "Crammed together in the darkness we became just a single mass of bodies, and with each explosion we swayed along with the shaking bunker walls."[29]

The conditions inside some bunkers on this first night of bombing were truly appalling. Many of these structures were little more than a series of narrow tube tunnels in the ground, with wooden benches along their concrete walls. Even the larger, overground bunkers were often extremely cramped inside. They became so overcrowded that sometimes they were reserved exclusively for women and children, and some overzealous bunker wardens also excluded foreign workers. There were simply not enough places to go round.

Paul Elingshausen, who also witnessed the bombing on this night, was shocked by the terrible conditions inside the air raid shelters. After trying, and failing, to save his house from the hail of incendiary bombs, he eventually joined his wife and two young children in the nearby bunker.

Imagine around 1,000 people crammed into the small rooms, a real heat inside, sweat running down our bodies, the bunker full of smoke from outside, not a drop of water to drink, no food and no light. The electricity went straight away. Torches were all flat; the few tallow candles were soon finished. And the whole time there was such an atmosphere; outside the bombs roared, often so close that the bunker shook. Can you imagine this with women and babies?[30]

Despite such conditions, few complained. They were aware that the alternative—to weather the storm outside—was infinitely worse. Occasionally those near the doors would hear reports on what was happening outside as those on fire duty returned with messages for the bunker warden. In general, no news was good news. Fire wardens rarely beat on the door of the shelters unless it was time for everyone to evacuate.

Descriptions of what it was like to be in the streets at the time of the bombardment are rare, for the simple reason that very few were foolish enough to risk it. With over 1,300 tons of high-explosive bombs falling on the city, there was a great danger of being caught by the blasts. Incendiary bombs also struck the ground at high speed, and the most fearsome of these would spill liquid phosphorus as they landed. The threat of being hit by falling masonry was also very real.

One of the first to discover why it was so important to seek shelter during an air raid was Wanda Chantler, in the makeshift earth bomb shelter on one side of her labor-camp compound. Beside her, sitting patiently on the benches, was the handful of women that she had managed to rouse from their beds earlier.

> Suddenly there was a gust of wind that blew the door in. There was a terrific noise. It was like a winter's night when the wind comes howling through the door and through the window, and you sit in the kitchen hoping it will go away—that sort of noise. And this wind blew our wooden door right open and we were exposed to a terrific blast of hot air. Until then we didn't hear the bombs falling. We didn't even *know* they were falling.[31]

The blast knocked Wanda off her feet, and the other girls had to help her up. Shaken by the explosion, they all huddled in the open doorway of the dugout wondering what to do. Since their shelter no longer seemed to provide much protection they eventually decided to venture back across the compound to see if the other women were all right. But as soon as they stepped through the door they could see that something truly dreadful had happened.

> The barracks were not there. They just were not there. I looked, and then I looked down, and it was all there in a heap. That was all that was left of the barracks. . . . We stood, the six of us, and we didn't know what to do.

Numbed by shock, they did not move for a while, but eventually they were drawn forward to the rubble that had once been their sleeping quarters by the sound of some cries.

> It was light, you could see everything, because it was burning, because the firebombs were falling down as well, and the phosphor bombs. We saved lots of girls, but some of them died. We just kept pulling them out of the rubble. There were bits of flesh everywhere. Bits of flesh. And there was one arm, just an arm, sticking out of the debris. One hundred and twenty-three girls died that night.

Throughout Hamburg, similar destruction was being wreaked on countless other streets and houses. While those who had sought shelter in the larger public bunkers were generally safe, many more people had hidden in the cellars of the larger houses. When one of these received a direct hit, or caught fire, those in the cellar often found their exit blocked by rubble or flames. In such cases the only escape was to try to break through to a neighboring cellar in the hope that there might still be a way out.

Sometimes the only option was to run through the fires, and this was the most terrifying choice of all. Despite being only a small child at the time, Klaus Müller remembers doing exactly that. He lived with his parents and grandparents, who owned a milk shop on Marthastrasse, right in the center of one of the areas that was worst hit. As the bombs began to subside he was sheltering with his family in a cellar beneath his grandfather's apartment. After a while it became apparent that the whole house was on fire, and that the only way out was through a burning passageway into the inner courtyard. Fortunately, Klaus's grandfather kept several milk churns filled with water in their cellar for just such emergencies.

> As a small child one remembers everything as being far larger—it was probably only a few meters—but it was an inferno. The entire entrance was filled with flames . . . my grandfather and the other men poured ten milk churns of water into the passageway, and this created a small path through which we could pass.[32]

As he and the rest of the group escaped through the inner courtyard to the street outside, they found the whole of Marthastrasse on fire—not only the houses, but the very tarmac on the road itself. Beyond, they could see Belle-alliancestrasse and the Eimsbüttler Chaussee, where there was a small park that would be safe; but to get to it they had to rush along the pavement beside the burning road. It was only twenty meters, but by the time they got there the right-hand side of young Klaus's clothes was alight—his parents had to beat out the flames before carrying him to safety in the park opposite.

A few streets away, the nine-year-old Liselotte Gerke was sheltering in a cellar on the Eimsbüttler Marktplatz. The street was home to a large tram depot, and tonight there was a line of stationary trams, nose to tail along the center of the road. As the young Liselotte came out of her shelter she saw that while her side of the street was relatively untouched by the bombs, the opposite side was burning brightly, and scores of people were trying to cross the road to escape the flames. But the trams were in the way, and there was not time for all of them to clamber into the cars and out the other side. The next day, when she and her friends went out to investigate the damage in the trams, she stumbled upon a pair of small, charred corpses. "This was the moment the war started for me. It was the first time I had ever seen anything like this."[33]

Descriptions like these are merely snapshots of what people experienced that night. The bombs spread out over the whole of the west of the city, and in many places to the east and south. Tens of thousands of people were affected, and since the bombs were indiscriminate, women and children found themselves caught up in the fire and explosions just as frequently as the city's workforce, who were the ostensible target of the attack. Even political prisoners and forced laborers such as Wanda Chantler were affected. Terrifying though their ordeal was, however, the bombing raid was no worse than many others that had taken place in other parts of Germany. Despite the widespread destruction, most people managed to escape with their lives, and even their belongings, intact. Hamburg had not yet been made special by its ordeal—it was just another name on the long list of towns that had suffered heavy bombing raids.

That said, the death toll was still extraordinarily high. Early estimates claimed that about 1,500 people died during this raid—far more than in any other previous attack on the city—and tens of thousands more had been made homeless.[34] For a city that had made such a huge effort to ready itself for an attack like this, these figures represented a crushing defeat.

The main cause of destruction was the fires, which in many areas had been allowed to get out of control. According to the official police report on the disaster, the performance of the emergency services had been exemplary, but in the heat of battle it was inevitable that many of the drills that had been practiced so often did not go quite according to plan. Hans Brunswig worked in the technical division of the Hamburg fire service, and noted that some of the Nazi Party volunteers who served in the fire brigade did not follow the drills properly, and were content simply to muddle through.[35] Many eyewitnesses on the night say the same thing: Erwin Garvens, for example, noted in his diary that it was almost impossible to put out the fires in his neighborhood because of a lack of leadership and direction. While the women cooperated admirably, many of the men, particularly the soldiers on leave, were quick to give up and abandon the burning buildings to their fate.[36]

To be fair, however, the huge destruction in the city, including the severing of many water mains, made it almost impossible for even the best-trained firefighters to do what they were supposed to do. Paul Elingshausen, the deputy air raid warden of his block, spent almost two hours fighting the fires in his and the neighboring houses before finally giving up.

> There was no running water, the Tommies had smashed the waterworks first. The small amount of water we had on the ground was quickly used up, and we had to abandon house after house. Finally Dr. Wilms's house caught fire, and I, as deputy air raid warden, stopped fighting the fire, since there was neither sand nor water, and the flames were already licking the side of our roof. We started to save what could be saved. . . . I had all of fourteen minutes to rescue the most important things, some clothes and other stuff. . . . One cannot imagine how fast fire is, and how easily it can cut off your escape route; this is why I also gave up, no matter how much I would have liked to have this or that. And so I stood below with what little stuff I had, and was forced to watch, full of impotent anger, as our beloved building burned.[37]

The British tactic of dropping a combination of high-explosive and incendiary bombs had worked: While the incendiaries started the fires, enormous explosions kept the local wardens from reaching them until it was too late. Further bombs on timer fuses continued to hamper the fire brigade well into the next morning.

The gas and water mains had been cut, and so had electricity supplies, making many pumps useless. Just as problematic was the damage to the telephone lines. In order to direct the emergency effort, the control room of the air protection leader needed to be in communication with all the affected areas—but while they were being swamped with calls from the south and east of the city, the worst-hit areas in the west were unable to inform them of how bad things had become. As a consequence, early on at least, the fire brigade was directed to the wrong parts of town. Once the mistake was discovered, the fire chief had no choice but to send out motorcycle dispatch riders, some of whom perished in the chaos. Officers sent out on reconnaissance were often forced to make long detours, making them unable to report back for several hours. Things were made even more difficult when the control room itself was engulfed in flames, and all its staff were compelled to evacuate to another building.[38]

Early that Sunday morning, the city's gauleiter, Karl Kaufmann, was compelled to declare a state of emergency. Immediately, the running of the city came under stronger Nazi Party control, and the SS were sent out to make sure that firefighters continued the effort to extinguish fires throughout the day. Kaufmann's worst fear was that the RAF would return the next night to stoke the fires up once again, in which case it was essential that tonight's fires be put out by nightfall on Sunday. In the event that proved impossible. Even after fire brigades from all the nearby towns had been drafted in to help, many fires raged for days. In some areas the fires were so huge that they were not finally extinguished for several *weeks*—many of the houses had already bought in their supplies of coal and coke for the winter, and when these caught fire it was next to impossible to put them out.[39]

Once the All Clear had sounded, the flak batteries across the city finally stopped firing. Unable to pinpoint the attacking airplanes, the best they had been able to do was to put up an unaimed barrage in the hope that they might be lucky enough to score a few hits. Now they had finally stopped, the barrels of the guns glowing with the heat of all their firing. Flak helper Rudolf Schurig claimed afterward that his battery alone had shot 547 rounds into the sky on that night.[40] In total, about 50,000 rounds of heavy flak were discharged into the heavens.[41] For all that, only a single Wellington had been shot down over Hamburg, and a Halifax of the Pathfinder Force seriously damaged.[42]

Now that the firing had stopped, the flak helpers in the worst affected parts of town were free to go and join in the emergency effort in the streets. In Altona, the wounded Johann Johannsen was finally given permission to stand down by his flak battery commander. He immediately went to look for his family. As he hurried off through the burning streets he narrowly missed being blown to smithereens by a high-explosive bomb: Even though the RAF planes had all returned home by now, such explosions were still going off throughout the city—partly because of the numerous bombs that had been dropped with timer fuses, and partly because of chemicals catching fire in factories. By the time Johannsen reached his house, he was a bag of nerves.

> Everything was in flames: houses, vehicles, trees. Burning phosphorus dripped from the roofs. Around my house it was empty of people— apparently they were sitting in the cellar even though the house was ablaze. I hurried into the stairwell, where glowing sparks were already coming down, and then in two, three leaps was down in the air raid cellar. On my question, "All okay?," I discovered that my son and another person who'd been sheltering in the cellar had broken through a wall cavity into a neighboring cellar.[43]

As he gathered up his family and took them through the streets to safety, the suitcase he had rescued from the cellar caught fire, set alight by a "huge rain of sparks . . . pouring down over everything."[44]

All across Hamburg people were beginning to emerge from their shelters, and the sight that greeted them was one of chaos. After several terrifying hours belowground, Rolf Arnold clearly remembers his first sight of the devastation that was unfolding outside his Harvestehude home:

> As we left the cellar after the regular tone of the All Clear siren, the first window in the stairwell presented us with a view over the courtyard toward Harvestehude: a terrible picture—everything we could see was on

fire. Grindelberg was burning on both sides, and the facing parts of Ober-
strasse, Werderstrasse, Brahmsallee, Hansastrasse, and Hallerstrasse—
they were all burning. It was a complete sea of flame.[45]

Just across the Alster in Winterhude, the picture of destruction was similar, as Mathilde Wolff-Mönckeberg recorded in her diary shortly afterward:

> Back in our flat we stand on the balcony and see nothing but a circle of
> flames around the Alster, fire everywhere in our neighborhood. Thick
> clouds of smoke are hanging over the city, and smoke comes in through
> all the windows carrying large flakes of fluttering ash. And it is raining in
> torrents! We go into the road just for a moment at 3:30 A.M. In the
> Sierichstrasse several houses have collapsed and fire is still raging. The
> sight of the Bellevue is dreadful, and the Mühlenkamp is nothing but
> glass and rubble. We go to bed completely shattered.[46]

The huge fires across the city were so numerous that they sparked off a
number of unusual meteorological events. To begin with the massive heat
had created strong winds. Johann Johannsen claims he had to struggle
against "a frightful storm, caused by the heat."[47] Liselotte Gerke remembers
her aunt telling her the next day that she was unable to fight her way
through the wind to the shelter at Osterstrasse station, and had to go to the
one at Emilienstrasse instead.[48] And then, amidst all the wind and fire,
another peculiar phenomenon occurred: It started to rain.

The full effect of these vast events could only be clearly seen from a distance. Professor Dr. Franz Termer, director of the museum of ethnology,
was watching the city burn from his home in Hochkamp in the far western suburbs.

> I will never forget the view over burning Hamburg. On a wide horizon,
> from north to south, a single fiery glow; above this, while we had a clear
> starry sky over us, an enormous cloud whirled and billowed upon itself
> over the city, reaching to the sky with sharp, threatening edges. I was
> reminded of a volcano eruption, and, to strengthen this, the phenomena
> it caused were similar to an eruption. Because of the hot air, which rose
> and then cooled and condensed in the upper atmosphere, a downpour
> fell over Hamburg from the 2,000–3,000-meter-high cloud of smoke....

In Hamburg the rain mixed with the ash and created a thick black mud, as we know of volcanic eruptions—a mixture which covered everything, distorted people's faces and matted their hair. I personally saw such creatures on the following day.[49]

As Sunday dawned the whole of Hamburg was wreathed in a thick black smoke. Perversely, the morning seemed darker than the night had been: At least during the night the people had had the fires to see by, but under the cloud of smoke there was nothing to light up the streets. Night had effectively become day, and day night, as Pastor Schoene of the Christuskirche in Eimsbüttel noted:

> By the morning everything was wrapped in black smoke, which was so thick that at nine o'clock in the morning it was still too dark to see anything indoors. Not until eleven o'clock did it become lighter, so that one was able to see what time it was. At three in the afternoon the sun appeared like a small ball shining through the smoke cloud.[50]

The houses and their coal stores were burning and so were numerous warehouses, storing everything from timber and grain to margarine.[51] The municipal gasworks was ablaze, and in Barmbek 3,000 liters of ethanol exploded in a liqueur factory.[52] The billowing smoke cloud caused by all these fires was blown by the prevailing winds eastward across most of the city. When Ilse Grassmann woke up in her Uhlenhorst apartment, she recorded in her diary the eerie effects of this huge cloud:

> The sun has no power today. It is already midday and it still hasn't managed to pierce through the layer of smoke and ash. An indescribable radiance: a wan, yellow light gives everything a feeling of unreality that is beginning to seem oppressive.[53]

Mathilde Wolff-Monckeberg, who lived a little farther north, noted the same thing in her diary:

> There is no proper daylight the following morning, the town is so shrouded in smoke. The sun cannot fight its way through, but looks like a bloodshot eye onto the devastation. It remains like that all through the

day; the smell of burning is all-pervading, so are the dust and the ash. And the siren never stops.[54]

Her husband, Emil Wolff, went for a walk into the city to see what had happened, and returned with depressing news.

> He was full of sad tales. His beloved cigar shop no longer existed, his favorite luncheon place, Michelsen, destroyed, huge devastation at the Gänsemarkt, a direct hit on the Opera, Eimsbüttel and Grindel wiped off the face of the earth.[55]

In fact the scale of the damage was beyond anything anyone on the ground could yet imagine. In Eimsbüttel whole streets had been destroyed, including post offices, schools, churches, the tram depot, the police station, and Schlump railway station. In Altona the damage included numerous factories and council offices, the military hospital, an electricity substation, the county courts, the police headquarters and barracks, and the old town hall.[56] Although no one area was quite "wiped off the face of the earth," the damage in the west of the city was extensive, and the dispersed nature of the bombing meant that there was not a single area of central Hamburg that was unaffected. Regardless of the material effects of the bombs, the effect on morale was devastating.

For Wanda Chantler this night would have an effect that would last a lifetime. She had spent most of the night doing what she could to help the wounded and dying in her forced-labor camp, even stepping through the barbed wire to help rescue a German family whose house on the other side of the street had also been hit. After a long night she finally returned to the rubble. Exhausted and confused, she wanted to see if any of her few belongings had survived the destruction, and she was particularly concerned about finding her Latin grammar book, which she had been studying in the evenings.

> I should have taken it with me in my pocket when the warning sounded, but it was so hot that night that I didn't put my coat on. So I'd lost my grammar, and I was looking for it in this terrific light from the fires. And there, in the debris, were five eyes on a plank, looking at me. Just five people's eyes. And I said "Go to sleep," and started crying. Five eyes on

a plank. I said, "Go to sleep, I'll come back." But when I came back they were not there.[57]

Over the coming week, the forced laborers of the Lokstedt fish-canning factory were completely abandoned by the authorities, forgotten among the mounting devastation. Wanda and many of the other surviving prisoners considered escaping—the barbed-wire perimeter of their camp had been blown down, and the guards were caught up in the wave of chaos that had swept over the city. But since they had nowhere to go most of them stayed where they were, waiting for someone to come and tell them what to do.

A few days later Wanda Chantler found herself in the factory dining room that had now become their makeshift dormitory, flailing her arms and striking out at anyone who came near her. When she was eventually restrained, she was diagnosed as having suffered a complete nervous break-down, brought on by the shock of all the horror she had witnessed. To this day she is still haunted by a single memory, that of five human eyeballs resting on a plank of wood in the debris of her barracks. There could be few more stark images of the reality of modern warfare.

On the afternoon of Sunday, July 25, Gauleiter Karl Kaufmann announced that nobody would be allowed to leave the city without special approval. It was an instruction that was to ensure the deaths of countless thousands in the coming days.[58] Certain that what had just happened was merely the beginning of something much larger, those who had strings to pull did so now. However, even those who were able to win permission to leave often found it difficult to do so. The train network had been severely disrupted, and those who had permission to leave often had to walk to the other side of town to find a station that was open. Those who had access to cars drove to safety, perhaps using gasoline that they had set aside for exactly such an emergency.[59] Parents who could afford to do so sent their children away to friends or relatives outside Hamburg. Some of the homeless, the *Ausgebombten*, as they were called, were evacuated to other parts of north-ern Germany in specially commissioned army trucks—others were forced to find shelter where they could within the confines of the city.

For the majority of Hamburgers the nightmare was only just begin-ning. They had nowhere to go, and no means of getting there in any case. There were thousands of people involved in emergency operations who could not leave the city because they were desperately needed—there would be no letup for these people for several days. For the rest there was little alternative but to stay in Hamburg and go to work as normal: Without the special permission to leave it would be impossible to find work, shelter, or rations elsewhere.

So the people of Hamburg did what the people of Essen, Bochum, Cologne, Warsaw, London, and countless other European cities had done before them—they gritted their teeth and got on with life as best they could. Though they fully expected another attack, nobody could have predicted what was about to befall them. The raids that were yet to come would be unparalleled in human history.

Chapter 11

THE AMERICANS
JOIN THE FRAY

*There is many a boy here today who looks on war
as all glory, but, boys, it is all hell.*

—GENERAL SHERMAN[1]

The people of Hamburg did not have to wait long for the second strike to come. The Allies had been talking about round-the-clock bombing ever since the Casablanca Conference in January: Now, for the first time, it was about to become a reality. Even as the British bombers were arriving home, American planes were already being prepared for a follow-up attack. Hamburg would be given just fifteen hours to recover before the bombs began falling all over again.

There were lots of good, sound reasons why the Americans were keen to attack the city again so soon. For a start, there was a chance that the general chaos caused by the British night raid might make it marginally safer. The staff at the USAAF bomber headquarters knew that the RAF had jammed German radar the night before, and they hoped that the chaos this had caused would give American crews a better chance of getting in and out alive. More important, they hoped their bombers would do greater damage by attacking immediately. Not only would a sudden daylight bombing keep the city in disarray, but they would be causing damage exactly when the city was least able to cope. Hamburg's firemen could not be in two places at once: While they were busy putting out fires in the west, U.S. bombers would drop their bombs in the south, in Hamburg's harbor district.

The man who made the decision to bomb Hamburg today was Brigadier General Frederick L. Anderson Jr., the head of the Eighth Air Force's VIII

Bomber Command. Anderson was one of Hap Arnold's "wonder boys," an energetic thirty-seven-year-old who had seen breathtakingly rapid promotion over the past few months. In mid-May he had been given command of 4th Bombardment Wing, but he had only stayed there six weeks before being promoted once again to his present job. By all accounts he was an enthusiast of long-range strategic bombing and, when later in the war it looked as though precision bombing might not be working, he was not at all averse to the idea of area bombing instead.[2] He was certainly interested in the way the British were conducting their bomber war: Tonight he would board one of the RAF planes bound for Essen to see for himself what area bombing looked like.[3]

Anderson regularly attended Sir Arthur Harris's planning sessions. RAF Bomber Command HQ was only a ten-minute drive from his own headquarters at Wycombe Abbey, and it seemed prudent to learn firsthand what his British partners were doing that night before planning his own follow-up for the next day. So when Harris had placed his finger on the map at Hamburg on July 24, Anderson was present. Later that same morning he had held a meeting with his own staff officers at which he, too, chose Hamburg as his target. Unlike Harris, however, Anderson specified exactly which buildings they were to aim for today. Out of all the possible targets in the city, Anderson picked two: the Blohm & Voss shipyards, and the Klöckner air-engine factory in the southeast of the city. According to the latest directive from the Combined Chiefs of Staff, these were two of the highest-priority targets in Germany.[4]

Anderson's staff knew that this mission was going to be their toughest yet. The USAAF had tried to attack the city only once before, exactly a month ago, and that mission had ended in disaster. The Germans had jammed their navigational aids, and the weather had been so cloudy that most of the American planes had been unable to find each other, let alone the target. They had only managed to get as far as the German coast before the Luftwaffe had arrived in such numbers that they had been forced to turn back. Eighteen planes had been shot down that day, and the American force had barely even crossed into German territory. As the 303rd Bombardment Group's lead pilot had said in his official report afterward, the whole mission had been "futile."[5]

The American planners were determined not to let the same thing happen today. The first thing they checked was the weather: There was no point in attempting an attack on Hamburg if the target was covered in cloud. The forecast was for clear skies—but to make sure, a reconnaissance flight was sent out to Heligoland early on the day of the attack. When this returned with reports of perfect conditions, the raid was given the go-ahead.[6]

The air force staff then devised a plan to confuse the Germans and to give their own crews the best possible chance of getting to the target and back again safely. Hamburg was not the only target they were bombing today, so it was important to coordinate all the different attacks to make sure they complemented each other. It was also important to conceal their true targets until the last possible moment: Once the Germans knew where they were heading they would be able to lie in ambush.

There were three separate forces flying today. The first was bound for the Heinkel aircraft factory at Warnemünde, on the Baltic coast. This wing would fly out toward Germany, but while it was still out at sea it would suddenly turn northward, as if it were heading for Denmark. The idea was to draw the German fighters out of their airfields too early, so that by the time the Americans actually crossed the coast they would be forced to return to their bases to refuel.

The second force was a smaller one—just three bomb groups, or about sixty planes—that was bound for the U-boat yards at Kiel. This force would fly across the North Sea with the Warnemünde wing, and also turn northward before suddenly switching back on itself and going back to the turning point. Then they would fly on to the target from there. Again, this was designed to confuse the Germans, conceal their true aims, and draw the Luftwaffe fighters out too early.

Following these forces, about forty minutes behind, were two combat wings bound for Hamburg. The first was to bomb the Blohm & Voss shipyards in the south of the city, while the second was to attack the Klöckner air-engine factory in the southeast. By this time, so the planners thought, the Luftwaffe would all be back at their airfields refueling, thus giving the Hamburg force time to make it to the target relatively unmolested. After the city had been bombed, both of these combat wings were supposed to join up with the Kiel force, and they would fly home together. By now the Luftwaffe would be back in the air, and it was much safer flying in larger numbers. The Hamburg wings and the Kiel wing would need to look out for one another on the way home.

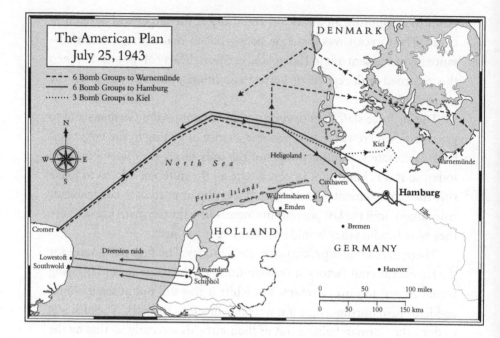

The American Plan
July 25, 1943

- - - - 6 Bomb Groups to Warnemünde
——— 6 Bomb Groups to Hamburg
········ 3 Bomb Groups to Kiel

The final piece of the jigsaw was a pair of diversionary flights, well to the south. A small force of fighters and light bombers would attack Holland and northwest France, making believe that they were the main danger. The idea was to hold down German fighters in these areas and prevent them from reinforcing the defenses in northern Germany.[7]

It was an ambitious plan, and one fraught with danger. If the various diversions did not work, the planes bound for Hamburg would find themselves the focus of all the combined fighter defenses of Germany, Holland, and northwest France. If either the Warnemünde or the Kiel forces aborted their missions then the Hamburg force would find itself isolated. And if the Hamburg and Kiel forces failed to meet up with one another on the way home they would both be more vulnerable to attack. The USAAF was taking a huge gamble by splitting up its force into four smaller units: Unless the plan worked perfectly, any one of these units might end up facing the full force of the Luftwaffe all alone.

The fact that the Americans believed they could attack a target as strong as Hamburg with a divided force, in broad daylight, without fighter cover, was perhaps an indication of how green they were. It is important to remember that this was still very early in the air war for them, and they had not yet had a chance to learn from their mistakes. General Anderson had been at his post for a mere three weeks, and his staff had planned only a handful of missions to Germany on this scale before. The bomber groups were just as inexperienced. None of the six groups that took off for Hamburg this afternoon had even existed when America joined the war, and four of them had been in England only for a matter of weeks.[8] In the past eight months they had been created, trained, transported across the Atlantic, accommodated in a foreign country, and thrown into the thick of the air war. By any standards, this was a baptism of fire.

It is easy to criticize the naïveté of their plans, but they had not yet had the opportunity to accrue long years of experience as the British had. That they were able to bomb Germany *at all* in the summer of 1943 is little short of a miracle.

The RAF watched the way the Americans planned their missions with a certain amount of curiosity. Despite superficial similarities with the British, it had become obvious by now that the USAAF was a very different air force from the RAF. The contrasts existed at every level—strategically, tactically, even right down to the very design of the airplanes themselves. But in the end it all boiled down to one basic difference: The British bombed by night, but the Americans bombed by day.

I have already touched on some of the practical and ethical reasons why the USAAF was determined to keep flying bombing missions in daylight. But the reason that they believed they would succeed at this hazardous enterprise, where both the British and the Germans before them had been forced to give up, was the quality of their planes. While the British and Germans had tried to fly through swarms of enemy fighters at the beginning of the war in outdated, poorly equipped bombers, the Americans would do so in something much more suited to the job: the Boeing B-17—easily the best daylight heavy bomber of the Second World War.

The B-17 was not nicknamed the "Flying Fortress" for nothing. It was equipped with bulletproof windows round the rear gunner's position, armor plating throughout, and it positively bristled with machine guns. The B-17F, which was the particular model in operation during July 1943, had up to sixteen .50-caliber Browning machine guns: four in the nose, two in the tail, four on the roof, two in the belly, and a pair on either side in the waist. When it was under attack, every member of the ten-man crew but the two pilots had something to shoot with. And most important, unlike the bombers of other nations, this one had no blind spots.

A single American bomber was therefore a pretty formidable opponent for any fighter. However, unlike the British at this stage of the war, the Americans did not fly one by one, but in groups of twenty or so, all flying together in close formation. Each group of twenty would be accompanied by two others: One group would fly in the lead, the next slightly higher and to one side, and the last slightly lower and to the other side. Any German fighter pilot who dived through the middle of a formation like this would have to be either extremely brave or extremely foolhardy: With anything up to a hundred guns firing at him at any one time, there was very little chance of his escaping unscathed.

To protect themselves from flak, the B-17s had been built to fly at heights of 30,000 feet and even higher. This was 5,000 to 6,000 feet higher than a pilot of heavy bombers in the RAF could dream of. It flew at speeds of just under 300 mph, which again was considerably faster than any RAF heavy bomber. True, it could carry less than half the bomb load of an RAF Lancaster, but the Americans reasoned that they did not *need* to carry such huge numbers of bombs. Their whole philosophy was built around dropping a few accurately placed bombs on specific targets—not, as with the RAF, on plastering the whole area with bombs. They were happy to sacrifice their bomb capacity for the ability to fly higher, faster, and more safely than any other air force in the world.

The only problem with these theories was that they did not quite work—at least, not yet. No matter how high or how fast the American bombers flew, they were not a match for the German fighters, and probably would not be until the introduction of long-range American fighter escorts later in the war. The USAAF was certainly not strong enough to commit to several targets at once, and they seriously underestimated the strength of the Luftwaffe. Their British counterparts warned them of these facts, and could not understand why the Americans refused to listen. To the British, it looked as though the USAAF was determined to repeat the same mistakes that they themselves had made.

The late Pierre Clostermann, one of the Allies' greatest fighter aces in the Second World War, once described to me the first time he ever saw a USAAF officer: He was wearing a cowboy hat and a revolver on his hip and "swaggering like he had just stepped out of the Wild West."[9] In fact, the whole American air force at that time was brash, confident in its abilities to the point of arrogance, and determined to live by its own rules. Eventually the brashness of their attitude would be vindicated—indeed, many have argued that it was only by forcing the Germans into a long-term, daylight gun battle that the Allies finally gained air superiority—but in the meantime some pretty harsh lessons had to be learned.

If there were close links between the RAF and the USAAF on a command level, there were fewer links between the airmen themselves. The Americans had separate airbases and rarely had the opportunity to meet their British counterparts. When they did meet, however, there was a strong mutual respect between them. Walter Davis of 91st Bombardment Group (BG) remembers a conversation he had in the summer of 1943 with an RAF man he met in a London pub. The British airman insisted on buying him a drink with the words, "You wouldn't catch me going over Germany in daylight!" In reply, Davis simply said, "Well, you wouldn't catch me going over there in the dark!"[10]

To a certain degree, Walter Davis was being generous to his RAF drinking partner. Of the two air forces, the RAF men unquestionably had the better deal—at least at this stage of the war. Sure, the Americans did not have to take off or land in the dark, they had their squadron colleagues all around them as they flew, and when danger came they could at least *see* it coming. But without the cover of darkness they were little better than sitting ducks, and their rigid adherence to formation flying meant that when the guns started firing they could not even take evasive action. As one U.S. veteran cogently put it, "We were ordered to fly in an aluminum crate, carrying 2,000 gallons plus of 100-octane gasoline, with a 6,000- to 8,000-thousand-pound bomb load, in tight formation, straight and level, while people shot at you."[11]

With tactics like this, life expectancy in the U.S. Eighth Air Force was not exactly high. The airmen knew this—it was one of the first things they learned when they got to Britain. For example, Samuel Fleming was told as soon as he arrived at Molesworth airbase that there was virtually no way that he was going to get through his tour alive.

What it boiled down to, according to the guys keeping score, was this: In 1943 and 1944, the average life span of an Eighth Air Force bomber and crew was fifteen missions. The assigned tour of duty for crew members, however, was initially twenty-five missions, and later increased to thirty and finally to thirty-five missions. . . . One did not have to be a brain surgeon to figure out one's odds of finishing a combat tour.[12]

Joseph Mutz was similarly demoralized when he arrived in England. He had been slightly delayed on his journey across the Atlantic, and got to his airbase a few days after most of the men he had trained with. One of the first things he did was to look up a friend, only to find that he had already been shot down. It was impossible not to come to the conclusion that the same fate awaited him. "I had a rock in my stomach, and I just knew that we were never going to make it. Just *couldn't* make it. I even went as far as writing my brother. I told him what to do with my insurance money."[13]

This was not what these men had signed up for. Most of them had joined the air force simply because they thought it would be better than serving in the infantry—they had been warned about the dangers of the trenches by their parents, some of whom had experienced the horrors of the First World War. But it was now beginning to look as though they might have made the wrong choice. While most of the infantry were still safe back home, and would not see action for almost another year, American airmen were dying in droves.[14] Nor were they safe from some of the more gruesome aspects of war, as anyone who experienced a direct hit on their plane soon discovered. Scott Buist, a USAAF gunner from New Brunswick, remembers having to pull the remains of his crewmate from the ball turret after it had received a direct hit. "We had to pull him out, an arm, a leg, pieces, his head; I put his head in the basket. . . . This is a kid that I slept next to."[15]

Perhaps the operative word in this quotation is the word "kid." Almost all the men who flew B-17s during the Second World War were in their late teens and early twenties. Most of them had never been outside the United States before, and yet here they were now, thousands of miles from home, fighting a foreign war for the sake of a noble principle. Many of them were lonely, and desperately missed their friends and family back home. They were all, to one degree or another, scared of the task that lay ahead of them.

But in general they were determined to do their best, if only for the sake of their own pride.

These, then, were the men who would bomb Hamburg during the afternoon of July 25, 1943. They faced the combined dangers of flak, fighters, mechanical malfunction, extreme cold, and lack of oxygen. More than 1,200 of them would take off that afternoon. One hundred and fifty would not return.

Chapter 12

THE LUFTWAFFE
STRIKES BACK

No plan survives contact with the enemy.

—FIELD-MARSHAL HELMUTH VON MOLTKE[1]

When the crews turned up at briefing on the morning of July 25 none of them knew what lay in store. For weeks now, unpredictable banks of cloud over northern Europe had prevented the USAAF from planning any missions to Germany, and most of the men hoped that it would stay this way—at least until they had finished their tours. Over the past month they had concentrated on targets in France and the Low Countries—mostly airfields and aircraft factories. Raids like this were the "milk runs" that every airman hoped for when he attended briefings like the one this morning: a relatively short trip across the English Channel, often with fighter escorts to keep them safe.

However, there were signs that things were beginning to change. A week ago some of them had been detailed to attack a synthetic rubber factory in Hanover—a mission that had been called off at the last moment due to bad weather. And then, yesterday, they had made their first trip to Norway—easily the farthest any of them had ever flown on a mission. There had been little or no opposition along the way, but that was not the point: The men were beginning to get the message that there was now nowhere in Europe that was beyond them. So, as they gathered in the briefing rooms of their various airbases this morning, there was a slight tension in the air. They knew that it was only a matter of time before they were sent somewhere truly dangerous.

The ritual at briefing was pretty much the same as it was for the RAF. There was the same blackening of the windows, the same locking of doors, and the same false bravado as some of the young men talked or joked their nerves away. And, just as in RAF briefings, all eyes were drawn to the large board at the end of the room. On that board, hidden behind a curtain, was the information they were all eager to know: the map of Europe, marked with a ribbon showing their route to the target and back.

After all the men had taken their seats, and the windows were covered, the briefing officer stepped up to the stage and the room descended into an uneasy silence. Without ceremony, he reached up and pulled aside the curtains on the target map. Philip Dreiseszun, who attended the 381st BG briefing in Ridgewell, remembers this moment with particular clarity. "Then came the moment of revelation! The board cover was removed as we heard the words, 'Gentlemen, the target for today is Hamburg!' A stunned silence gave way to utterances of dismay and alarm."[2]

Nobody liked flying to targets in Germany, but today the crews had real cause for concern. They all knew that Hamburg was one of the best-defended cities in Germany—they had been told so at their last briefing on this target, a month ago. Those who had flown on that unfortunate mission knew exactly what could go wrong—especially the men of the 379th BG, who had lost six crews that day. Even the crews who had not been around at that time had probably heard about it: It had been one of the USAAF's most disastrous missions to date.

As the men shifted uncomfortably in their seats, the briefing officer began to outline the strategy behind today's mission. The target for 379th, 303rd, and 384th BGs would be the Blohm & Voss shipbuilding yards: the most important U-boat manufacturer in Germany. For the 91st, 351st, and 381st BGs, the target was the Klöckner air-engine factory in the southeast of the city. The Luftwaffe had been stepping up production of fighter planes in recent months, and it was absolutely imperative that the Allies stop them from doing so further—the lives of the American airmen themselves depended on it.[3]

After his opening statement, the briefing officer went on to outline the specifics of the mission: the route they would be taking, the sort of weather they could expect, and so on. But the information every man in the room was waiting to hear was what sort of opposition they should anticipate. Of course, when it came the news was only what they expected. Fighter opposition would be fierce, so it was essential that all the groups did their utmost to stay in tight formations. And the flak would be almost continuous from the moment they crossed the coast. The briefing officer was particularly clear on this last point, and told the men that Hamburg alone had ninety-eight heavy AA guns trained on them that day. (As formidable as this sounded, the real number was actually more than three times this.) In any case, he advised the men to take evasive action wherever possible: "If you are able to observe the flashes of the AA guns," he said, "it will take the shell 20 to 30 seconds to reach you." That was the moment for the whole formation to try immediately to shift height and direction.[4]

The men listened to these details in silence, trying to calm their nerves enough to take in all the statistics and instructions. As one veteran from 384th BG remembers it, the dread in the room this morning was almost palpable. "There was definitely an air of apprehension about this briefing. It's always stuck in my mind that, after the target had been revealed, every navigator in the group prepared a course for the nearest friendly country. Sweden, I think it was, on this day."[5]

What Philip Dreiseszun remembers most was the reactions of his crew-mates. Some of them were downright despondent, but once they had all had time to digest the news, the main emotion seemed to be one of grim determination.

> Our bombardier, James H. Houck, gloomily expressed feelings of fore-boding. The rest of us, I believe, were in a state of numb awe, of mixed feelings of fear and wonder, and facing unknown qualities in ourselves. How would we react in confrontation with the might of the German Luftwaffe and the formidable antiaircraft fire we surely would meet? The bonds, fortunately, that held a crew together were a subconscious factor in helping us set individual concerns aside long enough to concentrate on the tasks that lay ahead.[6]

After lunch the crews went to get their gear: flight rations, escape kits, flight clothing, parachutes. Just as the RAF had done the evening before, they now milled around nervously, some of them talking or cracking jokes, others communing silently with themselves as they waited for the person-nel carriers to come and take them out to their planes. The only difference was that this was not taking place at twilight, but in the hazy sunshine of a hot summer's day. By the time the trucks came, everyone was beginning to overheat a little, particularly the gunners in their heavy, wool-lined suits.

Out at dispersal they would busy themselves inside the plane—but once everything was ready they would shelter in the shade of the wings, leaving their flight jackets off until the last possible moment as they stood around waiting for the signal that it was time to go.

It was not until after one o'clock that they finally climbed on board and the B-17s' engines roared into life. Edward Piech flew as a bombardier with the 351st BG during this time, and remembers the thrill he always felt as the line of bombers prepared to leave the ground.

> There was a green flare and then the first, the lead ship would take off. And then a few seconds after that each one, one by one, lined up in a column. . . . I will never forget the sound of those B-17s taking off. They just sort of leave a thrill up and down my spine: No matter where I am and I hear those sounds, I can't escape from it. It is actually, to me, it was a beautiful sound.[7]

As the planes took to the air, the first task was to gain height and assemble into proper formations. This sounds simple, but was in fact one of the most problematic tasks of the day. Slotting each individual plane into the correct position in the formation was quite time-consuming, and it could take an hour or even longer to get this right.[8] Veteran Donald Hillenmayer explains:

> These airplanes climbed at the rate of 500 feet a minute when they are fully loaded, so, to get up to, say, 12,000 feet to form, that's pretty close to half an hour just to get there. . . . So, the lead crew, he's up there, starts to circle and here comes the second plane and he cuts him off and gets into formation. Here comes the third one, he cuts them off, he gets into position. Now, you do that say eight or ten times. . . . It took us an hour-and-a-half to form.[9]

This was only the start of the problem. Once each individual group had arranged itself into proper formation they then had to find one another, so that they could accompany one another across the sea. The combat wing bound for Blohm & Voss managed to assemble without much trouble, but the Klöckner wing had some major problems. The 91st BG, which was supposed to be leading two of the other groups, was unable at first to find

either of them in the haze. In desperation, the lead plane made the whole
group circle back over England, firing flares to attract attention to themselves. They eventually picked up the low group in their formation (the
351st BG) this way, but the high group (the 381st BG) was still nowhere to
be seen. It was only after the formation leader gave up and set course for
Germany that they finally spotted the 381st BG up ahead. This group then
lost more time as it doubled back to fall in behind the leaders.[10] After all
these delays the whole wing was in a woefully ragged formation, and it was
still struggling to close up even as it crossed the German coast two hours
later.

While all these complicated maneuvers were going on there was little
that the crews could do but sit and wait. Conditions inside the B-17s were
far from comfortable, especially for those in the extremities of the plane.
They were climbing to an altitude of between 26,000 and 30,000 feet: At
these heights the temperature regularly drops to less than minus forty
degrees, and despite wool-lined boots and electrically heated suits it was
not uncommon for airmen to come home with frostbite. "The warmest I
ever flew on a mission was thirty below zero," says Albert Porter Jr., who
served as a ball-turret gunner later on in the war, "and the coldest was close
to sixty below. When we finished the mission, our whole front of our out-
fit was solid ice from the condensation of the oxygen, your breath."[11]

Flying at any altitude above 10,000 feet made them all reliant on oxygen. They got this by plugging their face masks into one of the plane's
central outlets, but there were spare bottles of oxygen stowed throughout
the plane in case of emergency. These could be the difference between life
and death. If for any reason the crew's air supplies were cut off, then anoxia,
and eventually unconsciousness, would soon follow. It was important to
react to any cut in oxygen immediately—after a minute or two the airmen
would be unable to perform even the simplest tasks. The worst thing about
anoxia was that those affected often would not realize it. As their reactions
slowed they often believed they were behaving quite normally, and by the
time they began fumbling with the oxygen bottles it was too late—they
were incapable of saving themselves. Experienced airmen kept a constant
watch on their fellow crew members, just to make sure that everyone was
still conscious.

Of all the members of the crew, those who were under the most constant
stress were the pilot and his copilot. They might not be forced to suffer the

cold like the gunners at the back of the plane, because the cockpits were at least heated, but the pressure of holding the bomber in close formation with twenty other aircraft for several hours on end was both physically and mentally exhausting. The other members of the crew—the navigator, the wireless operator, the bombardier—were also obliged to undergo prolonged periods of intense concentration. They had to keep a constant log of their position just in case anything went wrong, and all crewmen were supposed to keep a lookout for fighters whenever they were not otherwise engaged.

Of the 123 planes that took off for Hamburg that afternoon, fourteen were forced to turn back, mostly because of mechanical malfunctions. Unlike the British night bombers, who would often get away with flying to a target and back on just three engines, many B-17 crews were understandably reluctant to fly over German territory in anything but a fully functioning machine. After these fourteen fell away and returned to England, the remainder of the force continued their climb. It was imperative that they manage to attain their bombing altitudes before they reached the European coast.

As they rose through the haze they found themselves flying in the deep azure of the infinite sky. Soon even the haze beneath them melted away, and they were left with the perfect flying conditions they knew as CAVU—"ceiling and visibility unlimited." For a short while the heavens seemed a peaceful place: There were no enemy fighters to worry about just yet, and nothing broke the eternal blue but the vapor trails of a hundred Flying Fortresses. Some of the crew could be forgiven for taking a few moments to sit back and admire the view. Others would swap jokes and tease one another over the intercom in voices that were just that little bit too loud, or too merry; only as they approached the coast of Europe would they gradually lapse into silence, as all eyes began to concentrate on combing the heavens for the telltale glints of German metal.

The lead group of bombers first sighted the German coast around four o'clock. As the navigators searched for landmarks in order to pinpoint their position, everyone else watched the surrounding sky. It did not take long to find what they were looking for: the distant dots of fighter planes rising above the earth to meet them. As they approached the mouth of the river Elbe at about 4:15 P.M., the first German fighters attacked. They were halfhearted attacks at first, as if they were merely testing the Americans. But gradually Luftwaffe planes began to appear in greater numbers, hovering around the edges of the formations, waiting for a chance to pounce on any B-17 that strayed even slightly away from the rest. "You always had the feeling that you were in a chicken coop," said one veteran of these raids, "and the fighters out there are foxes or weasels."[12]

Darrell Gust was a navigator on one of the 303rd BG's Flying Fortresses. In his position just behind the bombardier in the nose of the plane, he could see exactly what was going on around the formation.

> We were hit by swarms of fighters as soon as we crossed the coastline. These guys were *eager*! Maybe twenty to thirty miles from the target, I looked out of the window over my navigator's table and saw an Me109 sitting out there out of range, but apparently flying the same course we were, and maybe 200 to 300 yards below our formation. I knew that fighter pilots sometimes did this, kind of looking us over. Then they would suddenly zoom up and ahead of us, positioning themselves for a 180-degree turn and a nose-first attack on the B-17 formations.
>
> I thought, "This bastard is up to no good and I'll keep my eye on him." He just kept flying parallel to us, but he seemed to be getting closer. He finally edged in to what I estimated to be about 700 to 800 yards. I grabbed the 0.50-cal above my navigator's desk and gave him about fifteen to twenty rounds. I could immediately see my tracers going behind him. I corrected my aim and gave him a burst of about thirty rounds. Suddenly, there was a plume of white smoke emerging from the Me109, and he started to drop in a vertical dive. I called to S/Sgt Virgil Brown, our tail gunner, that I had nailed an Me109 and asked him to keep his eye on it. He said he saw it go straight down and crash behind us.[13]

This was probably the first casualty of the day, an Me109 from III/JG26: it crash-landed at Stade airfield, but the pilot escaped unhurt. Two more German fighters from this *Gruppe* alone were also forced to land with combat damage in the next few minutes.[14] It was a good omen for the Americans, but these were still early days.

It might not have seemed like it to the bombers in the vanguard of the mission, but the American plan was actually working quite well. While the skies appeared to be bristling with German fighters, there were actually far fewer than there might have been. The force bound for Warnemünde, which had already approached northern Germany some forty minutes earlier, had succeeded in drawing many of the Luftwaffe into the air too early, and many of the Me109s and FW190s that might have been here to greet them were actually now back at their airfields refueling. The diversionary raids down in France and Holland had also worked: At least two Luftwaffe *Staffeln*, which might otherwise have been sent northward to defend Hamburg, were sent from Schipol and Woensdrecht airfields to deal with these attacks.[15] In fact, the only part of the American plan that had not seemed to work was the attack on Kiel. The three bomb groups in this wing had had such a hard time finding one another, and were so dispersed across the sky, that the wing leader had been forced to call the whole mission off. They returned home without dropping a single bomb on German soil. Nevertheless, the other deceptions had worked well. Not a single American bomber was shot down before they reached the target; and while the Blohm & Voss wing might have had to deal with German fighters, the Klöckner wing, which came in about fifteen or twenty minutes behind them, had a virtually free run into Hamburg.

However, the German fighters were only one part of the formidable Hamburg defense line: There was nothing the Americans could do to deceive the flak guns. Indeed, as they flew through the clouds of exploding shells, there was very little any of them could do to avoid being hit. Ironically, the very tactics they relied on to keep them safe from the fighters also made them very vulnerable to flak. A single B-17, weaving back and forth more than five miles above the ground, would have been an impossible target for the flak gunners. A group of twenty, forced to fly relatively steadily so that they could all keep together, was a much bigger target. After the failures of the previous night, the German flak gunners must have relished the opportunity to take their revenge this afternoon.

Many of the American aviators feared flak far more than they did fighters. Walter Davis, who was flying a plane in the Klöckner wing, was one of them: "Oh, the flak was much more worrying. You could *see* the fighters. And we had gunners on our airplane. Whereas you can't see the flak—you don't know when it's going to come. You can see it exploding, but you can't dodge it. . . . And they had so much of it over there. . . ."[16]

The antiaircraft fire began before they even reached the German coast, when two flak ships in the Elbe estuary opened up on them. A short while afterward, when the batteries of Cuxhaven also started up, the flak suddenly became both accurate and intense, "So thick you could get out and walk on it," according to Walter Davis. This carried on virtually uninterrupted for the next twenty minutes, but it was not until they reached Hamburg that it got really bad. "When we were going in to Hamburg it looked like a big black cloud over it. Actually what it was was the smoke from the flak coming up."[17]

This was far worse than anything the Americans had ever experienced before. The flak bursts seemed to create an impenetrable curtain before them, and they had no choice but to fly straight through it. As they approached the city they began to see the flashes in the air as the actual shells exploded—red or pink explosions, followed by small clouds of brown or black smoke, like thousands of firecrackers filling the sky. Some airmen found the sight mesmerizing. But there was never any doubt about the danger they were in. Some of the planes were literally thrown about the sky by the sheer force of the exploding shells. According to the men of the 381st BG, who were flying in the Klöckner wing, the antiaircraft fire was quite simply "the most intense we have ever seen."[18]

It took just twenty minutes for the Americans to fly from the coast to the outskirts of Hamburg, but they were under fire for the whole journey. By the time they reached the city many of them had had holes punched in their wings and fuselages, a handful had even lost one or more of their engines. Worse still, they were already beginning to take casualties. Flying in the lead group of the Blohm & Voss wing, the "Judy B" had taken a vicious blow to the side of the cockpit. Lieutenant Charles Bigler, the nineteen-year-old copilot, remembers what happened:

> It was five minutes before our bomb run over Hamburg. A Nazi fighter came in straight on my side and knocked out my oxygen. A shell glanced on the back of my seat and hit the pilot's back. The pilot slumped over and I tried to keep him up with one hand and hold the ship with the other. If I had let him slump I would have been unable to control the ship. We made our bomb run with me driving with one hand.[19]

The pilot, Willis Carlisle, had died instantly. For five minutes, without any oxygen to sustain him, Charles Bigler held the dead man up, only calling out for help once he had completed his bomb run. Over the next hour a desperate struggle ensued as the bombardier and the top-turret gunner

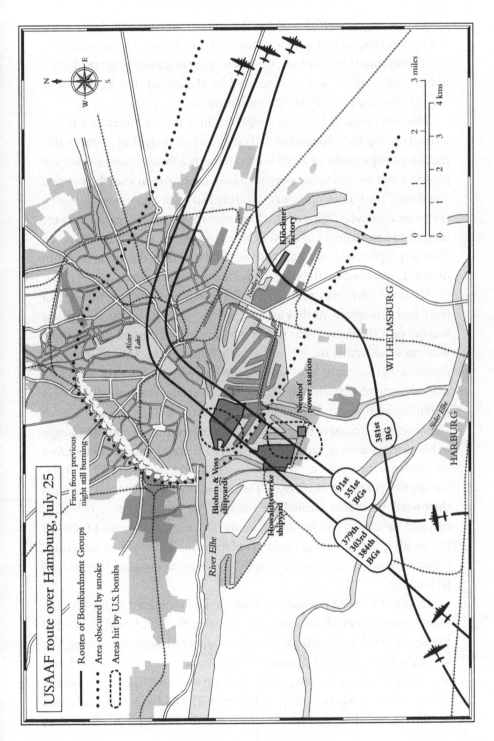

USAAF route over Hamburg, July 25

— Routes of Bombardment Groups

····· Fires from previous night still burning

··· Area obscured by smoke

⊂⊃ Areas hit by U.S. bombs

N
W — E
S

0   1   2   3 miles
0   1   2   3   4 kms

River Elbe

Alster Lake

Blohm & Voss shipyards

Howaldtswerke shipyard

Neuhof power station

Klöckner factory

Norder Elbe

Süder Elbe

WILHELMSBURG

HARBURG

381st BG

91st 351st BGs

379th 303rd 384th BGs

tried to get oxygen to Bigler, and at the same time remove the body of the dead pilot. Despite being under continual attack from German fighters, and falling almost 25,000 feet, Bigler somehow managed to get the Judy B home—although he was so exhausted by the ordeal that he had to be carried from the plane by the station's medics.

This was probably the most dangerous time for the Americans. If they wanted to drop their bombs correctly they had no choice but to stay in formation and fly straight and level toward the target. Evasive maneuvers of any kind to avoid the flak were now prohibited, because even a small deviation could send the bombs off-course. During this critical couple of minutes, they were effectively sitting ducks. Even after the bombs had gone they were obliged to keep straight and level just a little longer, until they had taken their target photographs. Only then could they follow the group leader in his gentle weave across the sky to avoid the flak once again.

However, there was another problem today, and not one that any of them had anticipated. As they approached the target it became clear that it was not only the sky that was filled with smoke from the flak shells—there was smoke all across the ground as well. Some of the American airmen assumed that this must have been a deliberate screen, set by the Hamburg authorities to obscure the city center. This is certainly what the 303rd BG's group leader thought: "There must have been a million square miles of smoke screen," he said to the press office when he returned home (although in his official report he reduced this claim to about fifty square miles). As a consequence, he went on, "the bomb results were unobserved."[20] Others, like the ball gunner of 384th BG's "Doris Mae," thought that the Americans themselves must have created the smoke: "The preceding group's bombs had sent up a lot of smoke. If they hit the target, we did too for I followed our bombs right down into the center of the mess." Unbeknown to this eyewitness, there *was* no previous group: The 384th BG was the first to drop its bombs.[21]

In fact, the smoke was coming from all the fires started by the RAF the night before. It is ironic that the very success of the British raid threatened to prevent the Americans from following it up with a second strike, but this is exactly what happened. A westerly breeze was blowing thick black clouds across the whole of the target area, making it almost impossible for the Americans to see where to drop their bombs. The Blohm & Voss yards were on the edge of this huge smoke cloud, but the Klöckner airplane-parts factory was right in the middle of it, so it was beginning to look as if neither wing would be able to find its target. In an effort to salvage the mission, two of the Klöckner groups decided to head for Blohm & Voss instead, in the hope that this target might be easier to see. The third group, the 381st BG, were still too far behind their leaders to realize what they were doing, and carried on with their planned route above the smoke cloud.

So it was that five bombardment groups, instead of just three, headed toward the U-boat yards on the banks of the Elbe. It was still not certain whether they would be able to bomb it, and for a short while the whole mission hung in the balance. But as the bomber formations made their final approach, by a piece of great good fortune, a gap in the smoke clouds opened up. Blohm & Voss was still obscured, but the quays and buildings of Howaldtswerke, one of Hamburg's other shipyards, were clearly visible. As they got closer the smoke began to close over the target area once more, so without wasting any time the 384th BG opened their bomb bay doors and unleashed 44,000 pounds of incendiaries on the dockyards. They were followed at roughly one-minute intervals by the 379th, the 303rd, the 351st, and the 91st bombardment groups, dropping wave after wave of explosives and incendiary bombs onto the buildings below.[22]

Meanwhile, the last group, the 381st, was still struggling to keep up with the rest of the force. Unable to see what the other Klöckner groups had done, the group leader decided to cut the corner off the designated route to save time, but as he flew across the south of the city he and his group found themselves alone. From here on he stuck to the planned route, heading eastward over the smoke clouds, but it rapidly became obvious that he was never going to find the Klöckner airplane-parts factory—the smoke was simply too thick. With the Klöckner mission looking like a lost cause, the group held on to its bombs and decided to seek out a target of opportunity on the way home. They finally settled on the railway marshaling yards at Heide, which they bombed at ten past five, half an hour after the other groups had already got rid of their bombs. Then they hurried to close up with their fellow bomber groups once again for the hazardous journey home.

By now all six bombardment groups were looking more than a little ragged. Of the 123 Flying Fortresses that had started out this afternoon, fourteen had aborted the mission before even reaching Germany. Almost half of those that remained now had flak damage of some sort or another,

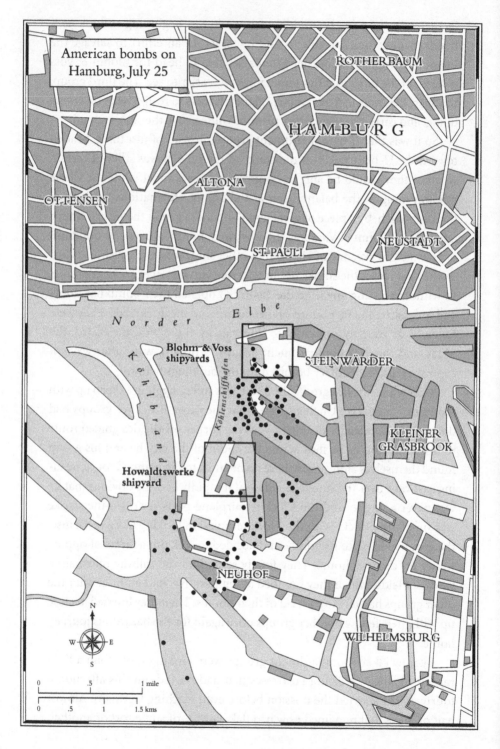

American bombs on
Hamburg, July 25

ROTHERBAUM

HAMBURG

ALTONA

OTTENSEN

NEUSTADT

ST. PAULI

Norder   *Elbe*

Blohm & Voss
shipyards

STEINWÄRDER

Köhlbrand

Köhlenschiffhafen

KLEINER
GRASBROOK

Howaldtswerke
shipyard

NEUHOF

WILHELMSBURG

N
W · E
S

0   .5   1 mile

0   .5   1   1.5 kms

and many more had been hit by cannon fire from the ever-present fighters.[23] Those American planes with major damage were now in serious trouble. If an engine had been hit, or any of the vital controls, it would become more and more difficult to keep up with the others. And stragglers knew that they would face a journey home that was doubly dangerous: Not only would they be the first to be targeted by the German fighters, but they would have to face those attacks alone.

As the bombers struggled to stay close together the Luftwaffe at last began to appear in force all around them. Fighters from Heligoland, which had been the first to contact the invading force, had now refueled and were coming in for a second attack. They were joined by fighters from Deelen, Husum, Jever, Nordholz, and Oldenburg.[24] Some American groups reported seeing as many as 100, 200, or even 300 fighter planes over the next hour or so. At times they seemed to fill the sky, attacking in waves from every conceivable angle; there was nothing the Americans could do but abandon all other duties and man the guns.[25]

With such huge numbers of fighters coming in at them, it was only a matter of time before some of the Flying Fortresses started to go down. Survivors of the two Hamburg wings unanimously claimed that the German fighters were far more ferocious than usual, pressing home their attacks with a terrifying determination.[26] The Luftwaffe had not yet learned that the best method of attack was to dive at the bombers head-on and try to get the formation to break up—but there were many cases of this happening, nevertheless. The largest number of attacks came up from below at the rear, and in general they were not by single fighters but by groups of three or four at a time.

It was the lower groups that took the brunt of all this ferocity, and particularly the straggling members of those groups. The worst hit was the 384th BG, which by now was limping forward with several disabled planes, their normally tight formation looking more and more ragged as the afternoon wore on. Some individual planes in this group were attacked twenty to twenty-five times by fighters alone, and yet somehow, miraculously, managed to stay airborne.[27] Others simply could not take the punishment the Luftwaffe was dealing out.

Brad Summers was one of the copilots with this group, and tells the story of what happened to his plane:

Before we got to the target we had one hit, knocked all the glass out of the top turret. The engineer, who managed the turret, I think his oxygen mask protected his face quite a bit. There was some little splinters in his neck and shoulders, but he went back to his gun. He couldn't put his head out because of the wind blowing through the turret, so he huddled over down inside trying to [aim] by the tracers (the gun sight was also destroyed), which is not a very accurate way to shoot. . . .

We proceeded on and got several other hits. I recall seeing a flash out of my window and I looked and there was a rip in the skin on the top of my wing. It must have been about eight or ten feet long, opened about four or five inches wide. The skin was peeled back where apparently a 20mm shell from a fighter plane had gone in and ripped it out. As I looked, I saw another hole open up. The only thing I could figure was, an 88mm shell had gone right through the wing without exploding.[28]

It was around this time that the tail gunner had a direct hit on his turret. The concussion from the explosion lifted him and threw him back into the body of the plane, but he seemed to be OK, so he crawled back to see if the tail guns were still intact. One of them was still working, so he went back to firing it until a second direct hit blasted him back through the doorway again. This time his guns had been blown out of the back of the aircraft altogether. There was nothing more he could do.

Under sustained punishment like this it did not take long before something vital was hit, and Summers's Flying Fortress was being hit from all angles. With no top turret, and most of the back of the plane blown away, they were an easy target for the fighters. The Germans kept coming. First an aileron went. Then they got some hits in the tail that knocked out the trim tabs, so that Summers had to lean forward on the stick to hold the nose of the plane down. And finally the stabilizer got blown away, leaving the two pilots powerless to fly the plane. There was nothing left to do but to bail out. Brad Summers continues:

I hooked my parachute on and I got my hat. I put that on, then I decided, well, heck, I'd probably lose it anyhow, so I threw that away and got a bail-out oxygen bottle . . . I don't know why all these silly thoughts went through my head, like wanting to get my hat, but anyway, I was beginning to feel the effects of the lack of oxygen—anoxia, we called it—getting a bit lightheaded . . . I decided I'd better get out of there right away. I just did a somersault right out the door and down I went.[29]

Summers fell several thousand feet before he pulled the ripcord of his parachute, and only did so when he thought it was likely that he might pass out. One of the waist gunners was not so lucky—he was killed in his position by flak. And Kenny Harland, the valiant gunner who carried on shooting despite having his top turret blown apart, died when he hit the ground. Everyone else survived to become prisoners of war. The fact that they did, and the fact that they had so much time to bail out, is a testament to the sheer strength of the B-17 Flying Fortress under punishment.

Some of the planes from the other groups were having just as tough a time of it. Philip Dreiseszun was a navigator in 381st BG when the full force of the German fighter formations attacked them.

The enemy swarmed at us from all directions. Our gunners, and Houck [the bombardier] and myself were all firing; new belts of ammunition were hurriedly installed as rounds were expelled. . . . Our plane lurched, shuddering heavily as 20-millimeter shells tore through the fuselage and Plexiglas windows. Houck spun around from his front firing stance, sinking to our little deck in a sitting position. I was slammed against the worktable but felt no pain. The attack ended, and I turned my attention to Houck. Above his chest-pack parachute was a gaping hole in his chest which spurted blood . . . I prayed for some sign of life; there was none.[30]

When the bail-out order came, Dreiseszun agonized over whether he should push his dead comrade out of the plane with his parachute on, so that he could be recovered for burial once he reached the ground. But, reasoning that the parachute might get caught on the tailplanes and endanger the rest of the crew, he eventually decided to leave him where he was. Pulling the cord on the emergency hatch, he kicked the door open and leaped through into 27,000 feet of cold space and nothingness.

I let myself fall free in the awesome quiet. I estimated about 2000 feet and then pulled the ripcord. The chute jerked violently as it unfurled buffeted by the strong wind at that altitude. The leg straps tightened painfully in the groin area. On seeing the 'chute unfold, I knew I was a goner! It was

full of large holes, small holes, and many tears. How it kept me afloat . . .
I'll never know. During the attack, a 20-millimeter shell had evidently
made a direct hit on my parachute. . . . The final 6000–7000 feet were like
a free fall. I hit the ground with such a jarring impact, it felt like every
bone in my body had shattered. I lost consciousness.[31]

When he came to there was a German soldier sitting on him, searching him
for weapons. He was lucky. Two of his crewmates who had landed nearby
were killed by an angry mob of civilians. The tail gunner went down with
the plane. The other five members of the crew survived to become prisoners of war.

A pattern was beginning to emerge in the attacks made by the Luftwaffe
fighters. First they picked off the stragglers—those planes that were
already crippled by flak and earlier fighter attacks. Then they concentrated
on the planes at the back of the formation—most of the B-17s lost were
ones that had started off the day at the back. And finally, once one or two
of the smaller formations were understrength (and therefore had fewer
guns with which to defend themselves), the fighters came in to finish off
the rest.

It was this last point that was to prove particularly devastating. While
some bomb groups made it home relatively untroubled, others suffered
attack after attack all the way across Germany and most of the way home
across the North Sea. Of the three bombardment groups in the Klöckner
wing, for example, two of them lost only a single plane on the way home.
The third, which had been severely depleted from the outset when seven of
its planes had aborted their missions, received the full brunt of the German
storm. This group, the 381st, lost three planes on the way home—and all
three were in the same squadron (Dreiseszun's 532nd Squadron).

The story was the same for the Blohm & Voss wing. The twenty-one
planes in lead group suffered just fifteen attacks, and lost two planes, both
of them stragglers. The high group was attacked nineteen times, and only
lost one plane out of twenty—again, a straggler. The low group was attacked
eighty times—more than twice the number of the other two groups put
together.[32] It lost seven planes that afternoon, six of them from the same
squadron. This desperately unfortunate unit, 544th Squadron, was all but
wiped out.

The reasons behind this loss were simple: The low squadron of the low

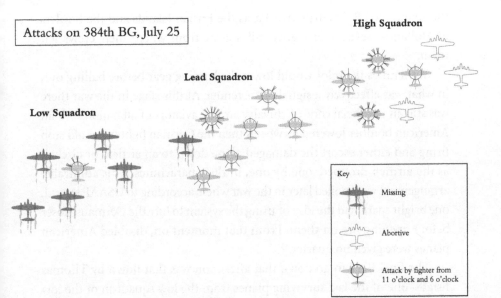

Attacks on 384th BG, July 25

High Squadron

Lead Squadron

Low Squadron

Key

Missing

Abortive

Attack by fighter from
11 o'clock and 6 o'clock

group was the most vulnerable place to fly in the whole formation, and was often nicknamed "Purple Heart Corner" or "Coffin Corner" because of the disproportionate number of planes that were always shot down there. After coming through Hamburg, the 544th Squadron had already been under relentless attack for forty minutes, and four of the seven planes were now struggling to keep up. They were picked off mercilessly by the German fighters. Once the squadron was down to just three planes it was easy prey—the fighters came in again and again until two more had been shot down. The only plane left struggled upward to fall behind the lead formation, but it had to suffer nine more sustained attacks before the fighters finally left it alone.

It goes without saying that every one of these stricken bombers went down fighting. Of the ten men in a B-17 crew eight of them had guns to fire, and they did so until the bitter end. The pilot would only give the order to bail out once all hope was lost. Switching the automatic pilot on, he and whatever crew were still alive would don their parachutes and leap from the plane, but with the automatic pilot still in control, the empty plane would often continue flying for dozens of miles before finally crashing. Some of the abandoned B-17s drifted as far as the Frisian Islands and the borders of Holland—seventy or eighty miles away from where their crews left them.

Sometimes the pilot would lower the landing gear before bailing out, in what was effectively a signal of surrender. At this stage in the war there was still an unofficial code of chivalry among aviators of all nations—if an American bomber lowered its wheels then the German fighters would stop firing and either escort the damaged plane down to an airfield or circle it as the airmen dropped, one by one, in their parachutes. This admirable arrangement was spoiled later in the war when, according to USAAF legend, one bright spark had the idea of using the system to lure the Germans closer before opening fire on them. From that moment on, disabled American planes were given no quarter.[33]

The final B-17 to go down that afternoon was that flown by Thomas Estes—one of the last surviving planes from the low squadron of the low group (544th Squadron, 384th BG). The crew had been under attack for well over an hour now, and had already watched several of their squadron comrades go down. They had seen at least one man falling from a stricken plane without a parachute, his arms and legs thrashing about as he fell.[34] They had fended off so many attacks from German fighters that both the tail gunner and the ball turret gunner had run out of ammunition: They had been reduced to tracking their attackers with empty guns in an attempt to make it look like they were still firing. As the crew told the story later, the assault was utterly ferocious: "They came in pairs, attacked down, slashing along our left side. . . . They totally disregarded our fire and pressed their attacks to within 100 feet of our plane."[35]

By the time Estes's plane was out over the sea he was barely able to fly it anymore. Three of the engines had been hit, the left wingtip was shattered, and the oxygen supply to the top turret had been knocked out. When 20-mm shells blasted a gaping hole in the nose of the plane, the bombardier and the navigator were thrown back into the tunnel by the explosion, ripping their helmets and oxygen masks off them in the process. Both men struggled back to their guns, but it was no use—the Flying Fortress was going down into the sea.

Staff Sergeant George Ursta was manning the ball turret when this happened, waving his guns at the attacking fighters to make believe he was still firing. He picks up the story:

I was still tracking ships when I heard an explosion and saw the no.2 engine smoking. I called up the pilot and asked him if it was a good idea to get out of the ship at this time. He said I should leave the ball turret and I went up to the radio room. I saw that the gang all had chutes on so I put mine on. . . . The engineer came back and told us that we didn't need any chutes as we were going to ditch, so I took my harness off and threw it out of the window. The engineer started throwing out ammunition and I helped him, and we both took the right hand gun and threw it out. . . . After that we were told to go into the radio room and find good positions so we wouldn't upset after we hit the water. I just sat there with my eyes closed and said a little prayer.[36]

As they glided inexorably downward the bombardier, David Davis, put his head out of the escape hatch at the top of the radio room to see how close they were to the water. Unfortunately, as he was doing so six Focke-Wulf 190s came in at the plane head on, and the pilot was forced to dive suddenly to avoid them. Davis was thrown through the top hatch and only managed to prevent himself from falling out of the plane by clinging desperately to the fuselage. All the others in the radio room quickly scrambled up to the hatch and did their best to pull him back in again, but there was nothing they could do. After falling 5,000 feet the plane finally leveled off, and Davis was at last thrown back into the radio room. Brute strength, and not a little luck, had saved him from being sucked out into the empty sky.

The B-17 finally hit the water a few minutes later. Even now the fighters continued to attack them: As the the shaken crew clambered out of the sinking plane 20-mm shells continued to burst on the wings and the water all around the stationary plane. One of these fighters doubled back to make another pass, but when its pilot saw the life rafts self-inflating beside the plane he decided not to strafe them and turned instead for home. That was the last that any of the crew saw of the battle of Hamburg.

After the sharp dive, many of the crew believed that their pilot, Thomas Estes, must have been killed. In fact he was dazed, but still alive—he was the last to crawl out of the plane before it sank. The ball turret gunner saw him crawl out of the side window of the cockpit and hauled him out of the water onto the life raft.

Miraculously, all ten men had survived the ditching. They spent two nights desperately trying to keep their dinghies, which had been peppered with holes by exploding flak fragments, afloat; eventually they were picked up by a Danish fishing vessel and brought back to the English coast. Against the odds they had all lived to fight another day.

German fighters continued harassing the American planes halfway across the North Sea. Some of them, such as the Focke-Wulfs of I/JG1 from Husum airfield, were already on their third sortie of the afternoon. As the Americans flew farther and farther out to sea they were eventually attacked by night fighters as well—a group of twin-engined Me110s from Leeuwarden. The fact that the German fighter controllers would commit these cumbersome night fighters to the fight shows exactly how committed they were to finishing off as many of the B-17s as they possibly could. Night-fighter crews were not properly trained to attack formations of Flying Fortresses, and their machines were not nearly so able to zip away should they be caught in the overlapping fields of American fire.

The radar operator of one of these night fighters explains what he saw as his pilot steered the Me110 toward the American formation:

> It was the first time I had seen Boeings from the air. From five or six kilometers away, they looked like a great heap, like a great swarm of birds. You couldn't see individual planes, only those at the front. We had been told that the Americans were very dangerous, that each plane had eighteen guns. We only had these little, slow, night fighters. When we saw a bomber at night, there was a feeling of joy but, in the day, it was a strange feeling because you knew that, instead of shooting at only one bomber, many bombers would now be shooting at us.[37]

Nobody expected these night fighters to attack a full formation of B-17s, but their controllers explicitly instructed them to keep a look out for American stragglers.[38] The only real advantage they had was that of surprise: If they headed out in front of the formation, they would be hidden by the brightness of the evening sun, which by now was shining right into the American gunners' eyes. Eventually they spotted one of the B-17s in the high squadron of 303rd BG that was lagging slightly behind the others, so they came in to attack.

Their tactics worked, but only to a degree. It was quite common for some of the gunners to rest easy around this time—they would take their oxygen masks off for a smoke, or for a few bites of the Hershey chocolate bars they kept among their flying rations. The Americans were indeed caught off-guard—their official reports refer to this last combat of the day as a "sneak attack"—but their superior fire power was enough to keep the Me110s at bay. Indeed, they even managed to shoot down one of the German fighters—that flown by Leutnant Eberhard Gardiewski and his radar operator Friedrich Abromeit. Both of the Me110's engines were hit, and it was forced to crash into the sea some twenty miles off the Dutch coast. The crew were eventually picked up by a British motor torpedo boat and brought back to England. This was the final encounter of the day: With their fuel running low, all the other German fighters were at last recalled to their airfields in Germany.

The Flying Fortresses did not get back to their various bases until after 7:30 that evening, more than six hours after they had first taken off. Battered and short of fuel, many of them had difficult landings—the final challenge in a mission beset with difficulties. Several planes were so short of fuel that they had to land at alternative airfields. Even those who made

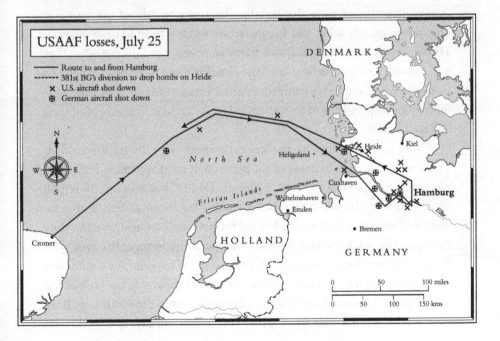

USAAF losses, July 25

——— Route to and from Hamburg
------- 381st BG's diversion to drop bombs on Heide
✗ U.S. aircraft shot down
✪ German aircraft shot down

it back to their own airfields did not have an easy time. One of 303rd BG's planes, the "Yankee Doodle Dandy," almost crashed at Molesworth airbase. The pilot found himself caught in the prop wash of another B-17 while he was coming in to land, and the sudden turbulence tossed the plane around in the air until one of the engines finally ran out of fuel. As they plummeted toward the ground the crew managed to avoid disaster only when the engineer, Stan Backiel, had the presence of mind to raise the landing gear, giving the pilot just enough lift to pull the plane back up again.[39] "Yankee Doodle Dandy" came round again and this time landed perfectly.

A few minutes later the last of the B-17s joined it on the ground. Their hazardous mission, the seventy-sixth in the history of VIII Bomber Command, was now officially over.

At each airfield, the station commander and his staff stood out in the dying evening sunshine and anxiously counted the planes in, just as they had counted them out six hours ago. They were not the only ones waiting to welcome the men home. The ground crews, who were particularly attached to both the airplanes and the crews, were anxious to see that both had returned safely. Most of them had a long night's work ahead, trying to patch up the aircraft so that they could be used again in the morning. Intelligence officers were also standing by, ready to debrief the men and note down exactly what had happened on today's troublesome mission. Those airmen who had not flown today were eager to find out what they had missed. And at one or two of the airfields there were newspapermen from the Associated Press and the United Press, ready to note down the immediate impressions of the exhausted crews as they climbed out of their battered B-17s.

Those who were first on the scene, however, were the station medics. There were casualties in many of the planes that returned today. For example, the radio operator of "Yankee Doodle Dandy" had run out of oxygen while manning the ball turret, but the battle had been so frantic that no one had been able to come to his aid for over half an hour. By the time they got him back to base he had swallowed his tongue, his eyes were frozen shut, and he was virtually blue from lack of oxygen. The copilot was also injured: As he was coming back to help his crewmate the base of the top turret had revolved violently, crushing his foot in the mounting. Both men would be nursed back to health over the coming days and weeks, and the radio operator, Richard Grimm, would even go on to earn himself a DFC later in the war.[40]

The crew of the "Judy B" were in even worse trouble as their plane came to a halt at Kimbolton airfield. Their pilot was dead, their copilot badly disabled by his ordeal in the air, and two of the other crewmen were almost unconscious from a lack of oxygen. At Ridgewell, the home of 381st BG, there were two more cases of severe anoxia, and two men from 384th BG had to be hospitalized at Grafton Underwood because of the wounds they had received during the day.

These were the lucky ones. Of the 123 crews that had started out this afternoon, fifteen had failed to return. As the survivors were driven back across the airfield to the debriefing rooms they could see for themselves how many planes were missing. Later, when they gathered for a meal, the empty seats spoke far more eloquently than any statistics. At Grafton Underwood the atmosphere was particularly somber: Seventy faces had been removed from the mess hall during the course of just one afternoon.

That night most of the men went to bed early, too exhausted to consider anything but sleep. Some of them were issued rations of whisky to calm their nerves, and perhaps cheer them up a little. Others were offered sleeping pills to help them shut off the effects of their adrenaline.[41] They were emotionally and physically worn out.

They would need their sleep. Every one of these bomber groups was scheduled for another maximum effort tomorrow, and most of the men would be up again before sunrise, to repeat the whole performance.

Chapter 13

THE AMERICANS AGAIN

*They know that if a flaming bullet comes through their gasoline tank
it immediately becomes a burning torch and they are gone. They
know that if a wing is torn off there is the same result. They know
that a dozen fatal things may happen any time, and that if they fall
two hundred or twenty thousand feet, existence is at an end.*

—BILLY MITCHELL[1]

While the men of VIII Bomber Command slept, American intelligence
officers worked late into the night analyzing the information they had
gathered during the various debriefing sessions. The statistics did not look
good.[2] To start with, fourteen of the planes bound for Hamburg had abandoned their mission before they had even reached the German coast. That
represented over 11 percent of the total force—an unacceptable figure. In
the case of the wing that was supposed to bomb Kiel the *entire* mission had
been called off because they had been unable to assemble into a safe formation. If the average is taken for all the American forces bombing that
day, more than a quarter of the B-17s had turned back before reaching
Germany. Something had to be done about this problem, and soon—every
plane that aborted its mission merely increased the risk of failure, and
worse, for those who carried on.

The loss rate was even more worrying. Fifteen planes out of 123 had
been shot down during the day: That was 12 percent of the total force
detailed for Hamburg, and nearly 14 percent of those who actually flew over
the city. Losses like these were simply unsustainable. Half a dozen more missions like this and the entire American bomber force would be wiped out.

Another concern was the number of planes returning home damaged.
Sixty-seven planes had been shot up, nine of them so badly that they
could now barely fly. To make things worse, twenty-three planes had been

damaged by their own squadron companions. This was probably inevitable—the Americans flew in such close formations that it was sometimes difficult not to fire at each other—but nevertheless, the loss rate was bad enough without adding to it by friendly fire.

Over the coming weeks the USAAF would do their best to overcome these problems. They would introduce "Splasher" radio beacons to help their bomb groups find each other before leaving the coast of England— that way there would be less chance of their having to abandon their mission because of an inability to assemble properly. They would insist on ever-tighter formation flying to reduce the risks of being attacked by German fighters. But in the end, nothing they suggested could hide the fact that they were being outclassed in the skies over Germany. No matter how formidable a group of Flying Fortresses was, it was no match for the combined forces of heavy flak and swarms of Me109s.

The final piece of the intelligence picture was perhaps the most discouraging. After all the losses they had suffered, it seemed that only 60 percent of the planes had actually bombed anywhere near the target. Seventy-three crews had dropped their bombs on or near the docks in Hamburg, another thirteen had bombed the railway marshaling yards at Heide—the rest had either been shot down, aborted, or dropped their bombs elsewhere. Of all the statistics, this was the one that had to improve most urgently. If the bombers were not hitting their targets there was little point in flying to Germany in the first place.

Needless to say, all of these figures were highly confidential and did not become public knowledge until long after the war. There was, however, one set of numbers that was advertised as widely as possible: These were the statistics for how many German fighters had been shot down. American claims for the day were huge: thirty-eight German fighters destroyed, six probably destroyed, twenty-seven damaged.[3] Some of the bomb groups had suffered terrible casualties, but with scores like these they could at least console themselves that they were giving as good as they got.

The only problem with these figures was that they were a complete fiction. It is quite understandable that the American airmen believed themselves so successful: Any German fighter that dived through a formation could have ten B-17s firing on it at the same time, and if it went down then every one of those B-17 crews would claim the victory. In the end, however, it was still only one fighter shot down, not ten. German records give an idea of just how inflated American claims could be. They suggest that only six fighters were shot down by B-17s *in total* that afternoon, and another handful damaged.[4] That is less than a sixth of the number claimed by the USAAF. American intelligence officials suspected this, but they let the numbers stand because they served as a much-needed morale boost to their men. At this stage in the war they needed every morale boost they could get.

As morning dawned on July 26, the USAAF crews assembled once again for a briefing on the day's target. They did not know it yet, but they were at the beginning of a seven-day roller coaster that would come to be known as "Blitz Week": almost 2,000 sorties on twenty-three towns and cities across northern Europe.[5] Today was the third maximum effort in a row.

The Americans had a policy of resting one squadron in every group for each raid, so only a few of the men flying today would have been on all three of these missions. However, two thirds of today's force had been through yesterday's ordeal. These men had only had about five hours' sleep and were still recovering from the battering they had received over Hamburg, so it goes without saying that they were hoping for an easier target today. They were to be sorely disappointed. Not only were they going back to Germany, but their mission would be exactly the same as the one that had just decimated them: Hamburg again. Their exact targets would also be the same: the Klöckner air-engine factory and the Blohm & Voss shipyards.

It is impossible to imagine the sense of dismay, not to mention déjà vu, that some of these men must have felt as the curtain went back on the target map. However, there were some major differences from the briefing yesterday. For a start, the wing that was to fly on the shipyards today was the one that had been detailed for Klöckner yesterday, and vice versa. The wings themselves would be organized differently, too: Today it would be the 381st BG leading the Blohm & Voss wing (with the 351st and 91st BGs in the high and low positions); the 303rd BG would lead the Klöckner wing (with the 379th and 384th BGs in the high and low positions). It was important to spread the responsibility around as much as possible, both to give the newer groups the opportunity to prove themselves and to give the established groups a rest. They would be flying a similar route to yesterday's, with the difference that they would turn southward after hitting the target, rather than northward, and head for the North Sea by flying between Bremen and Oldenburg.

Today's Hamburg raid was again just one part of a bigger plan involving several attacks on German territory. Three other combat wings would be attacking a rubber factory in Hanover and, just as yesterday, one of these was supposed to fly a feint off the German coast in order to draw the fighters from their airfields prematurely. There would again be a series of diversions over northern France and the Low Countries by a force of light bombers under fighter escort. Each of the various combat wings and diversionary forces would aim to cross into Europe at different points, simultaneously, in the hope of splitting the German defenses.

The American planners had done all they could to protect their forces—now it was up to the individual crews. It was a tired and apprehensive group of men who left their various briefings and made their way out to their planes. Unlike the day before, they now knew *exactly* what was waiting for them in the skies over Germany. Some of them were plainly demoralized, which may well have influenced events later on that morning.

The two Hamburg wings took off at around 9:00 A.M. into the hazy sunshine of another warm summer's day. They were in trouble almost immediately. While one of the wings managed to assemble without too many difficulties, the other was a shambles from the start. The 303rd BG, which was supposed to be leading the Klöckner wing, failed to find either of its two accompanying groups despite coming across several unidentified formations of B-17s. Eventually the 303rd BG leader, Major William Calhoun, gave up looking for them and fell in behind the Blohm & Voss wing.[6]

The 379th BG, meanwhile, spent half an hour wheeling and dispersing with various other groups of planes over the English coast but eventually gave up looking for their leaders and returned to base. The other missing group, the 384th BG, ended up following one of the Hanover wings most of the way across the North Sea, before turning back. It would have been quite possible for this group to bomb Hanover instead of Hamburg today, but the group leader was worried that, unlike his group, the formation he was following might be equipped with long-range fuel tanks. Given the possibility of the entire bomb group running out of fuel over the sea on the way home, he took the sensible decision to abandon the mission and turn back. So it was that only four bomber groups, rather than six, approached Hamburg this morning. Thirty-nine planes had turned back simply because they had been unable to form up properly.

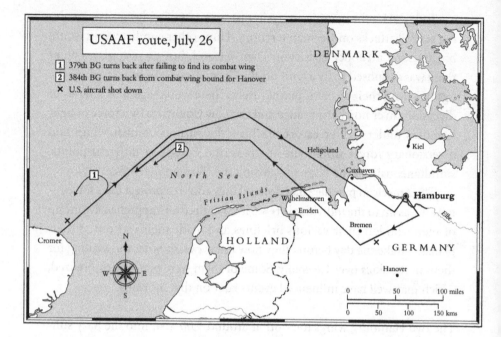

USAAF route, July 26

1 379th BG turns back after failing to find its combat wing
2 384th BG turns back from combat wing bound for Hanover
✕ U.S. aircraft shot down

DENMARK

Heligoland   • Kiel

Cuxhaven

North Sea

Frisian Islands   Wilhelmshaven •   ● Hamburg

• Emden

Bremen

Cromer   HOLLAND   ✕   GERMANY

Hanover
•

0   50   100 miles
0   50   100   150 kms

However, these were not the last of the planes to drop out today. The number of abortive flights, which had so concerned VIII Bomber Command HQ the night before, was escalating sharply. In the 303rd BG, five planes aborted their mission today—a quarter of the total number dispatched. In the 351st BG, nine planes turned back, and in the 91st BG the number was eleven—just over half of them. In fact, of the 121 Flying Fortresses that took off for Hamburg this morning, only fifty-four of them ever made it as far as the target. Just one of the sixty-seven planes that turned back did so because of any damage caused by the German defenses.[7]

One could be forgiven for asking what on earth can have caused such a phenomenal dropout rate. It was quite normal for there to be a few engine problems in any mission, but the number of technical malfunctions for the Hamburg wings today was twice what it was on any of the other wings. Some of the excuses for turning back were woolly at best: engines that were running a little rough, an erratic turbo, loose fittings on a pilot's oxygen hose, and so on. A few of the reasons given appeared to be outright inventions. For example, one 351st BG crew claimed that they had returned because of a malfunction of one of the supercharger regulators, but when the station mechanics investigated they were unable to find anything wrong. The number of "pilot illnesses" that occurred this morning frankly defies belief. The only real explanation for all this is that many of those who had experienced yesterday's ordeal could not face the thought of going through it all over again. They had simply lost their nerve.[8] This should not surprise us—it is human nature to avoid danger when given the opportunity. What should surprise us is that the *remaining* crews elected to carry on in the face of such severe danger despite their depleted numbers.

The four bomber groups that approached Hamburg around midday on July 26 were so badly depleted that they were in serious danger. Had the defenses been anything like as ferocious as the day before they might have suffered even worse casualties. But these groups were lucky today—most of the German fighters had been deployed farther south to tackle the B-17s that were flying on Hanover. While those wings were attacked mercilessly, the Hamburg force was allowed to fly across Germany relatively unmolested. That is not to say that there were no fighters around—on the contrary, there were thirty or forty German fighters waiting for the Hamburg force as soon as it crossed the coast—but unlike yesterday they seemed happy to sit back and wait for the flak to do its work, and pick off any stragglers later. Fortunately for the Americans, however, the flak did not seem to do nearly as much damage as it had done the day before, and almost the entire force was able to get to the target and out again without receiving any serious damage.[9]

Once the four bomber groups had arrived at the city, the next challenge was to find their targets. This was easier said than done, because, once again, the docklands were immersed in clouds of smoke. Unlike yesterday, however, most of this smoke was not caused by the fires in the city; instead it was a deliberate screen produced by German smoke pots on the ground. This time the Hamburg smoke-screen units had not been caught unawares; because much of the panic in the city had died down during the last twenty-four hours, they had had time to prepare for the coming bombers. Blohm & Voss was already completely obscured, as were several other areas of the city. In the event, the Blohm & Voss wing chose to attack Howaldtswerke again, just as they had yesterday, because this target was clearly visible on the ground beneath them. They scored several direct hits on the shipyard, as well as on the M.A.N. diesel-engine works.[10]

The 303rd BG wisely chose not to attempt an attack on the Klöckner

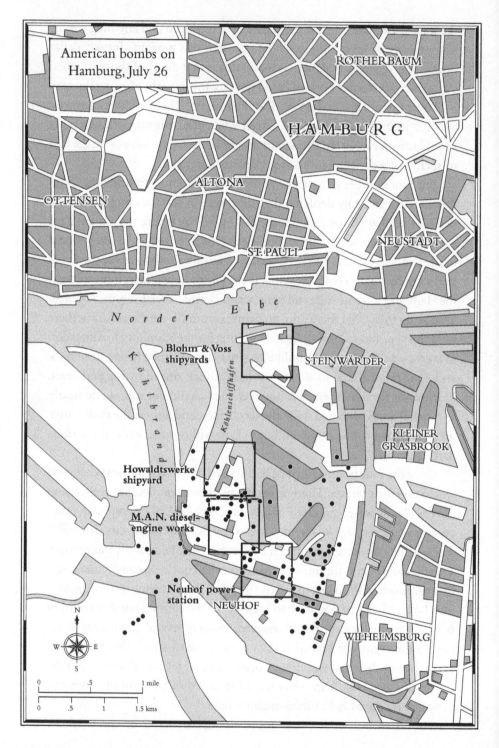

American bombs on
Hamburg, July 26

factory by itself, but instead flew over the Neuhof power station, which was just south of the targets the other bomber groups were striking. One of its bombs scored a direct hit, putting the plant out of action for more than two weeks—probably the single most important effect of the whole raid. This group then fell back in with the other bomber formations and turned southward for the long journey back home.

Unlike the RAF raid two nights previous, which had lasted almost an hour, this bombing run took just a single minute to execute. There were so few planes, and they were flying in such close formation, that as soon as the lead bomber dropped his bombs the whole of the rest of the formation were able to follow suit. More than 126 tons of incendiaries and high explosive fell in that one minute between 11:59 and midday, and then it was all over. This was exactly the way precision bombing was supposed to go: The all-important dock areas received dozens of direct hits simultaneously, but apart from those who were in the area at the time, most of the civilians in Hamburg barely knew that the bombing had happened at all.

The journey home was potentially even more dangerous than the previous day's withdrawal flight. Their route would keep them over German territory for almost twice as long, and by flying between Bremen and Oldenburg they would attract the attention of both flak and fighters all the way out. This was a calculated risk on the part of the American planners: The Hanover forces would also be flying through this area, and the USAAF was gambling on the fact that the Luftwaffe would not be able to attack both forces in great numbers. In the event, it was the Hanover wings that continued to suffer the brunt of the German storm. The Hamburg wings were barely bothered at all—since their formation had held up to the flak remarkably well, they were merely escorted out of German territory by a fighter force that was unwilling to do much beyond hover around the edges waiting for stragglers.

In the end, only one B-17 was unable to keep up with the others—an unfortunate plane called "Nitemare," piloted by First Lieutenant James W. Rendall Jr., which had been hit by flak both on the way into the target and on the way back out again.[11] With two of its engines on fire, it was only a matter of time before Nitemare was forced to drop away from the formation. German fighters lost no time in dealing with it, attacking the plane three and four abreast. The radio operator was killed by their machine-gun fire, and the B-17 was so badly damaged that there was no option for the rest of the crew but to bail out. The ball turret gunner did so, but his parachute failed to open and he died when he hit the ground after a fall of 26,000 feet. The navigator and bombardier reached the ground safely, but were shot while trying to escape shortly afterward. They both died from their wounds in hospital. The rest of the crew survived to become prisoners of war. Nitemare itself crashed near Nindorf, ten miles southeast of Rotenburg.

While this stricken plane was making its long descent to the ground, something unusual happened in the skies above. As the fifty or so remaining bombers were making their way back to the coast they were joined by nine strange B-17s, which tried to slot themselves into the American formation. They had none of the usual markings of an American plane, such as the call letters and identification letters, and their waist-gun windows were closed. When one of these tried to join 351st BG the other crews became suspicious and fired a few warning rounds at it—it immediately turned round and headed back into Germany. Presumably these were captured planes that the Luftwaffe hoped to slot into the American formation either to gather intelligence or to attack it—German records for that day are somewhat patchy and do not mention what they were hoping to attack. Whatever the case, after the Americans had crossed the coast, all of these strange B-17s turned away and returned to Germany accompanied by two twin-engined fighters.[12]

There was only one other loss for the Hamburg force. On the way home a second plane from 91st BG ran out of fuel and had to land in the sea. Its pilot, Lieutenant Jack Hargis, took the plane down gently, and the whole crew managed to get into their dinghies without much trouble. They were eventually brought home by an RAF rescue launch (which also had to tow home the two Walrus seaplanes that had originally come to rescue them, because rough seas prevented them from taking off again).

The Hamburg wings had been incredibly lucky. Their loss of just two planes and one crew made this one of the cheapest bombing raids the Eighth Air Force had ever flown over Germany. The wings that had flown to Hanover that day were not so lucky. Like the Hamburg force yesterday, they had attracted most of the German fighters, and sixteen B-17s had been shot down. A further six had been lost to a wing that never made it to Hanover, but bombed Wilhelmshaven, Wesermünde, and a convoy off the Frisian islands. Once these huge losses were added it took the shine off the Hamburg "milk run": The loss rate was still 12 percent of the effective planes today, well over twice the rate that was considered sustainable.

Losses like this would continue over the coming days. On Wednesday July 28, twenty-two American planes would be shot down over Kassel and Oschersleben. Another ten would be lost on Thursday, and twelve more on Friday, all over Germany. By the end of the week they would have lost eighty-eight Flying Fortresses, with another dozen so badly damaged that they had to be scrapped. Nearly 900 American airmen would be dead, wounded, or missing. VIII Bomber Command simply could not continue like this. On the following weekend they finally retired to lick their wounds, and for the next two weeks the American B-17s ceased flying altogether. Despite some good bombing results, including those at Hamburg, their attempts to make their mark in the skies over Germany had only left them depleted and demoralized. This was one battle that the Luftwaffe seemed to have won.

Chapter 14

THE EYE OF THE STORM

*First the left and then the right! . . . But he's held to his feet, held to
the ropes, looked to his corner in helplessness!*

—CLEM MCCARTHY[1]

The attacks by the USAAF on July 25 and 26 shocked Hamburg. The city
had not seen a daylight raid since the beginning of the war, and it had
certainly never seen American planes fly over the city: The fact that formations of Flying Fortresses were now daring to approach Hamburg during
broad daylight seemed to herald a new confidence in Germany's enemies.

Despite their losses in the air, the Americans had been able to do considerable damage to the Elbe port. The Blohm & Voss works had suffered
quite badly, with severe hits on the construction shops, the ship fitters'
shop, the engine erecting shop, the boiler house and power station, the
foundry and the tool stores. Two of the dry docks had also been very heavily damaged. In the Howaldtswerke factory several furnaces were now
completely out of action, as were the shipbuilding and machinery sheds,
and the diesel-engine works. The USAAF had also scored direct hits on the
Neuhof power station, the oil stores beside Rosshafen, and many of the
nearby railway sidings.[2]

While none of this would have directly affected most people in Hamburg, the effect on their morale is incalculable. They were still seriously
shaken up by the Saturday night bombing, and the fact that they would now
have to suffer daylight attacks as well was extremely alarming. Rudolf
Schurig was out in the center of Hamburg when the alarm went off for the
first American raid, and remembers how frightened everyone suddenly was.

The sirens sounded once more—the *Fliegeralarm*. Terror and dismay
played across people's faces all over again. Women grabbed their children,

men grabbed their wives, and they hurried to the nearest air raid shelter where whole crowds were gathering. I have never seen the people of Hamburg running in such panic because of an air raid siren![3]

Hiltgunt Zassenhaus remembered sheltering during the second American attack the next day. She described an atmosphere in the shelter made even more nervous than usual because of the destruction they had already witnessed:

> Shortly after ten we heard a distant hum over the clouds; the sound came nearer, became a roar. The sirens had failed, but the doom-laden drone in the heavens was warning enough. We hurried down to the cellar of the Institute. Professors, students, women and children, men in blue work overalls, covered in dust from laboring in the debris. The room had no windows. The power had failed. We stood pressed up close to one another in the dark and listened to the noise outside. It sounded like they were attacking the harbour. Then there was a crash nearby. We huddled together in breathless silence. Even the children said nothing.[4]

It was the incessant nature of the attacks that made them so difficult to bear. By attacking so soon after the British raid, the Americans had seriously hampered the rescue effort in the following days—and since the entire city was engaged in putting out the old fires there were few firemen left to deal with the new ones caused by the B-17s. To make things worse, the RAF had sent six Mosquito bombers to Hamburg on Sunday night, and again on Monday, with the sole purpose of causing as much nuisance as possible. After what had happened on Saturday night, nobody was taking any risks, and the entire city had huddled inside their air raid shelters for several hours on both nights. Among their very obvious physical woes, the whole population was now suffering from severe sleep deprivation.

It was not until Tuesday that the people of Hamburg got any peace. In the lull that day, the city authorities were finally able to get a clear picture of the damage that had been done. The picture was not a pretty one. Worst hit were the areas around Altona and Eimsbüttel in the west of the city, where whole districts had been burned to the ground. Barmbek had also suffered some fairly heavy damage, and the port area on the south shore of the Elbe had been hit by all three raids in succession. With the damage to power lines, and the destruction of the Neuhof power station, electricity was now severely limited. The gas and water mains had been breached in countless places, which was hampering the fire brigade's efforts to extinguish the fires. The transport systems in the worst-hit areas were now nonexistent, although the main lines in and out of the city were still functioning. There was major disruption to the telephone network within Hamburg, and after the destruction of the long-distance exchange in Rotherbaum all lines to the rest of Germany were cut.[5]

Almost all of the fires had now been brought under control, but doing so had required a Herculean effort. According to the Hamburg's chief of police, by the evening of Tuesday July 27, there were still fifty large fires burning across the west of Hamburg, and a further 1,130 smaller ones that the fire brigade had so far been unable to put out. Despite heavy reinforcement from other fire units across northern Germany, the sheer number of fires had been overwhelming. At the height of the crisis there had been eighty-seven kilometers of street frontage ablaze in the west of the city alone. There were several *single* fires that covered an area of four square kilometers or more: Such conflagrations were simply too big to deal with. The best the firemen could do was to put out the smaller outbreaks around the edges and stop the blaze from spreading. By nightfall on July 27, almost every fireman in Hamburg was still working in the west of the city. Most of them had had no rest and very little food for three days. But the situation, broadly speaking, was stable at last.[6]

With the fires under control, the heavy pall of smoke that had smothered the city all day on Sunday began to disperse and the damage slowly became clearly visible to everyone. Hiltgunt Zassenhaus described the scenes of utter devastation she encountered as she walked into the university on Monday morning to attend her physics exam:

> Along the way furniture was piled up outside the burning houses. Cushions and mattresses were singed, mahogany scratched and scorched. Their owners sat beside them, as if they were waiting for removal vans. But no vehicle could have come along the torn-up streets; and where the streets were clear cars and lorries drove through at top speed. Their vibrations sent a trembling through the broken walls; facades crumbled together and blocked off one street after another.[7]

The threat of falling facades was not the only danger she encountered as she tried to pick her way through the city.

> Rubble blocked the streets, so we had to go round it; we climbed over broken walls and charred wood, one after another, like a line of ants. . . . "Watch out!" shouted a voice from the side of a mountain of rubble. "There are unexploded bombs all over here!" But in blind indifference the crowd continued. What was the point of closing off the way? There were unexploded bombs everywhere. Each step back was just as danger- ous as each step forward.[8]

Because of the widespread destruction to electricity cables and gas and water mains, even those living outside the worst-affected areas now found their lives beset with difficulties, as Dr. Franz Termer described in a letter to a friend at the time:

> Organisation has quickly fallen apart. A shortage of bread is now begin- ning to take hold. One cannot cook, there is no gas as yet; one can only wash sparingly as there is no water in our homes. We cook at a neighbor's house who has an electric oven. We have the advantage that on one of the plots in our road there is a pump in the garden, to which the entire neigh- borhood traipses. My wife pushes the pram with water containers, I carry buckets.[9]

In the worse-affected areas this daily journey to the water hydrant was not only depressing, it was downright dangerous. Just south of the Hagenbeck Zoo there was a coal depot on Steenwisch that was still ablaze, and also a floor polish factory that had suffered a direct hit. There was floor polish flowing down the road: Residents had to step barefoot through the hot liquid, risking burns from the coal fires, just in order to get water from the hydrant on the other side of the road.[10]

There were other blows to morale. Not only had thousands of people's homes been destroyed, but so had the places where they worked, did their shopping, or spent their leisure time. In all the cutbacks ordered by Joseph Goebbels after his proclamation of "Total War," nothing had been done to restrict Germany's cinemas and theaters, because the Nazis recognized how important these places were for keeping up people's spirits.[11] Now many of

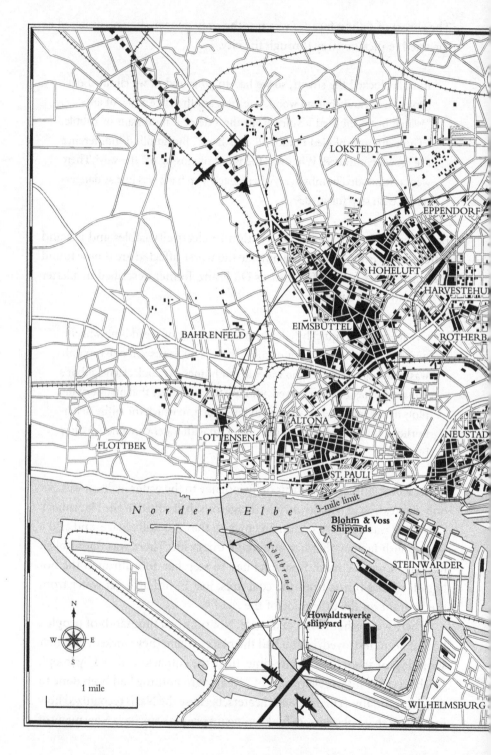

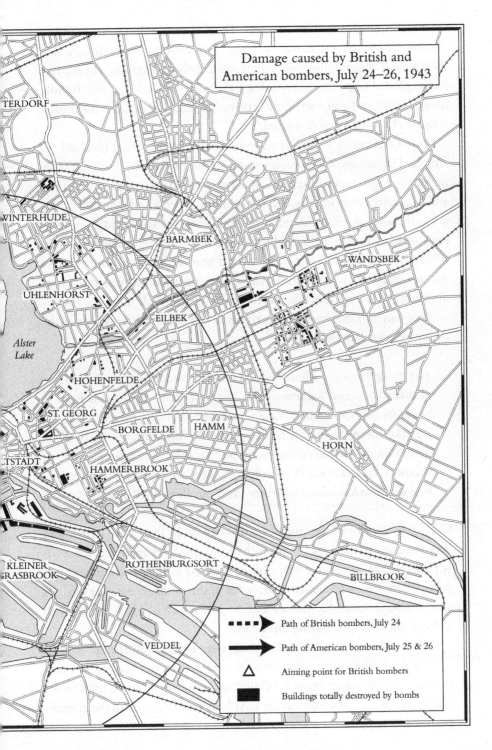

Damage caused by British and
American bombers, July 24–26, 1943

TERDORF

WINTERHUDE

BARMBEK

WANDSBEK

UHLENHORST

EILBEK

Alster
Lake

HOHENFELDE

ST. GEORG

BORGFELDE   HAMM

HORN

TSTADT

HAMMERBROOK

KLEINER
RASBROOK

ROTHENBURGSORT

BILLBROOK

VEDDEL

▪ ▪ ▪ ▶ Path of British bombers, July 24

⸻▶ Path of American bombers, July 25 & 26

△ Aiming point for British bombers

■ Buildings totally destroyed by bombs

the best-loved theaters lay in ruins. The Opera House in St. Pauli was completely burned out, as were parts of the Staatstheater, and the front of the Thalia-Theater in the town center was heavily damaged by a bomb that had exploded opposite. Many cafés and dance halls, such as the Trichter dance hall in St. Pauli, were now little more than rubble. Even the theater museum in Altona was destroyed.[12]

One of the most poignant episodes in this tragic period involved the famous Hagenbeck Zoo, which was hit in the British attack on Saturday night. Four zookeepers died during the struggle to put out the many fires, and five others were killed when the zebra house received a direct hit. But it was the animals that suffered most. One hundred and twenty large animals were lost during the night, along with countless smaller animals. When an 8,000-pound blast bomb landed near the big cat house several of the cats escaped: Two jaguars and a Siberian tiger had to be shot the next morning. All the big cats that stayed inside burned to death in the fire.

One can almost sense the weariness in the zoo's official report as the writer lists the damage done:

> Everything that was not burned down was destroyed by explosive bombs: the main buildings, both restaurants, the cattle sheds, the deer and goat house, the aviary, the walkways and superintendent's house, the zebra stalls, the ticket office, the country house opposite the main entrance, the business yards, the baboon enclosure, the monkey bath, the Rhesus monkey enclosure, the aquarium. The remaining buildings were partially destroyed by fire and explosion, and have been provisionally repaired by hand.[13]

Curiously, none of the animals were driven wild by their experiences, and very few even tried to escape from their broken cages and enclosures—it is probable that they were every bit as shocked as their human counterparts. There were a few exceptions: Some of the monkeys escaped into the surrounding area, and a stallion used his newfound freedom to play with a circus mare, despite having lost an eye.

In the following days, these animals were either rounded up or shot. The most valuable beasts were put onto a train, to be transported to safety in Bavaria. They never made it. While their train was on the sidings in the east of the city it was caught in the next heavy air raid, and all the animals perished.[14]

The city's spiritual institutions did not fare very well either. In destroying the city's churches, the RAF had succeeded where Hitler had failed. Christuskirche on Holstenplatz was a wreck, as was St. George's church to the east of the Alster.[15] The huge gothic Nikolaikirche was so badly damaged that Hamburgers to this day swear that it was the main aiming point of the British attack. The claim is without basis—the RAF Pathfinders were told simply to mark the area between the Alster and the river Elbe, and could not possibly have made out the spire of the church from 20,000 feet in the dark. But the church was, and is, such a potent symbol for the city that it was easy to imagine that the RAF would use it as their main target. In July 1943 many such rumors were born; indeed, the vicar of Michaeliskirche in the west of the city claimed after the bombings that *his* church was "undoubtedly the main target of the enemy attack."[16] The area around the church was so badly damaged that he could not help but take the raid personally, although the "Michel" itself (as the church is affectionately known) was the only major church in Hamburg to survive the war intact.

In the shocked and anxious city, rumors began to fly. People were claiming that Churchill had given Hitler an ultimatum: Capitulate, or Hamburg will be bombed into oblivion.[17] Others were saying that Turkey had declared war upon the Axis powers, or that Romania and Hungary were looking to make peace with the Allies.[18] It was not surprising the people believed these things—in the absence of any proper newspapers it was difficult to know what was fact and what was merely speculation.[19] The *real* news that Mussolini had resigned was scarcely more extraordinary than the false rumors. With such large parts of their city in tatters it was easy to believe that the whole Reich was falling apart.

Some of the most potent rumors concerned the clouds of foil-paper strips that the RAF had code-named Window. Whole bundles of these had landed all over the city, and nobody had the slightest idea what they could be. Children gathered them up enthusiastically, just as they collected shrapnel splinters, but the adults were more wary. Martha Bührich remembers seeing these strips everywhere while she was waiting for a tram on Monday afternoon:

The ground was covered with silver strips which the airplanes had dropped. A woman from the bank explained that a professor had said we should not touch them, as they had been covered with typhoid bacillus.

I told her that I had picked up countless strips on Sunday morning, and that she should not spread such rubbish.[20]

Fredy Borck, who was a schoolchild at the time, also remembers being told not to play with the piles of foil strips because they were poisonous.[21] In fact, so potent were these rumors that the *Hamburger Zeitung* used up precious space on its single sheet for an article entitled "The paper strips are harmless."[22] The following day it printed a further article entreating the people not to believe ridiculous rumors such as those claiming that the RAF had been dropping threatening leaflets, or that the water supply had been poisoned.[23] The fact that the city's only functioning newspaper was driven to print such articles is a measure of just how panic-stricken the people of Hamburg had become.

To prevent things getting further out of hand, the city's gauleiter, Karl Kaufmann, declared a "State of Major Catastrophe" early on Sunday morning, and a previously prepared disaster plan immediately came into effect. Police battalions were called in from surrounding areas in order to prevent any civil unrest, and signs were put up across Hamburg stating that any looting would be punishable by death. Huge cordons were placed around the worst-affected areas, both to stop people getting too close to the fires that were still alight and to prevent looters from helping themselves to the piles of personal belongings that now lined the streets. While the appearance of the SS on the streets caused widespread resentment among Hamburg's distraught civilians, there is no doubt that it also did much to ensure the smooth running of the rest of the disaster plan.[24]

Next came the clearance of the hospitals to make way for all the casualties. At first, everyone with a nonserious condition was told to go home—although when the night raids began again even the serious cases were evacuated in ambulance trains. In the meantime, most people were treated at one of the seventy-two air raid shelter clinics that dotted the city. Dr. Wilhelm Küper worked at one of these first-aid posts, and was surprised that, in general, the people managed to look after themselves remarkably well:

The vast majority of the dressings were so professionally applied—evidently the fruit of many training courses—that one could leave them as they were, if their usage was not for some of the more serious wounds.[25]

With the bursting of the water mains, and the requisition of all emergency water supplies by the fire brigade, the supply of drinking water became an immediate problem. People who had been hidden in shelters for long periods urgently needed water to drink, and yet they were frightened of taking water from the reservoirs in case they were arrested for it.[26] To try to prevent dehydration, emergency pumps and hydrants were made available around Hamburg, the city's many private wells were brought into use, and specially commissioned water trucks brought clean water to various locations across town.[27]

Emergency rations of food and cigarettes had been issued and were being handed out at various locations across the city. For those who had lost houses and apartments in the raids there was financial help available, and a special ration of clothes and shoes to tide them over until more permanent replacements could be arranged.[28] In the meantime, arrangements were being made to evacuate those who had lost everything. By the evening of Tuesday, July 27, 47,000 homeless people had already been sent out to Schleswig-Holstein by train.[29]

Despite the seemingly gloomy picture that the city presented, Hamburg's disaster plan was working well. In some of the lightly affected areas a measure of normality had already been restored, and work on returning the gas and water mains to service was well under way. Had they been allowed to continue, the city authorities would probably have been able to put Hamburg back in order within a matter of weeks.

They would not be allowed that luxury. Even as they were working, RAF Bomber Command was preparing to make another, even bigger strike on the city.

Chapter 15

CONCENTRATED BOMBING

The guiding principle of bombing actions should be this: the objective must be destroyed completely in one attack, making further attack on the same target unnecessary.

—GIULIO DOUHET[1]

The British had sent maximum-effort attacks to Hamburg on Saturday night, and to Essen on Sunday night. To mount a third that Monday would have been too much to ask of the exhausted crews, so the follow-up raid on Hamburg was postponed for twenty-four hours. With Monday evening to themselves, the airmen were free to do whatever they pleased, but there was little enthusiasm for carousing. Most of them took the opportunity to rest and went to bed early to catch up on sleep.

The people of Hamburg were not so lucky. After three raids in as many days they were understandably jumpy, and most people had abandoned their apartments for an uncomfortable night in one of the city's many shelters. For those who had dared to stay at home the slightest warning would be enough to have them out of their beds, running for cover. The British knew from experience that sleep deprivation could be almost as damaging to the economy as bombardment, so tonight the RAF sent six Mosquito aircraft over the city on a nuisance raid. The damage their few bombs caused was minuscule compared to what had gone before, but it was enough to keep the whole city awake.[2] It had the added effect of distracting the rescue workers and firefighters from their efforts. Much of Altona was still on fire from the raid two nights ago, and the approaching Mosquito pilots could see the city glowing from twenty miles away.[3]

The next day, Tuesday, July 27, it was the Americans' turn to have a rest. Officially, they cited uncertainty over the weather as the reason for taking the day off, but in any case the battered and harassed crews were in desperate need of a little respite. While the Americans recuperated, Butch Harris was eager to resume his attack on Hamburg. Whatever the Americans might have said about the weather, as far as he was concerned the forecast for the night looked promising. A Mosquito reconnaissance plane was sent out over Hamburg later that morning to confirm conditions: Its pilot reported back that, apart from a light smoke haze from the fires that were still burning, the weather was perfectly clear. So, without further hesitation, Harris ordered his second maximum effort on Hamburg to go ahead.

The plan for tonight was very similar to the one used on the night of July 24.[4] Once again the bombers would be using Window and flying in a tight stream through the German defenses. Zero Hour was again 1:00 A.M., and the aiming point was exactly the same as last time. The only real differences from the previous plan of attack were a slight change to the route and an alteration to the type of bombs they would be using.

Tonight, instead of flying down onto Hamburg from the northwest, the bomber stream would take a route right across the Schleswig peninsula, before coming back to approach Hamburg from the northeast. The idea was to make it look as if they were attacking Kiel or Lübeck—indeed, some historians have stated, wrongly, that the bomber stream passed directly over Lübeck as part of the ruse.[5] Whatever the case, it was not a very effective feint: Everyone in Hamburg was expecting another attack, and the defenses were still on high alert. However, it did mean that the run-in to the aiming point would be coming from a different direction from last time, so any creepback in the bombing would land on an entirely new part of the city. In the next few weeks the people of Hamburg would come to believe that the RAF had bombed the city with a methodical precision— ending their carpet of bombing with a particular street one night, and starting again with the next street along on the following night. Such accuracy was of course totally impossible, but there was an element of truth to the rumor. By coming at the city from different directions, the bombers could ensure that every suburb was hit over the series of raids. Over the course of their four raids on the city the RAF attacked in turn from the northwest, the northeast, the north, and the south. Effectively they were destroying the city one segment at a time.

The other main change to the plan was just as significant. Tonight the bombers would be carrying far more incendiaries than they had on the previous attack—to be precise, 240 tons more.[6] Some historians have

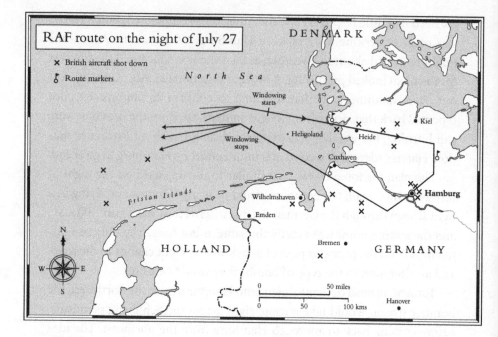

RAF route on the night of July 27

× British aircraft shot down

ʃ Route markers

DENMARK

North Sea

Windowing
starts

Windowing
stops

Heligoland

Kiel

Heide

Cuxhaven

Hamburg

Frisian Islands

Wilhelmshaven

Emden

HOLLAND

Bremen

GERMANY

N
W ← → E
S

0   50 miles

0   50   100 kms

Hanover

claimed that this change was made purely for operational reasons: The planes had farther to fly, so the Halifaxes and Stirlings had reduced the weight of their loads by replacing their high-explosive bombs with lighter incendiaries.[7] But this is not the whole story. Bomber Command planners were constantly revising the proportions of their bomb loads, and it was becoming increasingly obvious that incendiaries did far more damage than explosives. Hamburg was not considered a particularly flammable city— most of the old, wooden buildings of the city center had already been burned down in the great fire of 1842 and replaced by more modern brick and stone buildings—but when the planners of the operation saw how well the city had burned on the previous attack it seemed worthwhile to increase the proportion of incendiaries tonight. The Lancasters had already been ordered to carry "maximum economic incendiary loads" when the Hamburg raids were first conceived.[8] Tonight this order was extended to the Stirlings and Halifaxes as well.

As evening approached, morale was riding high at all levels of the RAF. Harris and his staff believed that they were at the start of a new era in the bombing war: Now that the German defenses had been blinded by Window,

Bomber Command effectively had complete command of the air, and Harris was convinced, more than ever before, that it would be only a matter of time before Germany was forced to surrender. The airmen were similarly enamored of their new radar-jamming device. The casualty rate had plummeted since they had started using it, and the drafty job of shoving bundles of silver strips through the flare chute had become by now a labor of love. A new spirit of optimism was spreading through airfields up and down the country. During their briefing for tonight's operation the crews were read out a message from Harris congratulating them on the success of their previous attacks on Hamburg and Essen. The message was greeted with great enthusiasm by the men, who were at last beginning to feel that they were making a difference. Perhaps their commander-in-chief had been right all along—perhaps they *would* be able to win the war by bombing alone.

Confidence was so high that officers of increasingly high ranks decided to join the crews on their trip tonight. Station commanders were not normally allowed to go out on more than a single operation each month, but this evening no fewer than five of them decided that it was time to see the effects of Window for themselves.[9] Two air commodores also decided to fly—Air Commodore W. A. Brooke of 4 Group and Air Commodore A. M. Wray of 1 Group. But the highest-ranking officer in the bomber crews tonight would be an American. Brigadier General Fred Anderson, the man in charge of the Eighth Air Force's bombers, was so eager to learn about how his allies operated that he decided to join a Pathfinder crew on their trip to Hamburg this evening. General Anderson had already been on the previous raid to Essen and had been extremely impressed. Tonight, flying as second pilot to Flight Lieutenant Garvey in a Lancaster from 83rd Squadron, he would witness destruction on a scale few people had ever believed possible.[10]

It had been a glorious summer's day, and when the bombers took off at around 10:00 the dying sun had painted the sky blood-red. All along the eastern edge of England the air was soon filled with the drone of 787 airplanes heading off toward the darkness of the North Sea. To most of those who lived along the coast it was a comforting sound. At this stage of the war bomber crews were still being treated as celebrities by the newspapers and newsreels, and as heroes by the general population: Apart from the army in North Africa and Sicily, they were the only force capable of taking the war to Germany. People who lived near airfields would often come out to watch the fleets of bombers take off into the evening, particularly on a fine, warm night like tonight. Children always waved cheerily, blissfully unaware of the realities of warfare.

Apart from a few minor mishaps, the whole of the bomber force managed to take off safely. A small proportion would turn back because of mechanical problems (only forty-two aircraft), but the vast majority congregated into three streams and headed out over the North Sea toward their rendezvous point, eighty miles off the German coast.[11] As on the previous raid, they began Windowing a few minutes later. And as on the previous raid the Pathfinder Force dropped yellow markers as they crossed the coast in order to concentrate the stream of planes more tightly. (A second set of route markers would be dropped later as well, to further concentrate the bomber stream.)

With their radar systems once again blinded by Window, the defending Luftwaffe fighters had only these route markers to guide them to the bomber stream. One of the Pathfinders in the vanguard of the stream had been shot down earlier, before Window had had a chance to take effect—but now that their radar screens had fuzzed over there was little that the freelancing German pilots could do but head for the lights in the hope that they might stumble across some British bombers in the dark. They were rewarded with just a single victory over a Lancaster from 467th Squadron. In return, one of their own Ju88s was shot down over Heide. In total, only five British bombers were shot down on their way to the target, at a cost of two German night fighters. So far, Window had proved every bit as effective as it had been on the first raid, three nights before.

However, the German defenses had not been idle over the past three days. Given how completely unprepared they were for the advent of Window, it is remarkable how quickly they responded to the crisis, and while their initial response was not enormously effective, it did mark the beginning of a long fight back against the RAF.

The first thing the German radar controllers did was to rely much more upon their long-range *Freya* radar, which was the only system not affected by the clouds of foil strips. While this was not nearly so accurate as the shorter-range *Würzburg* radar, and could not ascertain the altitude of the oncoming bombers, it could at least direct night fighters to the correct vicinity. Second, after two previous Window raids, the most-skilled *Würzburg* radar operators were beginning to notice some differences between the

images given off by Window and those given by real airplanes. At high altitudes, for example, when the bundles of Window had not yet dispersed
properly, the blips on their screens that moved more slowly were likely to be
small puffs of undispersed Window, while those that moved more quickly
were likely to be bombers. Airplanes on the fringes of the bomber stream
could also sometimes be distinguished from the fuzzy cloud of Window.

Changes were also taking place in German fighter tactics. While many
fighters were still held back in their boxes in the vain hope that some way
could be found to direct them toward the bombers in the old way, many
others were allowed to go freelancing. This was effectively a return to the
basics of night fighting, as it was before the advent of radar: Pilots would
have to rely on their own eyes and their intuition to find their prey. To help
them, a running commentary was broadcast by the German night-fighter
headquarters giving the pilots any information at all about the movements
and possible intentions of the bomber stream.

The single most important change that took place tonight, however, was
the advent of a brand new system of fighting: the *Wilde Sau* ("Wild Boar")
system created by Major Hajo Herrmann (*Wilde Sau,* is also a German
idiom meaning "crazy" or "reckless").[12] Major Herrmann was convinced
that British bombers were much more vulnerable to fighters than they were
to flak, so he devised a system whereby German day fighters could be used
to massively reinforce the much-beleaguered night fighters. His idea was to
fly his single-engined day fighters at high altitudes above the target, so that
they could see the outlines of the bombers silhouetted below them by the
fires, the searchlights, the marker flares, and any other illumination on
the ground. The German flak batteries would then be ordered not to fire
above a certain height, so that their fighters could swoop down on the
bombers safely from above.

After a great deal of opposition, Major Herrmann had finally been
given the go-ahead to try out his ideas on the night of July 3, 1943, over
Cologne.[13] After a limited success, Herrmann was granted permission to
raise a *Geschwader* of these new "Wild Boars" (i.e., three *Gruppen* of about
twenty-five planes each—see Appendix D). He immediately established a
Gruppe of modified Me109s at Hangelar airfield near Bonn, and two more
at Rheine and Oldenburg. Together they would make up the famous
Jagdgeschwader 300 (JG300).

Major Herrmann's new fighter force was still in its training period when the attacks on Hamburg began. On the first night of the battle, only a few planes from JG300 at Oldenburg had been sent over the city. On that night, many of the British crews had reported seeing a strange new type of flak shell bursting over the city, which looked "like large Catherine wheels." The official report remarks casually that these were not particularly lethal, and it now seems likely that these were employed as some kind of aerial signposting for the *Wilde Sau* fighters.

Today Major Herrmann's force was destined to take a much more important role in the battle for the skies over Hamburg. During the day, Major Herrmann received a telephone call from Göring instructing him to take his fighters out of training and employ them in full force tonight. When Herrmann protested that his men were not yet ready for such a task, he was overruled: Without proper radar cover, Herrmann's *Wilde Sau* were suddenly the Reich's most important form of defense.[14]

So it was that this fledgling force was employed in full for the first time over Hamburg on the night of July 27/28. While they would one day become an effective force, at this stage they would not be able to hold the bombers at bay. They simply did not have enough planes or pilots, and those pilots they did have were hopelessly undertrained for the huge task that now faced them.

At 12:55, two minutes ahead of schedule, the first Pathfinder dropped its load of yellow target markers, just a couple of miles east of the city center. Over the next five minutes salvo after salvo of yellow markers poured down onto the same spot, over the suburb of Hammerbrook. When the "backers-up" arrived with their green markers, they too dropped them onto the same area. Unlike the first raid, when the target markers had been spread out in four or five different areas, tonight they were unusually concentrated. The German defenders tried to put the bombers off by sending up decoy flares about ten miles to the west of the city, but nobody was fooled—they had chosen to use red flares, the only color *not* used by the British tonight.[15] Neither were they fooled when decoy fires were lit— compared to the real fires these looked positively minuscule.

If the Pathfinders arrived early at the target, the main force also started before they were due. Unable to contain their eagerness to get in and out of the target quickly, many aircraft had cut corners along their route, guided by the route marker flares that lit the way. By 1:02, when the main force was supposed to start their bombing, eighty-seven planes had already dropped their loads—almost all of them on the single concentrated spot over Hammerbrook. The fire they caused there became a beacon for those who followed. Wave after wave of bombers came in across the northeast of Hamburg to stoke up the fires still further, and with such a concentrated group of target markers to aim at there was at first very little creepback. As the later waves came in to bomb at around half past one, the fires were beginning to spread northward and eastward into the district of Hamm.

More than 2,313 tons of bombs were dropped within the space of just fifty minutes—another new world record. Unlike the last raid, however, when a similar amount had been dropped, tonight the bulk of these bombs were squeezed into just a few square miles. The mass of individual fires that had been started up by the opening wave now began to join up into one single conflagration. The firestorm had begun.

In all, 722 aircraft bombed the city that night—most of them in the same small group of districts to the east of the city center.[16] The scene below them was unlike anything any of the crews had seen before. According to Colin Harrison, who was flying a 467 Squadron Lancaster in the last wave of the attack, the flames were already visible from miles away: "We didn't need any navigation. We could see Hamburg from over the North Sea. We just flew where all the lights and the flares were. It looked hellish from on top. I mean, targets don't look very nice from on top, with all the colored fires and flames . . . but this was particularly awful."[17]

Above the fires, a pall of smoke rose so high that even the high-flying Lancasters found themselves flying through the fumes. "That was something frightful," remembers Bill McCrea of 57 Squadron:

I remember the clouds that were coming up about 30,000 feet. It was just one great volcano underneath. All I was thinking about was dropping my bombs and getting home—the same as everybody. . . . It was an appalling sight. Every so often it was just burbling up, just like a volcano. Every so often there was another explosion, another bomb went in, and there was another flash. And you could see the photo flashes going off, too—they were brighter and more sudden. They took the photographs that theoretically marked your aiming point. But of course that night you couldn't get anything, because there was no detail on the ground at all . . . there was just a whole sea, a mass of flame.[18]

RAF bombs dropped on Hamburg
on the night of July 27

Direction of approach

Alster
Lake

1-mile limit

2-mile limit

3-mile limit

☆ Target indicators dropped
• Bomb load
△ Aiming point

   Industrial areas

   Residential areas

Trevor Timperley of 156 Squadron also remembers the sights he saw that night:

> The firestorm still grips me most out of my whole tour—both tours. The very size of it on the ground: It was just a sea of flames . . . I remember I had a navigator who would never look out at all. He used to be head down in his little office, working out one thing and another, but he would never come and look up. I remember saying, "For Christ's sake, Smithy, look at this! You'll never see the like of it again!"[19]

For some of the airmen the thought of what was happening on the ground beneath them was quite harrowing. Leonard Cooper, for example, was a flight engineer in a 7 Squadron Lancaster that was flying at an altitude of around 17,000 feet that night. He estimated that the cloud of smoke was rising to about 20,000 feet—and they were flying directly through it. "We could definitely smell . . . well, it was like burning flesh," he says. "It's not a thing I'd like to talk about."[20]

With the German defenses in disarray, most of the bombers managed to make their bombing runs without running into difficulty. Some, however, were not so lucky. After the raid of the 24th/25th, the mobile railway flak batteries that Hamburg had sent to the Ruhr were rushed back to defend the city. There seemed to be more searchlights than ever, especially above the parts of town to the west and northwest that had been hit by the previous raid. Without radar to guide them, the vast numbers of guns and searchlights were unable to pose anything like the threat they used to—but even so, twenty-eight aircraft returned to Britain with serious flak damage.

On the rare occasions when an aircraft *was* caught by the searchlights, the speed with which the other lights and guns locked onto the victim could be terrifying. When the master beam caught a Lancaster piloted by Sergeant C. G. Hopton, the other lights zoned in almost immediately, lighting the plane up as if it were daylight. Within moments the full force of all the flak batteries in the area was focused on this one hapless aircraft as it turned and dived in an attempt to break free of the danger—with nothing else to aim at, the flak gunners were glad of any opportunity to bring down one of their attackers. As the Lancaster finally escaped the lights, a shell hit the port wing, and the inner engine was set on fire. The flight engineer immediately set about feathering the engine and extinguishing the blaze, but before he could do so they came under attack a second time, this time from a German fighter who had been attracted by the lights. Blinded by the brightness of the searchlights, none of the crew spotted him until he was already closing in from above. He sighted his cannon on the burning engine and raked the port wing, before being forced away by the Lancaster's two gunners. Miraculously, no one was hurt, and Hopton's aircraft was able to make it back to England on its three remaining engines.[21]

The plane that attacked Hopton's plane was an Me109, probably one of Major Hajo Herrmann's *Wilde Sau* fighters. These fighters were unquestionably more effective at shooting down RAF bombers than the flak was. As they roamed the sky high above the city they could see the bombers below them, clearly silhouetted against the glow of all the raging fires on the ground. It is ironic that until this point the British had suffered even fewer casualties than they had on their first raid; but now, with the fires illuminating them, a handful of bombers were about to become victims of their own success.

At 1:21 the German flak batteries were ordered to limit their fire to 5,500 meters (about 18,000 feet).[22] At a stroke the defense of the city, at least in the higher altitudes, was now entirely up to the *Wilde Sau*, who immediately swooped down to attack the bomber stream from above.

Appropriately, the first of their victims was claimed by Major Herrmann himself:

> The clouds of smoke over Hamburg were so dense that it made you shudder. I saw this great column of smoke: I even smelt it. I flew over the target several times and then I saw this bomber in the searchlights.... It was like daylight in those searchlights. I could see the rear gunner; he was only looking downwards, probably at the inferno below. There was no movement of his guns. You must remember that, at this time, the British were not generally warned to watch out for us over the target. I had seen other bombers over targets with the gunners looking down. I fired and he burned. ...As he fell, he turned and dropped away from the smoke cloud. I followed him a little but, as he got lower and lower, I left him. I watched him burst on the ground.[23]

Three more RAF planes were shot down over Hamburg that night. For these few doomed airmen, it was every bit as dangerous in the skies over

Hamburg as it was on the ground. The flames that engulfed the planes as they fell to earth were a savage echo of the inferno below.

The narrow margin between life and death was made brutally stark to one Lancaster crew from 460 Squadron. They were as inexperienced as a crew could possibly be: Their pilot, Reg Wellham, had been on the previous trip to Hamburg as a "second dickie" pilot, but for the rest of them this was their very first operation. Apart from their Australian navigator, Noel Knight, they were all in their early twenties.

They had reached the target without any mishap, but just after they had dropped their bomb load and were about to turn for home the whole plane was rocked by a massive explosion. The force of it turned the plane on its back, and it was soon dropping out of the sky like a stone.

Ted Groom, the crew's flight engineer, remembers the event vividly. He was at the back of the aircraft dropping bundles of Window down the flare chute, when he suddenly found himself floating in the air, surrounded by foil strips from burst Window packets:

> It all happened so quickly, in a matter of seconds. I didn't know where I was—I was just rolling around amongst all these bundles. My first thought was to get a plug in somewhere. I knew where all the intercom plugs were, right through the aircraft. I stumbled around in the pitch black, got hold of the lead, and plugged myself back into the intercom. Reg the skipper was shouting out for me to get up to the front as quick as possible. By that time we were right way up. I went past the wireless operator. I went past the navigator, who'd lost everything off his desk and was trying to find all his stuff in the semidarkness. Everyone was crying out, "What the hell's happening?!" I eventually got up to the front and Reg said, "Get this sorted out!" So I synchronized the engines at a normal climbing rate of about 2,850 revs a minute, plus seven or eight boost. I checked all the temperature gauges, and the fuel, even the oxygen to see if that was all right. I looked at the altimeter—you do this automatically when something goes wrong—and I saw that we were at 10,000 feet. I looked at the pilot, signaled to him that I didn't want him to speak, and I pointed at the altimeter.[24]

What Ted Groom was pointing out to his skipper, and what he didn't want to be broadcast to the others over the intercom, was the fact that their aircraft had dropped 9,000 feet in a matter of seconds. Just a minute more and they would all have died as they crashed into the fires on the ground below.

When they arrived back at Binbrook airfield just before five o'clock that morning, the ground crew checked the plane over for damage. The fuel pipes were hanging down out of the bottom of the aircraft, and there were loose panels where the rivets had burst, but there was absolutely no damage to indicate that they had been hit either by flak or by fighters. After an officer from the Air Ministry came to check the details, the unofficial explanation was that Reg Wellham and his crew had been directly above another British bomber when it was attacked by a German fighter. The other bomber had not yet dropped its bombs, so when it exploded the force was great enough to blow Reg Wellham's Lancaster onto its back. If this is indeed what happened, then that German fighter almost got two bombers with a single shot that night.

This was by no means the last such incident of the night. Dozens of crews returned with stories of combats and near misses: ten over Hamburg itself, and over a dozen more on the way home. Eight planes would be shot down on the return journey: six by German fighters, and two more by flak when they strayed off-course over the cities of Wilhelmshaven and Bremerhaven. Excluding four aircraft that were written off when returning crews crash-landed them, a total of seventeen British planes were lost that night: five more than on the first Hamburg raid. But this was still only half the number Bomber Command had become used to over the preceding months. Despite the rapid change in German tactics, Window was still working wonders for the British.

At 1:47 the last of the attacking aircraft dropped its mix of high explosives and incendiaries, and the tail end of the bomber stream finally made its way back toward the coast and over the North Sea toward England. Behind them they left one of the biggest man-made fires the world has ever seen, which even now was still growing in intensity. As one young rear gunner was to write in his diary that night: "If it had been a really clear night the fires would have been visible nearly back to our coast. As it was we could see it nearly half way back, about 200 miles, and a column of smoke about 20,000 feet, so Hamburg must have had it."[25]

Chapter 16

FIRESTORM

What if the breath that kindled those grim fires
Awaked should blow them into sevenfold rage
And plunge us in the flames? . . . what if all
Her stores were opened and this firmament
Of hell should spout her cataracts of fire?

—MILTON, *PARADISE LOST*[1]

To understand what happened on the night of Tuesday, July 27, 1943, one needs to know a little about how large fires work. Very few people have any direct experience of conditions inside a major conflagration, and even those who are unlucky enough to have lived through a house fire cannot possibly understand what it is like to be caught inside a firestorm. So before describing what happened in Hamburg that night, it is necessary to explain how firestorms come about, what exactly they are, and why they can be so deadly.

Large conflagrations are different from ordinary house fires in two important respects. First, because of their sheer size they produce such vast quantities of smoke that even those who are far away from the flames can often end up suffocating. This is particularly dangerous in city fires—anyone sheltering in the confined space of a basement or cellar runs the risk of dying of smoke inhalation or carbon monoxide poisoning, as all the oxygen is sucked out of the air and replaced with poisonous fumes.

Second, and more important, the incredible temperatures such fires reach—sometimes as high as 700 or 800 degrees Celsius—superheat all the air above and around the fire, causing it to rise rapidly. In some cases this can set off a chain reaction. As vast amounts of air rush skyward they leave behind a vacuum, which sucks new air from the surrounding areas to fill the space. This new air streams in bringing new oxygen, which in turn feeds the fire. The process gradually accelerates: The fire gets hotter, and the winds get faster, often reaching speeds of 60 or 70 mph. This is what gives the "firestorm" phenomenon its name: the combination of huge fires and storm-force winds. As long as there is enough fuel to keep the fire burning the winds will continue to blow, first rushing into the fire horizontally along the ground, and then shooting skyward with the heat.

As I mentioned in Chapter 10, Hamburg had already had one firestorm on Saturday night, where witnesses claimed to have seen "a frightful storm, caused by the heat," and winds that were so strong that it was impossible to fight one's way through them.[2] British aircrews on that night reported seeing clouds of smoke billowing up to 20,000 feet and beyond, forced rapidly into the sky by the strength of the heat. This was comparable to the devastating firestorm that had enveloped Wuppertal two months before the Hamburg bombings, and that which would consume Dresden eighteen months later.[3]

What happened tonight, however, was in a whole different league. The winds reached speeds of at least 120 mph, and in some places perhaps as high as 170 mph—the same speed as Hurricane Katrina, which devastated New Orleans in 2005.[4] To make things worse, these winds were not steady in their force—they swirled and changed direction rapidly from one moment to the next. In a forest firestorm the wind is generally free to take the most direct route to the center of the conflagration, spiraling inward in an anticlockwise direction, just like a cyclone. In a city like Hamburg, by contrast, the winds were forced away from their natural course by all the buildings that stood in the way. Instead they were channeled along streets, sometimes meeting head on at street junctions, causing eddies and swirls that could easily knock a human being off his feet. There are many reports of "fire-whirls" at such junctions—miniature tornadoes—that only added to the misery of the fugitives trying to find safety.[5]

Accompanying these hurricane-force winds were some of the hottest temperatures ever experienced in a city fire. The sheer amount of flammable material, stacked up in six-story buildings like huge charcoal ricks, produced enough heat to melt the glass in the windows of cars and trams in the street—which means the temperature must have approached the same levels as a glass furnace: that is, about 1,400°C.[6] Inside the buildings the temperature was much hotter still—it melted cutlery, glass bottles, and burned bricks to ash.

In the years that followed the catastrophe, the Hamburg firestorm came under intense scientific scrutiny, and it was concluded that no other large fire in recorded history has ever equaled it in intensity. It was far worse than any of the great forest fires that have engulfed large parts of America and Canada; greater even than the vast city fires that have consumed London, Chicago, or any of the countless cities bombed by the Allies across Germany. The reasons Hamburg's firestorm was so bad are as simple as they are tragic. The fault lay with the weather conditions of the time—a set of circumstances so unusual for the area that they have only rarely been repeated since.

Because of all the hot, sultry weather that Hamburg had been experiencing, there was an unstable pocket of warm air sitting directly over the city. This pocket of air was made warmer by all the fires that had been burning since Sunday, and was saturated with smoke particles, which retained the heat even further. All around Hamburg, however, and high above it, the air was much cooler. Surrounded on all sides by this colder air, the effect was like a huge, pressurized balloon, sticking up into the air some 10,000 feet. All it would take to burst the top off this balloon was a sharp rise in temperature. Once it *had* burst, the warm air over the city would rise unrestricted for thousands of feet, rapidly drawing newer air behind it, and setting off the perfect conditions for the greatest firestorm the world has ever seen.[7]

The final factor in this set of extremely rare conditions was the humidity—or rather, the lack of it. Being close to the sea, the air in Hamburg normally has a very high humidity—a seasonal average of about 78 percent. On July 27, 1943, the humidity was a mere 30 percent. After the long, dry summer most of the buildings in Hamburg were like tinder anyway, but with such low humidity there was nothing to stop the rapid spread of fire. Other historians have used the analogy of a furnace with a very tall chimney, just waiting for someone to light a match below.[8] That match was lit shortly before 1:00 A.M. when the RAF dropped the first of 1,174 tons of incendiaries into the eastern quarter of the city.

Part of the tragedy for Hamburg was the sheer bad luck of it all. The Allies had not specifically planned to take advantage of these weather conditions; indeed, they did not even realize that such conditions *could* lead to firestorms.[9] Their understanding was far more basic: The weather was good simply because it was clear, which made navigation to the city much easier, and because it was dry, which would make it easier to start effective fires. They had no idea exactly how perfect the conditions were for their purpose.

They did, however, have a very good idea of how to start fires, and how to keep them going. After years of practice, they had created a highly effective system. To start with, they knew that the most important factor in starting a really huge fire was concentration. If an attacking force dropped all of its incendiaries in a single area it would be impossible for the defenders to put out all of the individual fires. If enough of these fires were allowed to take hold, they would soon begin to join up into huge conflagrations. The fire brigades would be saturated: Unable to cope, they would be forced farther and farther away from the fire's center, and would struggle even to prevent the fires from spreading to other districts.

The second most important thing was the use of high-explosive (HE) bombs. Most people assume, instinctively, that the whole purpose of high explosives is to destroy buildings. Our perception is colored by our modern experience: The bombs used by terrorists, or even by conventional military forces, are almost always designed to cause the maximum damage to buildings by razing them to the ground. But bombing during the Second World War was carried out on such a huge scale that different tactics were required. Fire was far more efficient than high-explosive bombs at destroying large areas, so Allied tactics were aimed at getting the fires to spread as far and as quickly as possible. Military planners learned early on in the war that if they wanted their fires to spread it was actually counterproductive to blast buildings down because this would create fire breaks. The purpose of high explosives, therefore, was not to *destroy* buildings but merely to blow in as many doors and windows as possible, to allow the air to get inside and feed the flames. Buildings that were not yet burning could then catch fire as the sparks and embers from neighboring buildings floated in, setting curtains and furniture alight. By blowing off roofs, HE bombs also allowed the incendiaries to pierce through to the lower floors of a building, where they could do the most damage. The explosions had the added effect of keeping most of the firefighters inside their shelters long enough to give the fires a chance to take hold and putting craters in the roads that prevented fire engines from getting to the affected areas. So while it was the incendiaries that did the most damage, the high explosives had an essential role, and it was important to get the exact mix of the two different types of bombs right.[10]

One might be tempted to ask what kind of mind comes up with theories like this, but to be fair to the Allies a great deal of the research had already been done for them—or rather, *to* them. During the Blitz on Britain in 1940–41, the Luftwaffe had rained incendiaries down on London and other British cities, causing huge damage. The British, who had only really used HE bombs until then, soon learned that the fires were doing far more damage than the explosions and began experimenting accordingly.[11] Repugnant as it might seem now, the cruel logic of war requires such efficiency. By the summer of 1943, Royal Air Force planners had worked large-scale bombing down to a fine art.

The concentration of bombs on Hamburg that Tuesday night was so great that the civil defense organizations in the eastern quarter of the city had little chance of saving anything. "After only a quarter of an hour, conditions in these districts were terrible," claimed the official German report shortly afterward. "A carpet of bombs of unimaginable density caused almost complete destruction of these districts in a very short time. Extensive portions were transformed in barely half an hour into one sea of flame."[12] The bombs came down so thick and fast it was impossible to stop the spread of fire: Tens of thousands of individual fires very quickly joined up and became one vast conflagration.

The people of Hamburg had been expecting another attack at some point, but nothing could have prepared them for the hammering they were now experiencing, especially in the eastern quarter of the city. Even those who had lived through the first night of attacks must have been shocked at the intensity of tonight's bombardment. For Fredy Borck, the eleven-year-old child who lived in the riverside district of Rothenburgsort, it was the most terrifying night of his life.

> Suddenly it started to happen outside. It was a bombardment that is still indescribable, even today. . . . All around us were the crashes of bombs striking with appalling explosions—ear-shattering explosions that seemed to be right next to us, over us. You could even hear the howl of the nearer bombs before they hit, then the crash as they burst. It must have been hell outside! It got worse and worse. The walls of the cellar rose and sank. . . .

An inhuman screeching and groaning came from the walls. We screamed along with it, screaming out our terror! We lost all self-control, crouched on the benches, cowering together with our heads between our knees to cover our ears.[13]

Fifteen-year-old Herbert Wulff was sheltering in a basement in Süderstrasse, right at the center of the main attack. He was huddling with his mother and his sister when the sound of the bombs became unbearable: Unlike Fredy Borck, his instinct was to leave the shelter and take his chances outside. His sister was still recovering from a gall-bladder operation—she had been dismissed from Barmbek hospital early because the rooms where she had been recuperating were destroyed in the first night of attacks. Even so, she too was determined to get out of the basement shelter:

Shortly after everyone in the building had filled the cellar, the whole building shook, right down to the foundations, from the explosion of a huge bomb. I can still see it, how the foundation walls moved between the buttresses and swayed dangerously. Then the lighting went out abruptly, and a cry rang out through the cellar room, and I thought for a moment that my final hour had come. After that first terrifying second we had only one thought: to get out of here. Instinctively my mother, my sister and I grabbed each other's hands and pushed our way through to the cellar stairs.[14]

Some people—the foolish and the brave—were already outside their cellars watching events unfold. Most houses and factories had a fire warden who would make regular patrols for incendiaries and call for help from the shelters when a new fire needed to be put out.[15] Many of these brave men and women died before they had a chance to do anything useful. Those who survived found themselves quickly overwhelmed by the sheer numbers of incendiary bombs raining down around them. The German authorities estimated that 96,429 stick incendiaries fell on every square kilometer of ground, plus a further 2,733 larger incendiary bombs. This was over five times as concentrated as the previous large-scale attack.[16] To give some idea of what this meant on a human scale, imagine a large attic room, about ten meters long and ten meters wide. On average, in this attic room alone, ten incendiary bombs would fall, each of them crashing through the ceiling to set the roof timbers alight. With such a high concentrations of bombs it was impossible to put out all the fires as they occurred.

The incendiary bombs were of two main types. The most common were the four-pound thermite stick incendiaries. These would fall nose down, like miniature missiles, and strike the roofs of the buildings so hard that they would either lodge in the roof cavity or pierce right through to the rooms below, where they would then burst into flame. Some of these were also fitted with an explosive charge, so that if a fire warden came across one in time to shovel it out of a window it would explode, killing or maiming the person who was trying to rescue his building. The second type of firebomb was the bigger thirty-pound incendiary. This was heavy enough to crash straight through the roof space and into the apartments of the lower stories. These larger incendiaries were filled with a liquid mixture of Benzol and rubber, designed to splash across whatever the bomb hit, setting fire to everything within ten meters. German civilians tended to call these, and indeed all incendiaries, "phosphor bombs," which gave rise to a number of gruesome myths in later years. Phosphorus is a particularly evil substance, which sticks to the skin and is impossible to put out as long as it is in contact with the air. In fact, while a small number of bombs contained phosphorus, the vast majority were made of other substances, less immediately terrifying, but much more effective at starting fires.[17]

With dozens of apartments catching fire simultaneously, it is unsurprising that whole blocks were very soon ablaze. One of those who witnessed the burning of her own apartment was Henni Klank, a young mother who had ventured out of her shelter to see if she could rescue a few things.

> I don't know why, but suddenly the Devil possessed me; I wanted to go into our house one more time. Perhaps I thought I could still get some things out, like papers, photographs, and such things. But as I stood in the corridor the ceiling was already crackling, and I wanted to go to my father's desk in the living room, but there I saw only fire. The blazing and burning drapes flew in the room, the window panes burst and there was a hissing and crashing all around me. I couldn't manage the few steps to the desk, which stood at the window, my legs felt paralyzed. While dashing out of the apartment I hadn't grabbed even a single article out

of the wardrobe. I was in such a panic that I rushed back to the shelter as quickly as possible. The streets were already burning, the firestorm was now raging through all the streets![18]

Downstairs she found her friends and neighbors close to despair. They all knew that they must leave the building, but when one of them had tried to leave by the front entrance he had been blown away by the wind into the fire. The front of the building was ablaze, and opposite there was a timber business that was burning so fiercely that it was unlikely that they would be able to make their way through to the relative safety of the canal beyond it. Eventually somebody came up with the idea of breaking through the back wall of the building. Frau Klank's husband remembered a pickaxe that stood in the corner of the basement, so they smashed a hole through the wall big enough to push through the pram that carried their newborn baby.

The vision that greeted them on the other side of that wall was worthy of Hieronymus Bosch:

We came out at the Stadtdeich but into a thundering, blazing hell. The streets were burning, the trees were burning, and the tops of them were bent right down to the street, burning horses out of the "Hertz" hauling-business ran past us, the air was burning, simply everything was burning![19]

The bombardment had been so fierce that many people found themselves in similar situations: Their houses were on fire, and yet their escape routes were blocked by rubble or flames. This is exactly what happened to Erich Titschak, a professor of entomology who lived on Dimpfelsweg in the center of the suburb of Hamm. At 1:15 A.M., right in the middle of the attack, a firebomb set the cellar stairs alight making escape from their shelter virtually impossible. Worried about how they would get out, he and some others broke through to the neighboring cellar, only to find that the way out here was also blocked by flames. In desperation they broke through to the basement on the opposite side. This house, and the one beyond it, had already been burned down in a previous raid, so they thought it would be easy to find a way through to the street. In a letter to his children shortly afterward, he describes what he found.

A labyrinth of cellars, hallways, corners and sheds opens before us. . . . All kinds of useless junk blocks our way. We break through eleven doors, one by one, hoping to finally find the exit onto the Hammer Landstrasse . . . there must be a safe way out of here, the corner house, for our wives and children. Some cellar doors fly open at the first hit, but now we are faced with two heavy doors, which resist all our efforts. We take it in turns, sweat running in streams from our foreheads, but without success. The doors are probably lined with iron on the other side. The bolts are strong, our axe glances off the concrete without leaving a trace.[20]

Disappointed, Titschak and his companion, Herr Bläß, returned to their own cellar, knowing that the only way out was their burning stairwell. On the way back they caught a view of exactly what they were now up against.

In one of the adjoining rooms, I knock out the cellar window and catch my first glimpse of Dimpfelsweg and the gardens. What I see takes my breath away. Not just our building and the neighboring building: no, the entire Dimpfelsweg, the buildings opposite, the Wagnerische Villa, the big building by the cinema, the cinema itself, the Claudiastrasse—it all is one enormous sea of fire. A tornado-strength storm sweeps through the streets, pushing a rain of embers before it as thick as a snowstorm in winter. We were supposed to go through there? We'd never make it! Our clothes would instantly catch fire. The Hammer Landstrasse, which was supposed to save us—the same picture. As far as I could see through the iron bars of a small cellar window, all the big beautiful buildings were burning from top to bottom.[21]

Back in their cellar they instructed everyone to wrap wet towels around themselves and do their best to escape through the burning stairwell. It is important to remember that at this point, while everyone could see the immediate danger of the burning stairs, they had no real idea of the hell that lay beyond. Bravely, each person in the cellar made the short run through the flames, Titschak leading the way, but as they stumbled out onto the street, they suddenly found themselves confronted by the sight of their entire neighborhood on fire.

Another survivor in similar circumstances, Hans Jedlicka, claims that the shock of this sight left him completely numb:

I was still convinced that the fire bombs had only hit our doorway, that once we'd run through we'd be safe. As we came through, the sight that met us was like a blow. All I could see was flames. The whole of Hammerbrook was burning! A powerful storm took hold of us and drove us in the direction of Hammerbrookstrasse. That was wrong. We had to go toward Heidenkampsweg—there was water there, and the Stoltenpark. We stumbled over the first charred corpses. From there on it was like a switch turned in my head. It was like being in a dream. I saw and heard everything, crystal-clear, but in spite of the great heat felt no pain. We had to fight our way through the firestorm meter by meter. My mother's clothes caught fire. I put the flames out with my hands.[22]

In conditions like these, it is little wonder that many people chose to stay in their cellars in the unrealistic hope that the reinforced ceilings would afford them some protection from the flames in the buildings above them. Some people must genuinely have believed that they would be safer in their makeshift bunkers than they would be outside—this, after all, was what all the public information documents and broadcasts had told them. Others simply gave up in despair. When everything outside was burning, what difference did it make whether one stayed or left? Some air raid wardens reported having to bully people into seeking safety elsewhere with blows and kicks, even though it had become obvious that to stay put meant certain death.[23]

Part of the problem was that according to the conventional wisdom of the time, the safest place to be was still the shelters. In any normal raid, when the upper floors of a house were on fire it was still fairly safe down in the cellar, and certainly better than risking the explosions of the bombs outside—occupants of a burning building were encouraged to stay where they were at least until the All Clear had sounded. However, this was no normal raid. Once the firestorm took hold, the wind and all the flaming debris it carried would make it almost impossible to escape through the streets. Many of those who survived did so precisely because they left their cellars early. Perversely, it was those who initially appeared to be in the most danger who ended up being the most likely to survive. Those whose buildings caught fire later on in the raid found themselves trapped between their own fire and the hell of the firestorm outside.

In an interview with *Der Spiegel* magazine in 2003, the poet and songwriter Wolf Biermann described how agonizing the decision was to stay or to go. He was a six-year-old child at the time, but remembers the events of that night clearly, as if they were burned into his memory.

> I sat there alone with my mother. . . . She was sitting there as if she was paralyzed or maybe because she was smart—because in such a panic everything you do is a mistake. It's a mistake to leave: You run to your own death. It's a mistake to stay: Death will come to you. Nobody is ratio- nal in such a situation. In a sense I was rational: I pressed my little head into my mother's coat, into her lap, and thus I could breathe; the air was impossible to breathe elsewhere.
>
> Then my mother realized we'd burn there. She took a little leather suitcase with our papers and a few photos of my dad who, just a few months ago, had gone through the fiery oven in Auschwitz, as a Jew, as a communist. And she handed me a little bucket—a little aluminum bucket with a cover. There was mirabelle jam inside, my mother had made it. And I took my little bucket and then we got out. We crawled through the basement.[24]

As he stepped outside it was not so much the sight of all the flames that ter- rified him as the noise. The crash of the bombs going off around him, the roaring of the fires, the drone of the planes, and above it all the terrifying whine of the wind: "What a sound it was! It was hell, it was hell's fires. In hell it is not only hot but loud. The firestorm was screaming!"[25]

The odyssey that lay before people like the young Wolf Biermann and his mother defies imagination. In a conflagration this huge it was impos- sible to escape the fire—the distance to the edge was too great. The best anyone could hope for was to travel a shorter way to some open space that would act as an island in this terrible flaming sea—a park, or a set of play- ing fields where the fire could not properly take hold. In Hammerbrook people made for the Stoltenpark, or the banks of the many canals that criss-crossed the area. In Hamm those who were able made their way to the Hammer Park, and in Eilbek it was the Jakobipark, just north of Hassel- brook station. And yet even here the heat was so great that people were overcome. Without shelter from the storm of sparks their clothes and hair were still in danger of catching fire, and many people sustained such bad burns as they escaped that they perished shortly after reaching relative safety. In the smaller parks and open spaces hundreds of people died because they were unable to get far enough away from the incredible heat. In one green of about 120 meters long and a similar width, over a hundred people who had sought safety in the center were burned to death.[26]

The following account is by a man who was in his mid-forties. When the exit from his cellar was blocked by rubble he was forced to break through into his brother-in-law's pastry shop on the ground floor of the building. From that point on it became almost impossible to keep the family together as they ran through the burning streets in desperate search of shelter.

There were only two places that might be safe: either the sports field on Grevenweg or the Ankelmannplatz in the opposite direction. The escape route to the sports field was shorter, but was more likely to be in the middle of a sea of fire. I personally, with my family, chose the somewhat longer route, racing along the middle of the street, which was alight with flying sparks, in order to avoid some of the heat from the burning house facades.

Even on the short distance to the next corner, we saw the first people burning, desperately running figures, who suddenly fell, and as we approached, were already dead. We had reached the first crossroads. Here we saw a building whose roof had, exceptionally, only just caught fire. In the entrance to this building we took shelter for a few moments from the storm, the heat, the whipping whirl of sparks, and the glowing mounds of phosphor. We were in desperate need of this break. Although we had only traveled a short distance, our lips were already badly swollen. Our throats were incredibly dry. Our legs felt weak. . . .

All around people fled from burning buildings. Some came out with their clothes already alight, others caught fire outside, from the sparks, the blazing heat, or the phosphor. Again and again we saw burning people suddenly start to run, and soon after to fall.

After this, terrible cries were to be heard but they too grew rarer. I saw many burning people who ran and collapsed in silence. There were also people traveling in the opposite direction to us. Because of this we had only gone a few steps when I heard my sister call. We could not see her, because despite the bright fires close by, thick smoke and dust darkened everything. We followed my sister's voice, calling ourselves, but received no answer. For a short while it became lighter. Around twenty meters in front of me, I saw my brother-in-law appear from the darkness of a building's wall, and run into the middle of the street. I called to him. He turned to me. I saw from his badly swollen face, that he had already suffered heavy burns. Whether or not he recognized me, I do not know. My brother-in-law suddenly turned away again and began to run. I then saw that all his clothes were burning brightly. He fell in to a mass of three or four corpses which were already completely burned. When my wife and I reached there, our brother-in-law was already dead, burned. There was no way to save the people who were falling. He who fell over during his escape was lost. . . .

My wife's head began to burn. Her hair had caught fire. With a small amount of water that I had in a bucket with me I was able to put out her burning hair. At the same time I cooled my hands and face. . . . My wife complained: "I can't go on! My feet are burned! My hands!" . . . I also felt great pain in my right hand, caused by a severe burn. My left hand was beginning to hurt similarly as well. My head burned as if on fire, especially my face. I also noticed that my sight began to fade.

The stretch of road upon which we now traveled brought ever-worsening scenes of horror. I saw many women with their children held in their arms running, burning and then falling and not getting back up. We passed masses of people made up of four or five corpses, each probably a family, visible only as a pile of burned substance no larger than a small child. Many men and women fell over suddenly without having caught fire. Around us were hundreds of people. Some of them ran, some moved slowly, with a peculiar shuffling walk. All this happened in silence. The terrible heat had dried throats so much, that no one could scream. Silently and with the last of their force, women tried to save their children. They carried them pressed close. Many of these children were already dead, without their mothers' knowing.[27]

A tornado, a whirl of sparks, the tops of trees bent down to the street by the force of the burning wind—what these people were witnessing was the beginning of a unique phenomenon. The word *Flammenmeer*, "sea of flames," comes up again and again in accounts of the firestorm. While this is something of an idiom in German, it is also a literal description of what these people saw: a vast sea of fire in the grip of a hurricane. It is not surprising that when a local priest saw what had overcome his neighborhood in Eilbek he was reminded of the apocalyptic vision of St Matthew.[28] For most people, however, what they were witnessing was, quite simply, a picture of hell. With the fires spreading for miles in each direction there was literally no end to the flames in sight—it was as if their entire world had been transformed in a few short minutes into a blazing inferno.

The city authorities struggled vainly to keep the fires under control, but right from the outset they were fighting a losing battle. With most of the fire brigade still in the west of the city, there were actually very few teams of firemen to combat the flames. Those who did make it very soon gave up trying to put the fires out and concentrated instead on rescuing people caught within the burning buildings. In Rothenburgsort, for example, the fire brigade leader ordered his men to create an umbrella of water for the fugitives to escape beneath, and in this way brought between 3,000 and 5,000 people to safety.[29] Such rescue attempts were still possible on the outer edges of the main firestorm area—but once the fire brigade ventured into Hammerbrook, Borgfelde, and Hamm they were forced to abandon all hope of saving anyone. The head of one firefighting unit discovered that not only was he unable to help the fugitives, he was lucky to escape with his own life.

> In Hammer Weg there were people lying on the street. We climbed out of the car to rescue them. Then suddenly, along the Landstrasse there came a colossal sheet of flame, which I tried to escape by running ahead of it. The driver got away by turning the car down Horst-Wessel-Strasse. The firestorm was a hurricane. No smoke on the streets, only flames and flying sparks as thick as a snow storm . . . I ran until I was exhausted.[30]

Ludwig Faupel was another fireman who had rushed to Hamm only to find himself embroiled in the full force of the firestorm. After driving through a "roaring, boiling hell," he and his fire crew were finally forced to abandon their vehicle in the middle of the road and take whatever shelter they could find.[31]

> Closely pressed against the ground behind a heap of stones, the heat was unbearable. Again and again I had to put out my smoldering clothes. I put my gas mask on for lack of air. Bits of fire, dust and ash flew all around. In the howling and crashing of the wind people were blown over,

stumbled and lay there exhausted, doomed to die. Above it all the growling drone of hundreds of aircraft. Bombs exploding.

Our fire engine was burning. My comrades had disappeared in the storm and heat. In order to stop myself being pulled into the fire I struggled against the storm and landed up in a huge bomb crater, full of water from a broken pipe. Trapped, I ripped the gas mask from my face and clung to the edge of the crater for fear of drowning. The rim broke off, my helmet was gone, dread began to take hold of me. I ducked under the water in order to escape the glowing heat. There was an insane noise in the air.[32]

In this atmosphere, surrounded by incessant noise and unbearable heat, the terrifying scenes that took place before the stranded fireman's eyes began to take on a surreal quality.

With a glance over the edge of the crater I saw a man kneeling right in front of me—with big frightened eyes he fell forward. I pulled the dead man into the crater. Only those who had left the cellars by this time would now survive. They rushed over glowing mountains of rubble. Many were killed by the ruins collapsing, or torn to pieces by bombs, suffocated or burned. I could not believe what I was seeing. In the thunderous din none of them could hear the screams of the others. Each struggled for survival. Parts of a collapsing house facade poured down on the other side of the crater and into the water. The brown sludge splashed around the edge and meant the end for some of those seeking shelter.[33]

As he clung hold of the edge of his flooded crater in the road, Faupel began to lose all sense of time. He has no idea how long he stayed there, whether it was hours or merely minutes. Eventually, however, instinct told him that he had to move on.

At some point in the night I ran on once more with the dripping wet jacket of the dead man over my head. In this whirling fire I had lost all sense of direction. On my way out of the chaos I came across a burned-out tram. The windows had melted in the heat. Dead bodies lay naked on top of one another in the carriage. Their clothes had disintegrated into embers. The people had tried to shelter here from the firestorm. In

Eiffestrasse they struggled for survival. Sinking into the hot tarmac, they had tried to support themselves with their hands, and lay now on their knees. They ended their lives screaming with fear and pain. I could not help them.[34]

Although he was only a child, Wolf Biermann clearly remembered equally chilling scenes.

The firestorm was so strong that it converted streets into jets. Schwaben-strasse, where we lived, was in a good position, aslant to the suction of the fire. But once you got into a street which was part of the suction, people started to burn like tinder and they had no chance. So we ran close to the walls to escape the storm. I saw how roofs were flying through the air; it was like in the movies, like science fiction, but real. The asphalt was burn-ing and boiling. I saw two women running, a young one and an older one, whose shoes got stuck in the boiling asphalt. They pulled their feet out of the shoes but that wasn't a good idea because they had to step into the boiling asphalt. They fell and didn't get up again. Like flies in the hot wax of a candle.[35]

Ernst-Günther Haberland was another schoolchild who found himself witnessing this uniquely awful vision, after leaving the safety of the main bunker at about five o'clock the next morning.

We looked around us, at the area where we had once lived. All the build-ings burned brightly, it was a single wall of fire. One could hear the terrible cries of people seeking help for their wounds. One saw people on Heidenkampsweg trying to cross from one side of the street to the other, where there was a canal. The asphalt of the road had become almost liquid with the immense heat. They reached the middle, where their feet got stuck in the asphalt. Their legs began to burn because of the heat, the flames ate their way up and met again above their heads. At first they screamed, then became quieter, and finally, they gave a last rattling breath and were dead.[36]

Survival in the open streets of Hamburg was now a virtual impossibility. The hurricane was full of burning debris—roofs, the branches of trees, pieces of masonry and timber—and there are many accounts of people being bowled over by items that hit them.[37] The very air itself was so hot and so choked with smoke and poisonous gases as to be all but unbreathable. Sparks and embers caught on people's hair, setting it on fire. To make things worse, the fugitives could not allow themselves to be carried along by the winds: Since the hurricane was caused by the fire sucking air inward to feed itself, this would have been suicide. Instead they had to battle *against* the wind, and all the flaming debris that it carried, in order to reach anything resembling safety. Neither were they able to seek shelter in doorways—often the heat from all the burning houses was so intense that they were obliged to stick to the middle of the road, just where the force of the wind was strongest.

The only way for the fugitives to save themselves was to find some open space, away from the burning buildings. When that open space was too far, they had to try to get there in stages, taking what shelter they could along the way. One woman tells how she, her husband, and her daughter traveled from one burning cellar to the next, sheltering for as long as the flames were not immediately threatening, before moving on once again. They did this no fewer than seven times, before finally succumbing to despair.

So we had finished with our lives. There was too little hope of escaping this hellish cauldron. No way to break through this ring. We no longer said a word to one another, we did not cry either, nor did we whine or complain, we only stared silently in front of ourselves. Suddenly we were told there was an escape route by the railroad embankment, that we should get onto the rails, since no trains could come because the station had been destroyed. We then slid down a long rope onto the platform. Today I can't imagine how we managed to get down there—but anyway, we got down. Exhausted, we threw ourselves onto the embankment. However, the grassy knolls were so hot that one could not stay on them. The opposite embankment had already caught fire. Hannelore climbed to the top of the embankment with the last of her energy in order to see how thick the smoke above was. . . . She called to us, and we climbed with what little strength we still had to the top, our cramped hands in the hot grass. When we arrived at the top, we fled into a small corrugated metal toilet. Here people sat on top of each other in the disgusting air, safe only from the sparks, and in no way from the smoke.[38]

On such a hellish night, a public toilet could be an extremely welcome haven, particularly if the cisterns still had water in them. Erika Wilken and her husband, Willi, found shelter in a toilet under the street on Grevenweg, right at the center of the firestorm area in Hammerbrook. For a while they huddled with eighty or one hundred others, wetting a blanket in the water from the cisterns to drape over their heads. When that water ran out they even used the water from the toilet bowls. There was little they could do beyond staying put and hoping not to suffocate as all the oxygen was sucked out of the air by the fires. But worse was to come.

To our misfortune, a large phosphorus bomb fell directly outside the toilet entrance (whose door had been blown off on Saturday evening). The people nearest the door now gave way to an indescribable panic. The inner toilet doors were torn off and used as shields in front of the bomb. After a few minutes, these doors too were burning brightly.

Terrible scenes took place, since all of us saw certain death in front of us, with the only way out a sea of flames. We were caught like rats in a trap. The doors were thrown on to the canister by screaming people and more smoke and heat poured in. In the meantime, the water in the tank had been used up. . . . My husband was completely worn out and we crouched next to the bowl. The other people here sat down too; some collapsed and never woke up again. Three soldiers committed suicide. I begged my husband to beat back the flames with our blanket—the one object we had brought with us apart from our papers—but he was no longer able to do so. So with my last strength I did it. My hair began to singe and my husband extinguished it. . . .

What now? Our hearts were racing, our faces began to puff up and we were close to fainting. Perhaps another five or eight minutes and we would be finished too. On my question, "Willi, is this the end?," my husband decided to risk everything and try to reach the outside. . . . I took the blanket and he the little suitcase. Quickly, but carefully so that we would not slip on the corpses, we reached the outside, me first and my husband behind me. One! Two! Three! We were through the wall of fire. We made it. Both without burns; only our shoes were singed. But our last strength and courage had gone. We lay down on the ground at the side of the canal. . . . People swimming in it kept wetting our blanket for us.[39]

Without intending it, Erika and Willi Wilken had stumbled upon probably the last safe haven in Hammerbrook. Away from the relative security of the parks and open spaces the canals that criss-crossed the area proved to be the only salvation for thousands of people. Here beside the water they were just a fraction cooler, and the air near the water's surface was more breathable than elsewhere. Most of the fugitives did not stop at the canals' edges, but hurried to submerge themselves, cooling their burns in the life-saving water.

And yet even here it was not completely safe. There are many tales of people becoming drenched in liquid phosphorus and being unable to extinguish the flames, even by throwing themselves into the canals, since phosphorus burns as soon as it comes back into contact with oxygen. Most of these stories can be dismissed as repetitions of a particularly gruesome urban myth.[40] However, the British did indeed use liquid phosphorus in some of their incendiaries, and there are enough eyewitnesses to make one or two instances of this terrible story possible.

Just as dangerous, however, was the thin layer of oil on the water's surface. Ben Witter, who witnessed the firestorm as a local journalist, describes the circumstances some people found themselves in as they sought shelter in the canals.

> It is difficult to explain how water can burn. It was burning because very many ships, small ships, had exploded and oil had been released into the water and the people who were themselves on fire jumped into it and . . . I don't know, some kind of chemical must have been in it, . . . and they burnt, swam, burnt, and went under.[41]

The official report of the Hamburg police chief confirms that while the canals were often the only safe place to go, they were still by no means comfortable. Even those who stayed in the water throughout the firestorm suffered burns on their heads; they were obliged to keep wetting their faces to avoid perishing in the heat. "The firestorm swept over the water with its heat and its showers of sparks so that even thick wooden posts and bollards burned down to the level of the water."[42] Many people were obliged to stay standing or swimming in the water for hours, and some simply became exhausted and drowned. Others died from injuries caused by falling masonry and the other debris that rained down onto the water's surface.

Twenty-one-year-old Heinz Masuch was driven to the Süd Kanal after being forced to abandon every other place of refuge he'd come across. Having left his shelter in Robinsonstrasse (a street that was so badly burned that it has since been erased from the map), he tried in turn the docks, the Sorbenpark, and a space behind the pillars of a bridge—but in each case the temperature became so unbearable he and his companions began to fear that their clothes would ignite.

> So we sat in the canal, up to our necks in water and our wet jackets and coats over our heads. If we thought we had escaped the flames here, we were gravely mistaken, as there were glowing coal barges floating along, from which we had to protect ourselves. We must have spent two hours in the water, maybe more, until the fires had died down.[43]

Wolf Biermann's mother was likewise trying desperately to find a safe place to weather the storm. Having taken shelter in a factory for a short while, she was now steering her son toward one of Hammerbrook's canals, rightly assuming that it was the only place left that might offer them some level of safety. He was still clutching the little bucket of mirabelle jam that she had entrusted to him in the cellar.

> Back into the streets? To try that was to put yourself straight back into the blaze. That was suicide. Impossible. But we had to go. We turned left round the corner, there was a canal, a bridge. My mother tried to reach the water with me near the bridge. We crawled through the handrail, down the canal's bank. . . . We reached the water, found a spot in the group of people and stood in the water. I was standing next to an old lady who on every finger was holding a little suitcase or handbag, everything she could grab. And now that was all floating on the water. I saw that from my low point of view, my head was as the same level as her hand. And suddenly I could see right in front of me how the woman's fingers were losing their grip, how the suitcase was floating away, how the woman was sinking. Then she was gone.
>
> More and more pieces of debris were falling around us from above, and it became obvious we couldn't stay there. Some stayed because they could think of nothing better to do, but my mother had a feeling we had to leave. So she grabbed me by my shoulders and swam with me across

the canal. And on the other side it was idyllic! There was grass, there were shallow banks and there were a dozen other people who had escaped there. They were sitting there like in a theater box: Nothing could fall down from above, and around them there was the panorama of a burning city which they could watch from a safe position. How wonderful! Believe it or not, it's true, I still had my little bucket in my hand. And as there was a good lid on it nothing bad had happened to it even when I fell into the water. . . . We opened the lid and it was the most wonderful mirabelle jam of my life—little wonder when your throat is sore, from the smoke, from the fire, from all the dirt, from all the anxiety! We passed the bucket around, so that everybody could take a taste of its syrupy sweetness. It was paradise on earth, in the middle of hell![44]

From this position on the bank of the canal they had a grandstand view of the blazing buildings stretched on all sides as far as the eye could see. Directly before them lay Hammerbrook, the center of the firestorm, and the glow of Hamm beyond. To their right the docks were also in flames, all the way down to the riverside suburb of Rothenburgsort. To their left, Borgfelde, Hohenfelde, Eilbek, and Wandsbek—all in flames. It is unsurprising that the sight stamped itself on the young boy's memory.

It is impossible to tell precisely when the firestorm first started, but it certainly began long before the bombing had finished. The word "firestorm" was not written in the chronological record at Fire Brigade Headquarters until 2:40 A.M., but Hans Brunswig, who was the chief engineer on duty that night, remembers that by two o'clock the winds were so strong that it was impossible to walk through the fire station courtyard: The men had to get on their hands and knees and crawl.[45] From the study he made both at the time and after the war Brunswig estimates that the firestorm probably began as early as twenty or thirty minutes after the first bombs fell.[46] His suggestion is certainly backed up by the accounts of eyewitnesses.

By 1:30 A.M., the fires already extended from the Berliner Tor on the edge of the city center right out to the Hammer Park in the east, and from the banks of the river as far north as the Wandsbeker Chaussee. In just half an hour the RAF had created a single huge area fire that had engulfed several square miles of the city. Had this fire been left to itself it probably would not have spread any further. One of the features of firestorms is that,

The firestorm area

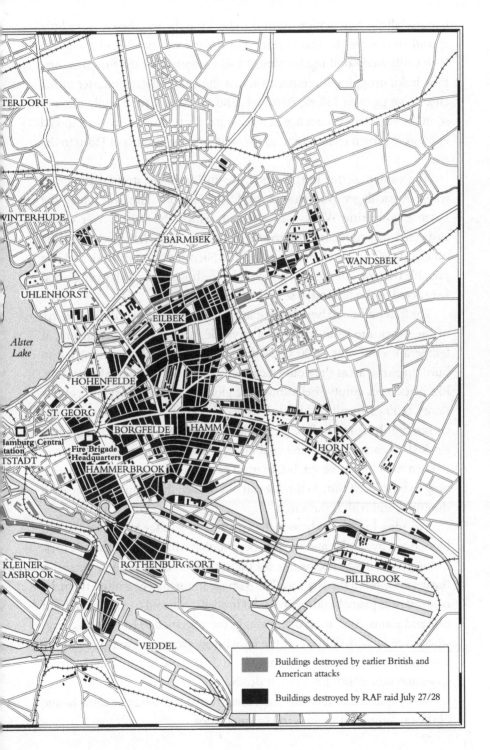

TERDORF

WINTERHUDE

BARMBEK

WANDSBEK

UHLENHORST

EILBEK

Alster
Lake

HOHENFELDE

ST. GEORG

BORGFELDE HAMM

Hamburg Central
Station
TSTADT

Fire Brigade
Headquarters

HORN

HAMMERBROOK

KLEINER
RASBROOK

ROTHENBURGSORT

BILLBROOK

VEDDEL

Buildings destroyed by earlier British and
American attacks

Buildings destroyed by RAF raid July 27/28

because all the winds blow *inward* to feed the flames, there is very little spread away from the main center. But the fire was not left to itself. The RAF continued bombing for almost half an hour after the firestorm first took hold, dropping incendiaries across the entire eastern quarter of the city. Large parts of Eilbek, Barmbek, and Wandsbek were badly hit, and soon the Fire Department began receiving reports that the fires had spread as far as the main train station to the west, and the suburb of Horn to the east.[47]

The center of this burning hell was in Borgfelde, around the point where Ausschläger Weg crosses the Mittel Kanal.[48] This was where the Lotze Engineering Works was situated, which the British War Office suspected of producing underwater mines for the Wehrmacht. On the other side of the canal, however, was the Nienstadt timber yard, and it is possible that the intense heat given off by the huge stacks of burning wood here acted as the first catalyst to the firestorm.[49]

For four and a half hours this unassuming corner of the city was the eye of the hurricane—the center of a citywide furnace that was burning at temperatures of over 1,000°C. By dawn there was hardly anything left to burn. In many areas the house facades were the only things left standing, like blackened, empty shells above the glowing rubble. Everything else—floors, ceilings, furniture, the stuff of people's everyday lives—all had been consumed. In some buildings, particularly those whose occupants had stocked up early on coke and coal for the winter, the fire would continue to burn for a long time yet, but in most cases the fire was gradually beginning to burn itself out. As the fire ran out of fuel, the raging heat began to diminish, and with it the winds.

Morning broke darkly over the city, just as Sunday had, with the sun blotted out by smoke, and no light beyond that which came from the fires. In the gloom it was impossible for the survivors to see yet how extensive the devastation to the city was. The damage immediately around them, by contrast, was plain: buildings reduced to shells, cratered roads, burned-out cars and trams. And, most distressingly, there seemed to be corpses everywhere one looked. Almost all the eyewitness accounts from this terrible morning have this factor in common—a deep sense of shock at the gruesome and ubiquitous presence of death.

Max Kipke remembers the sight that greeted him when he came to one of the underground shelters in Hammerbrook.

I went to the shelter and wanted to see if people had already come back out. But I saw only corpses, corpses, corpses. They must have wanted to reach the shelter, but did not make it. Even today, I do not understand why they were already dead. I was still in pretty good shape. The staircase which led down to the entrance of the shelter had a bend in it, and shortly after, another: the shelter was built practically two stories underground. The staircase was covered with bodies. The door to the shelter opened outward, and because it was blocked by the corpses, the people could not open it. After a while the next living being arrived, it was a marine. I asked him if he could help me. The shelter was full of people and they probably could not open the door. A third man joined us, and together we managed to clear the entrance enough, so that we were able to open the door a short way. The first people came out; they felt their way up, because there was no light—all the power lines were destroyed. Maybe it was better that they did not see anything.[50]

The sensitivities of those leaving the bunkers would not be spared for long. Once they found themselves at street level they were greeted with the most gruesome of sights, as Ruth Schramm remembers.

When we had clambered up the stairs, our first glance fell on the stacked corpses to the left of the shelter entrance. It was a double row, around ten meters long. I can still clearly see these completely blackened bodies before me. There was no time to waste thoughts on them; we were forced to protect our hair.[51]

Confronted with such sights on all sides, parents did whatever they could to shield their children from the horror of it all. Else Lohse was a young mother who had literally thrown her children out of a ground-floor window onto the Hammer Landstrasse to save them from the flames. Now she was doing all she could to keep them safe, both physically and emotionally.

The little ones kept asking, as we stepped over the dead: "What is that, mama?" I said to them, "Don't step on that or you will fall. It is a branch, fallen from a tree." "Mama, here is another one," and so it went on from Meuthien to Biederbeck, one after another. Some hugged themselves, others folded together or their limbs spread . . . you cannot imagine the scene, how the Hammer Landstrasse looked. Burned-out cars stood at angles in the road, dead upon dead.[52]

Traute Koch also remembers the corpses on Hammer Landstrasse. She had spent the night in a house that was relatively safe because it had been burned out in a previous raid—now her mother was trying to lead her away from the fires to safety.

> We came to the junction of the Hammer Landstrasse and Louisenweg. I carried my little sister and also helped my mother climb over the ruins. Suddenly, I saw tailors' dummies lying around. I said, "Mummy, no tailors lived here and, yet, so many dummies lying around." My mother grabbed me by my arm and said, "Go on. Don't look too closely. On. On."[53]

It is impossible to imagine the trauma such gruesome sights must have caused to these exhausted people, who were already in shock from their experiences of the night. Many were driven to the brink of madness. Erich Titschak, who had spent the night out in the streets, remembers seeing a woman screaming "They're coming to kill us!" repeatedly, despite the fact that both the bombers and the firestorm had long since gone.[54]

With so many people struggling to reach the open spaces, the parks were soon filled with the screams of the injured and the weeping of those who had been forced to leave loved ones behind. One woman describes sitting in what was left of the rose garden in the Stoltenpark, listening to all the terrifying sounds still around her.

> In front of me was the front of Heidenkampsweg, and I saw building after building collapse. Behind me was the animal sanctuary where the animals slowly burned. On top of the cries from the surrounding burned and wounded, the last calls of the dying, and the cries for help from the collapsing buildings, came the barking and screeching of the cats and dogs. It was enough to drive you to despair.[55]

Hans Jedlicka, who was also sheltering in this park, witnessed similar things.

Churchill and Roosevelt at the Casablanca Conference,
where the Combined Bomber Offensive was first agreed. (U.S. Army)

Sir Arthur Harris,
commander-in-chief of RAF Bomber
Command (Imperial War Museum)

Major General Frederick L. Anderson,
commander of U.S. VIII Bomber
Command (U.S. Air Force)

Hitler arrives at Hamburg's airport on one of his many prewar visits. He never returned to the city once war had broken out, despite appeals for a morale-raising tour after the city was destroyed. (Archiv Erna Neumann)

Karl Kaufmann, Hamburg's gauleiter and a loyal disciple of the Führer (Studio Schmidt-Luchs)

Hermann Göring (left) was head of the Luftwaffe, but it was Erhard Milch (right) who ran the show. Chief of Air Staff Hans Jeschonnek (center) shot himself shortly after the bombing of Hamburg. (Private collection)

The heart and soul of Hamburg:
The docks and shipyards were the main targets of the raids.
(Denkmalschutzamt Hamburg)

Hamburg before the war. Narrow
streets like this allowed fires to
spread rapidly. (RAF Museum)

RAF ground crew prepare bombs before loading them into a Stirling bomber. (Imperial War Museum)

Secret weapon: A factory worker cuts strips of "Window" to the right length. (Imperial War Museum)

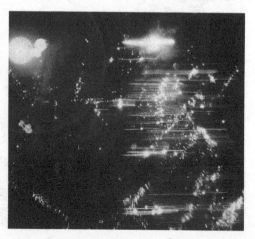

Hamburg from the air, on the night of July 24. The center of the picture shows the Neustadt on fire, with bombs spreading back toward Altona at the bottom. (Imperial War Museum)

Colin Harrison: "One minute I was a schoolboy, next minute they called me a man and put me in an aeroplane." (Private collection)

Bill McCrea: "When we were detailed on the first Hamburg raid we thought, 'Now we'll see what it's *really* like!'" (Private collection)

Doug Fry (center) hours before he was shot down at the end of July 1943. (Private collection)

The lead crew of the USAAF's 303rd Bombardment Group before their mission to Hamburg on July 25. The pilot, Major K. R. Mitchell, is second from the left at the back. (Mighty Eighth Air Force Museum, Georgia)

A group of men clears the rubble on Grosse Bergstrasse in Altona, shortly after the opening raids. (Denkmalschutzamt Hamburg)

A typical formation of B-17 Flying Fortresses,
with German fighter aircraft above. (U.S. Air Force)

American bombs fall on Howaldtswerke shipyards, July 26, 1943. (U.S. Air Force)

Hamburg women and children run for cover during an air raid warning.
(Studio Schmidt-Luchs)

Some of the city's 45,000 dead litter a street in the suburb of Hamm.
(Denkmalschutzamt Hamburg)

The changeful nature of the firestorm produced some gruesome contrasts:
This body of a pregnant woman could almost be sleeping, while the corpses behind
her are charred and mummified beyond recognition. (Imperial War Museum)

Even before the evacuation order was given, the *Ausgebombten* began to flee the city. Here a family struggles to rescue a few of their possessions. (Studio Schmidt-Luchs)

Survivors issued with emergency rations at one of the refugee assembly points. (Josef Schorer/Museum für Kunst und Gewerbe, Hamburg)

Elbstrasse (now Neanderstrasse) before the raids. (RAF Museum)

Elbstrasse after the raids. (RAF Museum)

The clean-up operation: Hamburg workers clear the entrance to a buried air raid shelter. (Imperial War Museum)

A prisoner from Neuengamme concentration camp loads charred body parts into a bucket. (Bildarchiv Preussischer Kulturbesitz)

Ruined landscape: After the Gomorrah attacks, Volksdorfer Strasse in Barmbek was little more than a pathway cleared through the rubble. (Denkmalschutzamt Hamburg)

In Hamm only the facades of buildings still stand; everything else had been turned to ash. (Imperial War Museum)

Life amongst the ruins: For the rest of the war, and for years afterward, families were forced to live in the most basic of conditions wherever they could find shelter. (Denkmalschutzamt Hamburg)

Just one of the four mass graves where 36,918 bodies are buried. Thousands more were never recovered. (Private collection)

How long we stayed in the Stoltenpark I no longer know. We watched the flaming hell of Hammerbrook. It still surprises me that anyone at all was able to make it through there alive. Again and again people came running over the bridge into the park. Screaming people with dreadful burns. One young woman especially stays in my memory. I still have the picture before my eyes. She came screaming out of the smoke over the bridge. She was completely naked and barefoot. As she came closer I saw that her feet were nothing but charred stumps. As soon as she found safety she fell down and died.[56]

Herbert Wulff, a sixteen-year-old boy who had spent the night huddling between an advertising pillar and the wall of a bridge, remembers the scene the next morning, after the fires had died down. Buildings were still burning, his city was utterly ruined, and there were horribly disfigured corpses scattered across the Heidenkampsweg.

But the most gruesome sight we must have seen was the people, lying on the ground completely naked, no longer recognizable as man or woman, with a centimeter-thick burned crust covering them, seemingly dead, but still giving their last signs of life through guttural sounds and small movements of their arms. This appalling sight will stay with me all my life.[57]

It is impossible to say with any accuracy how many people died that night. Rumors at the time put the death toll at 100,000, and for once the figure was not entirely far-fetched. Because of the chaos that reigned in the aftermath of the catastrophe German officials were never able to say for certain which deaths occurred during which air raid, but the official number for the whole series of attacks that week was eventually calculated at 42,600.[58] The vast majority of these deaths happened during the firestorm of July 27/28.

Terrifying as this total is, it is a miracle that the final figure was not higher still. One quarter of the population of Hamburg lived within the bombed area—427,637 people, according to official figures—and their numbers were swelled even further by the influx of people made homeless by the first heavy attack.[59] And yet more than 90 percent of this population managed to escape with their lives. Many of these people lived outside the edges of the firestorm, but even in Hammerbrook and Hamm the number who survived still outweighs the number that died.[60]

To survive the terrible conditions caused by the firestorm required not only incredible physical stamina, but huge courage and an unwavering determination to survive. Fugitives had to face the combined dangers of fire, high-explosive bombs (many of which were on time-delay fuses), falling masonry, and hurricane-force winds. Not only this, but they had to maintain the presence of mind to battle against the wind rather than let themselves be carried along by it, and to seek out shelter in the most unpromising of places. Many of these people refused to give up despite terrible injuries: More than 37,000 people were wounded during this series of attacks—again, the vast majority of them on the night of the firestorm.[61]

There was a strong element of chance involved in who survived and who did not: Sometimes a family would make a sensible decision over which way to run only to find their hopes crushed by the collapse of a building, or a sudden change in the direction of the wind. Even so, there were certain groups that were definitely more vulnerable than others. The very old and the very young were often the first to succumb to the force of the firestorm. According to the Hamburg Police Report the winds were so strong that "children were torn away from their parents' hands by the force of the hurricane and whirled into the fire."[62] Another eyewitness who described the "tornado-like storm" claimed it was so strong that it was almost impossible to fight it: "Elderly people, who were unable to walk well, were obliged to give up this impossible fight, and the flames greedily made their way over this prey."[63] A man in front of her was set alight like this, and "in less than ten seconds he, too, became a living pillar of fire."

The bodies of these people, along with hundreds of others, were later found where they had fallen. They were nearly always face downward, their arms thrown around their heads as if they were trying to shelter their faces from the heat as they died.[64] Most of the bodies were charred and shriveled to half their normal size. Some were so badly burned that the fat from their tissues had seeped out of them, forming pools around their bodies. Others, by contrast, were completely unburned. Absurdly, many of these were completely naked except for their shoes—the city coroner later concluded that they had probably tried to flee in their nightclothes, only to have them torn away or burned off in an instant by the heat of the storm.

But far more died in the shelters. In the east of Hamburg, there were relatively few purpose-built public bunkers—most people were forced to make do with the basements of their apartment buildings. When some of these were opened up the next day there was nobody left alive inside: They had all succumbed to the incredible temperatures generated by the fires. In some basements the heat had been so great that everything inside was charred beyond recognition, including the bodies of the occupants. But the worst killer was the smoke and carbon monoxide generated by the fires. One woman remembered afterward how the lack of oxygen had affected those in her shelter.

> The very small children fell asleep first, then the four-to-six-year-olds, then the slightly older, then the adolescents and finally the old. I knew what this sleep meant. Many never woke up, because our rescue came very late—we could not be saved sooner because of the terrible heat that raged on the street. . . . We owe our lives to an armaments factory worker who was looking for his wife, and looked in the Gothenkeller and found us all unconscious. This man then informed the police station on Nagelsweg. Consequently fifty soldiers were sent to carry us out and, in the first instance, lay us in the open in front of Gothenhaus so we could breathe some oxygen . . . I regained consciousness as three soldiers lifted me, and a fourth, who stood nearby, said: that is number 238.[65]

It is probable that as many as 70 percent of those who died were killed by smoke inhalation or carbon monoxide poisoning.[66] Their bodies were sometimes found piled up around the exits to the shelters, as if they knew that they were in danger but were unable to escape. More often, though, they were found seated at tables, or leaning peacefully against walls, as if they had simply fallen asleep.[67] These men, women, and children paid the price for following official advice not to leave their cellars until the All Clear was sounded. Had they done so, and taken their chances in the inferno, many more people might have been saved.

As the storm died down, those who had survived the night began to move once more. Often their first instinct was to leave the city as soon as possible, but many had become separated from their families during the frantic escape from their basement shelters, and to leave without them was too painful to consider. People began to mill about—some even venturing back toward the fires in the hope of finding friends and loved ones still alive.

Sixteen-year-old Herbert Wulff was one of the lucky ones. He had seen his sister run off several hours before, and had lost his mother in the smoke and chaos of the night. Now, in the gloom of morning, he was desperately trying to find them once more.

> It was a terrible twilight, as I now first began to make out the many corpses and the devastation all around. But of course my first worries were now for my family. Had they managed to survive? Luckily I found my mother again nearby, where I'd left her. She herself was unhurt, but beside her lay two dead bodies. Our joy at seeing one another again was huge. I took my mother with me to the other side of the street and started the search for my sister and father. And I was lucky. I found my sister nearby where we had last seen her during the night. She, too, had survived, albeit with bad burns on her legs caused by the devilish phosphorus. I myself had picked up some small burns, but nothing too bad. And then, like a wonder, my father turned up, relatively unscathed. He had had an unbelievable odyssey behind him. Our joy at seeing one another again was overwhelming, and we were simply indescribably lucky to have survived this purgatory.[68]

Others were not so lucky. Desperate stories began to emerge, of mothers losing their children in all the smoke and darkness, of children losing their parents when their buildings collapsed—stories that would be repeated again and again in the days to come. Countless others simply did not know what had become of their loved ones. They picked their way through the crowds desperately searching and calling out people's names. Occasionally family members were reunited this way, but for the most part their calls echoed round the parks unanswered.

Meanwhile, those who had no one to look for remained silent, dazed by the events they had just experienced. Many, including some of the eyewitnesses quoted here, were too badly injured or burned to do anything but stay where they were. Herbert Wulff and his sister both had fairly bad burns. "Albert H.," who had watched his brother-in-law die in the fire, was himself badly burned and suffering from exhaustion. Fredy Borck's eight-year-old brother fell into the flames as they were being evacuated from their Rothenburgsort cellar and burned his legs severely.

One of the most common injuries was burns to the eyes. After spending the night in the open, Erich Titschak complained that his eyes hurt so much he could no longer keep them open. Hans Jedlicka also had scorched eyes, as did Else Lohse and her son Peter, who very soon began to lose their sight.[69] Erika Wilken's eyes were so badly damaged during her ordeal in the Grevenweg public toilets that by the time she and her husband were being evacuated she could no longer see at all. "From Horn onwards our eyesight became worse and worse, and once we reached the compound we were already blind."[70] Perhaps it was a blessing in disguise. In most cases their eyesight would later return, but for now at least they were spared some of the gruesome sights others were having to endure.

Most of the injuries that occurred were caused by the incredible heat—inflamed lungs, scorched eyes, severe burns—but there were also many people who had broken bones through the strikes and blasts of high-explosive bombs and falling masonry. When the authorities finally arrived en masse to oversee the evacuation, these were the people who were taken away first, carried off in whatever vehicles could be commandeered: boats, trucks, and even horse-drawn carriages. Most people, however, were forced to walk to the edges of town before they could find transport. All the normal methods of escape—the trams, the subways, and the rail links—had been utterly destroyed. Most of the roads were also completely impassable. The only transport conduit relatively unaffected was the river, and even this was strewn with the debris of blasted boats and buildings.

As tens of thousands of people began to stream out of Hamburg, they left behind them a broken city, shrouded in smoke, in many places still burning. Despite the terror that they had all experienced there, it was impossible to leave without a last glance back at the place that had once been their home. For many it seemed like their final farewell. In a sense it was—although most would return to Hamburg in future months and years, it would never be the same city again. In the course of a single night almost a quarter of it had simply been erased from the map.

Henni Klank, who had escaped to the river with her newborn baby, was one of those who left by the city's most ancient form of transport—by boat. She remembers her departure as a final moment of supreme sadness.

> The boat was supposed to go to Lauenburg, and what took place aboard it on the journey is almost beyond description. There was no wound-dressing material, only paper bandages. I helped a young mother dress her half-burned baby with my makeshift gauze-nappy. We couldn't do more.... The woman and also the others were all in a state of shock. We glanced back once more at our broken and beloved Hamburg, across which a giant mushroom cloud was spreading. It was as if it wanted to say: I'll cover up all of this horror that descended on Hamburg tonight, for ever![71]

Chapter 17

THE "TERROR OF HAMBURG"

A stream of haggard, terrified refugees flowed into the neighbouring
provinces. In every large town people said: "What happened to
Hamburg yesterday can happen to us tomorrow."

—LUFTWAFFE GENERAL ADOLF GALLAND[1]

The events of July 27/28, 1943, shook the Nazi hierarchy to its very core.
Writing in his diary a few days later, Joseph Goebbels called the disaster
"the greatest crisis of the war."[2] For once, the normally resourceful propaganda minister seemed at a complete loss for what to do.

A city of a million inhabitants has been destroyed in a manner unparalleled in history. We are faced with problems that are almost impossible
of solution. Food must be found for this population of a million. Shelter
must be secured. The people must be evacuated as fast as possible. They
must be given clothing. In short, we are facing problems there of which
we had no conception even a few weeks ago.[3]

Many other key figures in the Nazi establishment were just as shaken. Albert
Speer, the minister of armaments and war production, told Hitler that if
the British managed to attack another six German towns on the same scale,
armaments production would be brought to a complete halt.[4] Erhard
Milch, the state secretary for air, went even further. "It's much blacker than
Speer paints it," he told the members of his ministry. "If we get just five or
six more attacks like these on Hamburg, the German people will just lay
down their tools, however great their willpower."[5]

The crisis of confidence became so bad that Hitler was forced to take
action to avert a collapse of morale in the party. A few days after the catastrophe, the Führer instructed Goebbels to speak to an assembly of ministers

and gauleiters to "inject some concrete into them." Ever faithful to his master, Goebbels did as he was told. It was a tense meeting. During the discussion, Milch repeatedly interrupted Goebbels with the almost treasonable outcry, "We have lost the war! Finally lost the war!" The propaganda minister had to appeal to his honor as an officer to make him quiet down.[6]

While those around him were in deep shock at the scale of the disaster, Hitler himself appeared to react to the situation in much the same way that he reacted to all such catastrophes: by remaining in denial. To Speer's announcement that further British attacks might halt German arms production, he simply said, "You'll straighten all that out again." Neither was he sympathetic to the victims of the firestorm. When Hamburg's gauleiter, Karl Kaufmann, repeatedly telegraphed him begging him to come and visit the stricken city, Hitler steadfastly refused. When Kaufmann asked him at least to receive a delegation of some of the more heroic rescue crews, Hitler refused that, too. He was simply not interested in Hamburg, nor the fate of its people.[7]

On the other side of the North Sea, the mood was precisely the opposite of the mood in Germany. While the Nazis imposed a virtual news freeze on all but the most general reports about the firestorm, the British and American authorities were quick to announce the details of their success to the international press. In London, the *Times* printed a large photograph of American bombs falling on the Howaldtswerke shipyards under the headline "Hamburg Battered": "Air bombing reached a new intensity on Tuesday night," it said, causing damage that would "far exceed that caused in any previous attack."[8] The *Daily Express* was even more graphic. "RAF blitz to wipe Hamburg off the war map" was the front-page headline on July 31:

> It now seems plain that Air Chief Marshal Sir Arthur Harris, our bomber chief, has set himself the task of wiping out completely the town of Hamburg from the enemy's war effort. . . . Bombs went down at the rate of about 50 tons a minute for 45 minutes, and nothing the guns and night fighters could do could stop them.[9]

In America, the headlines were equally triumphant: "Hamburg Pictured in Ruin and Death," wrote the *New York Times;* "Swedes Report Hamburg

Has 'Ceased to Exist,'" claimed the *New York Herald Tribune;* while the *Washington Post* went with "Heaviest Raid Dumps Death on Hamburg."[10] To add weight to their reports, they quoted statistics and eyewitness statements from the neutral press in Sweden and Switzerland. Lest the German people miss out on the news, propaganda leaflets were printed showing photographs of the devastation, to be dropped all over Germany in the next few weeks. The caption to the photograph read, *"Das war Hamburg"* ("This was Hamburg")—with the verb deliberately in the past tense.[11]

The Soviets also appreciated the propaganda value of the catastrophe. In the days after the firestorm, Russian soldiers erected loudspeakers along the front to broadcast the news across no-man's-land to the German troops. These announcements came with the suggestion that, since the Germans were suffering just as badly at home as they were at the front, they should simply surrender. Most of the German troops did not believe the announcements, of course; they were used to hearing such propaganda from their enemies. It was not until they were able to return to Hamburg on leave that they discovered the true extent of the devastation for themselves. As one veteran from the Russian Front remembers, despite the warnings, their first view of the city left them in a state of shock. "When we saw it [Hamburg] we just stood there in the train and thought, this cannot be. It was not only me, but all of us were completely shattered by it. We thought, that's it, the war's over."[12]

Soldiers who found themselves caught up in the bombing said that it was far worse than being at the front.[13] Some went further, claiming that it was worse even than the military disaster at Stalingrad. For example, Martha Bührich remembers meeting a soldier in the street who said that "he had witnessed the hell of Stalingrad, but that it was nothing compared to this terrible night." After the war, many others said exactly the same thing.[14]

Looking back, the implication of such statements is clear. If Stalingrad was the great turning point of the war for the German army, then Hamburg was the equivalent turning point for German civilians. Before the firestorm most people believed that their towns were largely safe from the Allied bombers; afterward they realized that these towns would be lucky to escape without being erased from the map. Hamburg made it clear that the Allies, and the British in particular, were intent on annihilating one city after another until Germany capitulated. It was beginning to look as though the terrible predictions Douhet had made in the 1920s were at last coming true: The home cities had become more dangerous than the very battlefields themselves.[15]

While government ministers were panicking over how they would handle the disaster, the city authorities in Hamburg could not allow themselves such a luxury. With vast swathes of the city still on fire, and tens of thousands already abandoning the city in panic, something had to be done immediately. Early on the morning of Wednesday, July 28, gauleiter Karl Kaufmann officially announced the evacuation of Hamburg. Women and children were told, not asked, to leave the city within the next few hours.

As Goebbels had suspected, the evacuation of Hamburg was to be a logistical nightmare. According to the city's disaster plan, displaced people were supposed to be evacuated by rail—but since all the train lines in the center of Hamburg were now down, and most of the city's stations were utterly destroyed, this was impossible. The roads were not much better. Throughout the main disaster area the streets were full of bomb craters, and rubble from collapsing buildings had made many of them completely impassable. To make things worse, there were still whole districts on fire. In such circumstances the only course of action was for refugees to make their own way to the edges of the firestorm area on foot. They would be guided by the emergency services, and the proper evacuation would take place from there.[16]

In an attempt to bring order to the chaos, the city authorities were forced to improvise wildly. Almost all the collecting centers for the homeless had been destroyed or damaged, so the authorities quickly designated four huge refugee camps: at the Moorweide Park, at the horse-racing courses in Horn and Farmsen, and at a large open space in Billstedt. Since nobody knew about these new refugee centers, loudspeaker vans were sent to roam the outer edges of the firestorm area telling people where they should go. At the same time dressing stations were set up on all the major exit roads in order to cope with the huge numbers of wounded people who were staggering out of the destroyed city. Enormous amounts of food and drink were brought in to feed everyone. On the first day alone half a million loaves of bread were given out, along with 16,000 liters of milk, beer, tea and coffee.[17]

Meanwhile, the authorities commandeered trucks, buses, and even horse-drawn carriages from every possible source in order to get people away from the city. Ten thousand men from the armed forces were brought in to help with the operation, along with all the police and SS forces that neighboring areas could spare. They shuttled people from the refugee camps to the nearest major stations—more than 750,000 people in total—before sending them on to cities throughout the Reich. A further 50,000 were evacuated on the river, and thousands more were flown out from Fuhlsbüttel airfield. Within just a few days over a million people were evacuated from the city, the largest such transfer ever carried out in Germany at such short notice.

When one looks at these figures they are undeniably impressive. On a grand scale it seems that the evacuation worked smoothly and efficiently—incredibly so, given the extent to which the authorities were forced to improvise. But this was not how most people experienced it. As they stumbled out of the burning suburbs, the streets strewn with corpses and rubble, many of the refugees were too exhausted to make it as far as the collection centers. Occasionally trucks arrived at seemingly random locations to help people on their way, but there were too few of these to make much of a difference, and many mothers were forced to stand with their children on street corners hoping to catch a ride on an army truck or in a private car.[18]

Huge numbers of people did not wait to be processed through the official collection centers, but made their own way to nearby towns and villages in the hope of finding shelter there. It is important to remember that not everyone was supposed to go: Officially, it was only the city's women and children who were evacuated, while the men were meant to stay behind to continue working. In reality, many of the men also left in order to take their families to safety. Nobody considered stopping them.

Within hours, all the satellite towns of Hamburg were utterly swamped with refugees. Even towns farther away were unable to cope with the numbers: It was one thing to take people away from Hamburg, but another thing altogether to find them places to stay. For example, when Heino Merck fled to his sister's house in Kellinghusen he found it already full of refugees.[19] Ilse Grassmann and her children were unable to stay with her sister-in-law in Wittenburg because the house was already jam-packed with other relatives in the same plight.[20] Erwin Krohn described the scene when he arrived in Neumünster as "an unparalleled chaos. Forty thousand inhabitants and 160,000 Hamburgers. Nobody knew where to go."[21]

With so many people on the move the city authorities were terrified of a breakdown in law and order. To prevent possible riots they stationed extra police and even SS units in the refugee collection points. Helmuth Saß describes the scene he witnessed when he arrived in the Stadtpark on Friday morning:

> On one side of the grass, I saw a detachment of the SS marching. They set up heavy machine guns every two meters. As I approached this row, I was curtly sent away. I asked Mr. Lukas what the SS were doing here. He answered: "They are supposed to guard us." And so it was that we, the *Ausgebombten,* were not to make a stand against the Nazi Party, otherwise we would be shot.[22]

However, the police could not be everywhere at once, and there are countless examples of ordinary people openly expressing their hostility toward the Nazi authorities away from the main collection points. Hans J. Massaquoi describes an incident at a station where "a man in a brown Nazi uniform came into sight, and a woman screamed at him from the train, 'You pigs, it's all your fault!'" She continued shouting similar state-threatening accusations until someone from her company "literally gagged her by holding a towel over her mouth."[23] He also tells the story of a soldier friend of his who was determined to desert the army, on the grounds that in the wake of this catastrophe "the war can't last longer than a couple of weeks, perhaps only a couple of days."[24] Another refugee, Lore Bünger, remembers hearing a man proclaiming loudly, "That Hitler! The pig should be hung!" before his wife warned him to be quiet.[25]

There was very little the authorities could do about such outbursts. They certainly could not have arrested everyone who voiced their anger—in the desperate atmosphere that prevailed in the wake of the firestorm, to do so would have risked causing riots. People no longer felt they had anything more to lose; consequently, for the first time in ten years, they were openly defying the Nazis without fear of reprisals. Hans Erich Nossack recounts a scene that speaks volumes:

> In the Harburg train station I heard a woman who had broken some rule or other screaming, "Go ahead, put me in prison, then at least I'll have a roof over my head!" and three railway policemen didn't know

what else to do but turn away, embarrassed, leaving the crowd to calm the woman down.[26]

Had they known how common such outbursts were, the Allies would have been delighted. This was exactly what was supposed to happen in the wake of a huge bombing raid: anger at the authorities leading to open defiance and, finally, revolution. But the final link in this chain never materialized. The speed and relative efficiency of the evacuation was certainly a factor in avoiding any serious civil unrest: By carrying people away from the city the authorities dispersed any potential trouble. And besides, the disaster had left most people too exhausted and apathetic to cause much more than a token fuss. It was simply too big an event to blame wholly on the Nazis. It seems that most people regarded the firestorm almost like an act of God: In such circumstances the state was "something completely irrelevant that could neither be blamed for a fate such as Hamburg had suffered nor be expected to do anything about it."[27]

The evacuation of Hamburg was a huge event for Germany, arguably more important to the course of the war than the firestorm itself. Terrifying as it had been, the firestorm affected only a single city. The evacuation, on the other hand, affected the Reich as a whole—indeed, until the Allied invasion in 1945, the mass migration of refugees from Hamburg was probably the biggest single event on the home front of the entire war. Until now, many ordinary Germans in the smaller towns and cities had known of the scale of Allied bombing only through what they read in the newspapers or heard on radio broadcasts. But as a deluge of refugees washed over the entire country, even those in rural areas now came face to face with people who had suffered the most unimaginable horror. The stories they brought with them could not be dismissed as mere rumors, and their message was clear: Nobody was safe anymore. What had happened in Hamburg would soon happen, in some degree, to every city in Germany.

The psychological effect this had on the country as a whole is incalculable. Years later, many would remember it as a defining moment of the war. For example, Adolf Galland, the Luftwaffe's most senior fighter general, claimed in his memoirs that the constant stream of shattered, frightened refugees spread what he called the "Terror of Hamburg" to even the remotest villages of the Reich: "A wave of terror radiated from the suffering city and spread throughout Germany. . . . Psychologically the war at that moment had perhaps reached its most critical point."[28]

Accounts from ordinary civilians certainly back up such claims. "I'll never forget the scene," says Margret Klauß, who was sixteen at the time. She had turned out at Lübeck station with the League of German Girls to hand out food and drinks to the refugees. "Most of them just sat there full of apathy, the horror still in their faces. Others hurried from wagon to wagon, calling the names of missing relatives in the desperate hope of finding their spouses, parents, or siblings again. It was heartbreaking."[29]

Hiltgunt Zassenhaus saw the beginning of the exodus after the first night of attacks, as lines of bizarrely dressed people traipsed past her window.

> There were women who dragged along in their winter clothes, who had draped themselves in fur coats. They panted in the heat. There were women in flimsy summer dresses with stockings of differing colors. The bombs had torn them out of their sleep. In their mad haste they had pulled on whatever they found, as they fell out of their burning houses. They pulled their children along with them: little feet that couldn't keep in step with their big ones. The men dragged suitcases and boxes tied up with string. They lay down on the paving stones. They pulled their shoes off. Or they lay down on the surface of the road and stared up into the darkened sky. Hardly anyone cried or complained. In their faces all life had been extinguished.[30]

Hannah Voss saw a later stage of the evacuation, on Wednesday afternoon, as trains full of refugees began to arrive in her hometown, ninety kilometers south of Hamburg. She and a friend went to the station to meet the hordes of people who were piling out of the trains; it was their job to lead the refugees to the school, where straw pallets had been laid out for them to sleep on. The sight that greeted her when she arrived at the station was pathetic in the extreme.

> They were just standing there with nothing except their bags and the clothes they were in. . . . One female came out of the train on to the plat-form, and all she had . . . was a budgerigar in a cage. I don't know how

the budgerigar survived the blast or whatever. But that is all this woman had in the world: a flimsy nightgown, no cardigan, no wrap, nothing except the cage and the budgie.[31]

Such images are certainly poignant, but they are nothing compared to the distressing scenes that occurred when some refugees had their luggage searched. One twelve-year-old boy fleeing Hamburg was stopped at the Danish border. He was traveling alone, and carrying two sacks. When customs officers made him open them they found that one contained the corpse of his two-year-old brother, killed in the raid; in the other sack were the bodies of the boy's pet rabbits.[32]

Since this is a thirdhand report, its veracity is perhaps questionable, but it is certainly true that many refugees did bring the bodies of their loved ones with them when they fled Hamburg. Friedrich Reck described seeing one such woman drop her suitcase as she tried to board a train in Bavaria. As it spilled its contents across the platform, among the toys, manicure case, and singed underwear was "the roasted corpse of a child, shrunk like a mummy, which its half-deranged mother has been carrying about with her, the relic of a past that was still intact a few days ago."[33]

Ernst-Günther Haberland described a similar event, when he met a man from his neighborhood shortly after the catastrophe.

> He had a small and a large case in his hand, and did not know where he should go. He opened the cases; in the larger one was something which looked like a burned tree stump, in the other two objects, smaller but otherwise similar. They were his wife and children, their bodies melted by the phosphor; he could not leave them behind.[34]

Many others brought the bodies of children who had suffocated as their families were in the very act of escaping.[35] It is unsurprising that they did so. In the hurry to flee Hamburg there was no time to bury them, and to abandon their bodies was unthinkable. As a consequence, many ordinary people across Germany did not merely hear about the deaths in Hamburg, they actually saw the corpses for themselves.

Despite the official suppression of all detailed news about the disaster, those who witnessed scenes like this could only conclude that what had happened in Hamburg must have been truly extraordinary in its horror. To their infinite credit, most people reacted by extending whatever help they could to the refugees. Families all over Germany immediately opened their doors and shared what they could with those who had lost everything. The state provided free food in all the major towns, but it could never have been distributed properly without the help of thousands of volunteers from the Hitler Youth, the League of German Girls, and many other community groups.

The outpouring of goodwill toward the refugees from Hamburg was as spontaneous as it was phenomenal. Hans Erich Nossack wrote shortly afterward of the "heartening experience of seeing those who had been most distant, sometimes the most fleeting acquaintances or business associates, voluntarily step into the breach with such kindness that one is shamed into asking oneself whether one would have done the same if the situation were reversed."[36] Inevitably, there were some exceptions, but in general refugees were accepted with open arms, and their welcome would not begin to wear thin for several weeks.[37]

Those who came into contact with the refugees could not help but be affected by them. The stories they brought with them were horrific. One woman told how a succession of badly wounded people had clutched at her feet and clothes as she scrambled through the fiery ruins, begging her to take them with her. She had been forced to kick them off her, because only by doing so could she escape death herself.[38] Another woman told how she had wrapped her children in pillows and thrown them out of the window to save them from the fire. Her baby slipped out of the padding and died when it hit the pavement. The mother who told this story "did not cry or complain; with the general fear, the thousands in agony, her pain was nothing special."[39] Tales like these were repeated ad infinitum all over Germany in the weeks to come.

Inevitably a feeling of gloom began to descend wherever the refugees gathered. Writing in the months shortly after the firestorm, Hans Erich Nossack claimed that the sense of total defeat was universal among the people of his city.

> I have spoken with several thousand people. . . . We were without excep-
> tion firmly convinced that the war would be over very shortly; there was
> no debating this point at all; for us, after all, the decision had already been

reached. There remained only the question of how and in what place of refuge we would be able to survive this brief interval.[40]

This sense of foreboding quickly spread throughout the nation, following the refugees along the railways to every city in the Reich. The general depression was directly comparable to the mood of the country after the defeat at Stalingrad—the difference was that, while the disaster at Stalingrad had happened over 2,000 kilometers away, Hamburg was right at the heart of northern Germany. The conclusion that everyone came to was that if Hamburg could not defend itself, despite being one of the most heavily protected cities in the Reich, then the same fate would soon come to other cities as well. Nobody in Germany was safe now.

As far as the Allies were concerned, this gloomy atmosphere was the greatest success of all. It was precisely what they had been hoping to achieve. The whole theory of area bombing depended on the spread of despair from one city to the next: The intention was to undermine the morale of the German people to such a degree that they would either abandon their workplaces or rise up against their government and demand an end to the war. Until now the Allies had been unable to deliver a blow hard enough to cause such a drop in morale. But with the destruction of Hamburg, the theory seemed at last to be working.

In order to produce the final "knockout blow" that would win the war, the RAF would have to do as Albert Speer had warned Hitler, and follow this up with the devastation of another major city. The most obvious target was Berlin, and everybody, including the Germans, expected the Allies to strike there next. The only thing that was stopping them was the fact that the nights were not yet long enough for the RAF bombers to get there and back under cover of darkness—but the nights were lengthening, and by the end of August the Reich capital would be within range. Soon observers in Washington were giving Berlin just "three weeks to live," and RAF officials in London were hinting that the city was about to get "the Hamburg bombing treatment."[41]

Germany was rife with similar speculation. In Berlin the people were so worried about what was coming to them that even the neutral press began to remark on the change of atmosphere in the city. "Fear approaching panic prevails in Berlin, and the people expect the city to be laid in ruins at any moment," claimed one correspondent from the Swedish *Aftonbladet*.[42] He described how trenches were being dug in the parks in order to protect people from the effects of a possible firestorm, and how frightened civilians were fleeing the city in fear. While the German authorities must have been dismayed at such gifts to Allied propaganda, there was nothing they could do to deny the reports. Indeed, a partial evacuation of the city had already been ordered by Joseph Goebbels himself, in his capacity as Berlin's gauleiter: In order to prevent an unauthorized exodus, the propaganda minister had instructed women, children, and nonessential civilians to leave the city at the beginning of August. When this event was finally confirmed in an official release to the Nazi *Völkischer Beobachter* a few days later, the British and American press could barely contain their glee.[43]

With the benefit of hindsight, however, all this speculation about Berlin's fate turned out to be hopelessly premature. The RAF could not possibly live up to what was now being expected of it: The firestorm they had created in Hamburg had been a matter of chance and would be virtually impossible to replicate in other cities. Nor were the Allies about to produce the "knockout blow" that would end the war. To do so they would have had to demonstrate the power to obliterate any city they wanted, at will. This meant destroying Berlin within days, not weeks, and then following it up with two or three other cities for good measure—only then would Speer's fears have the possibility of coming true. But the RAF had no intention of even trying such a feat. While Sir Arthur Harris certainly cherished hopes of teaming up with the USAAF to "wreck Berlin from end to end," he would not make the attempt until the winter of 1943–44.[44] In the meantime, there were very few suitable alternatives for a second strike: To find new targets even half Hamburg's size they would have had to fly as far as Breslau or Dresden—but during the short summer nights that would have posed too great a risk to RAF crews.[45] In the end, therefore, the concept of a knockout blow turned out to be nothing more than a mirage.

In the absence of other targets, the RAF was obliged to content itself with bombing those cities in western Germany that were within easy reach. There was nothing new about attacking Essen, or Remscheid, or Mannheim—they had all been bombed during the "Battle of the Ruhr" earlier in the year— but there was a general feeling in Bomber Command Headquarters that it was better to attack something than nothing. While important cities like

Berlin were still out of range, a return to the familiar targets might at least have the effect of destroying those industrial plants that had been missed on earlier visits.

With this in mind, Harris decided that he might as well finish the job he had started on Saturday night. So on the morning of Thursday, July 29, he ordered a third massive strike against Hamburg. If he could not finish the *war* by bombing, he would have to content himself with finishing off, once and for all, what was left of the city on the Elbe.

Chapter 18

COUP DE GRACE

I am in blood
Stepp'd in so far that, should I wade no more,
Returning were as tedious as go o'er.

—SHAKESPEARE, MACBETH[1]

Everybody in Hamburg knew that another raid was coming. In the areas that had not yet been hit, people began to stow away their most prized possessions in basements and cellars, in the vain hope that they might be spared when the bombs began to fall. Anything that was portable was piled into cars, or wagons, or even baby's prams, and the roads soon became jammed with people carting their belongings out of the city. Many traveled on foot, content to get themselves and their families away with little more than the occasional suitcase between them. The single thought that occupied everyone's minds was to get as far away from the city as possible.

While the exodus of civilians accelerated, there was also significant movement in the opposite direction. Not only were the emergency services pouring men and equipment into Hamburg, but the Luftwaffe was doing all it could to bolster the city's defenses. Mobile flak units were brought to the outskirts of Hamburg by train from all around, and huge numbers of searchlights were also beginning to arrive. Firefighters worked ceaselessly to control the flames before the Allies could return to stoke them up again, certain in the knowledge that the bombers would indeed be back. It was now merely a matter of time.

Whenever the air raid alarm sounded, everyone made directly for their shelters. The relaxed atmosphere that had prevailed just a week ago was now a thing of the past, and there was a new, frightened urgency to everyone's actions. On Wednesday night, not even twenty-four hours after the firestorm, the sirens sounded once again, and there was an immediate rush for the bunkers. It turned out to be a false alarm—the RAF was resting its crews tonight, and had merely sent four Mosquitoes over the city on a nuisance raid—but it meant that the remnants of Hamburg's exhausted population were deprived of sleep for a fifth night in a row. The next day there were no fewer than five major alarms, which repeatedly threw the rescue and evacuation effort into chaos. Some of these alarms were caused by British reconnaissance planes, but the most serious one was brought about by another large force of American B-17s heading straight for the area. It turned out that the USAAF was flying on to Kiel, so Hamburg was spared for another few hours, but the people of the city remained in a state of high anxiety for the rest of the day.

Despite being aimed at a different city, this last American raid did have another, unforeseen effect on Hamburg. Afraid that a disaster was about to overtake Kiel, the authorities suddenly withdrew all the motorized Air Protection battalions that had been drafted into Hamburg and sent them northward. In their absence, fires that had been left half-extinguished flared up, and the Hamburg fire brigade found itself hopelessly stretched all over again. The authorities had allowed panic to get the better of them, and for several hours in the middle of the day confusion reigned, before these units were at last sent back to where they were needed most.[2]

The fact that the Nazi authorities were so worried about this daytime raid on Kiel is a measure of how seriously they were beginning to take the new American threat. However, for the moment at least, the USAAF was a spent force. General Eaker had been fighting a desperate battle in the air over the past few days. On Wednesday he had lost twenty-two planes in two ill-fated missions over Kassel and Oschersleben. On Thursday he lost a further ten planes over Kiel and Warnemünde. By the end of this week alone the total loss would be one hundred planes, with the equivalent of ninety crews killed, wounded, or missing; Eaker would be forced to ground his shaken and exhausted crews for the next two weeks, just to give them time to rebuild their strength.[3]

As dusk approached on Thursday, July 29, the few people who remained in Hamburg headed straight for the bunkers—or at the very least made certain that they were within immediate running distance of somewhere safe should the alarm sound. Most of them no longer cared whether the shelters were comfortable or convenient—the only important criterion now was how safe they were. The huge *Hochbunkers* like those at Dammtor and the Heiligengeistfeld had become suddenly very popular, because of the way they had withstood the previous attacks. Few people trusted their basements any more—there was no longer any sense in taking risks.

As darkness fell, the streets quickly became deserted. A stillness descended on Hamburg unlike anything it had experienced in all its 750-year history. Almost a million people had fled, leaving whole districts empty, and soon there was nothing to disturb the silence but the wind that whistled through the glowing ruins. The city on the Elbe was little more than a ghost town.

While the remnant of Hamburg's population was seeking refuge for the night, the British were busy preparing to attack once again. For most of the day it had seemed unlikely that another raid on Hamburg would be worthwhile: Harris was worried that the smoke from the previous attack would obscure the target, making it impossible for the bomber force to locate it properly. But that afternoon a reconnaissance flight over the city had returned with the news that a light wind was blowing all the smoke inland, leaving the skies above Hamburg relatively clear. So Harris finally gave the order to proceed as planned.

For the 5,500 men who attended briefings that evening it was a case of déjà vu. Not only was the target the same, but the route there and back was fairly similar too. They would be taking off at the same time (around 10:00 P.M.), bombing at approximately the same time (shortly before 1:00 A.M.), and returning to base at the same time (at around 4:00 A.M.). The first and the last turning points were identical to Tuesday night's, and the final approach into Hamburg would be almost the same line they had taken on Saturday night.[4] In fact, everything was so similar to what had gone before that some crews began to feel that they were tempting fate. On the whole, however, most airmen seemed to think that tonight would be an easy ride, just as the previous Hamburg raids had been.

The RAF planners at High Wycombe knew that it was dangerous to cross into northern Germany so close to the points they had chosen on the two previous nights, but such was their faith in Window that they believed it was a risk worth taking. The route they had chosen was as short as they could practically make it, so that the 777 planes that took off that night could carry heavier bomb loads. In short, they believed that it was worth sacrificing a little security in order to deal Hamburg the hardest blow possible.

They knew exactly where the danger zones would be tonight. As the British Pathfinders crossed the German coast they were supposed to drop red route markers to show the way for the rest of the bomber stream. But these marker flares would be just as useful to the German night fighters in their search for prey—as soon as they were dropped, every night fighter in the area would flock to them like moths to a flame, certain that the British planes would all be passing through this one point.

The only way to protect the bombers from being ambushed, therefore, was to try to create a diversion. With this in mind, four Mosquitoes were sent to drop bundles of Window along an alternative route, to make it look as though a second bomber stream were approaching Hamburg from the direction of Bremen. To add to the deception they would also drop decoy route markers about sixty miles southwest of the bombers' real landfall.[5] The idea was that the Germans would have to split their defenses in two, making it twice as likely that the real bomber stream would slip through unmolested.

This then was the plan of attack for the night of Thursday, July 29, 1943, and with Window still working wonders nobody had any reason to suspect that it would be anything but a milk run.

Everything went according to plan until the bomber stream crossed the German coast. There were a few mishaps on takeoff, and a small percentage of early returns due to technical problems. By and large this was nothing to be concerned about, although one 100 Squadron Lancaster did collapse on the runway at Grimsby, blocking it so badly that the twelve aircraft behind it could not take off.[6] While ground staff tried to sort out the mess, the rest of the bomber stream was gathering over the North Sea and heading out toward Germany. They flew largely undisturbed until they reached their first turning point, about sixty miles northwest of Heligoland.

The problems started shortly after the Pathfinders began dropping the first route markers. As predicted, all the German fighters in the area headed straight for the markers, knowing that this was the one place they were guaranteed to find their prey. What the British had *not* anticipated, however, was how strong the German response would be. There had been a radical change in German tactics over the past five days, of which the introduction of the *Wilde Sau* fighters was only a part. Now that the

Luftwaffe could no longer rely on radar they had been forced to give their individual fighters a much freer rein. No longer were they expected to stick to their allocated "boxes" along the coast—they were now allowed to amass wherever they were most likely to find the British. German fighter controllers still gave a running commentary over the radio about the height and general position of the bomber stream, but it was up to the individual fighters to find and kill their prey, using nothing more technical than their own eyes.[7]

That the British took such a predictable route into Germany can only have helped the Luftwaffe. They were expecting the RAF to arrive at a similar point to last time, and had deployed their forces accordingly; the British decoy further south did not do much to divert their attention. With hindsight this is hardly surprising: No matter how many bundles of Window the four decoy Mosquitoes dropped, the image on the German radar screens could never have been as strong as that produced by the real bomber stream. While there is some evidence that the Germans did indeed think that a second bomber stream was approaching from the southwest, it must have been obvious that this was simply a diversion.[8] So most of the coastal night fighters seem simply to have remained in those areas where they expected the British to arrive. And as soon as the route markers went down, they pounced.

The first British bomber to be shot down was probably a Halifax from 78 Squadron piloted by Sergeant R. Snape, which crashed into the sea. Six other British planes soon suffered the same fate, all but one of them within a few miles of the first route markers.[9] The area around route markers had suddenly become the most dangerous part of the sky. Six other bomber crews were attacked here too, but were lucky enough to come back and tell the tale.[10] Out of the forty-nine crewmen shot down, only one survived— Flying Officer A. H. Boyle, who parachuted out of his 158 Squadron Halifax shortly before it crashed into the German countryside between Heide and Tellingstedt.

Veterans of the bomber war all agree on this fact: An attack from a night fighter came so quickly that there was very little time to react, and certainly no time to feel any fear. Within moments it was all over, one way or another. An attack on one Lancaster about this time showed what might happen. Flight Sergeant E. L. Pickles of 100 Squadron was approaching the coast of Germany when a burst of fire came from nowhere, blowing away the whole

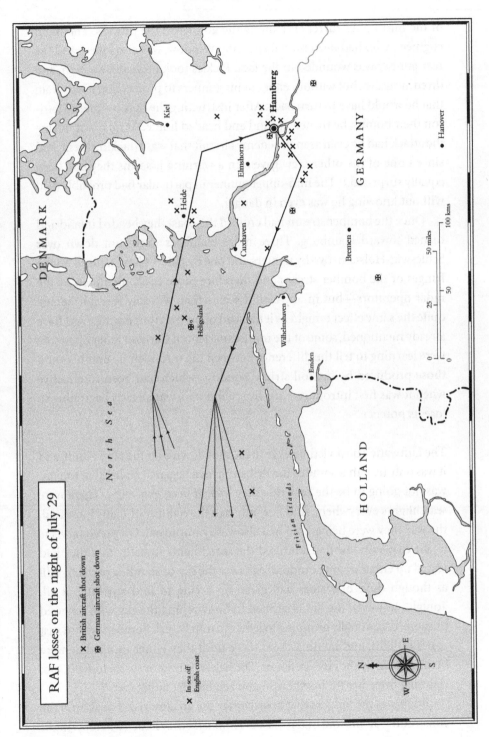

RAF losses on the night of July 29

✗ British aircraft shot down

✠ German aircraft shot down

✗ In sea off English coast

of the mid-upper turret and killing the gunner in the process. The flight engineer, who had been busy dispensing Window, was also killed, and the rear gunner was wounded in the face. Pickles took immediate action, and dived away fast, but without either of his gunners to protect him it was plain that he would have to turn back. After instructing the bomb aimer to jettison their bombs, he turned around and headed home. At no point during the attack had he even seen the enemy aircraft that was attacking them, and since none of the other crew gave him a warning it seems they had been equally surprised.[11] The mid-upper gunner in particular had probably died without knowing he was even in danger.

Once the bomber stream had crossed the coast they headed inland and turned toward Hamburg. Three more Halifaxes were shot down over Schleswig-Holstein, two by fighters and one by flak.[12] These were all on the fringes of the bomber stream and therefore more easily identified by the radar operators—but in any case it seems that Window was not having quite the same effect tonight as it had had on its previous outings. As I have already mentioned, some of the more experienced German radar operators were learning to tell the difference between the traces left by bombers and those produced by the foil strips. Window, which had been so effective when it was first introduced just five nights ago, was already beginning to lose its potency.

The Luftwaffe's next victims were those shot down over the target itself, and it was only here that some of the British airmen began to realize that tonight was not going to be the easy ride they had all been expecting. There were searchlights everywhere. And not only had the *number* of lights increased, the way they were being used had also vastly improved. On previous visits to the city, Window had confused the searchlights so badly that they had ended up either waving randomly all over the sky or standing perfectly still as though their operators had given up trying to find anything at all. Tonight, however, the lights seemed to be sweeping the sky with renewed purpose, occasionally grouping together to trap British bombers within vast cones of light, and holding them there until they either escaped or were blasted down by the city's defenses. The flak was more accurate tonight, too, claiming three British bombers in and around the target area.[13]

But it was the fighters that posed by far the greatest risk. Freed from the constraints of the old radar-based *Himmelbett* system (whereby night fighters were kept rigidly in separate "boxes" along the coast), conventional night fighters were taking enthusiastically to their new, freelance role—but the greatest successes fell to Major Hajo Herrmann and his *Wilde Sau* fighters. They were out in force over the city, and tonight was the night when they finally came into their own, lying in wait until they spotted a bomber silhouetted against all the fires before swooping down, sometimes even venturing into the flak zone to make good their attack. Of the nine bombers that were shot down above and around Hamburg, three of them were hit almost simultaneously by both flak *and* fighters, which shows how fearless this new breed of freelance fighters were.[14] There was a new determination in the way the Luftwaffe was prepared to defend its city, and it looked as though it was paying off: Halfway through the operation, the British had already lost far more planes than on either of their previous trips to Hamburg.

Flight Lieutenant H. C. "Ben" Pexton of 35 Squadron was one of the unlucky ones. As he was beginning the bombing run his Halifax was caught by first one searchlight and then several more, until the cockpit was lit up like day. He managed to release his bombs on target, but almost immediately afterward the plane was hit by flak, and the navigator was mortally wounded. Despite throwing the airplane around the sky, Pexton could not shake off the searchlights, which simply passed him on from one to another as he flew, and it was not long before a fighter came in to attack, attracted by the lights. A series of cannon shells blasted into the back of the plane, and both the rear gunner and the flight engineer were killed. As the fighter turned and came in for a second attack, Pexton's plane was virtually defenseless. Joe Weldon, the wireless operator, tells what happened next:

> It didn't seem long before we were being hit again and, this time, he got the starboard outer engine which was set on fire. Ben pressed the fire extinguisher but nothing happened. Then the fighter made another run and the pilot told us to bale out. "Better go, lads." Then, almost immediately, I think he was hit because he flopped forwards.
>
> All hell broke loose after that. The aircraft went over and must have gone into a spin. I was thrown into a heap and, when I was able to get to my feet, I found the open escape hatch above my head; it was normally in the floor. I can remember what I thought then. "Bloody hell! The wife's

going to get a telegram in the morning, saying I was missing." But I didn't think I was going to be killed; that was the last thought in my mind. There was someone else in there but I don't know whether it was the bomb aimer or the navigator. I went for that hatch; I didn't hang about, I can assure you.[15]

The crew member behind Weldon was in fact the bomb aimer, Frank Fenton, who gave him a push before following him out. These two were the only survivors of the attack. Their Halifax crashed a few miles outside the city they had just bombed.

By now it should be obvious just how dangerous the skies over Hamburg had become. However, for one small group of bombers the situation was even worse than for the others. Due to a mix-up at Scampton airfield, nine Lancasters of 57 Squadron had been sent out with the wrong "time on target"—while everyone else was due to have finished bombing by 1:30, this small group did not arrive at the target until twenty minutes later. The whole purpose of the bomber stream was to provide safety in numbers, and the Window that they dropped along the way could only provide a general screen for them all to hide behind. Deprived of this collective security, and brightly lit by fires that were so huge they could be seen for almost 200 miles,[16] this small group of 57 Squadron Lancasters was more vulnerable than they had ever been. The entire strength of the city's defenses was now aimed at them, and them alone.

One of the pilots of this group, Bill McCrea, still remembers the terror that gripped him once he realized that he and his comrades had arrived late.

The journey across and above a blazing Hamburg was one of the strangest I have ever undertaken. No one fired at us, no fighter attacked us, no searchlight was pointed in our direction. But as I turned away after dropping our bombs, I have never felt so exposed and so vulnerable. All I could do was to fix my eyes on the darkness beyond the fires and pray that we could reach that darkness before we were spotted by a fighter. Although we managed to fly clear without incident, one of our colleagues was not so lucky. I watched as a bomber just ahead and slightly below was subjected to a series of attacks from a fighter. It burst into flames and soon commenced its final fiery spiral into the earth below.[17]

The bomber that went down was a Lancaster piloted by Flight Sergeant E. F. Allwright, one of two planes in this small group that were shot down over Hamburg. The other, which belonged to Pilot Officer G. A. N. Parker, was hit by flak and crashed in the north of the city. Of the fourteen men in these two planes, only one managed to escape with his parachute on. The rest were casualties of an administrative bungle that had sent them out across Germany virtually unprotected.

The Luftwaffe fought the British all the way back to the coast, and then followed them far out to sea, giving up only when they reached the limit of their range. On this return journey a further four RAF planes were shot down, bringing the grand total to twenty-eight—almost the same number of planes that were lost on both the previous raids put together. In return, British gunners claimed to have destroyed four fighters, with another two probably destroyed and three more damaged.[18]

It had been a busy night in the skies over northern Europe, and one that the Luftwaffe could justifiably feel proud of. The German defenders, temporarily shocked into submission by the advent of Window, had not only reorganized, but had also learned an entirely new set of tactics in order to fight back. The general in charge of air defense, Generaloberst Weise, was so impressed with these new tactics that two days later he issued an order that they be adopted across the whole of the Reich.[19] The lessons learned by the Luftwaffe over Hamburg had a huge effect on the way they waged war, and would gradually win them the upper hand once more in the months to come.

Despite the Luftwaffe's relative success in the skies, there was little cause for celebration in Germany. The RAF's bombing had been much more scattered tonight, but even so it had been devastating. The chief of police claimed later that, in terms of physical damage at least, this was every bit as bad as the raid of Tuesday night. In Barmbek alone there was a single huge fire covering six square kilometers, where 167 kilometers of street frontage was burning. Other parts of the city had also been badly hit, especially the old town, the port, and some western suburbs like Eppendorf. In effect, "The whole of Hamburg had become one area fire."[20]

All this had happened despite the fact that the RAF had wandered off-course and marked the target fairly badly. The British plan had always been

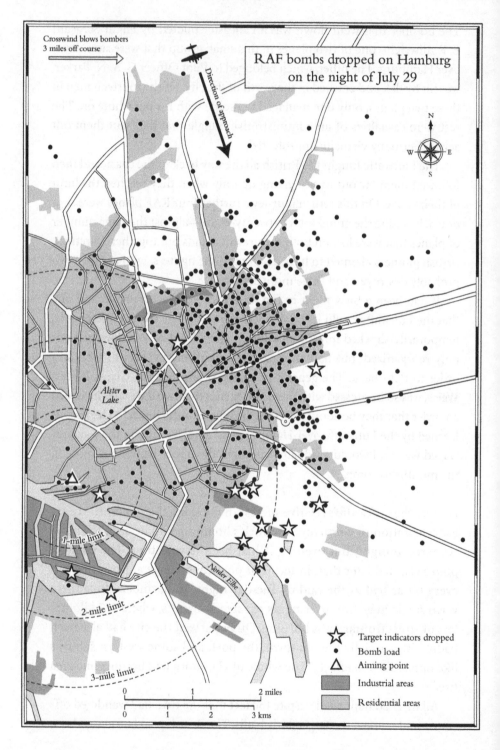

Crosswind blows bombers 3 miles off course

Direction of approach

RAF bombs dropped on Hamburg
on the night of July 29

N
W E
S

Alster
Lake

1-mile limit

Norder Elbe

2-mile limit

3-mile limit

0   1   2 miles
0   1   2   3 kms

☆ Target indicators dropped
• Bomb load
△ Aiming point
■ Industrial areas
▨ Residential areas

to concentrate their bombing in the northwest of Hamburg, in order to destroy the suburbs of Harvestehude, Rotherbaum, and Eppendorf. However, a cross wind had blown the Pathfinders off course, and they had ended up dropping most of their target indicators in the east of the city, directly over the same part of Hamburg that had already been bombed on Tuesday night. Indeed, many of the early bombs dropped on the suburb of Hamm, which was already so completely destroyed that a few more incendiaries could hardly have made much difference. But the bombing soon crept back over Eilbek and Barmbek, causing huge destruction over the northeast of the city. The original target to the west of the Alster was also badly hit, but only because the target markers were so scattered tonight.

After two whole days of desperate evacuation, there was hardly anyone left in the city to be killed. For those few who did stay behind, however, it was every bit as horrific as the night of the firestorm. Helmuth Saß was sheltering in a bunker beneath the Baptist church on Weidestrasse, but was forced to leave when a collapsing building blocked the entrance. He climbed out through the shutter openings only to find himself confronted with a mountain of burning rubble, a blizzard of sparks, and four-story houses burning all around him. As he made his escape down Vogteiweg with his mother and younger brother he suddenly became aware of the sheer absurdity of the situation.

> I thought that I was experiencing some sort of macabre play. Above in the airplanes sat the English, who were under orders to bomb us, while we ran through this burning hell for our lives. We did not know or hate each other. Suddenly, my brother's hair was burning. Shocked, we smothered the flames, but a welt remained. Shortly afterward, my mother screamed. A falling burning piece of wood had hit her calf, causing her to limp. We took shelter in the entrance to a shop, until a man who was hurrying past noticed that in the shop window firelighters, of all things, were on display. We had to get away from there.[21]

They struggled onward to an abandoned apartment building, where they found a barrel of water to douse themselves with. Then through the streets once more until they reached relative safety under a railway bridge on Barmbeker Markt. The absurdity of this kind of warfare manifested itself once more when they saw a group of men deliberately setting fire to a uniform shop at the start of the Dehnhaide. To perform an act of arson in the midst of a city that was already ablaze seems like madness, but the men justified their actions with the words, "When everything is burning, so the Party uniforms should burn too," and nobody bothered to contradict them.[22]

It was not only Helmuth Saß's shelter that was hit in this attack. Several of the larger "indestructible" public shelters were also struck. In Eilbek a high-explosive bomb hit the *Hochbunker* on the corner of Wielandstrasse and Schellingstrasse, blowing a hole through two and a half meters of reinforced concrete on the seventh floor. Two women were killed, and the other 2,000 shelterers were left in shock that such a thing was even possible.[23] But by far the worst calamity of the night was the collapse of the Karstadt department store on Hamburger Strasse, blocking the entrances to the store's two large air raid bunkers. Rescue workers managed to open one of the shelters the next day, releasing 1,200 employees from the debris. It took longer to reach the second bunker, and 370 people died inside from carbon monoxide poisoning.[24]

When such disasters were possible, it is not surprising that even in the biggest shelters people were afraid. Adolf Pauly took refuge in a bunker on the corner of Max Strasse in Eilbek when the bombers arrived.

> Hardly had we got there when all hell broke loose. In the bunker absolute darkness reigned, so we sat in our places, motionless, for hour upon hour upon hour. In the sweltering heat the air was suffocating. No matches, let alone a lamp, would light, so scarce was the oxygen. No ventilation flaps were allowed to be opened, otherwise the embers would have found their way in and 3,000 people would have suffocated in the bunker. Again and again the bunker shook under the resounding blows. Whether it was the collapsing walls of the neighboring houses, or (as was claimed) actual bombs falling on the bunker, I don't know. In the darkness we could hear general noise and cries in the floors below. There were burning people saved from the streets. Also that night two children were born in the bunker. Now and then the names of the missing would be called out. . . .
> For twelve hours I sat there with my wife in absolute darkness, fastened motionless to my place.[25]

When he came out the following day the whole of his neighborhood was on fire once again. His apartment, which had survived the previous two raids, was now ablaze, and there was no longer any choice but to follow the refugees who had gone before him. He was stunned by the whole event. The very reason he had not left the city earlier was that he did not think the British would bother to bomb his neighborhood a third time: "Yet another bomb attack on this field of ruins seemed senseless."[26]

Hans J. Massaquoi was just as shocked by the sight that greeted him when he finally left a public shelter in Barmbek.

> What awaited us was one of the saddest and most dreadful sights of our lives. The whole of Stückenstrasse—no, the whole of Barmbek, our beloved neighborhood—was practically razed to the ground. As far as the eye could see there was nothing but total devastation. In contrast to the ear-splitting noise of last night there was now a muted silence over the gruesome scenery. Here and there could be seen mummified, charred corpses. Obviously these people had decided to leave their apartments too late in order to get to a shelter. Most houses had burned right down to their foundations. Others were still in flames, and more still were nothing but burned-out ruins. One of these smoking heaps of rubble had been my home since childhood.[27]

Tonight's bombing had not caused anything like the human toll of the last attack. The official report did not attempt to put a figure on the number of dead—the city was in such chaos that it was impossible to separate the victims of one raid from those of another—but after the war a senior figure in the United States Strategic Bombing Survey made an estimate of about 800, and later estimates range between 1,000 and 5,000.[28] The material damage, however, was appalling. Only a few outlying suburbs now remained relatively untouched by the bombing—the rest were nothing but fire and ruins. There was seemingly nothing left to bomb.

And yet the RAF had still not finished with the city. In four nights' time they would direct a fourth and final massive raid against Hamburg, this time attacking from the south. That they should want to do so no longer surprised anyone in Hamburg. As the final survivors straggled out of Eilbek toward the fringes of the city they came across a scene that

Damage caused on the night of July 29

LOKSTEDT

EPPENDORF

HOHELUFT

HARVESTEHU

EIMSBÜTTEL

BAHRENFELD

ROTHERB

ALTONA

NEUSTAD

OTTENSEN

FLOTTBEK

ST. PAULI

Norder   Elbe

Köhlbrand

Blohm & Voss
shipyards

STEINWÄRDER

Howaldtswerke
shipyard

N
W   E
S

1 mile

WILHELMSBURG

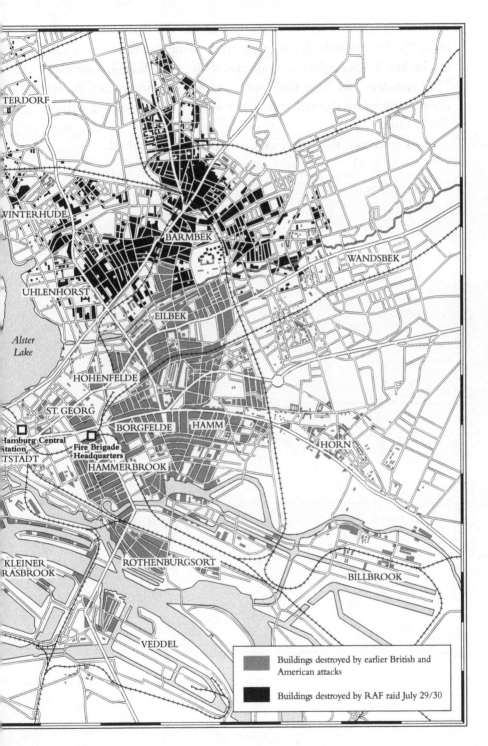

Buildings destroyed by earlier British and American attacks

Buildings destroyed by RAF raid July 29/30

seemed to symbolize the sheer insanity of the war that had overtaken them: The Jakobi Friedhof, a huge graveyard on the Wandsbeker Chaussee, was on fire. It was a sight that imprinted itself on Adolf Pauly's memory: "The cemetery had been laid waste, covered with incendiary bombs, the gravestones overturned, and there was thick smoke pouring out of a family vault."[29]

Now, it seemed, the British were even bombing their dead.

Chapter 19

THE TEMPEST

For my part, I have walk'd about the streets,
Submitting me unto the perilous night . . .
And when the cross blue lightning seem'd to open
The breast of heaven, I did present myself
Even in the aim and very flash of it.

—SHAKESPEARE, *JULIUS CAESAR*[1]

Hamburg, a proud Hanseatic city that had existed for over seven centuries, had been reduced to an endless field of smoking ruins in just a matter of days. Neighborhoods that had once been filled with bustling activity were now deserted, their streets filled with rubble, their houses reduced to empty, roofless shells. In many areas the only things left standing were the chimneys: "solitary chimneys," as Hans Erich Nossack recalled, "that grew from the ground like cenotaphs."[2]

This ghost town was populated only by small groups of soldiers, firemen, and rescue workers, with occasional gangs of concentration camp prisoners brought in to help recover the dead. Almost everyone else had gone. Thousands of wounded had been carried away to hospitals in other cities, some of them in specially commissioned hospital trains. Orphans had been gathered together and sent to join the other evacuated children in countryside schools where they would be safe from bombing. Even the inmates of the city's prisons had been either released, shipped away, or drafted in to help with the clean-up effort.[3]

There was one group of people, however, who were initially forgotten by the authorities. Many of the city's forced laborers were abandoned, while their guards fled Hamburg with their own families. Some made their way to the refugee camps, following the general exodus, but many simply stayed where they were, afraid to move without written authorization.

Wanda Chantler, a twenty-year-old woman from Poland, was one of those left behind. As mentioned previously, her barracks in Lokstedt had received a direct hit on the night of July 24, killing most of the women with whom she lived and worked. With nowhere to sleep, she had initially spent the nights outside on the grass of the factory compound, but eventually she and the few other survivors of her barracks moved into the communal dining hall instead. All were in a chronic state of shock and weak from lack of food and water. There was nobody left to provide for them; apart from the other forced laborers in other blocks, the entire city seemed to be deserted. It is therefore little wonder that Wanda's perception of the world around her began to take on an apocalyptic quality.

> All these dead bodies were lying about, and nobody knew what to do with them. And the weather was terrible. It was hot, and it was windy. It was as if all the walls had been taken away from the world, and all the clouds and the winds concentrated on Hamburg. It was terrible. It was light from the fires, but the smoke made it dark. I've never seen anything like it, and I don't think I ever will again. It was light, and yet it was dark. And you had no direction, you could not see. The smoke was choking.[4]

After three huge bombardments their whole world seemed to have been reduced to nothing but fire and smoke. On August 2, the elements finally conspired to complete the apocalyptic picture. A violent electrical storm descended upon the ruined city, its thunder and lightning a cruel celestial echo of the bombs that had been falling all week. By this point the abandoned girl had been living among the ruins of her barracks for over a week. As she and her few companions huddled together in the darkness of their factory dining hall, they watched the torrential rain outside with growing awe. "The elements seemed to have clubbed together to hit the earth at that particular point that was Hamburg," Wanda Chantler remembers. Tonight, after everything they had already been through, it was easy to imagine that these storm clouds had come here from "all around the globe," that the world war had given way to something even greater, that they were witnessing not merely the destruction of a city but the end of the world.

Astonishingly, this was the night that the British chose to launch their fourth and final major bombardment against the city. In among the thunder and lightning, the frightened girls could soon make out the distant

sound of sirens and the drone of planes, though it was sometimes difficult to tell the difference between the sound of the storm and that of the
bombs exploding. As the police report later made clear, this raid was the
final climax to ten days of terror, "in which the detonation of exploding
bombs, the peals of thunder and the crackling of the flames and ceaseless
downpour of the rain combined to form a hellish inferno."[5]

Other witnesses expressed similar dismay that the RAF should be
willing to brave such infernal conditions to pound the city all over again.
Franz Termer had fled with his family to Pinneberg, ten or twelve miles
outside Hamburg to the northwest, where he took shelter in a farmhouse.
The storm was so violent that it had woken him up, but as he and his wife
were checking on their children their attention was soon caught by a more
disturbing noise.

We had hardly finished when we heard the sirens sounding from
Pinneberg between breaks in the thunder. We couldn't believe our ears,
thought it must be a mistake. Surely the planes couldn't be coming now,
in such a heavy storm. But soon afterward a heavy flak barrage started up
a short distance away, and we could already hear the terrible buzz and
drone of heavy, four-engined bombers directly over our roof. Uninterrupted, one formation after another. The lightning flashed brightly, the
British flares shone yellow and red, and the muzzles of the flak guns
flashed like lightning in the dark night.[6]

Despite the strength of the electrical storm, the RAF had indeed arrived,
yet again, in the skies over Hamburg.

It should go without saying that Bomber Command HQ had never
intended to send their force into the face of this storm. No matter how
frightening the effect of the thunder and lightning on the shattered nerves
of Hamburg's civil population, the effect on the bomber crews, both physically and psychologically, was exponentially worse. Flying over German
territory was bad enough as it was without having to contend with weather
like this. And the likelihood of achieving a concentrated strike on the city
was virtually nil. So why were they here at all? What miscalculation or error
of judgment could have sent them into such danger?

Part of the blame at least must lie with Sir Arthur Harris. Ever since the previous attack on Hamburg on July 29 he had been itching to finish the job off, and it seems he originally intended to do so on the following night. However, he was prevented from doing so by political considerations—in the wake of Mussolini's downfall, Churchill had been keen to increase pressure on the Italians, and an urgent directive required him to plan immediate attacks on Milan, Turin, and Genoa.[7] On the night of August 1 Hamburg was back on the cards, but the raid had to be canceled because of bad weather. (Ironically it was this same storm that prevented crews from taking off—it passed through England on August 1 on its way to northern Germany, where bomber crews caught up with it twenty-four hours later.) By August 2, Harris's frustration was beginning to get the better of him. Tonight, if there was the slightest chance of destroying what was left of Hamburg, Harris was determined to take it.

The British held high expectations of this last raid. Their plan of attack was significantly different from previous operations, and reflected their growing confidence in their destructive abilities. Tonight, for the first time, they would approach Hamburg from the south, and they would have not one but two aiming points. The first waves were to drop their bomb loads on a point toward the north end of the Alster lake, with the idea that the creepback would sweep a curtain of destruction over Harvestehude and Rotherbaum—two districts that had suffered only lightly in the previous attacks. Then, halfway through the raid, the aiming point would be switched to the town of Harburg on the southern edge of the vast harbor complex.[8] It was an ambitious but well-thought-out scheme that would spell the end of those areas of the city that had so far escaped the bombs— provided everything went according to plan.

After all the postponements, Harris was keen to get started, weather allowing. As evening approached, a Mosquito was sent to check the weather conditions over northern Germany: If the storms had cleared the area then the RAF could head out for Hamburg a fourth time, otherwise they would have to scrap the whole operation yet again. To make sure they had the most up-to-date weather report, and to give themselves the greatest chance of sticking to their plan, Bomber Command delayed this weather reconnaissance flight until the last possible moment: The Mosquito did not leave Wyton airfield until 6:45 P.M. When it returned three hours later, the two-man crew told the Meteorological Office what they had seen: The skies over Hamburg looked relatively clear, but a huge cumulo-nimbus to the southwest of Oldenburg was moving briskly in the direction of tonight's target.[9] There was a chance that it would have moved on by the time the bombers reached Hamburg, but it would be a risk.

Bomber Command was fast running out of time to make a decision one way or another—if the squadrons were to get to Hamburg and back under cover of darkness they would all have to leave before midnight. After a hurried assessment, the Meteorological Office finally sent its weather report to Bomber Command HQ at 10:00 P.M. Crucially, they had watered down any worries about the storm: They claimed that there was only a "slight risk" that the bombers would encounter this dangerous weather on their journey.

Harris was normally fairly cautious when it came to the lives of his men, and on any other night he might have chosen an alternative target, or simply scrapped his plans altogether. Tonight, however, his impatience got the better of him: For such an important target a "slight risk" was one worth taking. The only concession to the weather was a modest alteration to the plan: Instead of attacking two separate aiming points in the city, the bomber force would concentrate on one, on the northwest shoulder of the Alster lake. Otherwise the raid would go ahead as briefed.[10]

Thus it was that 740 crews who had been on standby for the past couple of hours now made their way to dispersal, many of them astonished that the raid was actually going ahead. Some of them had already been told to expect violent weather, others were left to guess at the strength of the conditions from the vague warnings they had received at briefing. But all of them were about to experience a night they would never forget.

It was a blustery, overcast night when the bomber force finally took off. By midnight most of the planes were airborne and just beginning to break through the soup of cloud that covered the North Sea. For some crews the problems began almost as soon as they took off. At Scampton a Lancaster from 57 Squadron crashed on the runway and promptly caught fire, preventing six other Lancasters behind it from taking off.[11] Several planes from other squadrons did not even make it to the English coast before they were forced to turn back because of engine trouble—two of these landed so badly that they were written off, with injuries to seven crewmen.[12] A further shock came over the sea when a startled Royal Navy convoy mistook the bomber stream for a German force and opened fire on them. While it seems they did not do any damage, it was hardly a good omen.

Whatever happened on the journey across the North Sea, the real trouble did not begin until the bomber stream reached the German coast. Of all the operations that these airmen flew on, this is the one they universally remember, even to this day, and for those who finished their tour, there was nothing that even came close to the fear and confusion they were to experience tonight. It began with a sinister, almost surreal vision. Up ahead of them was a cloud unlike anything they had seen before: a huge, dark mountain of cloud, its sides cracked with deep fissures and chasms, and lit by the continual flashes of light that glinted from within its depths. Some of the crews thought that this vast cloud was in fact smoke, still rising from the burning ruins of Hamburg; many of them thought that the heavy flashes that lit it from within were some terrific new weapon in among the German flak. It was not until they got closer that they realized the truth, that this was the biggest and most violent electrical storm any of them had ever seen.

No pilot likes to fly through conditions this bad, but tonight there was nothing any of them could do to avoid it. To fly over the storm was impossible—the summit of this vast cloud rose to 30,000 feet, perhaps even higher, and apart from the handful of Mosquitoes from 139 Squadron, there was not an aircraft among them that was capable of flying that high while laden with bombs. There was no point in trying to fly around it either—to do such a thing would not only have isolated anyone who tried it, but taken him so far out of his way that he would never have had enough fuel to return home. One or two crews tried to fly under it, but gave up after sinking below 7,000 feet without managing to break free of the cloud. If they were to complete this raid there was only one choice: They must head directly into the face of the storm.

As they approached the lower peaks of this massive cumulo-nimbus the temperature began to plummet. Many crews chose this moment to turn around and head for home, sensing intuitively the danger that lay ahead. Of those that continued, most tried to delay flying through the cloud for as long as they could, choosing instead to follow the sinister rifts and valleys along its fringes. High walls of cloud loomed over them on both flanks, their dark bulk intermittently lit by sheets of lightning. Eventually these ravines would come to an end. Then there would be no choice but to head straight for the seemingly impenetrable wall before them and break through into the heart of the storm.

Bill McCrea, the same pilot who had found himself isolated on the previous raid when his squadron had sent him out twenty minutes late, remembers these moments as some of the most terrifying of his life.

The storm clouds that had been over England some 24 hours earlier were now dead ahead, dark and forbidding, and towering above the bombers by several thousand feet. I realised that what I first took to be flak were in reality lightning flashes emanating from the storm clouds that we were rapidly approaching. As we flew into the lightning-charged clouds the effect was immediate and terrifying. The air currents came first, throwing the aircraft from side to side as well as up and down. One could almost hear the airframe protest as it was subjected to these external forces. The lightning was continuous; as it flashed one could see that the clouds were sometimes broken up by eerie canyons and ravines.[13]

Major J. K. Christie, who flew a Lancaster with 35 Squadron, was another pilot who approached this storm with mounting anxiety. He recorded his impressions in his diary afterward.

Everything went smooth and according to plan until we approached Heligoland, where we started to run into clouds up to more than 20,000 feet. I carried on trying to keep above it and for some time just managed to keep popping in and out of the tops. By this time we were just about crossing the German coast. I saw numerous and colossal flashes all over the sky and for a long time I believed that the Germans had brought into action a new and terrific anti-aircraft weapon. After a certain while, we did not manage to keep on the top of the clouds and had to continue flying blind, shaken every ten seconds by terrific flashes which totally blinded me for many seconds afterwards. We got fairly heavy icing and very heavy statics.

In addition to this I had a new and very spectacular experience as the whole aircraft seemed to be completely electrified. There were huge luminous rings around the propellers, blue flames out of the wing-tips, gun muzzles and also everywhere else on the aircraft where its surface is pointed. For instance, the de-icing tube in front of my window had a blue flame around it. Electrical flowers were dancing on the windows all the time until they got iced up, when the flowers disappeared. The Wireless

Operator told me afterwards that sparks were shooting across his equipment all the time and that his aerials were luminous throughout their
lengths. I didn't feel a bit happy and tried to go down below the clouds.[14]

These mysterious blue flames were in fact St. Elmo's Fire, the phenomenon
that had mystified seafarers during the golden age of sailing ships. The
storm cloud through which they were flying was so highly charged with
electricity that it had begun to materialize in the form of a ghostly blue
light all around the aircraft.

Christie was not alone in seeing this unearthly sight; almost everyone
who flew through the storm tonight experienced this same phenomenon.
"Blue electrical discharges flashed between the muzzles of the guns," says
Bill McCrea, "and our propellers looked like Catherine wheels, as if a torch
had been fastened to the end of each blade. From time to time the whole
aircraft became shrouded in a blue shimmering light."[15] Colin Harrison of
467 Squadron still remembers the sight with awe: "We were lit up in blue
lights . . . sparks in all directions, jumping from one thing to another. And
the props—there was a beautiful blue arc where the props were turning."[16]
James Sullivan, a Wireless Operator with 156 Squadron, remembers the
same thing: "The lightning was sparking all along the fuselage and along
the guns. It looked like an electrical aircraft!"

When all around them was pitch dark, the effect of this luminous blue
light could be extremely unnerving—but it was virtually harmless. Much
more dangerous was the ice that suddenly began to build on all the leading edges of the aircraft: If enough was allowed to accumulate it could
destroy the planes aerodynamics, and the aircraft would literally fall out of
the sky.

This is precisely what happened to one Stirling of 620 Squadron, as one
of its crew members recalls:

I have never been as scared in my life and never will be again. I sat there,
petrified, then called to the skipper, "For Christ's sake, get out of this."
He started to climb more steeply but, as the Stirling's ceiling was only
about 15,000 feet loaded, we reached our maximum height and we were
still in cloud. Suddenly, we started icing up. The wings of the kite were
a white sheet. Great chunks of ice were flying from the propellers and
hitting the fuselage like machine-gun fire. Then the port wing went

down and we started dropping like a stone. After what seemed a lifetime,
I heard a distant voice whisper, "Jettison. Jettison." I have prayed very few
times in my life but this occasion was one of them and, thank heaven,
someone was listening.[17]

Ted Groom, a flight engineer with 460 Squadron, remembers a similar
thing happening to his Lancaster.

The propellers appeared like huge Catherine wheels, with ice forming
and static electricity. Chunks of ice were hitting the aircraft, and the
props and the control surfaces were being covered with ice. . . . All this
time we were losing height. This happened frighteningly quickly, and the
pilot and myself were overwhelmed with these conditions. The rest of the
crew wanted to know what was happening. Eventually, after losing several thousand feet we were back in control again. But the aircraft was still
in thick cloud. As we could not see any sky markers the decision was
made to drop the bombs and return to base.[18]

The only way to regain control of the plane was to lose as much weight as
possible, as quickly as possible, to stop the rate of fall. That is why both of
these planes jettisoned their bombs. It was also important to get rid of as
much ice as they could, especially since it could jam up the ailerons and
elevators, making it virtually impossible for the pilot to control the plane.
Ted Groom did this by desynchronizing the engines, which caused such a
vibration in the aircraft that it shook much of the ice free. It was a dangerous thing to do for any length of time, but in their case, fortunately, it
worked.

In such conditions it was a battle just to keep the aircraft controls working. The flight engineers found themselves dealing with several dangerous
problems simultaneously, as Sergeant Dennis Brookes recalled shortly
afterward.

The lightning was terrifying, flashing from one end of the kite to the
other. Both gun turrets went u/s [unserviceable] owing to ice and the
lightning. We were thrown about by thunder, and the outer hatch was
struck and wrenched open. Ice formed everywhere, and I was sweating
to help keep the controls free. . . . Great quantities of flak were bursting

all around but could not be distinguished owing to the lightning. Both
the compasses went u/s and very little control of the aircraft could be
kept. It was impossible to keep the engine tempo up and the boost
suddenly dropped off as the intake became clammed up with ice. Skipp,
whom I was standing by, told us the controls were getting very stiff to
handle and was far beyond the control of George [the autopilot]. We
were all expecting the worst and were ready to abandon aircraft, when
suddenly at 7,000 feet Skipp managed to pull her out of the dive and
began to climb again, having lost 10,000 feet in a few seconds.[19]

Tales of falling like a stone in these conditions were frighteningly common.
Sergeant J. Benny of 15 Squadron managed to pull out of his dive only at
4,000 feet. His squadron colleague Flight Lieutenant G. Bould was a mere
500 feet above the ground when he managed to regain control of his plane;
finding himself over Bremerhaven he immediately dropped his bombs and
hedge-hopped his way back to the German coast.[20]

One Halifax of 35 Squadron paid the ultimate price for these horren-
dous conditions. Sergeant A. Stephen, the mid-upper gunner, could only
watch helplessly as the aircraft's wings and propellers became coated in
thick ice, before his turret became so iced up that he could no longer see
out of it. The whole process had taken only a matter of seconds.

> I got out of the turret quickly to get my 'chute, for I felt we were not going
> to get out of this, and I was no sooner inside the fuselage when we went
> into a spin. The G force was very strong; I could not even lift my arm. I
> was in the centre section at this time and I felt someone kicking to get to
> the exit but he was pinned down like me. The spin seemed to go on for
> hours but, then, there was a crash and everything was thrown about.

After dropping through three miles of sky, Sergeant Stephen's Halifax had
crashed into the German countryside. Miraculously, he and the flight
engineer were still alive.

> When I came round . . . it was daylight and I saw that I was sitting in a
> heap of wreckage and Bert, the engineer, was lying beside me. I could not
> move but I heard someone talking outside and gave a shout. They were
> German soldiers and they came and lifted Bert and me out of the remains

of the Halifax. I remember cursing them for lifting me by the legs because they were fractured. The soldiers put us down in a field about a hundred yards from the wreckage and I saw that the part I had been in was just the two wings and the centre section. The Target Indicators were hanging out and the petrol tanks were right above them. How the lot did not blow up, I'll never know.[21]

Sergeant Stephen was the only one to survive this crash. His friend Bert eventually died in his arms a short time later; the rest of the crew had all been killed instantly.

At least four British planes were lost directly because of the ice tonight: They came crashing down into the sea, or into the German countryside, their pilots unable to do a thing to save them.[22] Another bomber was struck by lightning so badly that the pilot lost control. It crashed without ever reaching the target, killing everyone on board.[23]

The only consolation for the British was that the terrible conditions were just as bad for the German fighters as they were for the RAF. Wilhelm Johnen, a fighter pilot with III/NJG1,[24] later recorded his thoughts on the conditions he and his fellows had to endure on that terrible night.

When gusts of wind at gale force flung the machine about the sky; when in a fraction of a second the propellers, wings and engines were swathed in thick, heavy ice. . . . When devilish St. Elmo's Fire began to dance on the aerials, cockpit panes, and propellers, blinding the pilot. . . . In these moments is born the airman. . . . Pilots trust in God far more than people would believe.[25]

Without the use of their radar, German night fighters had to rely on their eyes to find their victims, but this was almost impossible in the midst of the stormclouds that filled the sky. Every now and then one of them would find a British bomber, and an extraordinary game of cat-and-mouse would develop as each aircraft weaved in and out of the clouds to escape the shots of the other.[26] Visibility was so bad that one Dornier Do217 of II/NJG3 actually collided with the bomber it was trying to attack: The pilot, Feldwebel Krauter, could not see to pull out of his attacking run before it was too late and crashed into Flight Sergeant J. A. Couper's 75

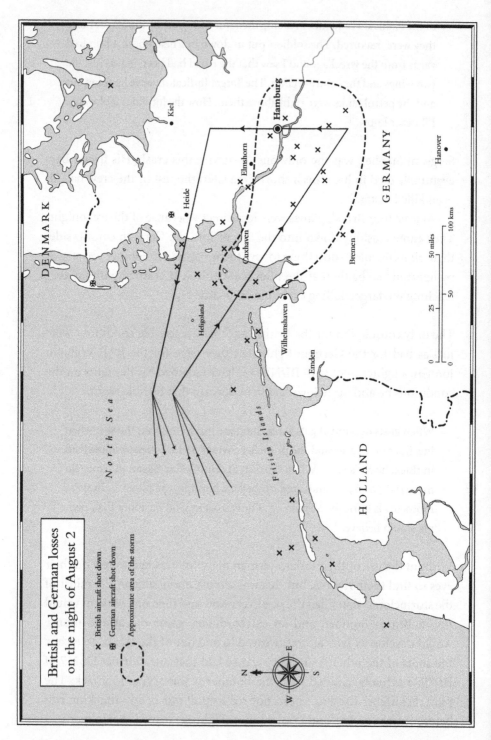

British and German losses on the night of August 2

× British aircraft shot down
✠ German aircraft shot down
⟋ ⟍ Approximate area of the storm

GERMANY

DENMARK

HOLLAND

North Sea

Friesian Islands

Kiel

Hamburg

Hanover

Bremen

Heide

Elmshorn

Cuxhaven

Wilhelmshaven

Emden

Helgoland

100 kms

50 miles

25

50

N E
W S

Squadron Stirling. Both planes went crashing to the ground. Herr Krauter escaped alive, but the crew of the British plane died in the crash.[27]

As the British bomber force approached its target it became steadily more ragged—what had begun as a tight stream was now degenerating into a dispersed scattering of individual airplanes. This was the final and perhaps most deadly effect of the storm. As the British planes were blown about the sky, their navigational instruments rendered useless by the effects of static electricity, many of them were separated from the bunch. Since Window only worked when the bomber stream was fairly concentrated, these isolated planes showed up on German radar screens. Consequently they were now in more danger than ever.

The German defenses wasted no time in picking them up. The fighters were also beginning to pick up lone bombers on their *Lichtenstein* airborne radar sets. Flak batteries began to win back some of their old accuracy, and it seems that at least four British planes were brought down by flak alone, and many more seriously damaged.[28]

Barely half the bombers that set off that night ever made it as far as Hamburg before they turned back. By the time they arrived they were in serious trouble. Hamburg's flak batteries had been heavily reinforced since the night of the firestorm, and they now let loose with a barrage that rivaled the storm itself. According to Rudolf Schurig, the commander of a flak battery in the northeast of the city, "the storm paled in the diabolic noise" given off by the German artillery. His battery alone fired 776 rounds into the sky (compared with only 547 rounds on the night of the first attack—or more than 40 percent more).[29]

Not only was there *more* flak for the British to contend with, it was now far more concentrated than before. Two days earlier Generaloberst Weise had decreed that all flak above a target city should be limited to 4,500 meters (14,700 feet), to give the German fighters space to attack the bomber force from above. The skies above Hamburg had therefore become doubly dangerous. Above the flak level the bombers faced the combined perils of ice, lightning, and the gunpower of every fighter aircraft for miles; and yet if they tried to venture out of the bottom of the storm cloud they faced an alternative storm of shells from Hamburg's greatly reinforced flak batteries.

As the raid progressed, the British situation only became more miserable. When a greatly depleted force at last turned for home, it was so broken up that any protection they might have gained from their radar-jamming bundles of Window was long gone. Many of the crews were completely lost, scattered across the sky from Holland to Denmark. One 405 Squadron Halifax was so badly damaged by flak that its pilot decided to fly to Sweden—he and his crew eventually bailed out over Malmö, and were interned by the Swedish authorities for the rest of the war. At the opposite extreme, six bombers were shot down just off the coast of Holland, some of them more than fifty miles off-course. Alone, damaged by flak, and forced to lose height by the power of the storm, they were no match for the fighter aces of the Luftwaffe's coastal squadrons.

Of these final six crews there was just one survivor. Peter Swan, a bomb aimer with 44 Squadron, was the only member of his crew who managed to bail out before his Lancaster crashed into the sea: Despite hitting his head on the escape hatch and passing out in midair, he managed to regain consciousness just in time to pull the ripcord of his parachute. After four hours in the cold waters of the North Sea, he was eventually picked up by a German E-boat. He spent the rest of the war in a prisoner of war camp.[30]

It was not until almost six o'clock the next morning that the last of the battered British force finally returned to the ground in England. As the tired, shaken crews climbed down from their aircraft, they were immediately taken off to the debriefing rooms, where a fairly depressing picture of the night's operations began to emerge. Some of them described being attacked by night fighters, many more described the increased intensity of the flak—but *all* of them spoke in awe about the violence of the storm.

It soon became obvious that many crews had not even attempted to bomb Hamburg, having been prevented from doing so by the conditions. To make things worse, even those who had made it to the target had been unable to bomb it properly. They had been instructed to drop their loads on the green target markers, but often there were none to be seen.

Trevor Timperley, who flew one of the Pathfinder aircraft that night, explains what went wrong. It was his job to mark the target using the Wanganui method—in other words, rather than illuminating the target on the ground he was to drop markers into the air above the aiming point, which would float down gently for all the other bombers to see. This was the method the Pathfinder Force used when there were clouds obscuring the target. The problem was that even in relatively still conditions the sky markers tended to drift away from where they were supposed to go. In a storm they were simply blown all over the sky. Even so, this was the least of Trevor Timperley's worries.

> They had forecast some cumulo-nimbus cloud, but nothing like the scale that was encountered. I was supposed to be towards the end of the raid, illuminating with this Wanganui air marker. There was no point unless it was *outside* the cloud: If you drop it in a cloud, nobody will be able to see it. As we got closer, and we were climbing up to get over the top of it, I realized that I was still going to go in the cloud ... I decided that if I kept my markers only, which was the important thing, and jettisoned the bombs, I would get the height [to break out of the clouds]. This turned out in the end to be 29,000 feet, which is pretty good in a Lancaster. Anyway, I just managed it. ... There were big gaps between the cloud, and I dropped my markers into one of them. But whether my markers slowly drifted into cloud as they went lower, I don't know. It was the best I could do.[31]

With the impossible conditions, their instruments failing all around them, and target markers that ended up drifting into the clouds, it is no wonder that many of those who battled their way through the storm failed to find Hamburg. Colin Harrison was one pilot who was completely disillusioned with the attack.

> I never saw the target. I was weighted down—the aircraft was badly iced up—and battered from all the thunder and turbulence and the like. I got knocked down from the 20,000 feet where we used to fly most of the time, to about 10,000 feet, and I came into a sort of a clear area. We were below cloud—it was practically a hole in the cloud—and there was no sign of the target. And I thought, well, this is a waste of time.[32]

Other pilots are even more outspoken about the seemingly pointless nature of the ordeal they were going through. Bill McCrea, who was still understandably upset about being sent to Hamburg twenty minutes late on the previous raid, is unforgiving about being sent into such danger a second time.

> The fourth raid was a shambles. An absolute shambles—entirely the fault of the Met men. We should never have gone, because this electric storm

came through England the previous day. . . . They said it would have
cleared Hamburg in 24 hours—well it hadn't, it was right across the city.
I think I flew in it for five minutes and I could feel the ice building up, so
I turned round the other way. I got what I thought was a source of light
coming from down below, so of course I dropped my bombs on that. I
think it was Bremerhaven but I wouldn't be sure.

He and his crew no longer really cared what they had bombed. Shaken and
silent, they were merely glad to be on their way home.

If the previous raids had been uniquely devastating in the history of
bombing, tonight's operation was nothing but an expensive RAF flop: a
miserable performance conducted in miserable conditions. The RAF had
lost thirty aircraft, at least a handful of which were defeated by the sheer
force of the storm.[33] One hundred and six planes had dropped their bombs
in the sea, fourteen had jettisoned them over land, and 197 had given up
on Hamburg and attacked targets of opportunity elsewhere.[34] Some crews
had bombed Bremen, more than fifty miles to the southwest of the place
they were supposed to be bombing; other crews had bombed Kiel, about
fifty miles to the north. In fact, only 393 aircraft had even made it as far
as the target, barely half the total British force, and even those planes that
did reach Hamburg did not manage to attack the areas they were supposed
to. In the words of the Hamburg police chief, "No focal point of the raid
was observable. . . . Casualties among the population remained small."[35]
In other words, the city had been spared the final, lethal blow that everyone had been dreading.

It seems that many of the crews that made it to Hamburg had dropped
their loads early. In the poor visibility, and with their instruments affected
by the storm, many navigators had been forced to calculate where they
were by dead reckoning: Most of these crews dropped their loads well
south of the city, but a few managed to hit Harburg. This southern part of
the port area had been one of the two original target points, and it is ironic
that it should have been taken off the target list that afternoon only to have
several bombers hit it by mistake.

A large number of planes also overshot the city. About twelve miles to
the northwest of Hamburg was the small town of Elmshorn; tonight there
was a large fire burning in the town center, caused either by the lightning

or by some of the initial stray bombs. Drawn toward the fire, as many as seventy British planes dropped their bombs on this hapless town, destroying more than 250 houses and severely damaging 200 more. Elmshorn was one of the evacuation points from the previous raids, and was still packed with refugees, some of whom could be forgiven for thinking that the British were deliberately targeting them as they fled.[36] Fifty-seven people were killed here.

As for Hamburg itself, a few fires were started in the center of town and in the eastern part of the port—but they were very scattered and the city's firefighters were able to deal with them relatively easily.[37] Some bombs fell into areas that had already been destroyed, and many more fell uselessly into the surrounding countryside. For the few people who still remained in the city, like Wanda Chantler and her friends huddled in the remains of their forced-labor camp, it was a blessed relief. Far from being a threat, the awesome force of the storm had come to their rescue.

The raid of August 2/3 brought an end to Operation Gomorrah, and also, for the moment, the devastation of Hamburg. The city would not have to suffer another large Allied raid for almost another year. After dropping nearly 10,000 tons of bombs on the city there seemed little point in repeating the attack. As far as the Allies were concerned, the job had been done.

PART III

THE AFTERMATH

Chapter 20

CITY OF THE DEAD

*Who could ever, even with unbound words, tell in full
of the blood and wounds that I now saw, though
he should narrate them many times?*

—DANTE, INFERNO[1]

In the days following Operation Gomorrah, the Hamburg authorities found themselves facing one of the biggest cleanup operations in history. Hundreds of miles of city streets were now buried beneath mounds of rubble. The city center had been transformed into a collection of smashed monuments, broken church spires, gutted architecture. The famous waterways that criss-crossed the city were now choked with floating detritus, charred wood, sunken boats. And the harbor itself—the very heart and soul of the city—appeared to be just as bad. Those parts of it that were visible across the river, such as the Blohm & Voss shipyards and the surrounding docklands, had been reduced to a mess of burned-out warehouses, sunken ships, and the mangled remains of some 122 cranes.[2]

At the center of the wasteland, like a huge black hole in the landscape, lay the charred remains of what would soon become known as the "dead city." It was here, in the districts of Hammerbrook, Rothenburgsort, and Hamm, that the worst damage had been done. Streets that had once teemed with activity were now a virtual moonscape, utterly devoid of life. The whole area was fundamentally unstable: Unexploded bombs still rested beneath the rubble, fires still raged in coke stores and lumber yards, and some of the house facades that had not already collapsed swayed visibly whenever there was a change in the wind. Bodies were scattered across the streets, many so badly scorched that they were indistinguishable from the blackened trunks of trees torn up by the force of the firestorm.

In the face of such devastation, not only here but in many other parts of the city, it was difficult for the authorities to know what to prioritize. The rubble certainly had to be cleared off the roadways before any of the major work could even be begun. Many of the damaged house facades were so unstable that they had to be torn down immediately, to prevent them collapsing on rescue workers. Supplies of drinking water had to be restored as quickly as possible to prevent outbreaks of disease, and there was pressure from Berlin to get the city's damaged war industries back up and running. There were still fears that some of the larger fires might once again get out of control. Indeed, some of these fires would not be put out until the beginning of October, a full two months after they had first been set alight.[3]

However, the authorities very quickly realized that the first priority, for everyone's sake, had to be the recovery and burial of the dead. This was easier said than done. The sheer numbers involved meant that it was impossible to recover more than a fraction of the bodies within the first week. So they decided to concentrate on those that the population would find most distressing—those bodies that were strewn, visibly, throughout the streets of the firestorm area. In this they were motivated by a genuine desire to spare the people of Hamburg any further anguish: The ordeal they had experienced was great enough already without their having to contend with the gruesome sight of bodies lining the roadways.

Of course, it was inevitable that many people were not spared this sight—especially in the early days. Annegret Hennings was one of those who ventured through the district of Hamm just a few days after the firestorm. What she saw there shook her to the core.

> In the Hammer Landstrasse I saw something lying there that looked like a charred tree trunk, and next to it another, smaller thing. They were a mother and child. Totally charred, so that they were unrecognizable. The dead lay everywhere. With some of them you couldn't tell if they had been burned to death or killed by the blast. None of them had any body hair left. After some time these streets were closed off, walls were built across them. Prisoners had to go into the cellars and fetch the people out. I felt very sorry for them.[4]

Gretl Büttner also describes making a journey into the "dead city." She and her companion, Dr. Maack, were investigating what had happened in these areas, and looking for the remains of some colleagues in the Air Raid

Protection Service. After clambering over the rubble for a short way, they found themselves overlooking a sea of corpses.

On a little open square near Boonsweg—I shall never forget the sight— there lay hundreds of men and women, soldiers in uniform, children, old people. Many had torn the clothes from their bodies shortly before their death. They were naked, their bodies seemed unmarked, the faces showed peaceful expressions, like in deep sleep. Other bodies could hardly be recognized; they were charred, torn to pieces, and had shattered skulls. . . . There an old woman lay. Her face was peaceful, soft, and tired. . . . And there, a mother with a child on each hand. They were all three lying on their faces in an almost gracefully relaxed position. . . . And there, a soldier, with charred stumps for legs. There a woman with a torn body, on whose bulging-out intestines the flies were feeding. And there a child, clutching a bird cage in his hand. And there, detached from the body, a boy's foot with a black boot; a small, brown girl's hand with a blue ring. . . . The heart almost stops beating at such sights.[5]

Scenes like this were only the tip of the iceberg. There were literally hundreds of streets and squares in the affected areas, and many of these were strewn with corpses. Most of the bodies, however, were out of sight, hidden away in the cellars where they had succumbed to the combined effects of the heat, the smoke, and carbon monoxide poisoning.

Hamburg had a very efficient system for collecting, identifying, and burying those who died in air raids; but in the summer of 1943 the authorities found themselves completely overwhelmed by the sheer number of bodies they had to collect, by the inaccessibility of the areas in which people had died. With rubble strewing the streets, often the only way to get to them was on foot. Corpses in the worst-affected areas had to be left for days or even weeks until the roads were clear enough to get the trucks in to take them away. Many were buried beneath piles of stone, requiring heavy lifting equipment before they could be recovered. Those bodies that were still underground were especially difficult to recover. Sometimes the inrush of air as cellars were opened caused fires to break out afresh, and many cellar shelters had to be left for up to ten days before they were cool enough for the disposal squads to enter.[6]

In the first few days after the firestorm, 10,000 corpses were collected from the streets for burial. This was the sort of work normally carried out by the Air Protection Police, but the sheer scale of the cleanup operations meant that hundreds of auxiliary workers had to be drafted in to help. Most of these extra helpers came from the armed forces, but the SS was also called in, as were prisoners from the concentration camp at Neuengamme. The bodies were gathered without ceremony: There was barely even time to identify them before they were taken away. After their details were logged, along with a description of where they were found and any possessions they had, they were merely piled onto the back of a truck and transported to Ohlsdorf cemetery.[7]

Ludwig Faupel was one of those who found himself dealing with the bodies of the dead. The company at which he was apprenticed had been completely destroyed, so he and his surviving colleagues were immediately drafted by the Rescue and Repair Service to help clear up the city. This, inevitably, involved a certain amount of recovering of corpses.

> The cleanup work went on. The streets had to be rubble-free, burned-out facades had to be leveled. . . . With the rest of our group we were obliged to join in with the cleanup work, in which the mountains of corpses were regarded as the worst work. It was not the sight of it, but the smell that made this activity so hard. As you walked through the ruins every now and then the smell of burnt flesh, or the sickly sweet stink of decomposing tissue, would bring on a strong and immediate nausea.[8]

Corpses everywhere were sprinkled with chlorinated lime, partly as a hygiene measure, but mostly in an attempt to counteract the terrible stench of advanced decomposition. Soon whole areas of the city smelled of this powder—it was the only way that the recovery squads were able to keep their nausea at bay. Cleanup crews entering the cellars had a particularly hard job. Here the stench was so bad that some military detachments insisted on blasting the cellars with flamethrowers before entering.[9] Recovery squads were issued with gas masks, in which the filter had been replaced by a pad soaked in rum or cognac. The mental and physical strain on these men was so great that many of them took to drinking the rum instead, and extra rations of alcohol and cigarettes were freely distributed throughout the Decontamination Service in order to keep the men working.[10]

The most unpleasant jobs were often reserved for the concentration camp inmates. Jan Melsen had been in Neuengamme ever since 1942, when he had been arrested as a member of the Dutch resistance. By the summer of 1943 he was already a virtual wraith. Perversely, it was his work clearing up corpses that probably saved his life, since it allowed him access to extra food—often stolen from kitchens and factories among the ruins. However, as he explained after the war, this extra food came at a high price.

> Later a truck came. Then we formed a chain and passed the corpses along until they were laid on the back of the truck. . . . After we had carried the corpses out of the cellars we had to start afresh with searching through the rubble for body parts, because they wanted to know approximately how many dead there were. We fetched ourselves bowls and buckets—there were enough lying around—then dug through the rubble and put whatever body parts we found in the buckets. In the evenings an SS doctor came with his assistants, and then we had to spread the body parts across the ground. From this he would estimate the number of men and women.[11]

As Melsen goes on to explain, it was not always easy to guess at the number of people who had died, simply because of the extreme circumstances of their deaths.

> I had just cleaned up a cellar when a civilian came up with the unit leader and said, "My wife and daughter were here—they must be in this cellar." But we had found nothing. The man cried out, "They must be here inside." It was nothing to do with me, but I had a pickaxe beside me, so we went back and forth, scraping around the entrance with the pickaxe. As I dug at the ground a bracelet sprung up. The people had been burned right down to their hair and skin—there was nothing left but this piece of gold.[12]

With some shelters they could only make vague estimates of between 250 and 300 dead—greater accuracy than this was completely impossible.[13]

In such circumstances, identification was a real problem. In a rather harrowing account, Ben Witter also describes pulling body parts from the rubble, along with wallets, ID cards, wedding rings, and all kinds of other material that might be used to identify the bodies. (In the end he was taken off this duty, because his hands were covered in staphylococcic blisters, brought on by continual contact with the cadavers he was handling.)[14] Gruesome though this work was, it took on a much more personal dimension when he discovered his own grandparents among the dead.

> My grandmother was a really stately lady, rather fat. A fat dead lady without a head was lying there: I wondered if it could be her and came to the conclusion it was. My grandfather I found later in the Harbour hospital. A lot of unknown bodies had been brought there—parts of bodies too … I examined all of them, and in a basin there was a belly with a watch sticking out from it. That was my grandfather's watch. There was only so much left of him … the rest was God's.[15]

Originally the plan was to burn all these corpses and body parts in the open. But when it was discovered that they did not actually pose much of a health risk after all, the authorities decided to bury them instead, and four mass graves were prepared in a corner of Ohlsdorf cemetery in the north of the city. Jan Melsen was one of the concentration camp inmates who was sent to dig them.

> I thought that all the corpses had been put in graves already, but that was not so—they had simply been laid out in a huge heap and doused with lime and chlorine, nothing more. The same people who had fetched the corpses out of the cellars now had to dig mass graves for the corpses. So we dug mass graves in the form of a cross. They are still there, in exactly that form, just as we lay them.[16]

Ben Witter also witnessed the way the graves were filled. From the back of one of the trucks he saw concentration camp inmates standing inside the graves among the dead, stacking literally thousands of bodies on top of one another. Round the top of the grave there was a circle of SS men, standing, for obvious reasons, with their backs to the corpses. They were all drinking, and two of them had become overpowered by the combined effects of the alcohol, the heat, and the stench. While they were thus distracted, a few of their prisoners took some clothes from the corpses, climbed over the edge of the grave, and disappeared into the trees. "I don't know how many escaped but I believe half a dozen managed it."[17]

*   *   *

During the first two weeks of August, the authorities became increasingly anxious about the possibility of epidemics breaking out. It was not only the vast number of corpses in the city that fueled their fears, but several other factors as well. With the city in ruins, those people who remained found themselves living in extremely close quarters and eating from communal kitchens. The conditions were ideal for the spread of disease, and in an attempt to stop typhus breaking out, free vaccinations were offered to anyone who wanted them.

The most worrying thing was the lack of drinking water. Instructions were issued repeatedly through the press telling everyone to boil all water before drinking it, but without any gas or electricity available this was often impossible. The city's toilets were another problem. The main sewers, remarkably, had remained intact, but without water for flushing, toilets everywhere were becoming hopelessly blocked. The authorities suggested that each surviving house community should dig latrines, with strict instructions that they should be sited at least fifty meters away from any of the city's 7,000 artesian wells, which had become so important in recent days for supplying water. But such outdoor latrines were never popular, especially during spells of rain, and many people simply poured their waste into the canals, despite the fact that this was strictly prohibited. The resulting stench merely added to the catalogue of repugnant smells that were now filling the city.[18]

Since most of the city's garbage trucks had been destroyed in the raids, and the streets were impassable in any case, the garbage collection service was virtually nonexistent. Soon, huge piles of rubbish mounted up everywhere.[19] At the end of August, Mathilde Wolff-Mönckeberg described the streets being "full of dirt and rubbish" all around town. She was still complaining of the same thing at the beginning of the following year.

> In the streets mountains of rubbish are piling up. The big metal dustbins are never emptied and garbage is bursting out all over the place. Paper, potato-peel, cabbage leaves—the muck-containers open their lids like gaping throats, vomiting out their evil contents. Then the wind takes it all and scatters it over the wet roads, leaving a stale, foul stench. We are told that every street must dig its own rubbish pit to avoid further contamination.[20]

A plague of flies and rats was soon swarming throughout Hamburg. They fed off the corpses, the rubbish, and the huge amounts of rotting food that had been abandoned in the ruins. Hans Erich Nossack describes the revulsion he felt whenever he saw these pests:

> Rats and flies were the lords of the city. Bold and fat, the rats frolicked in the streets. But even more disgusting were the flies, huge and iridescent green—no one had ever seen flies like this before. They swarmed in great clumps on the roads, settled, copulating, on top of the ruined walls, and basked, weary and satiated, on the splinters of window panes. When they could no longer fly they would crawl after us through the tiniest of cracks, soiling everything, and their buzzing and whirring was the first thing we heard in the mornings. This didn't stop until October.[21]

The increasing plague of flies began to pose a serious health risk, particularly where latrines and garbage dumps were located close to communal kitchens. Despite the exhortations for people to bury all their rubbish, this was actually very difficult: There was a distinct lack of picks and shovels, and the earth had been baked hard by weeks of hot sunshine.[22] So the plague continued to get worse. Supplies of chemicals for killing flies did not appear until the end of September, but in the end it was the onset of the colder autumn weather that brought a stop to the plague. The rats, on the other hand, remained. With piles of rubbish lining the streets there was little anyone could do to get rid of them.

Once again, the center of all this devastation and squalor was the "dead city," where the highest proportion of buildings had been destroyed, and where the remaining buildings were most unstable. People were warned to walk in the middles of the streets in all parts of the city, just in case of collapsing house facades, but they were told not to come into this part of town at all.

The sheer scale of the damage here was so great that even those eyewitnesses who did venture inside the "dead city" often found it impossible to describe what they saw. Most contemporary descriptions do not even attempt to give an impression of the vast field of ruins—instead they invariably focus on smaller details in a series of broken images. For example, Gretl Büttner is able to describe what she saw only by giving a list of images:

Ruins everywhere, as far as the eye could see. Debris on the streets, collapsed house fronts, farflung stones on curbs, charred trees, and devastated gardens. Over it all a bright blue sky, little white clouds, and a bright sun. This made the picture of endless grief and terrible devastation even more noticeable. And always the sound of new buildings collapsing and the crackling of the ravenous fire still feeding could be heard. Poor, beautiful, beloved, raped city! One was without words.[23]

It is revealing that eyewitnesses like this, who were otherwise eloquent, found themselves so tongue-tied by what they saw. It is as if the scale of the destruction was so great that the only way to make sense of it was by seizing on a handful of tangible details.

According to Hans Erich Nossack, the reason people did this was that the bigger picture was so completely unrecognizable. When he himself tried to take it in he was struck by a sense of unreality: It was as if the city he knew had not merely been destroyed but taken away entirely, and replaced with something completely alien. "What surrounded us did not remind us in any way of what was lost," he says. "It had nothing to do with it. It was something else, it was strangeness itself, it was the essentially not possible."[24] So complete was the transformation that he was totally unable to navigate his way through the dead zone, even in areas he knew well.

I have gone through all these districts, by foot or by car. Only a few main streets were cleared, but mile after mile there was not a single living house. And if you tried to work your way through the ruins on either side, you immediately lost all sense of time and direction. In areas I thought I knew well, I lost my way completely. I searched for a street that I should have been able to find in my sleep. I stood where I thought it must be and didn't know which way to turn.[25]

This was why people, on the whole, focused on little things. It was impossible to mourn a city that had become so alien: much better to concentrate on something specific—a particular street corner, or a ruined shop—as a tangible fragment of a lost past.

If mourning the city was difficult, then mourning the people who had died here was often impossible. The bodies had been removed so hastily that there was often nothing left to mourn—no proof that those people had died at all. Indeed, with almost a million refugees spread out across Germany, most Hamburgers had no way of knowing whether their friends and relatives were not in fact alive. There are countless stories of people fearing the worst, only to discover that their wife, or father, or daughter was alive and living somewhere in Bavaria. Equally there are stories of those who refused to believe that their loved ones were dead, even to the point of madness.

In the days after the catastrophe, signs appeared all over the city, chalked onto the walls of ruined apartment buildings: "Where are you Hilde?" "We are alive," "Aunt Anna is living in Blankenese." Soldiers on leave traveled from town to town, desperately searching for families that had disappeared.

In an attempt to bring order to this chaos, the police authority began cataloguing the names of the missing and the dead. It was hoped that the central register they created would become the first port of call for those looking for loved ones; it was also a way of re-establishing the party's grip on the exact whereabouts of the roving population.

There were two main catalogues. The first was a card index of all the refugees that had fled Hamburg in the days after the firestorm. All refugees were required to register themselves with the local police when they arrived at their destination, so that details of where they had moved to could be sent back to Hamburg. In the first week alone the Hamburg police received more than a million such communications, and even in November they were still receiving 2,000 to 3,000 each day. They used this information to produce a fairly accurate record of where everyone had gone.[26]

The second card index listed the details of all the dead, starting with where their body had been found, and any belongings they had had that might help with identification. Each time some unfortunate relative or friend recognized the details on one of these cards, a name could finally be matched to one of the bodies that had been buried, without ceremony, in the mass grave at Ohlsdorf. It was a painstaking process. By the end of the year they had still not discovered the names of even half of the 31,647 corpses that they had buried.[27] Indeed, many remain nameless to this day.

Some of the missing proved just as difficult to track down. By the end of the war there were still 2,000 names unaccounted for.[28] Some of these,

presumably, were people who were happy to slip off the Nazi registers, perhaps disappearing under pseudonyms in other areas of the Reich. But it is
likely that the vast majority were—and perhaps some still are—buried,
undiscovered, beneath the ashes of Hamburg.

At the beginning of August the "dead city" was cordoned off with barbed
wire, and dry stone walls built with blocks of rubble from the collapsed
buildings. Signs appeared all around the perimeter: "Forbidden zone. Entry
allowed only with written police permission."[29] The few roads into it that
remained open were guarded day and night to prevent people coming in.
The initial reason for this perimeter fence was to prevent the possible spread
of disease from the corpses, and to stop looters from disturbing the few
remaining belongings of the dead. But it was also done for moral reasons:
It was considered indecent that the recovery of cadavers should be carried
out in public.

Needless to say, the forbidden area soon gained an almost mythical status among the surviving population, and terrifying rumors about it began
to grow up. Some said the voices of the dead could still be heard, crying out
with the same screams they had uttered as they perished in the flames.
There were stories of children who had sneaked into the ruins coming
home with sores all over their arms and legs. Although this was probably
brought on by chemical residues in the rubble left by all the incendiaries,
some children seemed to believe it was a kind of curse put upon them by
the malevolent spirit of this "forbidden city."[30] Worse, it was said that
decontamination squads had to use flamethrowers, not only to cremate the
decomposing bodies where they were, but because "the flies were so thick
that the men couldn't get into the cellars: they kept slipping on maggots the
size of fingers, and the flames had to clear the way for them to reach those
who had perished in flames."[31]

For the rest of the war, the forbidden zone sat in the center of the eastern quarter like a dark reminder of the catastrophe, emanating a sense of
horror and a stench of death to the rest of Hamburg. For years afterward,
the reality of what had happened there, hideous enough in itself, was
routinely exaggerated into the grotesque. Myths grew up about the whole
area having been doused in a "rain of phosphor" during the attacks—
myths that were repeated well into the 1960s.[32] Official death tolls were
ignored in favor of higher figures—60,000, or 80,000, or 100,000—as if the

city were afraid to admit the truth that nobody really knew how many had died: The number was simply not quantifiable. Even sixty years after the event the final count is uncertain, though the most reliable figures put it somewhere around 45,000.[33] However many had died, the one thing everyone knew for certain was that the bulk of these deaths had taken place in the shattered streets of Hammerbrook, Rothenburgsort, and Hamm. This was a "dead city" in every sense of the phrase.

Chapter 21

SURVIVAL

Look not behind thee ... lest thou be consumed.

—GENESIS, 19:17[1]

Gradually, people started returning to the city. Foreign workers and slave laborers had no choice—they were herded back to Hamburg and allocated new barracks to live in among the ruins. Workers in essential industries were also required to return and help get the city back on its feet: If they did not, they would be denied ration cards. But the majority drifted back here because they felt they had nowhere else to go. They were tired of being tolerated as refugees in other parts of the country—they just wanted to come home. Nossack described it as a law of inertia: "The drops that were hurled in all directions by the city's collapse now flooded back to fill the crater."[2]

The return to this shattered city was a universally miserable experience. Even those who found their apartments intact were heartbroken by the destruction to their neighborhoods. All the places where they had once done their shopping, where they had worshiped and socialized and relaxed— everything was gone. It was a transformation that struck even the forced laborers as tragic:

> The damage from July's bombings was, of course, not confined to the restaurants. There were no more music halls or cafés with orchestras. The clowns were gone, the pom-pom of the Teutons' music had been silenced and the horses that circled around a ridiculous rink were nowhere to be found. The brothels had disappeared; there was no more wrangling on the street outside forbidding entry; the whorehouses were diminished to piles of bricks and the women who had not managed to escape in time had perished. Only two cinemas were still working, as a last testimony of former happy times for Hamburg society. The public baths had also vanished.[3]

Most of those who returned found that they now had nowhere to live: They were forced to sleep in the bunkers every night until they found friends or relatives with space to put them up. Those whose houses were still standing often found that other families had moved in while they were away. Rather than turn these people out they were often obliged to let them stay, at least until they had found somewhere else to live—but with the sheer lack of living accommodation in the city, this sometimes took months. It was common to find two or three families sharing even the smallest of apartments.[4] For those who could not find such shelter there was little choice but to return to the ruins. Gradually a shanty town grew up, as people found old cellars to live in, or stacked the debris up around ruined walls to create makeshift dwellings.

Mathilde Wolff-Mönckeberg described the spirit of this grim time with a mixture of incredulity and admiration for the ordinary people of Hamburg.

> It is amazing how these poor human beings manage to create some-thing, some kind of homestead, out of the rawest of materials, charred wooden boards and broken bricks. Everybody lends a hand: the hus-band if he is at home, the wife and all the children. And they are so proud of their achievement, preferring to live like Robinson Crusoe in one single room on the lonely heath, rather than be billeted out amongst strangers.[5]

They lived without electricity or gas, cooked on open fires as if they were out camping, and washed in the open at water pumps or from buckets. In the absence of any kind of transport, people walked everywhere, often clambering through the rubble-lined streets for three or four hours each day just to get to work and back.[6] And while the adults were at work, the children ran wild, as Mathilde Wolff-Mönckeberg continues: "There are children everywhere, hordes of them. There is no school and they roam the streets all day long . . . they forage in the garbage, dig tunnels in the rubble, and imitate the siren to perfection."[7] Johannes Schoene, the pastor of Christuskirche in Eimsbüttel, also wrote of "countless children" running around the ruins and "getting into mischief."[8]

Generally speaking, it was these children who were the first to adapt to the new realities of the war. In her diary of the time, Ilse Grassmann tells a story about her son and daughter playing a game of "Air Raids" under the kitchen table. The table itself was their shelter, and while one of them hid beneath it, the other dropped building blocks all around, claiming that they were bombs. The sight of her children playing like this filled her with a unique kind of dismay. "Is there no escape from this dreadful time?" she wrote. "Not even for the children?"⁹ But no matter how disturbing such games were, they demonstrated a fundamental truth: Huge bombardments were part of everyday life. What had once been considered "normal" no longer existed. There was a different "normality" now: one of bombs, and sirens, and ruins surrounded by barbed wire.

The children accepted this without thinking. The younger ones could not remember a time before the war—they had never known a time when the threat of British or Allied bombs had not hung over their city. Even the older ones found it difficult to imagine how things could be different. Since they were powerless to change the way things were, they had to get used to the devastation that now surrounded them.

For most of the adults it was not so different. Gradually they were forced to follow their children's lead: It was surprising what one could get used to, given time. The shock of the first few weeks very quickly began to wear off, to be replaced instead with a numb insensibility to all but the most traumatic sights. In varying degrees, everyone was slowly becoming accustomed to the terrible conditions in Hamburg: "Gradually you get used to the sight," wrote Maria Bartels to her husband at the front, "it's only when you go through Hamm that you realize once again what we've lost."¹⁰ Soon, people like this no longer noticed the rubble. They walked past ruins without seeing them. They no longer even noticed the smell, which hung over the city in a permanent fug. They learned how to cope by keeping themselves busy so that they would not have to stop and think about what had been lost. Maria Bartels continues:

> There is no radio (I dare not think of all the other wonderful comforts we've lost); it is too hopeless. It is best to work as much as possible, or go to the cinema for a change; that is the best medicine, so that you don't need to think. But on Sundays I will come out to see you, to recover, and gradually the year will come to an end and we'll look forward to a new spring. Hopefully that will bring something better than this year.¹¹

* * *

Life did get better, after a while. The bombed-out population were soon issued new ration cards, and provided with beds, warm clothes, and even furniture for their new homes among the ruins. Soon there were all kinds of little signs that a degree of normality was being restored. By August 10 several main stretches of road had been cleared and were open to traffic once more. The following day the post office reopened, and a week later the city's three daily newspapers were back in circulation. New shops were opened, a few small bars began to appear again, and some of the destroyed cinemas were re-established. On August 20, the Ufa-Palast cinema opened to show *Geliebter Schatz* (*"Beloved Sweetheart"*), a romance starring Ursula Herking and Sonja Ziemann, and people like Maria Bartels could lose themselves for a couple of hours in the harmless flickering of the big screen.[12]

The city's utilities were a major priority, and work on these was remarkably rapid. As the Americans discovered after the war, this restoration of the city's electricity "did much to reverse the original pessimistic outlook that fell over Hamburg after the raids."[13] It took only three and a half days to repair Tiefstack power station, and Neuhof power station was back in service after only twenty days, despite having been the main focus of 303rd BG on the second American raid. Even Barmbek power station, all but demolished on the night of July 29, was back in service by the end of October.[14]

Hamburg's other utilities were restored just as quickly. The air raids had hit the gas industry so hard that in the days after the catastrophe they were incapable of delivering even 3 percent of preraid levels. By the end of November, however, they were back up to 80 percent, and gas services had been restored to all but the worst-hit areas in the east of the city. It was the same story with the water supplies. The raids had destroyed the city's main pumping station in Rothenburgsort, and put 847 breaks in the water mains throughout the city, but within four months most of these breaks had been repaired, and the pumping station was back up and running. By the following spring the network of water mains was working at 97 percent of its previous capacity. The telephone system was less of a priority, but even so many of the phone lines, for business use at least, were working again as early as mid-August.[15]

It was not long, either, before the most important war industries were back up and running. By the end of the year, the aircraft industry was operating at 91 percent of its previous capacity. The production of electrical goods, optics, and precision tools was soon surpassing its previous level, and even the badly hit chemical industry was back up to 71 percent of its original output.[16]

The recovery of the all-important U-boat industry was even more miraculous. The Blohm & Voss shipyards had been the original target for both U.S. raids, and had also been hit by British bombs on the first night of attacks. And yet, despite the complete destruction of the administration building, workshop, and store buildings, the factory was back up and running almost to capacity within two months.[17] René Ratouis, a French laborer who had been in the shipyard when it was hit, could barely believe his eyes when he returned to work there at the end of September: "To our great astonishment, the Blohm & Voss factory hardly seemed to have suffered from the bombardments of July at all. We were completely bewildered by the thought that the incendiaries could have missed the most important factory in Hamburg."[18] The recovery of the U-boat yards was underlined on September 28 when the first Walter U-boat Wa 201 entered the water. Far from being knocked out of the war, the Blohm & Voss yards appeared to be flourishing once more.[19]

In the wake of all the physical recovery, it is only natural that the morale of the people of Hamburg also began to pick up. Hannah Kelson lived in the west of the city at the time, and she remembers the atmosphere becoming quite positive fairly soon after the disaster.

> Slowly some form of order returned. In fact, it returned remarkably quickly. I remember reading afterward that the intention of these air raids had been to break the spirit of the population. And I think I can say with total authority that this absolutely did not happen. People's spirit was quite tremendous. I know much is made of the spirit of the British during the Blitz, no doubt with every justification, but I think the same could be said about the civilian population, certainly as I saw it and knew it in those days, and I was right in the middle of it. There was no question of defeatism, or a sense of wanting to give up. In fact, if anything I think it strengthened people's resolve and gave them more backbone.[20]

Even in the east of the city the recovery in morale was remarkable. By the end of the year, Pastor Jürgen Wehrmann was able to look back with a certain amount of pride at the way his parishioners had dealt with the crisis.

The population of Eilbek was growing from day to day. One met ever more people in the street, their faces lit up with joy over the reclamation of their home town. I spoke with them and began to visit them in what they often sincerely called their apartments. It was now becoming quite apparent: Eilbek was beginning to rise up out of the ruins.[21]

The people of Hamburg were coping surprisingly well.

In an attempt to bolster this fragile new sense of resolve, a whole succession of party leaders came to visit the city. The first was Göring, whose visit on August 6 was the first item of news in the *Hamburger Zeitung* the following day. This was followed by visits from Himmler on the thirteenth, and Goebbels and Wilhelm Frick on the seventeenth. Admiral Doenitz also visited the docks to survey the damage done to the Blohm & Voss shipyards. The general panic and dismay that had gripped the higher echelons of the Nazi Party in the days just after the catastrophe had now subsided— so much so that they were already trying to put a positive spin on events. On August 19, State Secretary Georg Ahrens, who had accompanied Doenitz on his visit, was already writing to his relatives about what he called the "Miracle of Hamburg":

The intention of the enemy to strike a blow at the very foundations of the Reich has failed, and though Hamburg and the Hamburgers have received wounds that will bleed for a long time yet, the fact they have survived this blow in relative safety means that the enemy's method of murdering women and children in the major cities will not succeed in bringing down the Reich, not even if he makes the same attempt on other major cities. Amidst all the pain and hardship there is perhaps a positive thing that has come out of this: many would have believed that such a blow would have meant a complete breakdown. . . . Now we are all convinced not only that our city, our bleeding city, will live, but that the eternal German Reich will never come to an end when the people show such faith, such strength and such courage.[22]

Rhetoric like this might well have provoked a sneer from most ordinary Hamburgers, but the essence of the state secretary's words was undeniably true: The Allies' grand strategy of trying to undermine the Reich by bombing had not worked. Nor would it work in the coming years. Despite all they had been through, and all they were still suffering, the people of Hamburg had not given up.

The symbols of their determination to survive were all around them in the gradual clearance of the rubble, the restoration of electricity and water, and the stubborn pockets of life among the ruins. Throughout the city there were messages written in chalk on the fronts of bombed-out houses, saying, "*Wir leben*" ("We are alive"). These had originally been messages of reassurance to friends and neighbors in the direct aftermath of the catastrophe—now they began to seem more like a statement of defiance.

Then, at the beginning of September, just a month after the firestorm, something happened that had a huge psychological effect on the people: The trees began to bloom. There are numerous accounts of this strange, natural phenomenon.[23] Presumably it was some kind of defense mechanism in the tree population to ensure the survival of the species—but for the people of Hamburg, the sight of these apparently dead trees springing into glorious life became a unique symbol of hope. As autumn approached, Gretl Büttner wrote the following:

A miracle happened in the "dead city." By the end of August and the beginning of September the charred, burned trees sprouted new life; light green leaves dared to come out. So close to autumn, it was spring once again over the endless horrors. White lilacs bloomed in the destroyed gardens of the houses. Chestnut trees once more lit their white candles. And in this continuing life something mild and comforting, a change from helpless hatred to sorrow or resignation took place. One not only saw the dark, accusing debris. One saw the future again and learned to hope once more in the midst of the worst time of grief. Like a mantle . . . nature spread her strangest spring over the thousands of still bleeding wounds of the city. Hamburg was not dead. Hamburg must not die.[24]

Chapter 22

FAMINE

*Eating no longer seemed a pleasant necessity, but rather a dark law
that forced them to swallow, to swallow at any cost, in a hunger that
was never satisfied but appeared instead to swell.*

—HEINRICH BÖLL, *THE SILENT ANGEL*[1]

Hamburg held on for almost two years before the city was finally forced to surrender. There were many more raids—a further sixty-eight, to be precise, involving a combined total of over 11,000 aircraft. There were many more casualties, too: 5,666 men, women, and children lost their lives, and a further 6,463 were wounded.[2] The numbers could have been far worse, but the people of Hamburg were no longer prepared to take any risks with air raids. At the first sound of the siren they now headed directly for the nearest reinforced bunker—few people dared rely on the basement shelters anymore. Even when the sirens were not ringing they could not feel entirely safe in their ruined apartments and makeshift homes: "It is like lying in a coffin," said one survivor, "waiting for the lid to snap shut."[3] "We live through a fearful symphony of horror," wrote another. "There is no day, hardly a night without air-raid warnings. . . . The end is bound to be near, whichever way it comes."[4]

The long endgame of the war began in June 1944, when the British and American armies finally launched their invasion of mainland Europe. By March the following year they had fought their way right across France to the Rhine River, and by the end of April they had reached the west bank of the Elbe, overlooking Hamburg. Along the way they had captured hundreds of thousands of German soldiers, completely crushed the Luftwaffe, and inflicted a second devastating firestorm on the beautiful city of Dresden. By now it was obvious even to Hitler that the end was in sight. On April 30 he retired to the back room of his bunker and committed suicide.

One of Hitler's last instructions was a message to all his troops "not to give up under any circumstances, but . . . to continue the fight against the enemies of the Fatherland." As always, they were to resist the Allied advance to the last man.[5] Hamburg's gauleiter, to his eternal credit, disobeyed these instructions almost immediately. Having seen his city devastated from the air, he was unwilling to stand by while the Allies finished the job off from the ground. So, on May 3, Karl Kaufmann handed the city over to the British Second Army without so much as firing a shot. In the midst of a brutal, often insane war, it was an admirable example of common sense. Five days later, the rest of Germany followed suit, and surrendered unconditionally. The Second World War in the West had finally come to an end.

The scenes that greeted the British troops as they marched into the city were shocking in the extreme. Even battle-hardened soldiers were appalled by what they found. Tommy Wilmott, who had fought his way across Europe with the 2nd Fife and Forfar Yeomanry, sums it up succinctly: "All I remember about Hamburg was the smell. Even where we were, standing back looking on it, the smell from Hamburg was awful. The smell of death. It was terrible."[6]

Alongside this frightful odor was the terrifying physical devastation. Dr. P. J. Horsey was used to some fairly disturbing scenes—he was one of the group of medics sent to help the victims of Belsen concentration camp in the final days of the war—but he, too, was shocked by the sight of Hamburg when he visited in mid-May.

> The city itself was the scene of utter destruction. In the dock area, with one or two exceptions, there were acres and acres of rubble, which showed little evidence of having once composed houses. In many places even the streets were buried. Of the few buildings which did still stand, the majority had been gutted with fire, or were so badly damaged as to be uninhabitable. In spite of this the streets were full of Germans walking about purposefully: what they were doing or where they lived I cannot think.[7]

There is an implied feeling of guilt in Dr. Horsey's account, especially when he describes the people he came across in the street:

Some of the Germans looked away when we passed them: the children looked at us with great curiosity, but were kept well out of our way by their mothers, as though we might kick them. Most of the women looked at us with hate in their faces, but the men looked more cowed and ashamed.[8]

The truth is that men like Dr. Horsey had no idea what to expect when they came to Hamburg. They might have read in the newspapers about how the city had been "wiped off the war map," but they had no concept of what that meant, and the reality was beyond their wildest imaginings. Another British eyewitness, Philip Dark, remembers the Hamburg landscape with horror. Lieutenant Dark was a prisoner of war who found himself being transported through the city in mid-April, just before the surrender. What he saw there would stay with him for the rest of his life.

We swung in towards the centre and started to enter a city devastated beyond all comprehension. It was more than appalling. As far as the eye could see, square mile after square mile of empty shells of buildings with twisted girders scarecrowed in the air, radiators of a flat jutting out from a shaft of a still-standing wall, like a crucified pterodactyl skeleton. Horrible, hideous shapes of chimneys sprouting from the frame of a wall. The whole pervaded by an atmosphere of ageless quiet, a monument to man's power of self-destruction. . . . Such impressions are incomprehensible unless seen . . . Coventry and Bath, any bombing in England, just can't be compared to this.[9]

It is this last point that is perhaps the most important of all. Until they arrived in Hamburg, most British soldiers honestly thought they knew the worst of bombing—they had witnessed it at home in London, Glasgow, Southampton, and countless other cities. But the German Blitz on Britain was insignificant compared to what they saw here. The rubble, the ruins, the smell—as one British official wrote in 1946, it seemed "impossible ever to rebuild this city. . . . Another site must be developed for the traffic of the Elbe, to replace the essential heart of this historic port."[10]

Of course, it was not only Hamburg that was affected. By the end of the war the devastation had spread to every corner of the Reich—just as the refugees of 1943 had predicted—and postwar descriptions of Germany's other cities are equally devoid of hope. Cologne was a city "recumbent, without beauty, shapeless in the rubble and loneliness of complete physical defeat."[11] Dresden no longer resembled "Florence on the Elbe" but was more like "the face of the moon," and planning directors believed that it would take "at least seventy years" to rebuild.[12] Munich was so badly devastated that "it truly did almost make one think that a Last Judgment was imminent."[13] The damage in Berlin was so great that a former envoy to President Roosevelt described it as "a second Carthage."[14]

This then was the final result of the bomber dream, the fruit of decades of investment and research. The Allies had perfected the art of devastating cities. As a consequence there was barely a town in Germany that remained untouched by destruction.

In the aftermath of war, the Allies set about trying to rebuild the shattered country. Under the Marshall Plan the Americans agreed to pour $29 billion into Western Europe, and by far the biggest share was to go to Germany.[15] Along with the British and the French, they steered the western half of the country toward recovery, and eventually to prosperity. However, while the Allies are fond of congratulating themselves for creating the foundations of the German "economic miracle," it is important to remember that things got much, *much* worse for Germany before they improved.

When the Allies took over they inherited an extremely efficient economic system. British observers were astonished to find that, despite all the bombing and disruption, Germans were still spending evenings at the theater and the opera, hair and beauty salons were still open, and food was still relatively plentiful. The welfare system ensured that every German citizen was fairly well looked after, no matter what had happened to their homes. After Dr. Horsey visited Hamburg in May 1945 he was able to write that "all the Germans I ever saw were well dressed and looked very well fed."[16]

Under Allied control, however, the situation changed dramatically. By the autumn of 1946, when celebrated British publisher Victor Gollancz arrived in Hamburg, the people had been reduced to scavenging for food, malnutrition was rife, and children could attend school only on alternate days because they were obliged to share their shoes with their brothers and sisters.[17] Worse still was the threat of disease, which was much more of a danger than it had ever been in the aftermath of the firestorm. Tuberculosis was five times as prevalent as it had been before the war; penicillin was in short supply; there was only enough insulin available to treat a third of the diabetics in the city, and only enough bandages for a fifth of those who needed them.[18] One British medical officer, who mistook Gollancz for a visiting politician, came up to harangue him:

> What on earth are you politicians in London up to? Do you realise what's going on here? Ignoramuses see some people in the streets looking fairly well nourished but don't realise that they are living on carbohydrates and have no resistance, and they forget that the most seriously undernourished people are at home. The present figure of tuberculosis is appalling, and it may be double next year. An epidemic of any kind would sweep everything before it. We are on the edge of a frightful catastrophe.[19]

Katherine Morris, who worked for the British administration in the city, backs up Gollancz's observations. When she arrived here in 1946 the faces of many Hamburgers "were almost yellow with malnutrition."[20] Crowds of German children routinely gathered outside the British clubs and barracks in order to beg for food, while other, even more hopeless people, were forced to scavenge in the city's garbage cans:

> Spectral figures, gaunt and ragged, were moving with the lifeless gait of some macabre nightmare along the pavement . . . drifting from ash-can to ash-can, poking among the contents for something to eat, their rags flapping in the wind. (It became increasingly obvious why one never saw a cat in this city.)[21]

Germans had never suffered like this while the war was on. Until now, hardship to this degree had been confined to foreigners and forced laborers— but under Allied occupation, everybody suffered.

The fault lay directly with the policies of the British and American occupying forces. One of the first things the Allies did in the direct aftermath of the war was to arrest senior members of the Nazi Party and remove all party members from positions of influence. It is understandable why they did this, but the immediate effect of their actions was a complete breakdown of order. Getting rid of all the party members meant sacking virtually the entire administrative workforce, practically overnight. At a stroke, all the systems that had been keeping the German economy going so miraculously throughout the war were removed. The efficient German welfare network collapsed. The ration cards issued by the Allies were worthless, because there was no food in the shops—all the food distribution systems had disintegrated. The torturously slow German bureaucracy was replaced by an even slower and less well-organized Allied one. And in the administrative chaos that ensued, all those people who would once have been looked after by the state—not only the armies of orphans and homeless people, but now also concentration camp victims and literally millions of refugees from the East—were effectively left to fend for themselves.

The next thing the occupying forces did was far more shameful. Partly to prevent the Germans from rearming, but also to eliminate Germany as an economic rival, they began systematically to dismantle the country's industrial infrastructure. Factories that had survived the war were now closed, or even dynamited, in the name of preventing any of the German war industries from starting up again. The docks in Hamburg were blown up, the warehouses emptied, the cranes dismantled and used for scrap. Even fishing vessels were scuttled, just in case someone might try to convert them into minelayers—and this at a time when food was becoming desperately short. It can only have looked to the people as though the Allies were trying to carry on where the bombs had left off. In the words of Rudolf Petersen, Hamburg's first Bürgermeister after the war, "The sea's full of fish, but they want to starve us."[22]

In conditions like these, unsurprisingly, the black market flourished. Just as with other cities, the population of Hamburg had no option but to go "hamstering"—that is, taking day trips to the countryside in order to find food for themselves. Consequently, the price of food began to skyrocket. Hamburgers would barter anything for a few extra rations of meat or eggs: watches, jewelry, even their all-important winter clothes. There was soon a rather bleak saying doing the rounds in Hamburg: "All the farmers need now are Persian rugs for their pig-sties."[23] But the black market was now the only thing keeping many people alive. Official rations at the beginning of this winter provided people with only 1,550 calories per day—less than 60 percent of the recommended amount needed to keep them healthy. In reality, most people were receiving only between 400 and 1,000 calories per day—a comparable amount to the inmates at Belsen.[24] Without the black market to supplement their rations, the population of Hamburg were facing famine.

In desperation, the people began to threaten riots over food, just as they had done after the First World War. Martial law was declared in many parts of the country, and in Hesse the U.S. military governor was forced to issue warnings that the death penalty would be invoked for anyone rioting over food shortages.[25] A curfew was strictly enforced to keep the streets clear after dark. There was a growing sense of irony that such draconian methods were being used by the very people who were supposed to have liberated Germany from a totalitarian regime. Throughout the country there were serious concerns that the youth were becoming embittered, and even "renazified," out of disillusionment.

Things began to improve in 1948, but in 1946 they looked impossibly bleak. There was widespread despair about what the future might bring, and the goodwill that many in Germany once had for their liberators had vanished. In Victor Gollancz's words—which were frequently echoed after the occupation of Iraq nearly sixty years later—the Allies might have won the war, but they had "all but lost the peace."[26]

As if the situation were not bad enough, the winter that followed Gollancz's visit to Germany turned out to be one of the worst on record. At the beginning of January 1947 the temperature plunged to a terrifying minus 28°C, and remained below minus 10°C for several weeks. It was so cold that the Alster lake literally froze solid—according to one British soldier, who was detailed to drill holes through it, the ice was three feet thick.[27] The surface of the Elbe froze, too, and large ice floes began to appear in the North Sea around the Elbe estuary, making it nearly impossible for ships to enter. Such conditions would be dangerous at the best of times, but in the aftermath of the war they were almost catastrophic. Even those people who had proper homes had no means of heating them. All domestic electricity was cut between 7:00 A.M. and 8:00 P.M. in order to conserve power, and coal was in such short supply that goods trains from the Ruhr were routinely plundered by hordes of children trying to gather fuel.[28]

The temperature did not rise above zero until mid-March, more than three months after the cold snap began. For some people who lived through both events, this terrible winter was every bit as soul-destroying as the night of the firestorm itself—they were as powerless against the cold as they had been against the heat. Nobody knows how many people perished during this terrible winter, but the number is certainly in the hundreds, and perhaps even higher.[29]

For the city of Hamburg, things did get better—eventually. Over the next ten years the bulk of the rubble was cleared away, and the huge holes blasted into the cityscape were gradually filled with new streets and buildings. Slowly, the city showed signs of returning prosperity. The shipbuilding industry re-established itself on the banks of the Elbe, and the port began to flourish once more. A new bridge was built across the Alster. In 1948 the Deutschmark was introduced as a stable currency, and a larger variety of goods at last appeared in the shops. By the beginning of the 1950s the city was free to concentrate once more on what it had always been good at—trade—and the only major battles it was forced to fight were those against the ever-fickle floodwaters of the Elbe.[30]

Over the coming decades, Hamburg would again become one of the richest cities in Europe. The port on the southern banks of the Elbe regained its status as one of the biggest in the world, and was soon the city's principal employer. Trade worth billions of dollars every year now passes along the river. The city's proud tradition as the media capital of Germany has also re-established itself: National newspapers and magazines such as the Die Welt, Die Zeit, Stern, and Der Spiegel are based here, as are several television and radio stations, and literally thousands of advertising agencies, film studios, record labels, and book publishers.[31] Today it is impossible not to be impressed by the wealth, the zeal, and the sheer industry of the place.

And yet, even now, one cannot visit the city without remembering what happened here. The bomb sites and the rubble have disappeared, but there are obvious gaps in the landscape where buildings once stood. Air raid shelters still dot the city like a pox. The huge bunker on the Heiligengeistfeld, with its four vast flak towers, could not be demolished—it was designed to be indestructible—and it remains on the site to this day, an embarrassing, windowless eyesore. In the town center stands the ruin of the Nikolaikirche, its Gothic spire pointing to the sky like an admonishing finger. There are memorials to the catastrophe in every quarter. In the east, in one of Hamburg's busiest shopping areas, there is a sculpture of a terrified figure cowering in the corner of an air raid shelter.[32] In the west, there is an "Anti-War Memorial," deliberately placed next to the old Nazi monument that glorifies the patriotism of war.[33] And in the north, in Ohlsdorf cemetery, is perhaps the best-known memorial to the countless victims of the firestorm: a sculpture of Charon, ferrying souls across the River Styx to the underworld. It sits in the midpoint between the four mass graves where over 36,000 bodies lie buried.[34]

But perhaps the most poignant legacy of the firestorm is in the attitudes of those who survived its horrors. Klaus Müller still has an irrational fear of fireworks. His sister, who suffered from blackouts in the overpacked bunkers as a child, can still never bring herself to board a full underground train.[35] Some of the people quoted in this book admitted to experiencing flashbacks, especially on the catastrophe's anniversary, when memories roll before their eyes "like some appalling horror film."[36] At least two experienced nervous breakdowns later in life that put them in the hospital.[37]

For these people, and for countless more like them, the firestorm is not merely something that happened over sixty years ago. It is a continual burden, like a disease without a cure, that they will carry with them for the rest of their lives.

Chapter 23

THE RECKONING

*You can't have this kind of war. There just aren't enough
bulldozers to scrape the bodies off the streets.*

—DWIGHT D. EISENHOWER[1]

After the war, the British and American governments spent a great deal of
time and energy trying to discover exactly how effective their bombing had
been in Germany. The Americans immediately set up the United States
Strategic Bombing Survey and traveled all over the country interviewing factory managers and gathering captured German documents that described
the damage caused by the bombs. Not to be outdone, the British set up a
Bombing Survey Unit of their own. Both groups looked very carefully at
what had happened in Hamburg in particular—partly because the attacks
on this city had been so dramatic, but also because the damage had been so
well documented by the Hamburg authorities at the time.

This is what they discovered: Over the course of these six British and
American attacks, the entire eastern quarter of the city and much of the western quarter had been razed to the ground. The number of homes that were
incinerated by the firestorm defies the imagination: 40,385 residential buildings were either completely obliterated or rendered so badly damaged that
they were uninhabitable. These buildings contained around 275,000 apartments, or roughly 61 percent of Hamburg's total living accommodations.
None was rebuilt until after the war. A further 109,471 homes were less badly
damaged, but the city's economy had been wrecked so completely that two
thirds even of these remained unrepaired until after the war was over.[2]

Among all these homes were the other buildings that make up a city:
shops, schools, offices, and so on. Most of these had also been destroyed.
According to the American bombing survey, 3,785 industrial plants were
destroyed by this series of raids, as were 7,190 small businesses employing

21,000 craftsmen. About 5,000 of the city's 7,000 retail stores were also destroyed.[3] The Hamburg chief of police also claims that 83 banks, 379 office buildings, 112 Nazi Party offices, 7 warehouses, 13 public utility premises, 22 transport premises, 76 public offices, 80 military installations, and 12 bridges were completely destroyed. All of these buildings could be considered military targets, at least to some degree. A further 437 buildings were destroyed that had nothing to do with the war whatsoever, including 24 hospitals, 277 schools, 58 churches, 77 cultural centers (cinemas, theaters, and opera houses), and one zoo.[4]

By any standards, Hamburg had ceased to exist. Even in those areas where the buildings were still standing, many of the streets were blocked with rubble, making travel all but impossible. The trams could not run, and all of the central subway and overground train stations were out of action. There was no running water, no electricity, and no gas. There was no radio, no postal service, and no telephones. But most important there were no people. In the wake of the firestorm almost the entire population had fled, leaving the ruins utterly devoid of human life.

If the material destruction was breathtaking, the human cost of the air raids was truly tragic in scale. In just one week, 45,000 people had lost their lives. A further 37,439 had been injured, while almost a million people had fled the city and were now officially homeless.[5] All that they owned—everything from clothes and furniture to ornaments, letters, and photographs—had been burnt or blown to pieces in the raids.

To put these numbers in context, the death toll at Hamburg was more than ten times greater than that of *any* previous raid. At Nagasaki, where the Americans dropped their second nuclear bomb, the immediate death toll was 40,000—about 5,000 less than at Hamburg.[6] The devastation of this Hanseatic city cannot, therefore, be compared accurately with the sort of destruction normally associated with conventional bombing: It is more akin to the annihilation that would soon become possible in the nuclear age.

The question remains as to what all this destruction actually achieved. Did it knock Hamburg's U-boat and aircraft industries out of the war? Did it prevent the rest of Hitler's war machine from working efficiently? Did it in fact shorten the war to any degree? Or did it merely take the lives of innocent civilians, who in any case contributed very little to Germany's war effort?

It cannot be denied that the immediate effect on Hamburg's industries was huge. Almost half of the city's 81,000 commercial and industrial buildings had been completely destroyed, and the majority of its workers had fled. By the end of the year 226,000 people had still failed to come back to work—that is, 35 percent of the city's entire workforce.[7] With no buildings to work in, and no people to do the work, the drop in industrial output was massive. In August 1943, Hamburg produced only half of the total output that it had done in July. By the end of 1943 the city was still producing only 82 percent of its normal capacity. To some degree Hamburg never truly recovered from the shock of these raids, and throughout the rest of the war industrial output never fully recovered.[8]

After the war, the Americans estimated that as a direct result of the raids, Hamburg lost 1.8 months of its entire industrial production, about half of which was intended for the armed forces.[9] This meant that fewer supplies were sent to the Russian Front, fewer aircraft took to the skies, and fewer U-boats were launched to attack British shipping in the North Atlantic. To be more precise about this last point, twenty U-boats that would otherwise have taken to the seas around Britain were prevented from doing so.[10] When one considers that U-boats had been responsible for decimating the British economy before 1943, any reduction in their numbers, by whatever means, was absolutely essential to the Allies.

However, impressive though such figures are, it is important to remember that they represented only a temporary setback for the German war machine. Despite the enormous destruction in Hamburg's residential areas, the main industrial areas of the city remained relatively untouched. Much of the harbor complex had been spared, and even those parts that had suffered quite badly were soon repaired. For example, the Blohm & Voss shipyard, which had been the focus of the first American attack, was soon back in business, and 7,500 of the company's 9,400 workers were back at their stations within three months.[11] The Neuhof power station, which suffered direct hits in the U.S. raids, was back up and running within twenty days.[12] The figures for shipbuilding as a whole are even more surprising: By the end of the year, shipbuilding output was actually higher than it had been before the bombings.[13] Far from being on their knees, the city's most important war industries were coping extraordinarily well.

According to the United States Strategic Bombing Survey, the effects of the 1943 catastrophe were nowhere near as disruptive to the war economy

Total damage to Hamburg in the
Gomorrah raids, July 24–August 3

LOKSTEDT

EPPENDORF

HOHELUFT

HARVESTEHU

EIMSBÜTTEL

BAHRENFELD

ROTHERB

ALTONA

OTTENSEN

NEUSTA

FLOTTBEK

ST. PAULI

N o r d e r   E l b e

Blohm & Voss
shipyards

STEINWARDER

Köhlbrand

N
W   E
S

Howaldtswerke
shipyard

1 mile

To Neuhof power station

WILHELMSBURG

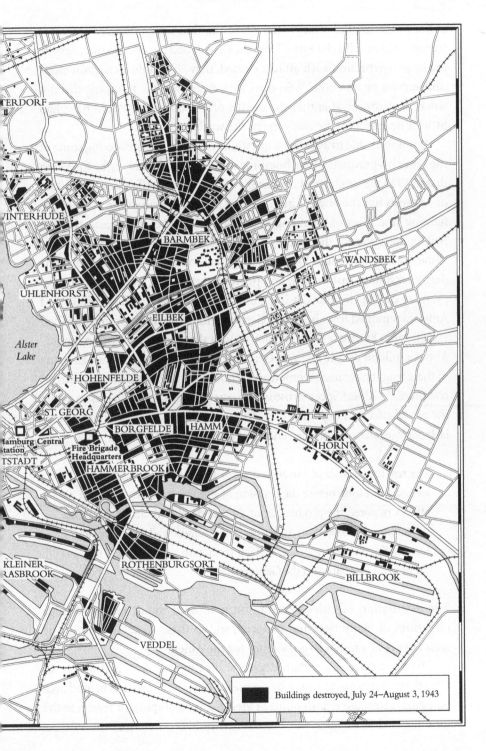

ERDORF

VINTERHUDE

BARMBEK

WANDSBEK

UHLENHORST

EILBEK

Alster Lake

HOHENFELDE

ST. GEORG

BORGFELDE **HAMM**

Hamburg Central station **Fire Brigade Headquarters** **HORN**

TSTADT

HAMMERBROOK

KLEINER RASBROOK

ROTHENBURGSORT

BILLBROOK

VEDDEL

Buildings destroyed, July 24–August 3, 1943

as the much smaller attacks later on in the war, which targeted the city's transport links with the Ruhr. Even the British had to concede that, despite the huge destruction such attacks caused, they "had only an irritant effect on German production."[14] So does this mean that the bombing did not work? Is it conceivable that the deaths of 45,000 people could have had little or no effect on the outcome of the war?

It is impossible to ask such a question without first considering some of the other by-products of the bombing war. First, it must never be forgotten that in 1943 the single most important member of the Allies was not Britain or America but the Soviet Union: It was they who were doing most of the fighting, and most of the dying, and as a consequence it was essential that Britain and America did all they could to show that the Russians were not alone. By bombing cities like Hamburg they could demonstrate their solidarity with their eastern ally, and prove that they, too, were exerting huge pressure on the Germans. It is a common argument that had Britain and America refrained from bombing Germany, the Wehrmacht would have had 10,000 more 88-mm guns to deploy against the advancing Russian tanks.[15] About a million people manned Germany's civil defenses, and though many of these might have been women and schoolboys, it was still a huge drain on resources. As Albert Speer wrote in his secret diary in Spandau prison, while the *actual* effects of bombing on German war industries were not particularly serious, these secondary effects of bombing were pivotal:

> The real importance of the air war consisted in the fact that it opened a second front long before the invasion of Europe. . . . defense against air attacks required the production of thousands of anti-aircraft guns, the stockpiling of tremendous quantities of ammunition all over the country, and holding in readiness hundreds of thousands of soldiers . . . this was the greatest lost battle on the German side.[16]

The devastation of cities like Hamburg ensured the diversion of huge quantities of manpower and materiel, and in these terms it can only be seen as part of a much larger victory for the Allies.

However, there is a certain degree of hindsight to such arguments: In 1943 these consequences were by no means the main intention behind area bombing. From the British point of view the most important reason at the time for such area raids was the effect they had on German morale. As explained earlier, the effect of Operation Gomorrah on ordinary Germans—not only survivors of Hamburg, but people across the whole country—was phenomenal. For the first time since the defeat at Stalingrad, people were beginning to speak openly about the possibility of Germany losing the war. The morale of the armed forces was similarly subdued. A new kind of war had opened up in the skies above their cities—one against which they were powerless to defend themselves—and for some the fighting now seemed utterly pointless. Despite their best efforts to push the battlefields far away from the borders of the Fatherland, their wives and children at home were being killed by the tens of thousands.

Of all the armed services it was the Luftwaffe that suffered most from this plummet in morale. It was they, after all, who were responsible for protecting the Reich, and it was they who had to shoulder the blame when their efforts failed. This failure was brought about by a huge shortfall in resources, manpower, and most important, adequate leadership. It had been obvious for well over a year that the Luftwaffe was incapable of defending Germany from the enormous fleets of bombers that were beginning to fly across the North Sea. To do so they needed a huge increase in the number of fighter aircraft they could put into the sky. But the only man capable of ordering this increase—namely Hermann Göring—had long since retreated into a life of debauched luxury. The various generals under his command seemed more concerned with political infighting than with defending the homeland, largely because they felt powerless to influence the way the air war was being run. For many, the catastrophe at Hamburg merely underlined the crisis that had existed in the Luftwaffe for years.[17]

General der Flieger Adolf Galland tells a very revealing story about the atmosphere in the higher echelons of the Luftwaffe just after the devastation of Hamburg. Galland was at a meeting in Hitler's headquarters when all the most important Luftwaffe commanders were present. With one voice they demanded an end to the emphasis on offensive operations, so that they could concentrate instead on a single purpose: the defense of the Reich. Most important, they wanted to start producing thousands of new fighter planes, fast, in order to stop the Allied bombers from getting through.

> Never before and never again did I witness such determination and agreement among the circle of those responsible for the leadership of the Luftwaffe. It was as though under the impact of the Hamburg catastro-

phe everyone had put aside either personal or departmental ambitions. There was no conflict between General Staff and war industry, no rivalry between bombers and fighters; only the one common will to do everything in this critical hour for the defense of the Reich and to leave nothing undone to prevent a second national misfortune of this dimension.[18]

But when Göring put their demands to Hitler, the Führer flatly rejected the idea. He merely repeated the mantra he had always followed: "Terror can only be broken by terror."[19] There was no point in trying to defend Germany; instead they should forge ahead with reprisal attacks against Britain. The fact that the Luftwaffe was barely equipped for any such reprisal attacks seems to have entirely escaped him. "In this hour," says Galland, "the fate of the Luftwaffe was decided."

Galland found Göring sometime later in an adjoining room, his head buried in his arms on the table, moaning like a wounded animal. It seemed that the Führer had lost faith in Göring's ability once and for all, and the dressing down he had given him sent the Reichsmarschall into a slough of self-pity and despair from which he never recovered. In the following days a cloud of gloom descended upon the Luftwaffe command. A few weeks later, Galland asked to be relieved of his post as C-in-C of Fighter Command, and Göring angrily granted his request.[20] One other senior Luftwaffe figure was so affected by the general depression that he went even further than Galland. On August 18, just two weeks after the catastrophe at Hamburg, Luftwaffe Chief of Staff Hans Jeschonnek put a gun to his head and shot himself.

However, the German situation was not all negative. Despite Hitler's refusal to defend the Fatherland from further attacks, there were others who made sure that the defense of the Reich was not neglected. The organizational brilliance of Erhard Milch (the state secretary of aviation) and Albert Speer (reichsminister of armaments and war production) ensured that German fighter production did, against all odds, increase dramatically over the coming months. With more fighters, the Luftwaffe was better able to defend the Reich, and it is largely due to the efforts of these two men that Germany was able to withstand the terrible Allied onslaught as long as it did.

Second, while Hitler might have prevented a wholehearted change in *strategy*, he did nothing to stand in the way of a change in *tactics*. The Luftwaffe changed its tactics to a remarkable degree over the next few weeks, and it did so as a direct result of what they had experienced at Hamburg. General Kammhuber's constrictive system of tying night fighters to specific "boxes" in a long, thin line along the coast was abandoned, allowing fighters to defend individual cities in larger numbers—especially the *Wilde Sau* fighters of Major Hajo Herrmann. An even more effective tactic was for German fighters to insert themselves into the bomber streams, so that they could follow their prey all the way to the target and out again. All this became standard practice as a direct reaction to what had happened at Hamburg: The disaster had not only united the leadership in their resolve to defend the Fatherland, but provided a long-overdue catalyst for change.

It is important to remember that it was not only Germany that suffered as a result of these raids. The cost to the Allies was also huge. In an extraordinary document produced a few months after the bombings, the U.S. government calculated the financial cost of attacking Hamburg. By giving a monetary value to the number of aircraft destroyed, bombs dropped, and even lives lost, the conservative figure they came up with was $46,412,700 (see Appendix K).[21] While this pales into insignificance next to the cost of rebuilding the whole of Hamburg (some 23,050 million Reichmarks, or $9,220 million), it was nevertheless a huge amount of money, equivalent to more than half a billion dollars today.[22]

When one considers that this level of activity was carried out night after night, it is little wonder that Britain ended the war virtually bankrupt. According to some estimates, the pursuit of the bomber war consumed as much as a third of the entire British economy.[23] When looking at figures like this the question naturally arises—was it worth it? With hindsight it seems inconceivable that this level of expenditure could ever have been considered good value for money. Even at the time there were serious doubts about the efficacy of bombing, and earlier in the war there had been many who had pushed for an end to bombing purely for financial reasons.[24] But we must remember that at the time, the politicians and planners had not yet seen the final result of the bombing war. They could only measure the cost against their predictions—or, more important, their expectations.

Their expectations were great indeed. In the summer of 1943, Sir Arthur Harris confidently believed that he could win the war simply by bombing alone. By destroying whole cities, so the theory went, the Allies were undermining the morale of the German people to such a degree that their "capacity for armed resistance" would be "fatally weakened." What they had achieved against Hamburg seemed only to prove that the theory was working. In September the Joint Intelligence Committee produced a report that compared the atmosphere in Germany to the atmosphere in 1918, when mutiny and revolution had swept the country. "A study of the picture as a whole," it said, "leads us inevitably to the conclusion that Germany is if anything in a worse position today than she was at the same period in 1918." The collapse of Germany might come "even this year."[25]

If bombing had lived up to these expectations, the cost, both in financial terms and in terms of human life, would have seemed a small price to pay. Had Harris been able to devastate a handful of other German cities in quick succession, his predictions of an early end to the war might indeed have been proven right. If Berlin had suffered the same fate within a few weeks, it is conceivable that this alone might just have tipped the balance. But neither the RAF nor the USAAF yet had the ability to do such a thing, let alone do it quickly, and the small window of opportunity created by their new, radar-jamming techniques soon began to close. By the time the Allies attacked Berlin in force that autumn the tactical advantage had already swung back toward the Luftwaffe.

The Allies did not achieve such air supremacy again for another eighteen months. It was not until February 1945, when they bombed Dresden, that they finally demonstrated the ability to replicate what had happened at Hamburg, seemingly at will. However, by this time few people believed in bombing as the ultimate weapon. With the Allies poised to enter Germany from both sides, the emphasis had long since changed to land operations. It is perhaps ironic that air bombardment only ever reached its full, war-winning potential after it was no longer required to deliver the decisive blow.

This, then, is the final tragedy of what happened at Hamburg. It did not herald an end to the war, as so many people in the RAF hoped and believed that it would—instead, it was merely the opening page of the most destructive chapter in the history of air warfare. While it was the forerunner of the catastrophes at Dresden and Tokyo, Hiroshima and Nagasaki, Allied air supremacy did not come soon enough to make Hamburg truly count. Instead, Germany was subjected to a death by a thousand cuts. The countless lesser destructions that took place in the following two years would spell the devastation not only of individual cities, but of an entire nation. By the time Germany capitulated in May 1945, the country was a virtual wasteland.

Chapter 24

REDEMPTION

This only is denied even to God,
The power to make what has been done undone.

—AGATHON[1]

I am aware that this book might have made uncomfortable reading for some. There is still a great deal of bitterness toward Germany, despite the decades that have passed, and many people simply do not care if the Germans suffered or not. During the course of my research I have spoken to scores of people—Jews, Gypsies, Poles, Danes, Dutchmen, Frenchmen, the list goes on—who have listened to my descriptions of the Hamburg firestorm and merely shrugged their shoulders. "It was their own fault," is the standard reply. "They started it." I would be surprised if even the most intransigent of these people could remain unmoved by some of the eyewitness accounts of the firestorm and its horrific effects; however, I do not imagine this will produce a change of heart, especially among those who have suffered directly as a result of the way the Germans themselves conducted the war. Indeed, some may resent being manipulated into feeling an empathy they had never intended. I make no apology for their unease. War is a horrific thing, and it would be unnatural to feel comfortable in its presence.

For readers from Germany, America, or the British Commonwealth there may be an added dimension to their discomfort. The legacy of guilt that surrounds the European bombings of World War II is a huge one, and both sides are still struggling to come to terms with it, even today. In Germany it remains virtually impossible to mention the bombs without the immediate acknowledgment that it was they who opened Pandora's box in the first place. A modern generation still feels duty bound to apologize for war crimes that were committed not by their parents, or even their grandparents, but by their great-grandparents. In the English-speaking world, feelings about the bomber war are even more complicated. While on the one hand there is a certain pride that they stood up to Hitler and rid the world of his particular brand of evil, on the other hand there is an unspoken sense of shame at the methods they were forced to use. There seems to be an underlying suspicion in the popular imagination that the RAF and the USAAF were able to defeat the Nazis only by descending, at least some of the way, to their level.

There are two events that encapsulate this discomfort. The first took place in central London, in May 1992, when hundreds of RAF veterans and their families attended a ceremony in honor of their old commander-in-chief, Sir Arthur Harris. The highlight of the day was to be the unveiling of a statue outside the church of St. Clement Danes in the Strand, followed by a reception at the High Court. However, among the crowd was a group of protesters who had turned out to voice their disgust that the butcher of Hamburg, Dresden, and countless other German cities should be so honored. They hurled abuse at the RAF veterans, and even at the Queen Mother, who was performing the unveiling ceremony. That night the statue of Harris was daubed with red paint. This was cleaned off, but the statue was soon attacked again, and it has been defaced several times since.

The second event took place a year later, in Hamburg. The Lutheran Church marked the fiftieth anniversary of the firestorm by organizing a series of meetings and memorial services to commemorate its victims. On the whole these were gentle, somber affairs, but during one service at the Michaeliskirche a group of students burst into the church and started heckling the mourners. What had angered them was the all-inclusive nature of the commemoration. According to the students, the Church should have made a clear distinction between civilians and everyone else: The deaths of civilians should be mourned; the deaths of soldiers, or members of the Nazi Party, should not. After unfurling a banner with the slogan "Operation Gomorrah—there's nothing to mourn," the demonstration finally became violent, and the protesters had to be forcibly ejected from the church.[2]

Both of these events caused a furor at the time, not only because they represented a younger generation questioning the deeds of their grandparents, but because they highlighted some of the deep moral questions that neither side has yet been able to come to terms with. The Germans, to their credit, at least recognize that this is a subject they cannot avoid—they even have a specific word for it: *Vergangenheitsbewältigung* ("the process of coming to terms with the past"). Britain and America, however, seem much less well prepared. They do their best to look back on the war in terms of black and white, good and evil, right and wrong—I am speaking not only of the veterans, but also of those who turn out to protest against the bomber war. When either group is confronted by the more ambiguous realities of bombing, few of them seem quite sure how to react.

The moral questions that surround the Allied bomber offensive are much deeper, and much more disturbing, than most people realize. During the course of my research for this book I have been asked repeatedly whether I thought the bombing of cities like Hamburg was justified. I have struggled to find an answer to this question, because it opens up so many difficult issues. It is certainly not a question that should be taken lightly: After all, if "War's glorious art" is murder on a mass scale, then bombing is one of its most efficient weapons.

To begin with, I have very little problem with the *fact* that Hamburg was bombed. The city was a huge center of industry, providing U-boats, aircraft, oil, chemicals, and all kinds of other materials that were essential for the German war effort. It was imperative that the Western Allies do everything in their power to disrupt these industries, both for their own sake and for the sake of the Russians, who were dying in their millions on the Eastern Front. Britain and America lived in constant fear that the USSR would one day give up their titanic struggle by coming to some arrangement with Hitler. Bombing was the only way to show them that the Western Allies were doing something to help, and successes like the devastation of Hamburg provided the Russians with a great boost to morale. As Albert Speer pointed out after the war, the value of bombing cities like Hamburg lay not only in the disruption it caused to German industry, but also in the huge resources it diverted away from the Russian Front.

A second issue is slightly more problematic. Toward the end of the war, and immediately after it, there was a great debate over whether the Allies were right to "blanket" bomb German cities, or whether they should have concentrated more on the *precision* bombing of specific factories and military installations. Most people agreed that precision bombing was preferable, partly because it was much more efficient, but also because it was much less likely to involve civilian casualties.

While I wholeheartedly agree that precision bombing should always be chosen over area bombing wherever possible, the RAF in 1943 did not have the luxury of that choice. They had already tried precision bombing, and the results had been disastrous. Flying in daylight, the British planes were easy targets for German flak and fighters, and they were quickly decimated. Moreover, even during daylight, their equipment was so primitive and their accuracy so bad that they rarely hit what they were aiming for. In short, if they wanted to survive, and if they wanted to destroy specific targets, there was no choice but to go in during the night and bomb the entire area.

When the Americans joined the air war they went through much the same process. They began with a determination to fly by day, and to employ precision-bombing techniques. By the summer of 1943 they began to pay for that decision with unsustainable losses. American planes were far less vulnerable to flak than British planes and far better equipped to defend themselves against fighters—but during the battle of Hamburg their day-time flights meant that, in percentage terms, they were losing up to four times as many planes as the British. By the beginning of August their losses were so bad that they were forced to stop flying altogether. Their policy of flying by day was rescued only by the advent of long-range fighters, which finally began to escort them over Germany toward the end of the year.

It is tempting to view the Americans as the good guys of this particular story, because despite all the pressure to give up daylight bombing they did stick to their convictions. One of the reasons they were so determined to do so was that they were convinced that the accuracy of their bombing made it worthwhile. The Americans were rightly proud of their Norden bombsights, which were vastly superior to anything developed by either the Germans or the British. However, this remarkable piece of equipment was only useful when the target was visible below. Whenever it was obscured by cloud or smoke, as it was at Hamburg, the Americans may as well have been flying by night.[3] So, for example, while they did hit the Blohm & Voss shipyards on July 25, they also hit the historic city center, the river, and a farmer's fields south of the city.[4] The only real difference that the people of Hamburg noticed between British bombs and American ones was that there were far fewer of the latter, so they did less damage.

The American decision to stick to daylight bombing over Germany was an incredibly brave one. However, I do not think it gives them any right to claim the moral high ground—and not only for the reasons given above.

For all their protestations about blanket bombing, they were not above employing this method when they thought it appropriate: Indeed, their bombardiers on July 26 were told that if they could not locate the port they were to drop their bombs anywhere in the "center of the city."[5] And while they may have exercised restraint in the European theater of operations, their intentions were not nearly so exemplary in the Pacific. In fact, they used their time in Europe to study British methods of bombing so that they could apply them with equal success in Japan. Their firebombing of Tokyo in 1945 was every bit as devastating as what happened in Hamburg, and the civilian death toll even greater.

The final moral issue brought up by the bombing of Hamburg is by far the most difficult to justify. It concerns the intentions of those who created the firestorm. The British always claimed that they were aiming their bombs at Hamburg's docks and military installations: This is what they told the press, who dutifully reported that the aiming point for the RAF was the Blohm & Voss shipyard; it is also what many of the British crews were told during their briefings. But this was not the case. The largest concentration of purely "military" targets, including the Blohm & Voss shipyards, was on the south shores of the river Elbe, and yet this was the only area of Hamburg that the RAF did not aim for. Instead they went exclusively for the residential areas, to the north of the river. The targets of the bombs were not military installations at all, but civilians.

Some might argue that it makes no difference whether the RAF aimed at civilians or not. The vast area over which the bombs were dropped meant that the results were quite likely the same: The town was still flattened, the civilians still dead. But there is a huge moral gulf between bombing a suburban street by accident and deliberately aiming for that suburban street. British planners justified this moral leap to themselves by pointing out that it was much more difficult to destroy factories than it was to kill the people who worked in them. As long as they destroyed the workforce it did not matter whether the Blohm & Voss shipyards were still intact—there would be nobody to build the U-boats in any case.

This idea makes me extremely uncomfortable, but I have to admit that the people who planned these raids do have a point. Why should there be any distinction between the German U-boat captain and the German factory worker who helped to build that U-boat? They were both working

toward the same end, which was to kill British sailors. And since oil workers produced fuel for that U-boat, surely they were also legitimate targets.
Farmers provided sustenance for soldiers at the front, textile workers produced their uniforms, and train drivers got them to and from the battlefield. In a "total war"—and we must remember that it was the Germans
who first proclaimed it as such—all these people are considered fair game,
as is anything else that supports the enemy's war economy.

The problem with this argument is that there is no clear place to draw
the line. Can we also justify the killing of actors and musicians, since they
contribute so much to the country's morale? And what about doctors and
nurses, who heal soldiers' wounds so that they can go back to the battlefield? As I mentioned in Chapter 7, some theorists even go so far as to say
that women and children are a legitimate target. German soldiers believed
they were fighting for their families, so by killing their wives and children
one took away their incentive to fight. Under this kind of logic the Second
World War was no longer a just and honorable struggle against an evil
regime, but a war of annihilation.

The only thing that saves this policy from the charge of total immoral-
ity is the fact that it was born from the very best of intentions. Those who
advocated bombing civilians sincerely believed that they were trying to
save lives rather than take them. Men like Harris, who had witnessed the
terrible bloodbath of the First World War, saw bombing as the only way to
spare British soldiers from total carnage. Fifty-five thousand RAF men and
26,000 USAAF men died during the course of the bombing war—a huge
total, but only a tiny fraction of the number who suffered in the First World
War trenches.[6] While the Russian army was paying most of the butcher's
bill on the Eastern Front, the Allied forces were able to keep them on their
side by paying a far smaller share until the Allied armies were strong
enough to launch a cross-Channel invasion. Also, so the theory went, it
was not only Allied lives that would be spared. The British Air Ministry
was convinced that bombing would save German lives, too, because it
would shorten the war—in fact, after the destruction of Hamburg there
were many in the government who believed the war would be over before
the end of 1943. Had the RAF achieved this, millions of people on both
sides would have been saved.

This line of thinking must have seemed incredibly seductive at the time.
But it is this very seductiveness that makes it so disturbing. The British

were so caught up in the bomber dream that nobody seems to have considered what would happen if the policy did not work. In the search for the elusive knockout blow the Allies carried on launching attacks on civilian targets for several years. Before Hamburg, they bombed Lübeck, Rostock, and Cologne. After Hamburg they bombed Mannheim, Kassel, Hanover, Munich, Berlin—the list of destroyed cities goes on and on. By May 1945 they had killed somewhere between 300,000 and 600,000 German civilians, most of whom had only tenuous links to the war.[7] The knockout blow—the final strike that would end the war and so save lives—was never actually achieved.

Perhaps the worst aspect of this policy is that it removes all the traditional distinctions between combatants and civilians. There has to be some line over which military men will not cross, even if it is an arbitrary one. The problem with the Allied air strategy during the Second World War was that it removed this line without even attempting to draw a new one. The failure to do so opens the door to the nightmare of unlimited warfare, where anything is allowed provided it gets the job done—war without rules, without principles, without conscience. I hesitate to make the comparison with the amorality that led to the Holocaust, as several historians before me have done, because that would be going too far. But, ethically speaking at least, we are only a few steps away.

It would be reassuring to report that the British people of the time at least considered these issues before they lent their support to the bomber war, but this was by no means the case. Few people ever spoke out against the bombing of German cities like Hamburg. George Bell, the bishop of Chichester, was one, as was the Labour politician Richard Stokes—but their speeches in Parliament were largely dismissed by the British press as unpatriotic. Basil Liddell Hart was another who objected: After writing enthusiastically about the theory of bombing, he was much less enamored of bombing in practice. As early as 1942 he claimed that it would be ironic if the so-called defenders of civilization could defeat Hitler only by depending on "the most barbaric, and unskilled, way of winning a war that the modern world has seen."[8]

Beyond these lone voices, however, the atmosphere was less one of regretful determination than of pure triumph, with ever-increasing superlatives emblazoned across the front pages of all the newspapers. The men who flew the bombers were regarded as heroes: Several British and American airmen have told me that they would often spend a night in a pub without ever having to buy a drink for themselves. Those who were recruited for morale-raising tours around British factories were treated like celebrities, and their descriptions of the huge fires created by Allied bombs were always greeted with enthusiastic cheers.[9]

By the end of the war, however, things had begun to change. Britain was already beginning to turn its back on the deeds of Bomber Command. After six long years of conflict the appetite for German blood was no longer what it had been in 1943, and nobody wanted to be associated with a policy that had killed hundreds of thousands of civilians. One by one, politicians, planners, and even the prime minister began to distance themselves from the decisions that had led to the "blanket bombing" of German cities. The only senior figure who openly accepted responsibility for the policy was Sir Arthur Harris, who had always been its outspoken champion. At the end of the war he became something of a pariah, and there are numerous examples of how the political establishment tried to distance themselves from him.[10] Rightly or wrongly, his reputation remains severely tarnished to this day—as the defacing of his statue makes clear.

In the United States the tide was also turning. The American people had always opposed the wholesale bombing of cities, so their reaction to the supposedly indiscriminate bombing of Dresden in February 1945 was one of outrage. Across the country, front-page reports appeared claiming that American airmen were engaged in the "deliberate terror bombing of great German population centers as a ruthless expedient to hasten Hitler's doom."[11] The people, and the media, were not pacified until General Arnold stepped forward to insist that the USAAF had not departed from its strict policy of bombing only military targets. Unlike in Britain, this assertion was generally accepted, and the idea that American involvement in bombing Germany had been anything less than exemplary did not really resurface until the 1960s.[12] Even today, Americans tend to reserve their distaste either for the way the British conducted the air war, or for how they themselves acted in the subjugation of Japan.

As popular revulsion for bombing has grown, the men who flew the planes and dropped the bombs have gradually become the scapegoats for our communal sense of shame. And since it was the British whose bombing was apparently more indiscriminate, it is the RAF who have received most of the blame. Almost every British veteran I interviewed for this book expressed indignation over the way the world has come to judge their actions since 1945. Indeed, I have often found it difficult to secure interviews with them in the first place, because many were worried at my intentions. They assumed that my wish to show the German side of the story meant that I was likely to do what countless people have done: that is, to blame them *personally* for the suffering that British bombs caused ordinary Germans. In short, they were worried that I would treat them in the same way as the protesters treated them at the unveiling of Harris's statue.

This is one of the saddest legacies of the bomber war. While I admit that I have a small measure of sympathy for *some* of the beliefs held by those protesters, I deplore their abuse of Bomber Command veterans. If it is wrong to punish German civilians for the sins of their political leaders, then it is equally wrong to attack British airmen for the planning decisions of their superiors. British bomber crews were almost always told at briefing that they were attacking military or industrial targets. They were motivated by a sincere desire to help their country, and to rid the world of a profoundly evil regime. Whatever we think of the way the bomber war was conducted, these men, who faced death daily, and witnessed the deaths of countless friends and comrades, deserve our utmost respect.

It seems fitting to record here what the veterans themselves have to say about the part they played in the Hamburg bombings. Most of the men I have interviewed seem to have demonstrated an understandable lack of imagination while they were actually flying over Germany: They were young, some of them still in their teens, and they pursued war with all the enthusiasm of youth. As they flew over the fires at Hamburg the typical reaction was not, "Oh, those poor devils down there!," but, "Cor, this is a damn good show tonight!"[13] They rarely spared a thought for the people beneath the bombs, and even if they did it was usually only to register the notion that Germany had asked for it. For those who had lived through the Blitz on Britain, the Germans thoroughly deserved what they were getting.

Some of the veterans I have spoken to are unrepentant to this day. The following is one of those who see no reason to regret the part they played in the bombing: "I don't care about their cities. I was glad to see them burning. . . . My only regret was that we got shot down when we did, because I would much rather have done a lot more."[14]

Others seem to have softened over the years, if only to acknowledge the suffering of those who were, nevertheless, still legitimate targets. A few have taken this process further, and seem genuinely troubled by the thought of those who had to fight their way through the firestorm. In the years since the war they have had time to reflect on the terrible consequences of the fires, and even to question the part they played in events.

Colin Harrison of 467 Squadron is one such man. Some time after the war he came across a photograph of an old man and his wife, dead, on the street in Hamburg, and the image still haunts him to this day. "I often thought about these two old people," he says. "The street was clear—all the rubbish had been cleared to one side. There was no rubble on the road. And I often wondered whether they had anything to do with me ... I wondered if I'd done it."[15]

If we are ever to lay this painful subject to rest, we could do worse than take a leaf out of Colin Harrison's book. I do not wish to imply that he is right to feel any guilt for his part in the Hamburg bombings—far from it— only that his capacity for empathy is to be praised. The legacy of the last war will never be left behind until both sides learn to acknowledge the consequences of their actions, as he has done, regardless of whether we believe that those actions were justified.

And what of the people of Hamburg themselves—how do they view the ordeal they went through? Do they blame the British and Americans for the devastation that was wreaked upon their city? Are they angry? Whenever I have asked this question of anyone from Hamburg, I have invariably received the same answer, and one that exactly mirrors the sentiments of their enemies: "We started it." Or, even more tellingly, "We deserved it." Anger, resentment, indignation—even sadness—seem for most people to be irrelevant, because what *really* matters is that Germans are sorry.

Even during the war, many people in Hamburg realized that they were not blameless, and that, to a degree at least, they had brought this disaster upon themselves. Many saw the catastrophe as the logical consequence of the Luftwaffe's attacks on Britain; some even believed it to be a just retribution for the way Hamburgers had treated the city's Jews.[16] In any case, an unspoken sense of shame was already embedded in the German psyche long before the end of the war. As Hans Erich Nossack recorded shortly after the firestorm, it was difficult to view the Allies as anything other than the agents of some kind of divine justice:

I have not heard a single person curse the enemies or blame them for the destruction. When the newspapers published expressions like "pirates of the air" and "arsonists," we had no ears for that. A much deeper insight forbade us to think of an enemy who was supposed to have caused all this; for us, he too was at most an instrument of unknowable forces that wished to annihilate us.[17]

After the war, the sense that Germany had deserved this retribution grew, fueled by the news of what had happened at Belsen, and Auschwitz, and Hamburg's own concentration camp at Neuengamme. The coldbloodedness of these atrocities seemed to dwarf anything the Allied air forces might have done. As the Nuremberg trials came and went, Hamburg's capacity for anger was smothered beneath a huge burden of communal guilt.

In such an atmosphere it was the Nazis, not the Allies, who were blamed for the catastrophe that had consumed the city in 1943. For example, when the famous memorial to the dead was unveiled at Ohlsdorf cemetery in 1952, the city's first postwar mayor, Max Brauer, gave a speech in which he denounced the "inhuman dictatorship" that had led the people like lambs to the slaughter. "This mass grave is a warning to us," he said. "We must recognize the danger [of extremism]. We must know that, in the end, as soon as mankind gives up its rights and freedoms it is stepping onto the road to self-destruction."[18]

These sentiments have been repeated in one form or another in every memorial since. On the fiftieth anniversary of the firestorm, Elisabeth Kiausch, the president of the city council, implored her audience never to forget the horrors of war, and the "sorrow that Nazism brought to innumerable people."[19] That same day, even as the student demonstrators were clamoring outside her church, the bishop of Hamburg was praying for forgiveness for the wrongs that Germany had committed in the past— particularly against eastern Europe, against the Jews, and against Gypsies. Her sermon was primarily an appeal for world peace, but also a plea that we should never forget the time of the Third Reich, when the "political blindness" of the German people had led to war and atrocity.[20]

However, there is a feeling in Germany that such attitudes might slowly be changing. While newspapers, politicians, and community leaders maintain the official line that Germany herself was responsible for the firestorm and its aftermath, many privately hold different opinions. It is not only those who lived through the bombings—German society has always made concessions for *personal* anger against the former Western Allies, so long as it is not voiced too loudly—there is now much more widespread resentment. A younger generation, which is not quite so intimately acquainted with German war guilt, has begun to question the readiness with which the Allies bombed civilians. Since 1989 there has also been an influx of ideas from the former East Germany. Understandably, the East Germans have never been quite so well-disposed toward the way Britain and America bombed their country—an attitude that was encouraged by the country's communist leaders for over forty years.

These feelings came to something of a head in 2002, when Jörg Friedrich published an extremely controversial history of the bombing war.[21] Friedrich openly claimed that the British insistence on area bombing made both Harris and Churchill no better than war criminals. Even more controversially, he deliberately described the bombings in terms usually reserved for Nazism and the Holocaust: So, for example, cellars are described as *Krematoria* ("crematoria"), cities as *Hinrichtungsstätten* ("places of execution"), and the destruction of libraries as *Bücherverbrennung* ("book burning"). Needless to say, the book's publication created a media storm in Germany and abroad. It also created enormous concern, because it appeared to strike such a chord with the German people: There were immediately worries that Germans were beginning to see themselves as the victims rather than the perpetrators of war crimes, and that books like this might even become a clarion call for neofascists.

While this last point seems unlikely, it is important to note that Germans seem to live in constant fear of a resurgence of right-wing extremism. Nowhere is this fear more prevalent than in Hamburg. In 1992 neo-Nazi violence provoked an antifascist demonstration on the streets of Hamburg 400,000 strong. There were more demonstrations when the American neo-Nazi publisher Gary Lauck was tried and sentenced here in 1996. I myself experienced a hint of the city's anxieties when I first visited Hamburg in 2001, during a book tour. A complete stranger approached me and asked me to wear a badge bearing an antifascist slogan: He had heard that I would be appearing on local television and wanted his slogan to appear with me. Being entirely unaware of Hamburg's political landscape at the time, I declined—but not without a measure of surprise at the strength of his feelings. It struck me then, as it has struck me many times since, how politically active Hamburgers seem to be when compared to my own countrymen. Sometimes it seems as though the city is vigilant to the point of paranoia when it comes to avoiding the political mistakes of the past.

It is against this background that the demonstration in the Michaeliskirche took place. The antinationalist students claimed to be protesting against the fact that churchgoers were mourning *all* of the deaths that took place during the catastrophe, rather than making a distinction between the guilty and the innocent. However, as they blew their whistles and sounded their horns, their objections seemed to go much further than this. Their banner claimed that there was no reason to mourn *whatsoever*, thus implying that every Hamburger that died in 1943 got what he or she deserved. Since all of Germany stood by and allowed the Nazis to march to power, all of Germany was to blame.[22]

As an outsider, this strikes me as a bizarre form of self-flagellation. I find it shocking that a group of Germans will go as far as to deny their countrymen the right to mourn the deaths of thousands of undisputed civilians, simply in the name of expiating their guilt. Even the most hard-hearted proponent of British bombing expressed regret at what they felt forced to do. Even those theorists who claimed that women and children were a legitimate target recognized that bombing them was a horrific idea—indeed, they believed that the very horror of it would prevent civilized nations from going to war in the first place. None of these groups would ever consider denying Hamburgers the right to mourn their dead. I doubt that such a denial would get much support in Germany either, but the fact that a group like this can suggest it at all seems significant. If German war guilt has grown so great that it takes precedence over the city's capacity to mourn, then it is unsurprising that there has been a right-wing backlash against it.

The more rational reasons behind the demonstration—that there should be a distinction between the civilian victims of the firestorm and those people who were legitimate targets for the bombs—are also much more interesting. *Should* such a distinction be made, or should we avoid distinctions, in the same way that the bombs themselves did? Since it is Christian doctrine to pray for *all* sinners, are churchgoers right to mourn the soldiers, the arms manufacturers, and the Nazi Party members along with the housewives and the children who were killed? And further, is it possible to go so far as forgiveness, even for those who went so enthusiastically to war in 1939? Or would this merely lend legitimacy to the atrocities the Nazis committed?

To consider these questions, the first thing we must do is to draw a distinction between public and private mourning. This is important because they are two very different acts. A private act of mourning is exactly that—something personal, unique to the individual who suffers through loss. A public act of mourning is a statement to the world, declaring openly the values that we collectively hold dear. The same person, commemorating the same event, can profess very different sentiments, perhaps even conflicting ones, depending on whether he is acting in a private or a public capacity.

Privately, of course, any individual has a right to mourn whomsoever they choose. A mother will naturally mourn her son even if he turned out to be a murderer. A husband might forgive his wife things in death that he could never forgive her while she was alive. Love, as Nietzsche wrote, is beyond good and evil; mourning for a loved one, therefore, takes no account of whether they were worthy of that mourning.

The same is true of Christian love for one's neighbor, whoever that neighbor might be—a civilian, a soldier, or even a Nazi. A storm trooper in the firestorm was no less human than a Hamburg housewife, and also deserves some empathy—if not for the *fact* of his death then at least for the *manner* of it. A Nazi prison guard may have committed countless crimes during his lifetime, and may even have intended to commit more, but at the point of death he was merely a human being undergoing a form of hell, and for this he, too, can be pitied. From a Christian point of view it is every individual's *duty* to try to forgive others, even those who have committed the most heinous of crimes.

In a public ceremony, however, this duty dissolves very much into the background. The whole point of a public commemoration is, first, to remember what happened, second, to explain why it happened, and third, to show the world what it is you have lost. When commemorating an event as huge as the Hamburg firestorm, the ceremony is as much about the loss of ideals as it is about the loss of human life. In the years since the war, the firestorm has come to be symbolic of an even greater tragedy: the fact that civilians, not only in Hamburg but all over Europe, should involuntarily have found themselves caught up in the fury of aerial bombardment. The loss that is being commemorated, therefore, is not simply human life, but *innocent* human life.

During a ceremony like the one that took place at the Michaeliskirche in 1993, the Church authorities have to walk a fine line: On the one hand they need to provide a venue in which people feel able to express their private grief at what happened, but on the other hand they have an obligation to present the tragedy of the firestorm in terms of the public symbol it has become. If the firestorm is to be seen as a tragedy for the innocent, the Church cannot also include the guilty in their prayers. In short, a distinction must be made.

Furthermore, it is the duty of the Church to direct the moral values of the community it leads. In an atmosphere where there is already a widespread fear of a resurgence of neo-Nazi activity, any public forgiveness of the sins committed by the Nazis during the Second World War is unthinkable. Indeed, anything that goes even a tiny way toward an implied acceptance of Nazi crimes must be vigorously shunned. These things are important not only for those Hamburgers who happened to be present at the commemoration, but for the whole city, and indeed the whole of German society. Such ceremonies are a template for the way the German people think about themselves, and for the way they remember both what they did during the war and what they suffered.

For these reasons, I believe the protesters at the Michaeliskirche were right to demand a distinction between those who should be publicly mourned and those who should not (although I am less sympathetic about the methods they used to get their point across). One would never consider having a ceremony devoted *only* to those militant Nazis who died in the firestorm—so why include them at all in a ceremony that should have been devoted to the innocents? I have argued that the Allies should have drawn a line between combatants and noncombatants, even if it were an arbitrary one; likewise it is fitting for the Germans to draw a line between those who should be mourned, and those who should not.

However, *where* exactly that line should be drawn is extremely problematic. Some people believe that all the genuinely innocent victims of the firestorm should be painstakingly named, in the same way that Berlin's Jews were listed for the Holocaust Museum, so that any future commemoration will be for them and for them only. They argue very passionately that this is the only way to avoid the cloudy thinking that mixes the guilty with the innocent, and that thereby devalues any commemoration of Hamburg's tragedy.[23]

Personally I do not believe this is the answer. If such a register were ever created, it would necessarily have to include many people who do not fit in with the spirit of the idea. For example, there were countless men and women in Hamburg who supported Hitler, who believed in "final victory," and who hated Jews, but who were never required to do anything active for the Nazi Party. It would make me very uncomfortable if such people were included among the innocent victims of the firestorm, but how could they possibly be excluded? Freedom of speech and freedom of political association are two of the cornerstones of democratic society—by this token even the most ardent supporters of Nazism must be deemed innocent if they have not committed any actual crime.

Equally, some people for whom such a register seems designed might easily find themselves left off. Many soldiers privately hated the war, and despised Nazi policies—and yet they still took up arms for their country. Hans Scholl is a perfect example. As the founder of the White Rose movement, Scholl was executed for printing anti-Nazi leaflets—and yet he had also served as a soldier in the German army. Most Germans would say that Scholl was a victim of the Nazi regime rather than one of its perpetrators. But if he had been killed by a bomb before he had had the chance to print his leaflets, or while he was still in the army, would he have ended up on the other side of the dividing line?

The problem with listing the innocent is that everyone not listed then becomes guilty by default. The distress that this would cause to countless families in Hamburg is surely too high a price to pay. In any case, I doubt that a register of the innocent would in reality remove all ambiguity: Disputes would inevitably arise, causing yet more distress, and in the absence of absolute proof it would be impossible to make a decision one way or the other. Guilt and innocence are rarely clear-cut concepts, no matter how much we would like them to be, and we must be prepared to allow for a rather broad gray area between the two.

If a line must be drawn, it should therefore be a broad conceptual one. Those people who both supported the Nazi Party and actively involved themselves in furthering its goals cannot, *must* not, be mourned publicly. Those who resisted the Nazis both in thought and deed should be remembered in our prayers. Everyone else should be left to God, in the faith that He will know His own.

I have written here about blame, about guilt, about morality, but in the end this book is not about any of those things. My main intention has never been to judge the events of the past, only to offer a reminder that they happened. One can always argue about who should be commemorated, and how, but in the end the most important thing is that a commemoration takes place at all, otherwise these terrible events will be forgotten. The world is already beginning to forget. Once the generation that lived through those events has gone, there will be nobody left to tell the story firsthand. This is perhaps the most dangerous thing of all. When the power of their direct experience is lost, there will be very little to prevent us from stumbling into exactly the same mistakes all over again.

The purpose of this book, therefore, has been to try to give an impression of what bombing actually means to those who are unlucky enough to be caught up in it. There was nothing particularly special about any of the people whose experiences are recorded here. The men who flew the Allied bombers or the German night fighters were perfectly ordinary young men—a fairly typical cross-section of the societies from which they came. The people of Hamburg were also ordinary people trying to go about their daily business in the same way they always had. And yet they were forced to live through some of the most terrible events the world has ever seen, simply because they happened to be born in the wrong time and place. In another time it could have been any of us.

Despite this, there are many who continue to harbor grudges—on the one side toward the Allied airmen who unleashed their bombs upon Germany, and on the other side towards the German system, the German war generation, even Germany itself.

To those who continue to blame the Allies, and particularly the RAF veterans, for the way they conducted the war, I would say this: Do not be too quick to judge history with the benefit of hindsight. What might seem obviously wrong to us today was not nearly so clear-cut in 1943. Their commanders might have made errors of judgment, but on the whole the men themselves acted honorably, and selflessly, at a time when civilization itself stood on the brink of the abyss. For this, if nothing else, subsequent generations owe them a debt of gratitude.

Likewise, for those who still harbor prejudice toward Germany, I have just one thing left to say. The bombs left their mark not only on Germany's cities, but also on its population. In the aftermath of the firestorm the German appetite for war quickly began to crumble, not only in Hamburg but across the whole country, and by the summer of 1945 it had completely disappeared. It has never really returned since. A nation that was once proud of its martial tradition is now one of the most pacifist countries in Europe, and one that is quick to admonish others for rushing into war.[24]

It is this innate pacifism that is perhaps the most lasting single effect of the bombing war. Since 1945, Germany has only deployed its troops in peacekeeping operations. This is in marked contrast to the United States, Britain, France, and the USSR, who between them have waged wars in almost every corner of the planet. Hamburg has returned to its traditional role as a city of commerce, and its many newspapers and television companies remain fervently antiwar. The old U-boat yards at Blohm & Voss now work only in the repair and conversion of trade ships and passenger liners. Whatever else can be said about Germany—and much is still said—it cannot be denied that her people have learned their lesson.

ACKNOWLEDGMENTS

I am extremely grateful to the staff at the many institutions that have become essential to the creation of a book like this. The most important of these were, in no particular order, the Air Force University in Alabama, the U.S. National Archives in Washington, the Reichelt Oral History program at Florida State University, Rutgers Oral History Archive of World War II, the British Library, the Imperial War Museum in London, the Royal Air Force Museum, the U.K. National Archives, the Museum für Hamburgische Geschichte, and the Forschungsstelle für Zeitgeschichte in Hamburg. I have been consistently surprised at the knowledge and helpfulness of the staff in such institutions on both sides of the Atlantic, and am truly grateful for their existence.

Special mention must be made of the various Geschichtswerkstätten and Stadtteilarchive in Hamburg, most of which are run with extremely limited funds, and rely on the unbounded enthusiasm of the people who run them. I am particularly indebted to Grunhild Ohl-Hinz of the St. Pauli-Archiv and Sielke Salomon of Galerie Morgenland Geschichtswerkstatt Eimsbüttel, both for giving me access to unpublished material and for introducing me to survivors of the firestorm. Tim Bottoms at the Mighty Eighth Museum in Georgia and Robin Sellers at Florida State University should also be mentioned for assistance above and beyond the call of duty. Also Klaus Gille of the Carl Hagenbeck Archiv, who kindly provided me with information about the destruction of Hamburg's zoo.

Where possible, I have tried to restrict myself to quoting contemporary diaries and letters in this book, since the details they give are more likely to be accurate. However, stories told face to face have an immediacy that can sometimes be lacking in written accounts. I would therefore like to express my deep gratitude to the men and women who have both shared their diaries and consented to be interviewed for this book, especially: Leonard Bradfield, Wanda Chantler, Leonard Cooper, Walter Davis, Lishman Easby, Ted Edwards, Doug Fry, Liselotte Gerke, Ted Groom, Colin Harrison,

Kenneth Hills, Norman Jones, Beege Margot, Wallace McIntosh, Bill McCrea, Gordon Moulton-Barrett, Ted Neville, F. H. Quick, James Sullivan, Denys Teare, Trevor Timperley, and Louis P. Wooldridge.

There are several individuals whom I must thank for their help with research. I could not have covered the German side of the story in nearly so much detail without the help of Malte Thießen and Mirko Hohmann. David Isby got me started on the American research, and Paul Wolf was an enormous help at the U.S. National Archives. Harry D. Gobrecht was very helpful with information relating to the USAAF's 303rd BG. Although I did not have time to follow up all the leads they gave me, Penny Ash and Keith Hill were generous with their own lists of contacts. The irrepressible Peter Hart of the Imperial War Museum not only helped with oral history sources but kept me smiling as well. Thanks must also go to H. E. Batchelder of the RAF Ex-Prisoner of War Association, Nigel Parker of *Bomber Command News* and Frank Haslam of the British & Commonwealth Air Unit Register, and Oliver Clutton-Brock. My wife, Liza, gave me excellent advice on ways to improve the manuscript, as did Ion Trewin and Ian Drury. I must also thank Sonia Stammwitz, Jenny Piening, and Sylvia Goulding for their help with translating some of the denser German documents.

As always, I am very grateful also to my agents: Simon Trewin and Claire Scott at PFD; Nicki Kennedy, Mary Esdaile, and all at ILA; and Dan Mandel at Sanford J. Greenburger Associates.

I must thank Methuen for permission to quote from Bertolt Brecht's "To Those Born Later" in Chapter 5; and Farrar, Straus & Giroux for permission to quote from Primo Levi's "Give Us" in Chapter 6.

Lastly I must thank all those at my publishers who have made this book possible. After working for several years in the publishing industry myself, I know what an enormous amount of effort goes into the creation, publicizing, and marketing of a book, and I am grateful to everyone at Simon & Schuster for all their hard work. In particular I must thank my editors Lisa Drew, Roz Lippel, and Sam Martin for all their patience, their excellent advice, and their constant enthusiasm for this book throughout the publishing process.

APPENDIX A

Chronology of Hamburg

Year	Date	Events and description
808		Charlemagne begins building a fortress called Hammaburg at the point where Alster meets the Elbe.
831		Franconian emperor Ludwig the Pious sends Benedictine monk Ansgar to pitch tents on the Elbe and appoints him bishop.
845		Viking marauders reduce Hammaburg to rubble.
9th–13th C		Reign of Schauenburg counts allows city to flourish and expand to south of the Elbe.
1186–87		Adolf III von Schauenburg parcels out wasteland to west of old town, and a mercantile settlement and harbor are constructed. This becomes Neustadt.
1189	May 7	According to tradition, Emperor Frederick Barbarossa grants Adolf III the right to duty-free trade all along the Lower Elbe to the point where it flows into the North Sea.
1190		Inhabitants revolt and try to free themselves from aristocratic rulers.
1201		Hamburg is invaded by Danes.
1227		Danes expelled by Adolf III's son, Count Adolf IV.
1235		Alster is dammed.
1250		Population 5,000.
1265		"Barbarossa's Charter" is formally drawn up.
13th C		Hamburg joins Hanseatic League.
1400		Population 7,500.
early 1400s		Klaus Stoertebeker and Godeke Michels, Hamburg's equivalent of Robin Hood, wage buccaneer war against Hanseatic fleet.

1510	Emperor Maximillian I declares Hamburg an Imperial City—an important step in gaining emancipation from Danes.
1558	Founding of Hamburg Stock Exchange. Population around 20,000.
16th C	Lutheran reformation in city carried through by Johannes Bugenhagen. Influx of Protestants to city to avoid persecution elsewhere.
early 17th C	Influx of Sephardic Jews from Portugal and Spain to avoid persecution.
1619	Founding of Bank of Hamburg.
1800	Population 130,000.
1806	Napoleon invades Hamburg.
1814	Napoleon's troops repelled.
1815	Congress of Vienna guarantees freedom of the city.
1842	The Great Fire.
1847	Founding of HAPAG (Hamburg-Amerikanische-Packetfahrt-Actien-Gesellschaft)—to become the biggest ship business in Germany.
1867	Hamburg joins North German League.
1871	Integration into German Reich under Bismarck.
1872	Opening of rail bridge across the Elbe—followed by New Elbe Bridge for road traffic in 1887.
1881–88	Erection of Speicherstadt, a harbor storage city district.
1888	Hamburg joins German Customs Union. "Free port" established, enabling Hamburg to become one of the largest storage locations for coffee, cocoa, spices, and carpets.
1892	Cholera epidemic kills 8,000.
1895	Construction of Baltic–North Sea Canal.
1897	Inauguration of new Rathaus.
1900	Population exceeds 1 million.
1912	Hamburg becomes the third-largest port in the world, after London and New York.
1914–18	40,000 citizens die in WWI.
1918	Revolution starts with mutiny of sailors in Kiel, and quickly spreads to Hamburg. On November 6 they form

"Workers and Soldiers Council," and seize political power. After the elections the following spring, they hand over power to city parliament on March 16, 1919.

1919		University of Hamburg founded. Treaty of Versailles requires coastal towns to hand over majority of merchant fleets to the victors of the war.
1923		Hyperinflation cripples Hamburg.
1927		Links with U.K. and U.S. help Hamburg to recover quicker than most of Germany. Blue-collar workers' pay reaches prewar levels again at last. White-collar workers' pay would do the same by 1929.
1929–30		World slump hits Hamburg hard. Companies go bankrupt. City's welfare expenditure spirals out of control.
1932		Unemployment almost 40 percent—radicalism returns.
1933	January 30	Hamburg's senate implements persecutions ordered by Nazis, so as not to give new government any pretext to intervene in the running of the city.
	February 28	Orders issued to carry out arrests.
	March 1	75 Communist Party functionaries arrested, to be followed by Social Democrats, trade unionists, and other opponents of National Socialism.
	March 5	Nazi vote in Hamburg rises by 100,000, giving them 38.8 percent of vote.
	October 14	Hamburg's parliament, the City Council, is dissolved.
1935	January 1	Nazi Party has 46,500 members in Hamburg, 3.8 percent of population. Air raid training begins.
1937		Greater Hamburg Act (Gross Hamburg Gesetz) incorporates Altona, Wandsbek, Harburg, and twenty-seven other municipalities under Prussian control until then. As a result, Hamburg nearly doubles in size, and population rises 41 percent to 1.68 million inhabitants.
		Hamburg–Lübeck autobahn is completed.
		Blackout drills started.
1938	April 1	Merger of Hamburg and other towns comes into being.
	December	Neuengamme concentration camp is completed.
1939	July	Air raid shelters start to be built—108 completed by September 1942, but still only enough for 10 percent of population.

1940	May 18	Hamburg bombed for the first time.
1943	April 20	Hamburg leaders draw up a disaster plan in case of heavy air raids.
	May 27	Sir Arthur Harris unveils plans to destroy Hamburg.
	June 19/20	Hamburg defenses carry out rehearsal for their disaster plan in Altona. Their worst-case scenario involves some 3,000 dead, 1,000 wounded, and 110,000 homeless.
	June 25	USAAF flies on Hamburg for the first time. They fail to reach the city, and lose eighteen planes.
	July 6–12	A week of consultation by Hamburg's leaders over the city's disaster plan, concluding in another rehearsal.
	July 27	Firestorm (see Appendix C).
	August	Göring, Goebbels, Frick, and others visit the stricken city, but Hitler refuses to come.
1944	end	Antitank obstacles erected in streets, and territorial army of old men and adolescents called up.
1945	April 29	Commanding officer Brigadier General Alwin Wolz establishes contact with British troops outside Hamburg.
	May 3	Wolz signs unconditional surrender. British troops enter the city.
1946–47	winter	Severe and sustained freeze sees temperatures drop to minus 28°C. Famine in the city.
1949		Hamburg becomes a federal state in the Federal Republic of Germany.
1962		Storm causes flooding that ruins old town and kills 300 people.
1993	July 24	Student protesters interrupt the fiftieth-anniversary commemoration of the firestorm, proclaiming, "there is nothing to mourn."
2003		The British ambassador addresses sixtieth-anniversary commemoration, expressing regret at events of 1943.

APPENDIX B

Chronology of World War II

BEFORE THE WAR

March 5, 1933—the Nazis win the German elections.

October 1933—Hitler withdraws from the World Disarmament Conference and the League of Nations.

March 16, 1935—Germany denounces the Treaty of Versailles clauses on disarmament.

June 1935—the Luftwaffe is re-created, with Hermann Göring at its head.

March 7, 1936—Germany reoccuppies the Rhineland, taken from it by the Treaty of Versailles.

July 1936–March 1939—the Spanish Civil War.

April 26, 1937—the Basque town of Guernica is destroyed by German bombers.

March 12, 1938—German army marches into Austria, a day ahead of the *Anschluss*.

October 1, 1938—with French and British agreement, German troops march into the Sudetenland in Czechoslovakia.

March 10–16, 1939—Germany annexes Bohemia and Moravia.

August 23, 1939—Germany and Russia sign a "nonaggression" pact.

1939

September 1—Germany begins the invasion of Poland.

September 3—Britain and France declare war.

September 17—Soviets invade Poland from the east.

September 13–26—Warsaw is bombed.

November 29—Soviets attack Finland.

1940

April 9—Germans begin the invasion of Denmark and Norway.

May 10—Winston Churchill becomes Britain's prime minister.

    `—German invasion of Belgium, Luxembourg, Holland, and France begins.

May 14—Rotterdam is bombed.

May 15—RAF begins strategic bombing offensive with attacks on oil and transport targets in the Ruhr.

May 18—Hamburg bombed for the first time.

May 26—the evacuation of British forces at Dunkirk begins.

May 31—Roosevelt introduces a massive rearmament program for the United States.

August 8—Battle of Britain begins.

August 24—the Luftwaffe accidentally bombs central London.

August 25—in retaliation, Churchill orders bombing raid against Berlin.

September 17—after failing to win air supremacy, Hitler is forced to postpone the invasion of Britain indefinitely: The RAF has effectively won the Battle of Britain.

September 30—Germany switches tactics to night bombing.

November 14/15—Bombing of Coventry devastates the city.

1941

March 24—Rommel begins advance in North Africa.

April 5/6—Germany invades Yugoslavia and Greece.

May 10/11—the final heavy bombing raid on London marks the end of the Battle of Britain.

June 22—Germany begins Operation Barbarossa: the invasion of Russia.

December 7—Pearl Harbor is bombed by the Japanese.

December 11—Hitler declares war against the United States.

December–May 1942—Japanese army sweeps across southeast Asia, taking Hong Kong, the Philippines, Malaya, Singapore, Burma, and the East Indies.

1942

January–May—the Japanese army sweeps across southeast Asia.

February 22—Sir Arthur Harris becomes C-in-C of RAF Bomber Command.

March 28/29—RAF firebombs Lübeck, destroying 60 percent of the old city.

April 23–26—RAF devastates Rostock.

May 30/31—the RAF attacks Cologne with its first 1,000-bomber raid.

July 4—the USAAF flies its first mission in Europe, against German airfields in Holland.

November 4—the "end of the beginning" of the war: The British win their first major land victory against the Germans at El Alamein.

1943

January 14–26—the Casablanca Conference, where Churchill and Roosevelt outline their bombing strategy. They agree on a policy of accepting nothing less than unconditional surrender from the Axis powers.

January 27—the first USAAF raid against a German target: Wilhelmshaven.

February 2—the surrounded German army at Stalingrad finally surrenders.

February 18—Reichspropagandaminister Goebbels declares "total war."

April 20—Hamburg leaders draw up a disaster plan in case of heavy air raids.

May 27—Sir Arthur Harris unveils plans to destroy Hamburg.

June 10—Pointblank Directive is issued, and the "Combined Bomber Offensive" against Germany begins, the USAAF bombing by day, the RAF by night.

June 19/20—Hamburg defenses carry out rehearsal for their disaster plan in Altona. Their worst-case scenario involves some 3,000 dead, 1,000 wounded, and 110,000 homeless.

June 25—USAAF flies on Hamburg, but never reaches the city; eighteen planes are shot down.

July 5–13—the last German counteroffensive in the East fails at Kursk.

July 6–12—a week of consultation by Hamburg's leaders over the city's disaster plan, concluding in another rehearsal.

July 10—British and American troops land in Sicily.

July 24–August 2—Operation Gomorrah destroys Hamburg (see Appendix C).

July 25—Mussolini is deposed.

August 1—Goebbels orders the evacuation of women and children from Berlin.

August 6—Göring visits the ruins of Hamburg.

August 17—Goebbels, Interior Minister Frick, and half a dozen gauleiters visit Hamburg.

—disastrous USAAF attack on Schweinfurt and Regensburg, in which they lose sixty aircraft.

August 18—Hans Jeschonnek, Luftwaffe chief of staff, commits suicide.

September 3—the Allies begin the invasion of the Italian mainland. Italy surrenders unconditionally.

October 13—Italy swaps sides, and declares war on Germany.

November 14—RAF begins the "Battle of Berlin."

1944

June 6—D-Day: The Allies land on the beaches at Normandy.

June 13—the Germans launch their first V-1 flying bombs on London.

July 20—Hitler survives assassination attempt.

September 8—the first V-2 rocket hits London.

October 16—Soviet forces enter East Prussia.

November 6—President Roosevelt is re-elected for a fourth term despite failing health.

December 16—opening of the German Ardennes counteroffensive.

1945

January 26—Soviet troops liberate Auschwitz.

February 3—Berlin suffers its worst air raid of the war when 1,500 USAAF bombers drop more than 2,000 tons of bombs on the city.

February 4—Yalta Conference begins.

February 13–15—Dresden is bombed, killing tens of thousands in a firestorm similar to that at Hamburg.

March 7—the Americans cross the Rhine into Germany.

March 9/10—Tokyo is firebombed, destroying sixteen square miles of the city and killing almost 90,000 people.

March 18—the RAF drop an incredible 4,000 tons of bombs on Berlin.

April 12—President Roosevelt dies.

April 11—concentration camp Buchenwald is liberated by Americans.

April 13—concentration camp at Belsen is liberated by British.

April 16—Russians begin their final push across the river Oder toward Berlin.

April 30—Hitler commits suicide.

May 3—Hamburg surrenders to the Allies without a fight.

May 7—unconditional German surrender.

May 8—VE Day.

August 6—the first atomic bomb is dropped on Hiroshima.

August 9—the second atomic bomb is dropped on Nagasaki.

August 15—the Japanese emperor informs his people that he will surrender.

September 2—VJ Day: the signing of the Japanese surrender brings World War II to an end.

AFTER THE WAR

September 30, 1946—Nuremburg Tribunal on war crimes delivers its verdicts.

Winter 1945–46—cold temperatures cause problems across occupied Germany.

Winter 1946–47—severe and sustained freeze across Germany sees temperatures drop to minus 30°C.

May 27, 1947—the British and American zones of control in Germany merge to form the "Bizone."

July 1947—Sixteen western European nations form the Committee for European Economic Cooperation. The Marshall Plan begins to take effect.

June 20/21, 1948—the Deutschmark is introduced in Germany, signaling the beginning of the *Wirtschaftswunder*.

APPENDIX C

Chronology of Operation Gomorrah

July 24

12:18—public air raid warning, set off by American B-17s heading for Norway.

Night of July 24/25—first RAF raid

22:00—791 British aircraft set out for Hamburg.

00:19—air raid danger (thirty minutes) sounded.

00:30 approx—RAF begins dropping Window, creating confusion for German radar.

00:33—main air raid alarm.

00:57—marker flares (*Tannenbäume*) rain down on western suburbs of Hamburg.

01:02—the first bombs begin to fall.

01:50—the last of 2,300 tons of bombs falls on the city.

03:01—the All Clear is sounded in Hamburg.

July 25—first USAAF raid

13:20—123 U.S. B-17s take off for Hamburg.

16:15—the Luftwaffe begins attacks on the U.S. formations.

16:20—main air raid alarm sounded in Hamburg.

16:36—384th BG drop the first bombs on Howaldtswerke shipyards.

16:40—the last bombs drop on Hamburg.

17:10—381st BG, unable to locate Klöckner factory, drop their bombs on Heide on the way home.

17:22—the All Clear is sounded in Hamburg.

18:10—after almost two hours, the Luftwaffe finally stops harrassing U.S. formations.

20:00—the surviving B-17 crews return to base.

NIGHT OF JULY 25/26

00:35—main air raid warning in Hamburg.

00:40 approx—six RAF Mosquitos bomb Hamburg in a nuisance raid.

JULY 26—SECOND USAAF RAID

08:50—121 American B-17s take off for Hamburg; 379th BG and 384th BG abort mission, leaving only four bomb groups to do the job.

11:32—main air raid alarm sounded in Hamburg.

11:59—fifty-four B-17s drop their bombs on harbor district. The bombing lasts one minute.

12:50—All Clear is sounded in Hamburg.

15:08—American bombers return to base.

NIGHT OF JULY 26/27

00:20—main air raid alarm sounded in Hamburg.

00:30 approx—four RAF Mosquitos (of six dispatched) bomb Hamburg in nuisance raid.

00:55—All Clear is sounded.

JULY 27

Five false alarms keep much of Hamburg in panic throughout the day.

NIGHT OF JULY 27/28—SECOND RAF RAID

22:00—787 RAF bombers take off for Hamburg.

23:40—main air raid alarm sounds in the city.

00:55—RAF Pathfinders drop yellow markers.

01:00—first bombs begin to fall in the east of the city.

01:20—the firestorm first begins to develop.

01:45—the last bombs fall.

02:00—firestorm so strong that men outside main fire station can only crawl on their hands and knees against the wind.

03:00–03:30—climax of firestorm.

02:40—All Clear is sounded.

05:00 approx—British planes return to base.

July 28

Morning—Karl Kaufmann orders the evacuation of women and children.
     —almost 1 million people begin their exodus from the city.

Night of July 28/29

00:15—main air raid alarm sounds.
00:25 approx—four RAF Mosquitos bomb Hamburg on nuisance raid.
01:03—All Clear is sounded.

Night of July 29/30—third RAF raid

22:00—777 RAF planes take off for Hamburg.
23:58—main air raid alarm sounds in the city.
00:37—first marker flares fall on the city.
00:43—first bombs begin to fall.
01:30—the last bombs fall.
02:00—a second firestorm develops in the northeastern suburb of Barmbek.
02:15—All Clear is sounded.
04:30 approx—RAF bombers return to base.

Night of August 2/3—fourth RAF raid

23:20—740 RAF bombers set out for Hamburg.
00:59—main air raid alarm sounds in the city.
01:30 approx—British force begins to encounter violent electrical storm.
02:07—scattered bombing begins all over northern Germany.
02:10—some marker flares fall over Hamburg, but most are misplaced or lost in cloud.
03:30—All Clear is sounded.
06:00 approx—battered RAF force returns to base.

APPENDIX D

Comparison of British, American, and German Terms

1. AIR FORCE UNITS, 1943

British (bombers)	American (bombers)	German (fighters)
RAF	USAAF	Luftwaffe
—	U.S. Eighth Air Force	*Luftflotte*
Bomber Command	VIII Bomber Command	*Jagddivision*
Group (8–12 squadrons)	Wing (6–9 groups)	*Geschwader* (3 *Gruppen* plus 1 *Stabschwarm*)
Squadron (3–4 flights)	Group (4 squadrons)	*Gruppe* (3 *Staffeln*)
Flight (6–7 aircraft)	Squadron (7 aircraft)	*Staffel* (9 aircraft)
—	—	(*Stabschwarm* [4 aircraft])

NB: The three air forces were very differently organized, and comparing them in this way is slightly problematic. For example, Allied bomber units are being compared to German fighter units. And, while RAF Bomber Command might have been similar to the American VIII Bomber Command, in 1943 the British organization was much larger than its American counterpart. The above is therefore only a very rough guide.

2. RANKS

British	American	German
Aircraftman	Private	Flieger
LAC	Corporal	Obergefreiter
Corporal	Staff Sergeant	Unteroffizier
Sergeant	Tech Sergeant	Feldwebel
Flight Sergeant	Master Sergeant	Oberfeldwebel
Warrant Officer	Warrant Officer	Hauptfeldwebel
Officer Cadet	Officer Cadet	Fähnrich
Pilot Officer	Second Lieutenant	Leutnant
Flying Officer	First Lieutenant	Oberleutnant
Flight Lieutenant	Captain	Hauptmann
Squadron Leader	Major	Major
Wing Commander	Lieutenant Colonel	Oberstleutnant
Group Captain	Colonel	Oberst
Air Commodore	Brigadier General	Generalmajor
Air Vice Marshal	Major General	Generalleutnant
Air Marshal	Lieutenant General	General der Flieger
Air Chief Marshal	General (or Four Star General)	Generaloberst
Marshal of the RAF	General of the Army (or Five Star General)	Generalfeldmarschall

APPENDIX E

British Order of Battle, July 24, 1943

RAF BOMBER COMMAND

1 GROUP (HQ BAWTRY HALL)

Unit	Airfield	Type of Aircraft
12 Squadron	Wickenby	Lancaster
100 Squadron	Grimsby	Lancaster
101 Squadron	Ludford Magna	Lancaster
103 Squadron	Elsham Wolds	Lancaster
166 Squadron	Kirmington	Wellington
300 (Polish) Squadron	Ingham	Wellington
305 (Polish) Squadron	Ingham	Wellington
460 (RAAF) Squadron	Binbrook	Lancaster

3 GROUP (HQ EXNING, NEWMARKET)

15 Squadron	Mildenhall	Stirling
75 (NZ) Squadron	Mepal	Stirling
90 Squadron	West Wickham	Stirling
115 Squadron	East Wretham	Lancaster
149 Squadron	Lakenheath	Stirling
214 (FMS) Squadron	Chedburgh	Stirling
218 Squadron	Downham Market	Stirling
620 Squadron	Chedburgh	Stirling

Special Operations

138 Squadron*	Tempsford	Halifax
161 Squadron*	Tempsford	Halifax, Hudson, Havoc, Lysander
192 Squadron	Feltwell	Halifax, Wellington, Mosquito

Nonoperational

196 Squadron*	Witchford	Wellington/Stirling
199 Squadron*	Lakenheath	Wellington/Stirling

4 Group (HQ Heslington Hall)

10 Squadron	Melbourne	Halifax
51 Squadron	Snaith	Halifax
76 Squadron	Holme-on-Spalding-Moor	Halifax
77 Squadron	Elvington	Halifax
78 Squadron	Breighton	Halifax
102 Squadron	Pocklington	Halifax
158 Squadron	Lissett	Halifax
466 (RAAF) Squadron	Leconfield	Wellington

5 Group (HQ Morton Hall, Swinderby)

9 Squadron	Bardney	Lancaster
44 (Rhodesia) Squadron	Dunholme Lodge	Lancaster
49 Squadron	Fiskerton	Lancaster
50 Squadron	Skellingthorpe	Lancaster
57 Squadron	Scampton	Lancaster
61 Squadron	Syerston	Lancaster
106 Squadron	Syerston	Lancaster
207 Squadron	Langar	Lancaster
467 (RAAF) Squadron	Bottesford	Lancaster
617 Squadron*	Scampton	Lancaster
619 Squadron	Woodhall Spa	Lancaster

6 (Canadian) Group
(HQ Allerton Park Castle, Knaresborough)

408 Squadron	Leeming	Halifax
419 Squadron	Middleton St. George	Halifax
427 Squadron	Leeming	Halifax
428 Squadron	Middleton St. George	Halifax
429 Squadron	East Moor	Wellington
432 Squadron	Skipton-on-Swale	Wellington

Nonoperational

426 Squadron*	Linton-on-Ouse	Wellington/Halifax
431 Squadron*	Tholthorpe	Wellington/Halifax
434 Squadron*	Tholthorpe	Halifax

8 (Pathfinder) Group
(HQ Castle Hill House, Huntingdon)

7 Squadron	Oakington	Stirling, Lancaster
35 Squadron	Graveley	Halifax
83 Squadron	Wyton	Lancaster
97 Squadron	Bourn	Lancaster
105 Squadron*	Marham	Oboe Mosquito
109 Squadron*	Marham	Oboe Mosquito
139 (Jamaica) Squadron	Wyton	Mosquito
156 Squadron	Warboys	Lancaster
405 (RCAF) Squadron	Gransden Lodge	Halifax
1409 (Meteorological)	Flight Wyton	Mosquito

RAF FIGHTER COMMAND

Intruder Operations

10 Group

307 (Polish) Squadron*	Fairwood Common	Mosquito
456 (RAAF) Squadron*	Middle Wallop	Mosquito

11 Group

157 Squadron*	Hunsdon	Mosquito
418 (RCAF) Squadron*	Ford	Mosquito
605 Squadron*	Castle Camps	Mosquito

12 Group

25 Squadron*	Church Fenton	Mosquito
141 Squadron*	Wittering	Beaufighter
410 (RCAF) Squadron*	Coleby Grange	Mosquito

*Not directly involved in bombing Hamburg, either because they were nonoperational, or because they attacked other targets.

APPENDIX F

American Order of Battle, July 24, 1943

U.S. EIGHTH AIR FORCE

VIII BOMBER COMMAND (HQ WICKHAM ABBEY)

1st Bombardment Wing (HQ Brampton Grange)

Unit	Airfield	Type of aircraft
91st Bombardment Group	Bassingbourne	Boeing B-17
92nd Bombardment Group*	Alconbury	Boeing B-17
303rd Bombardment Group	Molesworth	Boeing B-17
305th Bombardment Group*	Chelveston	Boeing B-17
306th Bombardment Group*	Thurleigh	Boeing B-17
351st Bombardment Group	Polebrook	Boeing B-17
379th Bombardment Group	Kimbolton	Boeing B-17
381st Bombardment Group	Ridgewell	Boeing B-17
384th Bombardment Group	Grafton Underwood	Boeing B-17

4th Bombardment Wing (HQ Elveden Hall, Thetford)

94th Bombardment Group*	Bury St. Edmunds	Boeing B-17
95th Bombardment Group*	Horham	Boeing B-17
96th Bombardment Group*	Snetterton Heath	Boeing B-17
100th Bombardment Group*	Thorpe Abbots	Boeing B-17
385th Bombardment Group*	Great Ashfield	Boeing B-17
388th Bombardment Group*	Knettishall	Boeing B-17

*Detailed for other targets, and therefore not directly involved in the bombing of Hamburg.

APPENDIX G

Luftwaffe Order of Battle of Fighters in the West, July 24, 1943

1 Jagddivision (HQ Deelen, Holland)

Night fighters

Unit	Airfield	Type of aircraft
Stab NJG1	Deelen	Me110 (aka Bf110)
I/NJG1	Venlo	Me110
II/NJG1	St. Trond	Me110
III/NJG1	Twenthe	Me110
IV/NJG1	Leeuwarden	Me110

Day fighters

Stab JG1	Deelen	Me109 (Bf109), FW190
I/JG1	Deelen	FW190
II/JG1	Woensdrecht, Schiphol	FW190
III/JG1	Leeuwarden	Me109
I/JG26	Grimbergen, Wevelghem	FW190
III/JG54	Schiphol	Me109

2 Jagddivision (HQ Stade)

Stab NJG3	Stade	
I/NJG3	Vechta, Wittmundhafen	Do217, Ju88, Me110
II/NJG3	Schleswig, Westerland	Do217, Ju88, Me110
III/NJG3	Lüneburg, Wunstorf, Stade	Me110
IV/NJG3	Grove, Kastrup	Do217, Ju88

NJ-Kommando 190	Aalborg	FW190
Stab JG11	Jever	FW190
I/JG11	Husum	FW190
II/JG11	Jever	Me109
III/JG11	Oldenburg	Me109
10 Staffel/JG11	Aalborg	FW190
Jagdstaffel Heligoland	Heligoland	Me109
III/JG26	Nordholz	Me109, FW190

3 Jagddivision (HQ Metz)

Stab NJG4	Metz	Do217, Me110
I/NJG4	Florennes	Do217, Me110
II/NJG4	St. Dizier	Do217, Me110
III/NJG4	Juvincourt	Do217, Me110
Stab JG26	Lille Nord	FW190
II/JG26	Vitry-en-Artois	FW190
Stab JG300 (Hajo Herrmann)	Hangelar, Rheine, Oldenburg	Me109, FW190

NB: This Order of Battle contains only units in western Europe between Denmark and northern France, and is the best estimate for July 24, 1943. Luftwaffe fighter units were moved around a great deal, and because of a lack of reliable documentation it is impossible to be completely certain where any one particular unit was on a given day. Those fighter groups that were too far from Hamburg to assist in its defense are not listed.

APPENDIX H

Air Force Casualties

FIRST RAF RAID, JULY 24, 1943

GERMAN LOSSES

Unit	Aircraft	Losses
II/NJG3	Ju88 C6, 360334	Lt. W. Töpfer shot down into sea off Sylt by Mosquito of 25 Squadron. Two men killed.
	Do217N, 1414	Ofw. W. Ziegler shot down, probably by Halifax of 51 Squadron. Two men killed.

BRITISH LOSSES

51 Squadron	Halifax II, HR940 MH-	Shot down by night fighter (Oblt. Günter Köberich of IV/NJG3). Sgt. W. J. Murray and 6 crew were all killed.
75 Squadron	Stirling III, EE890 AA-L	Shot down by night fighter (Fw. Meissner of II/NJG3). Three survived as POWs, but pilot W/O H. Nicol and 3 others died.
76 Squadron	Halifax V, DK187 MP-M	Lost over North Sea, probably by night fighter. Pilot F/O G. G. Such and 7 crew all died.
102 Squadron	Halifax II, JD316 DY-X	Shot down by night fighter. One survived as POW (P/O F. G. Smith), but pilot F/L T. Bakewell and 6 others died.

103 Squadron	Lancaster I, ED389 PM-J2	Shot down by night fighter (Hptm. Rudolf Sigmund, IV/NJG1), crashed in North Sea. Pilot W/O G. E. B. Hardman and 6 crew all died.
103 Squadron	Lancaster III, ED878 PM-V	Shot down by fighter (Oblt. Hermann Greiner, IV/NJG1). Pilot W/O F. F. O'Hanlon and 6 crew all died.
103 Squadron	Lancaster III, JA886 PM-E	Lost without trace. Pilot F/S R. A. Moore and 6 crew all died.
158 Squadron	Halifax II, HR941 NP-A	Shot down by night fighter (Lt. Böttinger, II/NJG3), crashed near Schleswig. Pilot Sgt. W. H. Bolam and 6 crew all died.
166 Squadron	Wellington X, HZ314 AS-P	Hit by flak, crashed at Buchholz. Pilot W/O G. Ashplant and 4 crew all killed.
214 Squadron	Stirling III, EE902 BU-P	Shot down by fighter and crashed at Barchel. Two survived as POWs, but pilot P/O R. W. Belshaw and 5 others died.
218 Squadron	Stirling III, BF567 HA-P	Shot down by night fighter, crashed near Neumünster. One survived as POW (F/O H. C. Eyre), but pilot W/C D. T. Saville and 6 others died.
460 Squadron	Lancaster III, W4987 AR-	Hit by flak and crashed near Cuxhaven. Pilot F/S A. G. Ashley and 6 crew all died.

In addition, one Halifax II (HR803 TL-P) from 35 Squadron piloted by F/S N. J. Matich crash-landed a minute after takeoff, without any of the crew being hurt; and F/S S. M. Grzeskowiak's 305 Squadron Wellington X (HF472 SM-S) crash-landed because of insufficient fuel, but again no one was hurt.

FIRST USAAF RAID, JULY 25, 1943

GERMAN LOSSES

III/JG1	Me109 G-6, No. 207	Maj. K.-H. Leesmann shot down by unknown American bomb group.

II/JG11	Me109 G-6, No. 20026	Lt. W. Gloerfeld collided with stabilizer of 379th BG B-17 and crashed near Bliedersdorf. Pilot wounded.
	Me109 G-1, No.14147	Lt. E. Kämpf shot down by B-17, possibly of 303rd BG. Crashed near Itzehoe. Pilot wounded.
	Me109 G-1, No. 14125	Uffz. W. Riedmann shot down by B-17, crashed at Sauensiek. Pilot wounded.
III/JG26	Me109 G-6, No. 16447	Pilot unknown. Crash-landed at Stade after combat, pilot unhurt.
IV/NJG1	Me110 G-4, No. 6343	Night fighter of Oblt. E. Gardiewski shot down into sea by B-17s of 303rd BG.

American losses

91st BG	B-17, 42–29813	Shot down by flak and fighters. One killed, but 2Lt. Marshall L. Pilert and 8 others survived as POWs.
303rd BG	B-17, 42–29606	Shot down by flak and fighters, 4 killed (including pilot Lt. John A. Van Wie), 6 survived as POWs.
351st BG	B-17, 42–3272	Shot down by fighter, 6 killed, but 4 survived as POWs (incl. pilot Lt. Edwin S. Boyd).
379th BG	B-17, 42–23175	Shot down by fighter. All 10 (incl. pilot Lt. Frank A. Hildebrandt) survived as POWs.
	B-17, 42–5917	Shot down by fighter: 4 killed, but 6 survived as POWs (incl. pilot 2Lt. Philip A. Mohr).
381st BG	B-17, 42–30013	Shot down by flak over Hamburg: 4 killed, but 6 survived as POWs (incl. pilot Lt. William R. Moore).
	B-17, 42–29976	Shot down by flak and fighters. All 10 crew (incl. pilot Lt. Jack H. Owen) survived as POWs.

	B-17, 42–30153	Shot down by flak, crash-landed at Südmoor. All 10 crew (incl. pilot Capt. Joe E. Alexander) survived as POWs.
384th BG	B-17, 42–3122	Shot down by fighters. All 10 crew (incl. pilot 2Lt. Ralph J. Hall) survived as POWs.
	B-17, 42–3069	Shot down by flak and fighters. All 10 crew (incl. pilot Lt. Gordon J. Hankinson) survived as POWs.
	B-17, 42–3024	Shot down by flak and fighters: 7 killed, 3 POWs (incl. pilot 2Lt. P. J. Ward).
	B-17, 42–3088	Shot down by fighters: 5 killed (incl. pilot Lt. Clarence R. Christman), but 5 survived as POWs.
	B-17, 42–29670	Shot down by flak and fighters: 2 killed, but 8 survived as POWs (incl. pilot Lt. Kelmer J. Hall).
	B-17, 42–3075	Shot down by flak and fighters: 7 killed, but 3 survived as POWs (incl. pilot Lt. John M. Hegewald).
	B-17, 42–5883	Shot down by fighters, crashed in sea. All 10 (incl. pilot Lt. Thomas J. Estes) were rescued by Danish fishing boat and returned to England.

In addition, Lt. Willis C. Carlisle Jr. of 379th BG was killed by a fighter—his crew brought the plane back safely.

2ND USAAF RAID, JULY 26, 1943

AMERICAN LOSSES

91st BG	B-17, 42–3031	Shot down by flak and fighters: 4 killed, but 6 survived as POWs (incl. pilot Lt. James W. Rendall Jr.).
	B-17, 42–42709	Ditched in North Sea after fighter attack. All ten (incl. pilot Lt. Jack A. Hargis) rescued and brought back.

In addition, Lt. Sidney Novell, a navigator with 381st BG, was killed when flak hit his B-17.

2ND RAF RAID, JULY 27, 1943

British losses

12 Squadron	Lancaster III, EE142 PH-G	Shot down by night fighter (Oblt. Willi Schmale of I/NJG3), crashed near Vechta. One survived as POW (Sgt. P. J. Bartlett), but pilot W/O W. Salthouse and 5 others were killed.
15 Squadron	Stirling III, EH893 LS-J	Shot down by flak and fighter (Uffz. Lüschner, III/NJG3). One survived as POW (Sgt. E. Hurley), but pilot F/L J. R. Childs and 6 crew died.
50 Squadron	Lancaster I, R5687 VN-D	Shot down by flak over Bremerhaven. Pilot F/S N. P. I. Castells and 6 crew all died.
78 Squadron	Halifax II, JD148 EY-A	Shot down by flak near Wilhelmshaven: 4 survived as POWs but pilot Sgt. L. E. Maidment and 2 others died.
100 Squadron	Lancaster III, EE169 HW-O	Lost without trace. W/O R. Gafford and 6 crew all killed.
101 Squadron	Lancaster III, JA863 SR-U2	Shot down over Hamburg by fighter (Maj. Hajo Herrmann, Stab/JG300). F/S D. P. P Hurst and 6 crew all died.
102 Squadron	Halifax II, JB864 DY-B	Shot down by fighter over Hamburg: 3 survived as POWs, but pilot F/O G. McF. Clarke and 3 others all died.
	Halifax II, JD150 DY-A	Shot down by fighter (Fw. Hans Meissner, II/NJG3). Sgt. G. H. Brown and 6 crew all died.
106 Squadron	Lancaster I, ED303 ZN-	Lost without trace. Sgt. E. G. McLeod and 6 crew all died.
	Lancaster III, ED708 ZN-	Lost without trace. F/S J. B. Charters and 6 crew all died.

156 Squadron Lancaster III, EE178 GT-R Shot down by fighter. At 13,500 feet the plane exploded, throwing pilot F/S G. W. Wilkins clear. All 6 others died.

Lancaster III, JA709 GT- Shot down into sea by fighter. F/O L. R. Crampton and 6 crew all died.

207 Squadron Lancaster I, W4962 EM-B Bar Shot down by fighter (Maj. Walter Ehle, II/NJG1): 2 survived as POWs, but pilot F/O C. Burne and 4 others died.

408 Squadron Halifax II, DT749 EQ-O Shot down by fighter (Lt. Sachsenberg, II/NJG3): 3 survived as POWs, but pilot F/L C. C. Stovel and 4 others died.

429 Squadron Wellington X, JA114 AL- Shot down by fighter near Neumünster. Pilot W/C J. A. Piddington and 2 others died, but 2 survived as POWs.

467 Squadron Lancaster I, W4946 PO-U Shot down by fighter (Hptm. Hans Joachim Jabs, IV/NJG1), and crashed in sea. F/S J. T. Buchanan and 6 crew all died.

Lancaster III, W5003 PO-H Shot down by fighter: 2 survived as POWs, but pilot P/O J. L. Carrington and 4 others died.

In addition 4 aircraft crashed in England:

7 Squadron Stirling III, EF369 MG-Z Lost power and crashed into a tree while preparing to land. Pilot P/O G. R. Wood and 6 crew all slightly injured.

15 Squadron Stirling III, EF437 LS-Z Hit by flak, and on return both engines cut out. Hit trees near airfield and crashed. Sgt. D. Jackson and 6 crew all injured, but not seriously.

76 Squadron Halifax V, DK188 MP-J Badly damaged by fighters, killing 1 and wounding 2 of the crew. On reaching England, 4 crew bailed out, but pilot P/O W. E. Elder crash-landed at Shipdham.

90 Squadron Stirling III, BK693 WP-A Damaged by flak. On return it swung off runway and crashed into parked Stirling. P/O R. Whitworth and crew escaped injury.

The following aircraft were lost on operations in the same area:

139 Squadron Mosquito IV, DZ458 XD- F/O E. S. A. Sniders and S/L K. G. Price both survived to become POWs.

3RD RAF RAID, JULY 29, 1943

GERMAN LOSSES

I/NJG3	Me110 G-4, No. 5468	Crashed at Stukenborg, possibly after combat with Stirling of 90 Squadron. Crew unhurt.
III/NJG3	Me110 G-4, No. 6277	Ofw. W. Kurrek shot down near Lüneburg by Mosquito of 605 Squadron. Two men killed.
II/JG300	FW190	Hptm F. Angermann shot down over Hamburg, probably by Lancaster of 467 Squadron. Pilot killed.
	Me109	Uffz. H. Fritz shot down near Oldenburg, possibly by Lancaster of 467 Squadron. Pilot killed.

BRITISH LOSSES

7 Squadron	Stirling III, EF364 MG-X	Lost without trace. P/O A. L. Forbes and 7 crew all died.
9 Squadron	Lancaster III, JA692 WS-D	Hit by flak and crashed in Hamburg area. F/L C. W. Fox and 7 crew all died.
35 Squadron	Halifax II, HR851 TL-T	Shot down by flak and fighter: 2 survived as POWs, but pilot F/L H. C. Pexton and 4 others died.
	Halifax II, HR906 TL-L	Shot down by fighter. F/L W. L. Breckell survived as POW, but pilot F/S R. Spooner and 5 others died.

51 Squadron	Halifax II, JD309 MH-	Shot down by night fighter over the sea. F/S A. Fletcher and 6 crew all died.
57 Squadron	Lancaster III, ED616 DX-	Shot down by flak, crashed north Hamburg. P/O G. A. N. Parker and 6 crew all died.
	Lancaster III, ED931 DX-C	Shot down by fighter and crashed at Tostedt. F/O B. G. N. Kennedy survived as POW, but pilot F/S E. F. Allwright and 5 others died.
61 Squadron	Lancaster III, ED782 QR-	Shot down by fighter, crashed into sea near Heligoland. P/O J. M. Phillips and 6 crew all died.
76 Squadron	Halifax V, ED244 MP-X Bar	Shot down by flak and fighter, crashed near Oberndorf: 5 POWs, but pilot Sgt. A. R. Bjercke and F/O C. Daniel died.
77 Squadron	Halifax II, JB956 KN-O	Shot down by fighter (Oblt. Gerhard Kath, II/NJG3). F/S G. H. Sutton and 7 crew all died.
78 Squadron	Halifax II, JB798 EY-P	Hit by flak, crashed at Bad Oldesloe. F/S P. A. Fraser and 6 crew all died.
	Halifax II, JD252 EY-W	Lost over sea. Sgt. P. F. Snape and 6 crew all died.
97 Squadron	Lancaster III, ED862 OF-P	Lost without trace. P/O D. J. Marks and 6 crew all died.
	Lancaster III, EE172 OF-O	Shot down by fighter. P/O C. Shnier and 6 crew all died.
102 Squadron	Halifax II, W7883 DY-R	Shot down by fighter (Lt. Sachsenberg, II/NJG3), crashed at Todesfelde. F/S Macquarie and 6 crew all died.
	Halifax II, HR711 DY-C	Crashed in sea near Heligoland. Sgt. J. S. Gaston and 6 crew all died.
156 Squadron	Lancaster III, ED598 GT-	Shot down by fighter. F/L B. F. Smith and 6 crew all died.
	Lancaster III, ED822 GT-	Shot down by fighter. F/S M. T. Hall and 6 crew all died.

158 Squadron	Halifax II, JD277 NP-G	Shot down by fighter (Oblt. Gerhard Raht, II/NJG3). F/O A. H. Boyle survived as POW, but pilot F/S N. R. McDonald and 5 others died.
166 Squadron	Wellington X, HE810 AS-Y	Lost without trace. P/O Birbeck and 4 crew all died.
214 Squadron	Stirling III, EF407 BU-A	Shot down by fighter over sea. F/O H. P. Shann and 6 crew all died.
218 Squadron	Stirling III, BF578 HA-A	Shot down by flak and fighter (Uffz. Walter Rohlfing, III/NJG3), crashing at Ahrenswohlde. Pilot Sgt. R. S. Pickard and Sgt. E. C. Bray died, but 5 others survived as POWs.
	Stirling III, EE895 HA-S	Hit by flak and crashed in east Hamburg. Sgt. J. Clark and 6 crew all died.
428 Squadron	Halifax V, DK239 NA-Q	Shot down by fighter, and exploded near Lüneburg. Sgt. P. Demcoe survived as POW, but pilot Sgt. D. H. Bates and 5 others died.
432 Squadron	Wellington X, LN294 QO-E	Shot down by fighter and crashed near Lüneburg. Sgt. J. H. Smith survived as POW, but pilot W/C H. W. Kerby and 3 others died.
460 Squadron	Lancaster III, ED535 AR-	Shot down by fighter (Hptm. Egmont Prinz zur Lippe-Weissenfeld, III/NJG1). F/O A. J. Johnson and 6 crew all died.
	Lancaster III, JA689 AR-	Shot down by fighter (Uffz. Lovenich, II/JG300). F/S H. L. Fuhrmann and 6 crew all died.
467 Squadron	Lancaster III, ED534 PO-R	Lost without trace. F/S R. W. Park and 6 crew all died.

NB: All the general RAF summaries of this operation claim only 27 planes were lost tonight, but the squadron records clearly list the 28 above.

In addition, the following planes crashed in England:

15 Squadron	Stirling I, EF339 LS-Y	Crash-landed at Coltishall on return due to engine failure. F/L G. Bould and crew unhurt.

50 Squadron	Lancaster III, ED468 VN-	Crashed on takeoff and caught fire. Sgt. E. W. A. Clarke and crew all escaped unhurt.
83 Squadron	Lancaster III, R5625	Hit by flak over Hamburg. On return P/O K. A. King mistook Sibson for Wittering airfield and crashed off very short runway. Crew unhurt.
90 Squadron	Stirling III, EE916 WP-F	Crashed shortly after takeoff. F/L C. G. Crew and crew all escaped injury.

4TH RAF RAID, AUGUST 2, 1943

GERMAN LOSSES

II/NJG3	Do217, No. 1493	Hptm. H. Baer shot down (possibly by Mosquito of 418 Squadron), crash-landed near Westerland. Crew injured.
	Do217N, No.1419	Fw. Krauter crashed at Wiemerstedt, possibly after collision with British bomber.

BRITISH LOSSES

9 Squadron	Lancaster III, ED493 WS-A	Shot down by fighter (Ofw. Karl-Heinz Scherfling, IV/NJG1), crashed into sea off Dutch coast. Sgt. D. Mackenzie and 6 crew all died.
12 Squadron	Lancaster III, DV224, PH-G	Shot down by flak over Hamburg. F/O S. Norris and 6 crew all died.
35 Squadron	Halifax II, HR863 TL-V	Crashed due to severe icing. Sgt. A. Stephen survived as POW, but pilot Sgt. E. Solomon and 5 others died.
44 Squadron	Lancaster I, W4778 KM-T	Shot down by fighter (Hptm. Hans Joachim Jabs, IV/NJG1), crashed in the Waddenzee. Sgt. P. L. Swan was picked up by German boat, but pilot Sgt. A. R. Moffatt and 5 others died.

51 Squadron	Halifax II, HR859 MH-	Lost without trace (possibly shot down by Maj. Radusch of II/NJG3). Sgt. E. R. Sklarchuk and 6 crew all died.
57 Squadron	Lancaster III, JA696 DX-J	Crashed at Nindorf. Sgt. A. C. Browning and 6 crew all died.
61 Squadron	Lancaster III, W5000 QR-B	Lost without trace (possibly shot down by Lt. Leube of I/NJG3). F/O R. Lyon and 6 crew all died.
	Lancaster III, JA873 QR-	Shot down by fighter, crashed near Lüneburg. F/L B. McM. Laing and 7 crew all died.
75 Squadron	Stirling III, BF577 JN-M	Collided in air with Do217 flown by Fw. Krauter of II/NJG3. Crashed at Kaiser-Wilhelm-Koog. F/S J. A. Couper and 6 crew all died.
	Stirling III, EH928 AA-A	Shot down by fighter (Hptm. Hans Joachim Jabs, IV/NJG1) and crashed into sea off Terschelling. P/O C. P. Bailie and 7 crew all died.
76 Squadron	Halifax V, EB249 MP-E	Crashed into woods at Hesedorf. F/O S. I. Dillon and 6 crew all died.
100 Squadron	Lancaster III, ED688 HW-A	Shot down by fighter (Oblt. Hermann Greiner, IV/NJG1), crashing in sea off Frisian Islands. W/O A. R. Wilden and 6 crew all died.
	Lancaster III, ED705 HW-C	Shot down by fighter and crashed in sea near Heligoland. F/L R. R. Howgill and 6 crew all died.
103 Squadron	Lancaster III, ED645 PM-F	Crashed south of Harburg. W/O J. S. Stoneman and 6 crew all died.
	Lancaster III, ED922 PM-C	Crashed into the Elbe, off Herrenfeld. W/O R. Dash and 6 crew all died.
115 Squadron	Lancaster II, DS673 KO-V	Shot down by fighter, crashed into sea off Wilhelmshaven. Sgt. R. W. Bennett and 6 crew all died.
	Lancaster II, DS685 KO-A	Lost without trace. F/S C. Button and 6 crew all died.

	Lancaster II, DS715 KO-Q	Struck by lightning, fell out of control, crashed near Harburg. P/O R. J. Mosen and 6 crew all died.
158 Squadron	Halifax II, HR751 NP-J	Hit by flak, crashed in east Hamburg. Sgt. C. K. Davie and 6 crew all bailed out, but Sgt. R. B. Farmery's parachute failed to open and he died. All others became POWs.
166 Squadron	Wellington X, HE464 AS-W	Shot down by fighter (Oblt. Hermann Greiner, IV/NJG1), crashed in Waddenzee. Sgt. H. Nash and 4 crew all died.
214 Squadron	Stirling III, EF409 BU-V	Iced up and crashed in sea off Wilhelmshaven. Pilot Sgt. A. A. R. McGarvey and Sgt. A. B. Grainger survived to become POWs, 5 others died.
300 Squadron	Wellington X, HF605 BH-P	Hit by flak, and forced down by severe icing. Pilot F/O Smyk and P/O T. S. Skalisz both died, 3 others survived to become POWs.
305 Squadron	Wellington X, HZ467 SM-C	Shot down by fighter, crashed Elksop. F/S Grzeskowiak and 4 crew all died.
405 Squadron	Halifax II, HR849 LQ-E	Hit by flak over Bremen. Sgt. A. F. Gregory and 6 crew all died.
	Halifax II, HR871 LQ-B	Hit by flak and storm, and eventually abandoned over Swedish territory. Sgt. J. A. Philips and 6 crew were all interned.
	Halifax II, HR917 LQ-G	Lost without trace (possibly shot down by Do217 of Hptm. R. Schönert of II/NJG5). F/L H. W. J. Dare and 6 crew all died.
419 Squadron	Halifax II, DT798 VR-T	Crashed due to heavy icing and storm: 3 survived as POWs, but pilot Sgt. J. S. Sobin and 3 others died.
428 Squadron	Halifax V, EB212 NA-U	Lost over sea. P/O V. T. Sylvester and 7 crew all died.

Halifax V, EB274 NA-H   Lost without trace (possibly shot down by Hptm. H. Jabs IV/NJG1). Sgt. M. Chepil and 7 crew all died.

432 Squadron   Wellington X, HE906 QO-H Crashed in the sea. P/O D. R. C. McDonald and 4 crew all died.

In addition, the following planes crashed in England:

7 Squadron   Stirling I, R9260 MG-O   Returned to Oakington with serious misfire. While landing, the undercarriage collapsed. Pilot P/O W. E. Stenhouse and Sgt. G. Breedon were injured, 5 others unharmed.

10 Squadron   Halifax II, DT792 ZSA-O   Badly damaged by fighter, crashed
               Farouk   on return to base. F/O J. G. Jenkins and crew unharmed.

57 Squadron   Lancaster III, LM322 DX-X Crashed on takeoff and caught fire. F/O E. T. Hodgkinson and crew unharmed.

166 Squadron   Wellington X, HF455   Crashed shortly after takeoff. W/O J. A. C. Newman and crew unharmed.

300 Squadron   Wellington X, HE807 BH-O Developed engine trouble after takeoff and crashed in field near Worksop, before bursting into flames. F/L J. Spychala and 4 crew injured.

The following plane crashed on another operation in the same area:

166 Squadron   Wellington X, HE578 AS-G Laying mines in Elbe estuary when lost without trace. W/O R. R. Burton and 4 crew all died.

APPENDIX I

Tables

Hamburg statistics

Date	Time of air raid alarm	Duration of alarm	No. of dead (all raids)	No. of wounded (all raids)	No. of homeless (all raids)	No. fleeing Hamburg (all raids)	No. fleeing to outer suburbs (all raids)	No. of fires (all raids)	Street frontage on fire (km)	Houses destroyed (all raids)	Houses seriously damaged (all raids)	Houses lightly damaged (all raids)	Industrial buildings destroyed (all raids)
July 25	00.33	2hrs 28							87km				
July 25	16.20	1hr 02							—				
July 26	11.32	1hr 18	45,000	37,439	250,000	928,000	110,000	5,896*	—	35,719	9,000	18,062	39,285
July 27	23.40	3hrs							215km				
July 29	23.58	2hrs 17							167km				
August 3	00.59	2hrs 31							—				

*Number taken from Hans Brunswig's *Feuersturm über Hamburg.*

Sources: Unites States Strategic Bombing Survey, Hamburg Field Report, and Hamburg Police Report.

RAF Statistics

Date	Sorties	a/c attacking		Abortive sorties		Missing	Damage to bombers			Interceptions		Bombs carried (tons)	Tons dropped on Hbg (approx figures only)
		Hamburg	Alternative	Over enemy territory	Not over enemy territory		Flak	Fighter	Other	Attacked	Not attacked		
July 24/25	791	728	6	1	45	12	20	2	9	7	42	2,411.3	2,300
July 27/28	787	722	6	2	42	17	29	5	7	15	67	2,433.3	2,300
July 29/30	777	699	6	2	45	28*	23	6	14	22	72	2,396.3	2,200
August 2/3	740	393	197	14	106	30	37	5	9	11	38	2,048.1	1,000
Total	3,095	2,542	215	19	238	87	109	18	39	55	219	9,289	7,800

*Total given in RAF Summary reports is 27, but squadron records show 28 losses on July 29 (see Appendix H).

Source: Bomber Command reports on night operations, UK National Archives AIR 14/3410.

U.S. BOMB GROUP STATISTICS—JULY 25

Original target	Bomb group	Planes dsptchd	Abortvs	Plns efftv B4 losses	No. of bombs	Altitude	Planes lost	Planes dmged	KIA	WIA	MIA	Claims			Actual kills
												Dstryd	Prob dstryd	Damgd	
B&V	379*	21	0	21	200 x 500lb	27,600	2	12	1	0	20	15	2	4	
	303	20	0	20	200 x 500lb	29,220	1	11	0	2	10	6	1	8	
	384	21	3	18	176 x 250lb	27,000	7	10	0	2	70	10	1	13	
Klöckner	91*	18	1	17	170 x 500lb	28,000	1	14	0	0	10	1	0	0	
	351	20	3	17	680 x 100lb	26,550	1	13	0	0	10	4	2	1	
	381	23	7	16	170 x 500lb	29,100	3	7	0	1	30	2	0	1	
Totals		123	14	109			15	67**	1	5	150	38	6	27	6

*Lead group.

**Of these, 9 had major damage.

Source: 1st Bombardment Wing Report of Operations, July 25, 1943; U.S. National Archives.

U.S. Bomb Group Statistics—July 26

Original target	Bomb group	Planes dsptchd	Abortvs	Plns efctv B4 losses	No. of bombs	Altitude	Planes lost	Planes dmged	KIA	WIA	MIA	Dstryd	Claims Prob dstryd	Damgd	Actual kills
Klöckner	379	19	19	0	388 x 500 GP	27,000	2		0	0	0	0	0	0	0
	303*	20	5	15	+		0		0	0	0	4	0	0	0
	384	20	20	0			0		0	0	0	0	0	0	0
B&V	91	20	11	9	234 x 250 IB	28,800	0		0	1	10	0	0	1	0
	351	24	9	15			0		0	1	0	0	0	0	0
	381*	18	3 (1e/a)	15			0		1	1	0	1	0	0	0
Totals		121	67	54	126.25 tons		2	15	1	3	10	5	0	1	0

*Lead group.

Source: Bomber Command Narrative of Operations, July 26, 1943; U.S. National Archives.

APPENDIX J

Aircraft Specifications

BRITISH BOMBERS USED ON HAMBURG

Engines	Crew	Length	Height	Wingspan	Max Loaded Weight	Ceiling	Cruising Speed	Max Speed	Bomb Load (with fuel for distance)	Bomb Load (with fuel for distance)	Armament
Vickers WELLINGTON X											
2	6	64.6 ft	17 ft	86.2 ft	36,500 lb	22,000 ft	165 mph	255 mph	4,500 lb (1,200 miles)	1,000 lb (2,550 miles)	8 x .303 guns
Short STIRLING III											
4	7	87 ft	22.75 ft	90 ft	70,000 lb	17,000 ft	200 mph	270 mph	14,000 lb (590 miles)	2,010 lb (3,575 miles)	8 x .303 guns
Handley Page HALIFAX III											
4	7	70.1 ft	20.75 ft	104 ft	50,000 lb	20,000 ft	225 mph	277 mph	13,000 lb (980 miles)	6,250 lb (2,005 miles)	10 x .303 guns
Avro LANCASTER I and III											
4	7	68.9 ft	19.5 ft	102 ft	68,000 lb	20,000 ft	216 mph	266 mph	14,000 lb (1,660 miles)	—	8 x .303 guns
De Havilland MOSQUITO Mk IV											
2	2	40.5 ft	12.5 ft	54.17 ft	21,462 lb	33,000 ft	265 mph	362 mph	2,000 lb (1,620 miles)	—	none

AMERICAN BOMBERS USED ON HAMBURG

Boeing B-17F Flying Fortress

Engines	Crew	Length	Height	Wingspan	Max Loaded Weight	Ceiling	Cruising Speed	Max Speed	Bomb Load (with fuel for distance)	Bomb Load (with fuel for distance)	Armament
4	10	74.7 ft	19.2 ft	103.8 ft	56,500	37,500	266 mph	299 mph	6,000 (1,300 miles)	—	11 x 0.5 guns

GERMAN DAY FIGHTERS DEFENDING HAMBURG

Engines	Crew	Length	Height	Wingspan	Normal Takeoff Weight	Ceiling	Cruising Speed	Max Speed	Range			Armament
Messerschmitt Me109G (Bf109G)												
1	1	29 ft	8.2 ft	32.5 ft	7,491 lb	37,890 ft	260 mph	386 mph	620 miles	—	—	1 x 20/30mm cannon 2 x 13mm mchn guns
Focke-Wulf 190 A3												
1	1	28.9 ft	13 ft	34.4 ft	8,738 lb	37,400 ft	260 mph	416 mph	497 miles	—	—	4 x 20mm cannon 2 x 7.9mm mchn guns

GERMAN NIGHT FIGHTERS DEFENDING HAMBURG

Engines	Crew	Length	Height	Wingspan	Normal Takeoff Weight	Ceiling	Cruising Speed	Max Speed	Range		Armament
Messerschmitt Me110G (Bf110G)											
2	3	42.8 ft	13.7 ft	53.4 ft	21,800 lb	33,000 ft	250 mph	342 mph	1,305 miles	—	2 x 30mm cannon 2 x 20mm cannon 2 x 7.9mm mchn guns
Junkers Ju88C											
2	2 or 3	49.4 ft	16.6 ft	65.8 ft	27,225 lb	32,480 ft	263 mph	307 mph	1,230 miles	—	3 x 20mm cannon 3 x 7.9mm mchn guns 1 x 13mm mchn gun
Dornier Do217											
2	2	58.57 ft	16.24 ft	63.3 ft	29,101 lb	29,200 ft	260 mph	320 mph	1,553 miles	—	4 x 20mm cannon 4 x 7.9mm mchn guns 1 x 13mm mchn gun

APPENDIX K

Financial Cost of the Hamburg Bombings

BRITISH AND AMERICAN

AIRPLANES LOST

USAAF	14	@ $500,000	$7,000,000
RAF	87	@ $350,000	$30,000,000
		Total	$37,000,000

CREWS LOST

USAAF	13	@ $120,000	$1,560,000
RAF	87	@ $58,000 (approx)	$5,000,000
		Total	$6,560,000

GASOLINE CONSUMED

USAAF	375,000 gals	@ 23¢	$86,250
RAF	3,095,000 gals	@ 23¢	$711,850
		Total	$798,100

BOMBS DROPPED

USAAF	998	500lb G.P.	@ $94	$93,800
	416	250lb inc.	@ $75	$31,200
	680	100lb inc.	@ $50	$34,000
RAF	9478	2,000lb G.P. (or equiv)	@ $200	$1,895,600
			Total	$2,054,600
			Total cost	$46,412,700

Source: "Cost of Destruction of Hamburg," Statistical Control Division, Office of Management Control, September 1, 1943; Air Force Historical Research Agency, Maxwell Air Base, Alabama, Microfilm A1107, 1654–6.

GERMAN

Damage to public buildings	140,000,000RM
Damage to military structures	48,000,000RM
Damage to stations, post offices, and telephone exchanges	19,000,000RM
Damage to major industrial plants	200,000,000RM
Damage to residential housing and smaller plants	22,643,000,000RM
Total	**23,050,000,000RM**
Equivalent in U.S. dollars (1943)	**$9,220,000,000**

Source: United States Strategic Bombing Survey, Hamburg Report.

NOTES

Introduction

1. Friedrich Nietzsche, *Beyond Good and Evil* (London, 2003), maxim no.146, p.102.
2. Hans Erich Nossack, *Der Untergang* (Hamburg: Ernst Kabel Verlag, 1981), pp.18–19. Nietzsche's idea of gazing into an abyss was used as a central theme in this classic account of the Hamburg firestorm.
3. For a much longer discussion of this German reaction to the war, including Stig Dagerman's observations, see W. G. Sebald, *On the Natural History of Destruction*, trans. Anthea Bell (London: Penguin, 2003).
4. According to the British Bombing Survey Unit, Dresden suffered 1,681 acres of destruction, as compared to Berlin's 6,427. In Hamburg, a much smaller city than Berlin, 6,200 acres were completely destroyed during the course of the war—75 percent of the city's total built-up area.
5. Coventry was attacked dozens of times during the war, but the only major attack occurred on November 14–15, 1940, when 600 people were killed and 800 injured. Casualties at Hamburg were some seventy-five times greater.
6. The exception, of course, was the Cuban Missile Crisis of 1962—a threat that, fortunately, never materialized. During the Second World War, however, Cuba was an American dependency; and at the time of writing, more than fifteen years since the end of the Cold War, Cuba's ability to pose a threat to the United States has been vastly reduced.

Chapter 1: City on the River

1. According to Eckart Klessmann, *Geschichte der Stadt Hamburg* (Hamburg, 2002), p. 413.
2. Major fires have struck Hamburg in the years 1284, 1684, 1842, and 1943. See Eckart Klessmann, *Geschichte der Stadt Hamburg* (Hamburg, 2002), pp. 38, 170, 393–406, 545. For the Great Fire of 1842, see also Hans Brunswig, *Feuersturm über Hamburg* (Stuttgart, 2003), pp. 129–34.
3. While the Hanseatic League was based around western Germany and the Baltic, it also had offices in cities as far away as Bruges, Amsterdam, Antwerp, Staveren, London, Bergen, and Novgorod. See Eckart Klessmann, *Geschichte der Stadt Hamburg* (Hamburg, 2002), pp. 45–48.
4. For descriptions of these three fires, see Klessmann, op. cit., pp. 38, 170, 545.
5. See Anna Brenken, *Hamburg: Metropole an Alster und Elbe* (Hamburg, 2001), p. 24; and Klessmann, op. cit., p. 228.

CHAPTER 2: THE ANGLOPHILE CITY

1. Wilfred Owen, "Strange Meeting." In this poem Owen describes a descent into a subconscious "hell," where a forbidden empathy between the German and British enemies can at last be voiced.
2. Joseph Goebbels, *Die Tagebücher von Joseph Goebbels,* ed. Elke Fröhlich (München, 1993), vol. II, August 12, 1943.
3. See Eckart Klessmann, *Geschichte der Stadt Hamburg* (Hamburg, 2002), pp. 157–58.
4. For a fuller account of the city's involvement in the Napoleonic Wars, see David Chandler, *The Campaigns of Napoleon* (London, 2002), vol. II, pp. 133–34; vol. III, pp. 61–62, 90, 142. See also Eckart Klessmann, op. cit., pp. 312–17, 349.
5. Klessmann, op. cit., p. 414.
6. It was not only the rich who had close ties with Britain. For example, when Hamburg's dock workers went on strike in 1896 to protest against their shocking working conditions, British-based dock workers sent 30,000 marks to Hamburg to support them. See Klessmann, op. cit., p. 481.
7. For conditions in the slum districts of Hamburg, and also figures on emigration to the United States, see Klessmann, op. cit., pp. 442–50.
8. HAPAG was founded in 1847 by August Bolten, and began steam services across the Atlantic in 1856. See Anna Brenken, *Hamburg: Metropole an Alster und Elbe* (Hamburg, 2001), pp. 68–69.
9. Hamburg's international airport at Fühlsbuttel first became a civil airfield in July 1912. During the First World War, it temporarily became the headquarters of the German army's Airship Division, before a more permanent station was erected at nearby Nordholz. See Basil Clarke, *The History of Airships* (London, 1961), pp. 56, 92.
10. The Canadians followed Britain into the war against Germany in 1914, while the United States remained neutral to begin with. For a description of Canadian fears that German Americans would attack the Canadian capital at Ottawa, see Lee Kennett, *A History of Strategic Bombing* (New York, 1982), p. 37.

CHAPTER 3: CITY OF REBELLION

1. Karl Marx and Friedrich Engels, *The Communist Manifesto,* trans. Samuel Moore (Harmondsworth, 1967), p. 83.
2. For a summary of events in Hamburg during the November 1918 revolution, see the website of the Museum für Hamburgische Geschichte at http://www.hamburg museum.de. See also Klessmann, op. cit., pp. 535–36.
3. Gerhard Schultze-Pfälzer, *Hindenburg: Peace—War—Aftermath* (London, 1931), p. 175.
4. General Sir Leslie Hollis, KCB, KBE, *Random Reminiscences,* typescript memoirs, Imperial War Museum Department of Documents, 86/47/1.
5. See Klessmann, op. cit., p. 538.
6. See Richard Bessel, *Nazism and War* (London, 2004), pp. 9–14. See also Robert G. L. Waite, *Vanguard of Nazism: The Free Corps Movement in Postwar Germany 1918–1933* (Cambridge, Mass., 1952).
7. See Klessmann, op. cit., p. 538.
8. By the terms of the Treaty of Versailles, Hamburg was required to hand over the bulk of its merchant fleet to the Allies as war reparations, and its trading links with overseas countries were suspended. See Klessmann, op. cit., p. 559.

Chapter 4: The Rise of the Nazis

1. Hermann Okraß, *Hamburg bleibt rot* (Hamburg, 1934), p. 207.
2. Ibid., p. 202. Okraß gives a full rendition of the legend of this beer hall battle, which took place in the Am Stadtpark pub (pp. 201–7). An English translation is available on the German Propaganda Archive website at http://www.calvin.edu/academic/cas/gpa/okrass.htm.
3. Eckart Klessmann, *Geschichte der Stadt Hamburg* (Hamburg, 2002), p. 539.
4. In 1932 the NSDAP had 51 seats, the SPD had 46, and the KPD just 26. See Klessmann, op. cit., p. 539.
5. Victor Klemperer, *I Shall Bear Witness: The Diaries of Victor Klemperer 1933–1941*, trans. Martin Chalmers (London, 1998), p. 6 (March 10, 1933).
6. While the Nazis received almost 44 percent of the vote in the elections of March 1933, the Nazi vote in Hamburg never exceeded 39 percent.
7. On January 1, 1935, the NSDAP had 46,500 members in Hamburg, or 3.8 percent of the population. Many more Hamburgers were members of the party's sub-organizations. See the website of the Museum für Hamburgische Geschichte at http://www.hamburgmuseum.de/e/htm_e/textversion/t-20jhd-1-10.html. Last viewed March 30, 2005.
8. See Klessmann, op. cit., p. 587.
9. *Gesetz zur Behebung der Not von Volk und Reich*, v.23.3.1933 (RGB1.I S.173), available at http://www.documentarchiv.de/ns.html.
10. See *Hamburg Police Battalions during the Second World War*, in *A History of Jews in Hamburg*, trans. Struan Robertson, at http://www.rrz.uni-hamburg.de/rz3a035//police101.html (last visited October 4, 2002).
11. Wiebke Stammers interview, Imperial War Museum Sound Archive 9089/07.
12. Ibid. For examples of such textbooks, see the German Propaganda Archive at http://www.calvin.edu/academic/cas/gpa/ww2era.htm.
13. For more on the persecuted Hamburg jazz and swing movement, see Detlev J. K. Peukert, *Inside Nazi Germany: Conformity, Opposition and Racism in Everyday Life* (London, 1989), pp. 166–67, 199–201; see also Earl R. Beck, *Under the Bombs: The German Home Front 1942–45* (Lexington: University of Kentucky, 1986), pp. 17, 52–53.
14. This law was officially named the "Law for the Protection of German Blood and German Honor," and was passed on September 15, 1935.
15. See Richard Bessel, *Nazism and War* (London, 2004), pp. 70–71.
16. *Deutschland-Berichte der Sozialdemokratischen Partei Deutschlands (SOPADE) 1934–1940*, ed. Klaus Behnken (Frankfurt-am-Main, 1980), vol. 5, pp. 1352ff. See also Detlev J. K. Peukert, *Inside Nazi Germany: Conformity, Opposition and Racism in Everyday Life* (London, 1989), p. 59.
17. In the years after political parties were banned, the Communists and the SPD repeatedly tried to establish underground movements to help the victims of persecution. These were almost invariably found out and destroyed, and many of the members were executed by the Holstenglacis. See "Persecution and resistance in the National Socialist state" on the website of the Museum für Hamburgische Geschichte, at http://www.hamburgmuseum.de/e/htm_e/textversion/20jhd-1-12.html (last viewed March 30, 2005).
18. Mathilde Wolff-Mönckeberg, *On the Other Side*, trans. and ed. Ruth Evans (London, 1979), pp. 27–28.
19. Quoted by Richard Overy, *War and Economy in the Third Reich* (Oxford, 1994), p. 189.

20. See Werner Johe, "Im Glanz der Macht: Hitler in Groß-Hamburg" in Heinrich Erdmann (ed.), *Hamburg und Dresden in Dritten Reich: Bombenkrieg und Kriegsende* (Hamburg, 2000), p. 15; and "Towards a War Economy" on the website of the Museum für Hamburgische Geschichte, op. cit.

21. Along with Altona, Wandsbek, and Harburg-Wilhelmsburg came the municipalities of Bergstedt, Billstedt, Bramfeld, Duvenstedt, Hummelsbüttel, Lemsahl-Mellingstedt, Lohbrügge, Poppenbüttel, Rahlstedt, Sasel, Steilshoop, Wellingsbüttel, Lokstedt, Cranz, Altenwerder, Preußisch-Finkenwerder, Fischbek, Frankop, Gut Moor, Kirchenwerder, Langenbek, Marmstorf, Neuenfeld, Neugraben, Neuland, Rönneburg, Sinstorf, and Curslack. Conversely, Hamburg handed over several of its traditional outlying properties to Land Prussia, such as Cuxhaven, which lay sixty miles away at the mouth of the Elbe.

22. Hitler took a special interest in the construction of a new Hamburg, but his plans were never completed. See Albert Speer, *Inside the Third Reich* (London, 1970), p. 407. Illustrations of the architects' models can be found in Werner Johe, op. cit., pp. 13–25.

23. Between 1925 and 1939 he came here no fewer than thirty-three times. In the last three years before the war he made six visits. See Werner Johe, op. cit., p. 13.

24. The *Robert Ley* was originally launched as a *Kraft durch Freude* (the Nazi leisure organization "Strength through Joy") ship—but it was so constructed that it could easily be converted into a troop carrier, as it was in 1939. See Werner Johe, op. cit., pp. 15–16.

25. Speech quoted in the *Hamburger Tageblatt*, February 14, 1939. See also Werner Johe, op. cit., p. 23.

Chapter 5: Hamburg Prepares for War

1. Bertolt Brecht, "To Those Born Later," from *Poems 1913–56* (London, 1987).

2. See Ian Kershaw, *Hitler, 1936–1945: Nemesis* (London, 2000), pp. 200–221. Kershaw quotes, for example, William Shirer, an American correspondent in Berlin, who wrote at the end of August 1939 that he doubted the Nazis would actually go to war "with a population so dead set against it."

3. Mathilde Wolff-Mönckeberg, *On the Other Side* (London, 1979), p. 27.

4. These figures and the accompanying description of air raid precautions in Hamburg are taken from the *Secret Report by the Police President of Hamburg (as local Air Protection Leader) on the heavy air raids on Hamburg in July/August, 1943 (Geheim. Bericht des Polizeipräsidenten in Hamburg als Örtlicher Luftschutzleiter über die schweren Grossluftangriffe auf Hamburg im Juli/August 1943)*, translated by the British Home Office in 1946. UK National Archives, AIR 20/7287, p. 2.

5. Ibid., pp. 1–12.

6. Ibid., p. 99.

7. Eva Erna Coombes interview, Imperial War Museum Sound Archive 16789/2.

8. Joseph Goebbels, *The Goebbels Diaries*, trans. and ed. Louis P. Lochner (London, 1948), May 16, 1943, p. 301.

9. Mathilde Wolff-Mönckeberg, op. cit., p. 37. Despite the many warnings, there had only been seventy actual raids up to this point; see Hans Brunswig, *Feuersturm über Hamburg* (Stuttgart, 2003), p. 451.

10. For the conscription of women, restriction of vacations, and longer working hours, see Beck, op. cit., pp. 40, 45; and Goebbels, *Diaries*, entries for January 25 and December 11, 1942, pp. 15, 178.

11. Goebbels, *Diaries*, April 23, 1942, p. 131.

12. Wiebke Stammers interview, IWM Sound Archive 9089/07.
13. Ibid.
14. Else Baker interview, IWM Sound Archive 18582.
15. Hannah Kelson interview, IWM Sound Archive 15550/5.
16. Goebbels, *Diaries*, April 17, 1943, pp. 258–59.
17. Beck, op. cit., p. 53.
18. For example, when the Americans and British defeated Rommel and turned their attentions to Sicily, Mathilde Wolff-Mönckeberg, op. cit., p. 66, expressed the hope that the British and Americans would hurry up and win the war.
19. Between July 1942 and July 1943 there were only fourteen raids on the city, and most of those were merely nuisance raids performed by just a handful of bombers. See Brunswig, op. cit., pp. 453–54.
20. Police president of Hamburg, op. cit., pp. 1, 97. It is possible that the chief of police wanted to deflect any blame away from himself and those acting under him, but (with only a few exceptions) the air raid protection measures in Hamburg were exemplary. See Brunswig, op. cit., p. 165–86.
21. Fredy Borck, "Feuersturm über Rothenburgsort 1943" in Kerstin Hof, ed., *Rothenburgsort 27/28 Juli 1943* (unpublished booklet, produced by Stadtteilinitiative Hamm e.V.), p. 11. Although I have not found any British record of a mission to drop such leaflets on Hamburg, there are many other German accounts that this occurred. Such propaganda leaflets were regularly dropped all over Germany, and it's likely that the people of Hamburg only imbued them with portentous qualities after the event.

Chapter 6: A Brief History of Bombing

1. Primo Levi, "Give us," *Collected Poems* (London: Faber & Faber, 1988), p. 68.
2. H. G. Wells, *The War in the Air, and Particularly How Mr. Bert Smallways Fared While It Lasted* (Leipzig: Bernhard Tauchnitz, 1909), p. 312.
3. Ibid., p. 186.
4. Gustaf Janson, "A Vision of the Future," printed in I. F. Clarke, ed., *The Tale of the Next Great War 1871–1914: Fictions of Future Warfare and Battles Still-to-come* (Liverpool University Press, 1995), p. 279.
5. See the many examples given in I. F. Clarke, op. cit.; Michael Paris, *Winged Warfare: The Literature and Theory of Aerial Warfare in Britain 1859–1917* (Manchester University Press, 1992); and Lee Kennett, *A History of Strategic Bombing* (New York: Scribner, 1982).
6. See Kennett, op. cit., p. 14.
7. In 1899, at the first Hague Peace Conference, Britain's Lord Wolseley refused to agree to a motion to ban aerial bombing because he believed aerial bombing would shorten future wars and so reduce the total numbers of casualties in any future conflict. Not only that, but fear of the effects of bombing would make nations hesitate about going to war in the first place. (See Sven Lindqvist, *A History of Bombing*, trans. Linda Haverty Rugg [London: Granta, 2001], p. 58.) These claims were repeated eight years later by American commentators such as Major George Squier of the U.S. Signal Corps, who claimed that once politicians realized that aircraft could bypass the battle zone altogether—that in fact the politicians themselves could now become the target—they would be deterred from going to war in the first place. See Major George Squier, "Present status of military aeronautics" (1907), reprinted in *Flight*, vol. I, no.9 (February 27, 1909), p. 304. See also Michael Paris, op. cit., p. 164.

8. B. H. Liddell Hart, *Paris, or the Future War* (London: Kegan Paul, Trench, Trubner & Co., 1925), pp. 45–46.
9. Quoted in Andrew Boyle, *Trenchard: Man of Vision* (London: Collins, 1962), p. 229.
10. Quoted in the *New York Times,* October 14, 1917.
11. Andrew Boyle, *Trenchard: Man of Vision* (London: Collins, 1962), p. 312.
12. Quoted in Max Hastings, *Bomber Command* (London: Michael Joseph, 1979), p. 46.
13. Leon Daudet, *La Guerre Totale* (Paris, 1918). Daudet is reputed to be the first person to have coined the phrase "total war."
14. Giulio Douhet, *The Command of the Air,* trans. Dino Ferrari (London: Faber & Faber, 1943), p. 151.
15. Cicely Hamilton, *Theodore Savage* (London, 1922), p. 75.
16. Desmond Shaw, *Ragnarok* (London, 1926), p. 349.
17. J. F. C. Fuller, *The Reformation of War* (London, 1923), p. 70.
18. Douhet, op. cit., p. 52.
19. See Kennett, op. cit., p. 38, for a description of the air raid scares in Ottawa and New York in 1918; and Sir Arthur Harris, *Bomber Offensive* (London: Collins, 1947), pp. 65–66 for the various scares in 1942.
20. J. M. Spaight, *Air Power and the Cities* (London: Longmans, Green & Co., 1930), p. 162.
21. Sir Malcolm Campbell, *The Peril from the Air* (London: Hutchinson & Co, 1937), pp. 54–55.
22. For the reader who is interested in how the international community has tried to restrict the use of various weapons and military practices, I strongly recommend Michael Howard, ed., *Restraints on War* (Oxford, 1979). See also James Brown Scott, ed., *The Hague Conventions of 1899 and 1907* (London, 1915).
23. For a brief description of this international conference, see Philip S. Meilinger, "Clipping the Bomber's Wings: The Geneva Disarmament Conference and the Royal Air Force 1932–34," *War in History* (1999), vol. 6, no. 3. See also Sven Lindqvist, *A History of Bombing* (London: Granta, 2001), pp. 116 and 140.
24. See Richard Bessel, *Nazism and War* (London: Weidenfeld & Nicolson, 2004), whose main thesis is that "The ideology of Nazism was an ideology of war, which regarded peace merely as a preparation for war" (p. 1).
25. UK National Archives AIR 41/40, Appendix 4, Roosevelt message, September 3, 1939.
26. Prime Minister Neville Chamberlain's speech to the House of Commons, September 14, 1939.
27. See Max Hastings, *Bomber Command* (London, 1979), p. 59.
28. Quoted in Robin Neillands, *The Bomber War* (London: John Murray, 2001), p. 41.
29. See Max Hastings, *Bomber Command* (London: Michael Joseph, 1979), p. 64.
30. For a description of this *"ruchloser Terrorangriff auf die Zivilbevölkerung,"* see Hans Brunswig, *Feuersturm über Hamburg* (Stuttgart: Motorbuch Verlag, 2003), pp. 43–46.
31. See Cajus Bekker, *The Luftwaffe War Diaries* (New York, 1994), p. 172.
32. Hitler's speech in the Berliner Sportpalast on September 4, 1940, quoted in Uwe Bahnsen and Kerstin von Stürmer, *Die Stadt, die sterben sollte: Hamburg im Bombenkrieg, Juli 1943* (Hamburg, 2003), p. 72.
33. Sir Charles Webster and Noble Frankland, *The Strategic Air Offensive against Germany, 1939–1945* (London: HMSO, 1961), vol. 1, p. 157.
34. These statistics are taken from John Ray, *The Second World War* (London: Cassell, 1999), p. 95; and Neillands, op. cit., p. 44.
35. See, for example, Churchill's speech of July 15, 1941, claiming that the people of London would certainly wish to "mete out to the Germans the measure, and more than the measure, that they have meted out to us"; quoted in A. C. Grayling, *Among the Dead Cities* (London, 2006), p. 187.

CHAPTER 7: THE GRAND ALLIANCE

1. During the German Blitz on London, Sir Arthur Harris claims that he stood on the roof of the Air Ministry watching the fires and said, in an echo of this biblical quotation, "Well, they are sowing the wind." Portal also swore at this time that "the enemy would get the same and more of it." See Sir Arthur Harris, *Bomber Offensive* (London, 1947), pp. 51–52.

2. Stanley Baldwin's famous quotation about the bomber always getting through did not account for the difficulties of navigating at night and over thick clouds, which meant that the target was often not even found, let alone bombed. When the Butt Report was published in September 1941, it showed that even when the bombers found their targets only a third of them managed to bomb within five miles of it. See, for example, Robin Neillands, *The Bomber War* (London: John Murray, 2001), p. 58.

3. Professor Pat Blackett, quoted in Max Hastings, *Bomber Command* (London: Michael Joseph, 1979), p. 111.

4. Quoted in Hastings, op. cit., p. 120.

5. See Sir Arthur Harris, *Bomber Offensive* (London: Collins, 1947), pp. 9–69.

6. Quoted in Hastings, op. cit., p. 135. Harris's memoirs have the politer version "tanks that ate hay and thereafter made noises like a horse," p. 24.

7. Harris, op. cit., p. 66.

8. Quoted in Hastings, op. cit., p. 135.

9. Ibid.

10. Harris, op. cit., p. 52.

11. Harris, quoted in Hastings, op. cit., p. 147. The figure of 60 percent was a British estimate from reconnaissance photographs, see Robin Neillands, *The Bomber War* (London: John Murray, 2001), p. 112; German estimates directly after the attack were as high as 80 percent—see *The Goebbels Diaries*, trans. and ed. Louis P. Lochner (London: Hamish Hamilton, 1948), p. 109.

12. Goebbels, op. cit., diary entry for April 28, 1942, p. 142.

13. These figures are taken from Hastings, op. cit., p. 152.

14. Their policy as regarded the Japanese was very different. The firebombing of Tokyo in 1945 owed much to the lessons the Americans had learned through observing British area bombing, and probably resulted in more casualties than Hamburg and Dresden put together.

15. See Roger A. Freeman, *The Mighty Eighth* (London: Cassell, 2000), p. 1.

16. Toward the end of the war the Americans themselves began to realize that their "pickle barrel" accuracy was a myth for these very reasons. See Summary Report of the United States Strategic Bombing Survey (European War), p. 4, U.S. National Archives. An exact reproduction of this Summary Report is available at the UK National Archives, DSIR 23/15754 and online at http://www.ibiblio.org/hyperwar/AAF/USSBS/ETO-Summary.html.

17. Quoted in Hastings, op. cit., p. 182.

18. Quoted in Neillands, op. cit., p. 201.

19. The German rumors are reported in Earl R. Beck, *Under the Bombs: The German Home Front 1942–45* (University of Kentucky, 1986), p. 59; the actual figures are taken from Neillands, op. cit., pp. 218–21.

20. Mathilde Wolff-Mönckeberg, *On the Other Side,* trans. and ed. Ruth Evans (London: Peter Owen Ltd, 1979), p. 65.

21. UK National Archives, AIR 24/257.

22. UK National Archives, PREM 3/11/8.

23. UK National Archives, PREM 3/11/8.

CHAPTER 8: THE BRITISH PLAN

1. Theodore W. Adorno, *Minima Moralia: Reflexionen aus dem beschädigten Leben* (Frankfurt am Main, 1962), chapter 19, p. 42. Adorno's philosophical work, written during the war, is about the annihilation of the individual by society. His argument that technology only serves to distance us from our humanity applies equally to the new weapons employed by the Allies during the next few days, as it does to the civilian technologies of everyday life.
2. See the descriptions of Sir Arthur Harris's "morning prayers" in Max Hastings, *Bomber Command* (London, 1979), pp. 247–49; for the specific meeting this morning see Martin Middlebrook, *The Battle of Hamburg* (London, 1980), pp. 97–98; and Gordon Musgrove, *Operation Gomorrah* (London, 1981), p. 1.
3. Bomber Command Intelligence Narrative of Operations No. 649, UK National Archives, AIR 24/257.
4. D Form, July 24/25, 1943, UK National Archives, AIR 24/257.
5. UK National Archives, AIR 55/158: *Report on German Flak Towers* by the Flak Disarmament Branch, Air division BAFO (December 1946).
6. See David Irving, *The Rise and Fall of the Luftwaffe* (Boston: Little Brown & Co., 1973), pp. 213–14.

CHAPTER 9: THE FIRST STRIKE

1. John Webster, *The Duchess of Malfi*, IV, ii, 254–55.
2. Quoted by Kevin Wilson, *Bomber Boys* (London: Weidenfeld & Nicolson, 2005), p. 245.
3. The average age of British bomber crews in 1944 was just twenty-three, which means that those just entering training were still twenty-one years old (an oft-quoted figure: see, for example, http://www.specialforces.co.uk/airgunners2.htm). In the event, many crew members could be much younger. Colin Harrison of 467 Squadron was a perfect example: He joined up when he was just eighteen years old, and was still only twenty by the time he was flying over Hamburg. "One minute I was a schoolboy wearing a cap, next minute they called me a man and put me in an airplane, next minute I'm a flight sergeant" (interview with author, December 8, 2004).
4. Interview of December 8, 2003, with Bill McCrea, who as a pilot with 57 Squadron took part in all four Hamburg raids in July and August 1943. See also his book *A Chequer-Board of Nights* (Preston: Compaid Graphics, 2003), pp. 77–85.
5. This speech was exactly the same in briefings across the country. Window was considered such an important innovation that each intelligence officer was given an identical document that they were told to read out verbatim at briefing. See UK National Archives, AIR 24/257.
6. Interview with Colin Harrison, pilot in 467 Squadron, December 8, 2004.
7. Interview with the author, December 8, 2004.
8. Letter to the author, December 1, 2004. Kenneth Hills's first operation with 9 Squadron was actually on the next Hamburg raid, on the night of July 27, 1943.
9. Quoted in Max Hastings, *Bomber Command* (London: Michael Joseph, 1979), p. 161.
10. While this job was usually allocated to the flight engineer, in some crews it would be the bomb aimer or wireless operator.
11. See Martin Middlebrook, *The Battle of Hamburg* (London: Allen Lane, 1980), p. 126.
12. Ibid., p. 120.
13. For exact times of all air raid alarms, see the Hamburg Police Report, UK National Archives, AIR 20/7287, p. 13.

14. The German 2nd Fighter Division (*Jagddivision*) had fighters stationed at Stade, Vechta, Wittmundhafen, Schleswig, Westerland, Wunstorf, Lüneburg, Grove, Kastrup, Aalborg, Jever, Husum, Oldenburg, Heligoland, and Nordholz.

15. See Adolf Galland, *The First and the Last*, trans. Mervyn Savill (London: Methuen & Co., 1955), p. 209; see also Hastings, op. cit., p. 234; Neillands, op. cit., p. 147.

16. Wilhelm Johnen, *Duel Under the Stars* (London, 1957), pp. 62–63.

17. UK National Archives, AIR 27/492. See also Middlebrook, op. cit., p. 131.

18. See Mathilde Wolff-Mönckeberg, *On the Other Side*, trans. Ruth Evans (London: Peter Owen, 1979), p. 61.

19. Interview with Colin Harrison, pilot with 467 Squadron, whose bomb aimer used to do this, December 8, 2004.

20. See Martin Middlebrook, *The Battle of Hamburg* (London, 1980), p. 84. Middlebrook does not reveal his source for this information, but his numbers are backed up by a German website, www.lostplaces.de/flakhamburg, which has a map displaying the positions of each of the flak batteries in and around Hamburg (last viewed December 1, 2004).

21. Interview with the author, November 19, 2004.

22. Interview with the author, November 12, 2004.

23. Interview with the author, October 20, 2004.

24. Leonard Bradfield, who was also interviewed by Kevin Wilson, is quoted here from Wilson's book, *Bomber Boys* (London: Weidenfeld & Nicolson, 2005), p. 248.

25. A Wellington piloted by George Ashplant of 166 Squadron was shot down over Hamburg, and F/S A. G. Ashley's 460 Squadron Lancaster was also shot down by flak near Cuxhaven. See W. R. Chorley, *Bomber Command Losses* (Hersham, 2004), vol. 4 (1943), pp. 239–40.

26. Email to the author, June 22, 2004. See also Mel Rolfe, *Gunning for the Enemy: Wallace McIntosh, DFC and Bar, DFM* (London, 2003), p. 65.

27. See Interim Report on the Attack on Hamburg, July 24/25, 1943, UK National Archives, AIR 14/3012.

28. Interview with the author, October 20, 2004.

29. Interview with Trevor Timperley, pilot in 156 Squadron (PFF), November 17, 2004.

30. UK National Archives, 75 Squadron Operational Record Book, UK National Archives, AIR 27/646.

31. Operation Summary, in UK National Archives, "Royal Air Force Operations Record Book: Appendices," AIR 24/257.

32. Bomber Command Intelligence Narrative of Operations No. 649, "Royal Air Force Operations Record Book: Appendices," UK National Archives, AIR 24/257.

33. See Musgrove, op. cit., p. 37.

34. Grzeskowiak went missing nine days later, on another Hamburg raid. It was his second operation. See UK National Archives, AIR 27/1672.

35. Wallace McIntosh quoted in Mel Rolf, op. cit., p. 65.

CHAPTER 10: THE DEVASTATION BEGINS

1. Text from propaganda leaflet dropped on Germany in 1943, with the caption *"Das war Hamburg,"* courtesy of Lishman Easby, 100 Squadron RAF.

2. For rumors about the Ruhr, see Mathilde Wolff-Mönckeberg, *On the Other Side* (London, 1979), p. 65; for rumors about exploding fountain pens see *The Goebbels Diaries*, trans. and ed. Louis P. Lochner (London, 1948), May 20, 1943, pp. 304–05.

3. While it was illegal in Germany to tune in to the BBC, many people in Hamburg no longer trusted Nazi propaganda and preferred foreign broadcasts to their own. See,

for example, Earl R. Beck, *Under the Bombs* (University Press of Kentucky, 1986), p. 37; Hiltgunt Zassenhaus in Volker Hage, ed., *Hamburg 1943* (Frankfurt am Main, 2003), p. 167; Wiebke Stammers interview, IWM Sound 9089/07.

4. See, for example, "Die Festung Europa hat kein Dach"—leaflet dropped on northern Germany late July 1943, sent to the author by Lishman Easby. While it appears that these leaflets were not dropped directly on Hamburg until the attacks themselves, there were widespread rumors leading up to the attacks that the RAF had dropped leaflets specifically mentioning the coming devastation of Hamburg. See Wolff-Mönckeberg, op. cit., p. 65; and Ilse Grassmann, *Ausgebombt* (Hamburg, 2003), June 25–26, 1943, pp. 9–10.

5. Wolff-Mönckeberg, op. cit., p. 66. For the countrywide drop in morale, see also Goebbels, *Diaries*, May 22, 1943, p. 307.

6. Wolff-Mönckeberg, op. cit., p. 65. This rumor is uncannily similar to the actual arguments given by Sir Henry Tizard for not bombing Hamburg—see the end of Chapter 7 above.

7. It was not until after the attacks that Kaufmann was finally able to announce to Goebbels that Hamburg's anglophile attitude was a thing of the past. See *Die Tagebücher von Joseph Goebbels*, ed. Elke Fröhlich (München, 1993), August 12, 1943.

8. See Charles H. V. Ebert, "The Meteorological Factor in the Hamburg Fire Storm," in *Weatherwise*, vol. 16, no. 2 (April 1963), pp. 70–75. The gentle breeze described was instrumental in bringing about the eventual firestorm on the night of July 27/28.

9. Volker Böge and Jutta Deide-Lüchow, *Eimsbüttler Jugend im Krieg* (Hamburg, 2000), p. 21; Ludwig Faupel's diary, FZH 292–8, A–F.

10. See "Frau W." in Monika Sigmund et al. (eds.), *"Man versuchte längs zu kommen, und man lebt ja noch . . ."* (Hamburg, 1996), p. 29.

11. UK National Archives, AIR 20/7287: *Secret Report by the Police President of Hamburg (as local Air Protection Leader) on the heavy air raids on Hamburg in July/August, 1943*, p. 1; Hans Brunswig, *Feuersturm über Hamburg* (Stuttgart, 2003), p. 187.

12. Interview with Wanda Chantler (née Wanziunia Cieniewska-Radziwill), July 5, 2004.

13. Hannah Kelson interview, IWM Sound Archive 15550/5. Tonight, fortunately for her, she was on holiday in a village just outside Hamburg, and so missed the full force of the raid, although the noise and commotion were still enough to rouse the young girl from her bed.

14. Martha Bührich quoted in Renate Hauschild-Thiessen, *Unternehmen Gomorrha* (Hamburg, 1993), p. 25.

15. See, for example, Hanni Paulsen's description of a bunker in Martin Middlebrook, *The Battle of Hamburg* (London, 1980), pp. 149–50.

16. Hans Erich Nossack, *Der Untergang* (Hamburg, 1981), p. 17.

17. Ibid., p. 19.

18. Ibid., p. 13.

19. Broadcast according to Georg Ahrens's nephew, Hans Ahrens, quoted in Renate Hauschild-Thiessen, *Die Hamburger Katastrophe vom Sommer 1943* (Hamburg, 1993), p. 18.

20. St. Pauli Archiv, interview with Frau M., 2/26/1993.

21. Letter to the *Hamburger Abendblatt*, August 1, 2003.

22. *The Goebbels Diaries*, trans. and ed. Louis P. Lochner (London, 1948), March 9, 1943 (p. 215), and March 11, 1943 (p. 224).

23. Rudolf Schurig, quoted in Rudolf Wolter, *Erinnerung an Gomorrha* (Hamburg, 2003), p. 122.

24. Ibid., p. 122.

25. Johann Ingw. Johannsen, typescript account c/o Marga Ramcke, Ottensen Geschichtswerkstatt.
26. Hiltgunt Zassenhaus, "Feuer vom Himmel" in Volker Hage (eds.), *Hamburg 1943* (Frankfurt am Main, 2003), pp. 156–57.
27. Internet source, Henni Klank, "Operation Gomorra," last viewed September 1, 2005, http://www.seniorennet-hamburg.de/zeitzeugen/vergessen/klank1.htm.
28. Hiltgunt Zassenhaus, op. cit., p. 157.
29. Ibid.
30. Paul Elingshausen, typescript account, Forschungsstelle für Zeitgeschichte in Hamburg (FZH) 292–8, A–F.
31. Interview with Wanda Chantler, July 5, 2004.
32. Unpublished transcript of group conversation, "Klöntreff 'Eimsbüttel im Feuersturm'," Galerie Morgenland/Geschichtwerkstatt, p. 4.
33. Interview with Liselotte Gerke, April 6, 2005.
34. UK National Archives, AIR 20/7287: *Secret Report by the Police President of Hamburg (as local Air Protection Leader) on the heavy air raids on Hamburg in July/August, 1943*, p. 15. Later estimates put the death toll for this raid much higher, but it is almost impossible to say with any accuracy how many people died in any one particular raid during this intense period of attack.
35. Hans Brunswig, *Feuersturm über Hamburg* (Stuttgart, 1981), pp. 162, 167, 175.
36. Erwin Garvens, in Renate Hauschild-Thiessen, *Die Hamburger Katastrophe vom Sommer 1943*, p. 33.
37. Paul Elingshausen, FZH 292–8, A–F.
38. Secret Report by the Police President of Hamburg, op. cit., p. 15.
39. Ibid.
40. See Rudolf Winter, op. cit., p. 125.
41. Extrapolation from Bundesarchiv document RL 19/424, History of Luftgaukommando XI by General Flieger Wolff. See Martin Middlebrook, op. cit., pp. 154, 168.
42. The single Wellington shot down belonged to 166 Squadron. See W. R. Chorley (ed.), *Bomber Command Losses* (Hersham, Surrey, 2004), vol. IV (1943), p. 239.
43. Johannsen, op. cit.
44. Ibid.
45. Rolf Arnold, http://www.seniorennet-hamburg.de/zeitzeugen/vergessen/arnold1.php, last viewed September 1, 2005.
46. Mathilde Wolff-Mönckeberg, *On the Other Side* (London, 1979), pp. 68–69.
47. Johannsen, op. cit.
48. Interview with author, April 6, 2005.
49. Franz Termer in Renate Hauschild-Thiessen, *Die Hamburger Katastrophe vom Sommer 1943* (Hamburg, 1993), p. 47.
50. Pastor Schoene of the Christuskirche in Eimsbüttel, quoted in Volker Böge and Jutta Deide-Lüchow, *Eimsbüttler Jugend im Krieg* (Hamburg, 1992), p. 24.
51. Total damage report, UK National Archives, AIR 40/426.
52. Reconnaissance report on photographs taken by RAF 542 Squadron, at 1200hrs, July 27, 1943: UK National Archives, AIR 24/257; see also Franz Termer in Renate Hauschild-Thiessen, *Die Hamburger Katastrophe vom Sommer 1943* (Hamburg, 1993), p. 47.
53. Ilse Grassmann, *Ausgebombt* (Hamburg, 2003), p. 20 (July 25, 1943).
54. Mathilde Wolff-Mönckeberg, op. cit., p. 69.
55. Ibid.
56. Hamburg damage report, UK National Archives, AIR 40/426.
57. Interview with Wanda Chantler, July 5, 2004.

58. See the *Hamburger Zeitung,* July 25, 1943: "Das Verlassen des Lufschutzortes Hamburg ist bis auf weiteres nur mit einer besonderen Genehmigung gestattet."
59. See Mathilde Wolff-Mönckeberg, op. cit., pp. 69–70.

CHAPTER 11: THE AMERICANS JOIN THE FRAY

1. Speech at Columbus, Ohio, August 11, 1880, printed in the *Ohio State Journal* the following day; a photostat of the published speech can be found in Lloyd Lewis, *Sherman, Fighting Prophet* (New York, 1932), p. 637.
2. In March 1944, faced with high losses among his men, he was quoted as saying that he would like to bomb "those damn cities" until "there won't be a damn house left." See Ronald Schaffer, *Wings of Judgement: American Bombing in World War II* (New York, 1985), p. 68.
3. Anderson flew with F/Lt. Garvey of 83 Squadron; see UK National Archives, AIR 27/687.
4. The Casablanca Conference in January had designated U-boat manufacturers as the highest-priority target, but by the time of the Pointblank Directive in June this had taken second place to German air force targets, such as Klöckner, which were "second to none in immediate importance." See W. F. Craven and J. L. Cate (eds.), *The Army Air Forces in World War II* (Chicago, 1949), vol. II, p. 666.
5. Group leader's report on mission, June 25, 1943, U.S. National Archives, RG18, E7, Box 728, Folder 2. See also Roger A. Freeman, *The Mighty Eighth* (London, 1986), p. 52.
6. For details of this meteorological flight, see UK National Archives, AIR 29/867.
7. For all these plans, see VIII Bomber Command Report of Operations and 1st Bombardment Wing Report of Operations; U.S. National Archives, RG18, E7, Box 941. See also Martin Middlebrook, *The Battle of Hamburg* (London, 1980), pp. 176–80, and Gordon Musgrove, *Operation Gomorrha* (London, 1981), p. 56.
8. The 351st BG had arrived in Britain at the end of April and had flown its first mission in mid-May on Courtai (May 14); 379th BG had arrived around the same time (first mission: St. Nazaire, May 29); 381st BG and 384th BG had both arrived in May/June (first mission: Antwerp, June 22). See Roger A. Freeman, *The Mighty Eighth War Diary* (London & New York, 1981).
9. I had the great pleasure of working with Pierre Clostermann on the English translation of the millennium edition of his classic book *The Big Show.* This was one of his favorite anecdotes about the Americans he met during the war.
10. Walter K. Davis, interview with the author, July 28, 2005.
11. John F. Homan interview, July 25, 2002, Tape 3, side A, Rutgers Oral History Archives of World War II.
12. Samuel P. Fleming, *Flying with the Hell's Angels* (Spartanburg, South Carolina, 1992), pp. 49–50. In July 1943 the combat tour was still twenty-five missions.
13. Joseph E. Mutz interview, February 9, 2000, Tape 1, side A, care of Reichelt Oral History Program, Florida State University. Mutz flew as armorer/gunner for the 95th BG in the Warnemünde wing today.
14. American infantry were, of course, engaged in North Africa and Sicily in July 1943.
15. W. Scott Buist interview, September 27, 1995, Tape 1, side A, care of New Brunswick History Department, Oral History Archives of WWII, Rutgers University.

CHAPTER 12: THE LUFTWAFFE STRIKES BACK

1. This is the popular form of the quotation. The actual quotation is, "No plan of operations extends with any certainty beyond the first encounter with the main enemy

force." See "Über Strategie" in *Moltkes Militärische Werke,* vol. II (Berlin, 1900), part 2b, p. 291.

2. Philip P. Dreiseszun, 381st BG website, http://www.381st.org/stories_dreiseszun.html, last viewed April 5, 2006.

3. Ironically, the Klöckner air-engine factory had already evacuated before these raids took place, so it was a much less important target than the USAAF thought. The plant had changed function to that of a repair shop, with some continued production of gears and screws. See United States Strategic Bomb Survey, Hamburg Report, UK National Archives, AIR 48/19, p. 45.

4. Quotation and estimate of AA guns from 303rd BG "Mission to Hamburg, Germany: Estimate," U.S. National Archives, RG18, E7, Box 678, Folder 9. Martin Middlebrook lists the actual numbers of heavy flak guns in the city as 166 88-mm, 96 105-mm, and 16 128-mm guns—although he does not reveal his source for this information; see *The Battle of Hamburg* (London, 1980), p. 84. His numbers are backed up by the website http://www.lostplaces.de/flakhamburg (last viewed December 1, 2004), which says that, in addition, 20 128-mm guns and 48 105-mm guns were brought in on 17 railway flak batteries.

5. Howard L. Cromwell, quoted by Martin Middlebrook, *The Battle of Hamburg* (London, 1980), p. 183.

6. Philip P. Dreiseszun, "Gentlemen, the target for today is Hamburg!" 381st BG website, http://www.381st.org/stories_dreiseszun.html, last viewed April 5, 2006.

7. Edward Piech interview, c/o Shaun Illingworth, Rutgers Oral History Archive of World War II. Piech actually flew on the second Hamburg mission the following day, but his general comments are relevant to both missions.

8. Sometimes it took even longer. For example, the 91st BG took off at 1:20 but did not finally cross the English coast until 2:37. See 91st BG immediate narrative, July 26, 1943, U.S. National Archives, RG18, E7, Box 541, Folder 11.

9. Donald Hillenmayer interview for the Rutgers Oral History Archives of World War II, September 11, 2003, Tape 1, side B.

10. See Philip Dreiseszun, "Gentlemen, the target for today is Hamburg!" http://www.381st.org/stories_dreiseszun.html, last viewed April 5, 2006.

11. Albert S. Porter Jr. interview, February 9, 2004, Tape 2, side A, care of Rutgers Oral History Archives of World War II.

12. Edward Piech interview, op. cit.

13. Lt. Darrell Gust, quoted by Brian D. O'Neill, *303rd Bombardment Group* (Oxford, 2003), pp. 61–62.

14. See Donald L. Caldwell, *The JG26 War Diary* (London, 1998), vol. II, p. 121.

15. Ibid.

16. Walter K. Davis, interview with the author, July 28, 2005.

17. Ibid.

18. 381st Bombardment Group War Diary, July 25, 1943. See the group's official website, http://www.381st.org, last viewed April 7, 2006.

19. Charles R. Bigler quoted in Frank L. Betz and Kenneth H. Cassens (eds.), *379th BG Anthology* (Paducah, 2000), p. 17. Bigler mentions this as happening on the Sunday raid, but it appears these events happened on the Saturday; see Derwyn D. Robb, *Shades of Kimbolton: A Narrative of 379th Bombardment Group* (San Angelo, 1981), July 25, 1943.

20. Major Kirk Mitchell quoted in message from 303rd BG to 1st Bomb Wing, July 25, 1943, U.S. National Archives, RG18, E7, Box 678, Folder 9. For Mitchell's more realistic estimate, see U.S. National Archives, RG18, E7, Box 406, Folder 9.

21. Staff Sergeant F. C. Thurman, quoted in PRO Report, U.S. National Archives, RG18,

E7, Box 1081, Folder 8. As the lead group, the 379th BG was supposed to drop its bombs first, but it was not uncommon for whole squadrons or groups to drop their bombs slightly before or slightly after they were supposed to. For example, within 303rd BG, the 360th Squadron dropped its bombs about fifteen seconds before their own group leader (see 303rd BG's mission report, U.S. National Archives, RG18, E7, Box 406, Folder 9).

22. VIII Bomber Command Report of Operations, U.S. National Archives, RG18, E7, Box 941. As the lead group, 379th BG should have been the first to drop its bombs, but it appears that the low group (384th BG) dropped fractionally earlier on this occasion.

23. As always, accurate numbers are difficult to pin down, as different sources say different things. I have chosen to use the Reports of Operations of VIII Bomber Command and 1st Wing as my main references here, and have used Roger Freeman's *Mighty Eighth War Diary*, the standard work on the U.S. Eighth Air Force, to fill in any gaps. Out of the ninety-four B-17s that managed to bomb Hamburg and return home, forty-six sustained flak damage.

24. See intercepted German radio messages for July 25, UK National Archives, AIR 40–425.

25. Enemy Aircraft Attack Data for 103rd Provisional Bombardment Combat Wing, Mission July 25, 1943, U.S. National Archives, RG18, E7, Box 678, Folder 9.

26. See the Report of Operations for VIII Bomber Command, and for the 1st Bombardment Wing (U.S. National Archives, RG18, E7, Box 941), and especially the Enemy Aircraft Attack Data for 103rd Provisional Bombardment Combat Wing, Mission July 25, 1943, (U.S. National Archives, RG18, E7, Box 678, Folder 9).

27. See pencil charts, detailing attacks on each individual aircraft in 384th BG, U.S. National Archives, RG18, E7, Box 1081, Folder 8.

28. Brad Summers quoted in Ken Decker, *Memories of the 384th Bomb Group* (New York, 2005), 3rd edition, p. 15.

29. Ibid., p.16.

30. Philip Dreiseszun, "Gentlemen, the target for today is Hamburg!" quoted on 381st BG website http://www.381st.org/stories_dreiseszun.html, last viewed April 5, 2006.

31. Ibid.

32. Again, there are some slight discrepancies in the numbers. The 103rd Provisional Bombardment Wing data show that 379th BG was attacked only fifteen times, but the pencil charts prepared by the bomb group itself suggest that there were twenty attacks (see U.S. National Archives, RG18, E7, Box 940, Folder 14). Likewise, the 103rd Wing data show eighty attacks on 384th BG, but the bomb group records suggest that there were 122 attacks (see U.S. National Archives, RG18, E7, Box 1081, Folder 8). The lower estimate in each case is more likely, since there was a tendency for double-counting in the bomb groups.

33. While this myth cannot be definitely confirmed, Robert C. King, a B-24 pilot with 485th BG, claims he actually witnessed an instance where an American bomber from another group did exactly this, and "from that mission on, the Luftwaffe targeted that group and annihilated it." See Robert C. King interview, November 30, 1994, Rutgers Oral History Archives of World War II, Tape 1, side B.

34. This man was believed to be the navigator in a/c no. 075, flown by Lieutenant Hegewald. See the story of the attack on a/c 883, U.S. National Archives, RG18, E7, Box 1081, Folder 8.

35. Ibid.

36. Staff Sergeant George Ursta, Story of Attack, U.S. National Archives, RG18, E7, Box 1081, Folder 8.

37. Unteroffizier Friedrich Abromeit, IV/NJG1, quoted by Martin Middlebrook, *The Battle of Hamburg* (London, 1980), p. 215.

38. See the summary of intercepted German radio messages, July 25, UK National Archives, AIR 40/425.

39. See the description of Mission no. 53 on 303rd Bomb Group Association's CD-ROM, *The Molesworth Story* (2nd edition). Yankee Doodle Dandy was aircraft #42–5264.

40. For more on this story, see the description of Mission no. 53 on 303rd Bomb Group Association's CD-ROM, *The Molesworth Story* (2nd edition). Grimm's DFC was awarded in 1992, forty-seven years after the paperwork requesting it had gotten lost.

41. According to Paul Gordy, quoted in Martin Middlebrook, *The Battle of Hamburg* (London, 1980), p. 219.

CHAPTER 13: THE AMERICANS AGAIN

1. William Mitchell, *Winged Defense: The Development and Possibilities of Modern Air Power—Economic and Military* (New York, 1925), p. 163. Mitchell argued that to face such dangers required extraordinary moral qualities, so the fledgling U.S. Air Force should accept only men of the highest caliber.

2. For all the statistics in the following paragraphs, except where otherwise stated, see VIII Bomber Command Report of Operations, and the 1st Bombardment Wing Report of Operations, U.S. National Archives, RG18, E7, Box 941. Statistics for missions other than those to Hamburg are taken from Roger A. Freeman, *The Mighty Eighth War Diary* (London, 1990).

3. As always, there is some discrepancy in the statistics. These numbers are taken from the 1st Bombardment Wing Report of Operations for July 25; but the VIII Bomber Command "Analysis of Enemy Aircraft Encounters" for the day lists forty-four destroyed, six probables, and twenty-eight damaged (a copy of this is available in the UK National Archives, AIR 40/425). Either way, the figures are vastly inflated.

4. These figures for German fighters lost are Martin Middlebrook's—see *The Battle of Hamburg* (London, 1980), p. 218. Middlebrook's figures are not always reliable (for example, he says the Americans claimed forty-one enemy aircraft destroyed when the 1st Bombardment Wing Report of Operations lists only thirty-eight), but the main point still stands—American claims were vastly overinflated.

5. See Roger A. Freeman, *The Mighty Eighth War Diary* (London, 1990), pp.78–83 for exact figures: Between July 24 and 31, 1943, the USAAF dispatched 1,672 B-17s and 261 B-26s to twenty-three different target areas.

6. See 303rd BG Report on Mission of July 26, 1943, U.S. National Archives, RG18, E7, Box 729, Folder 2. See also VIII Bomber Command Narrative of Operations Mission No. 77, U.S. National Archives, RG18, E7, Box 941, Folder 1; and Martin Middlebrook, *The Battle of Hamburg* (London, 1980), pp. 223–24.

7. See VIII Bomber Command Narrative of Operations Mission No. 77, U.S. National Archives, RG18, E7, Box 941, Folder 1.

8. See 1st Wing Narrative of Operations, July 26, 1943, U.S. National Archives, RG18, E7, Box 941, Folder 1. For 351st BG reasons for abortive missions, see its Mission Summary Report, U.S. National Archives, RG18, E7, Box 1002, Folder 22.

9. The flak, though intense, was "somewhat lighter than that experienced in the raid of July 25." In 351st BG, for example, only a quarter of the planes were damaged by flak, compared with three quarters the day before. See Group Leader's Narrative, 351st BG, July 26, 1943, U.S. National Archives, RG18, E7, Box 1002, Folder 22; and Mission Summary Report (in same folder).

10. See Immediate Interpretation Report, No. S.A. 417, UK National Archives, AIR 40/426.
11. Martin Middlebrook wrongly claims that this plane was called "Local Girl" by her crew (see *The Battle of Hamburg*, p. 231), but the 91st BG website is adamant that it was called "Nitemare." See Lowell L. Getz's 2001 article, "Mary Ruth Memories of Mobile ... We Still Remember," on the 91st Group website: http://www.91stbomb group.com/maryruth4.htm, last viewed June 22, 2005. The name is backed up by Roger Freeman and David Osborne, *The B-17 Flying Fortress Story* (London, 1998), p. 88, aircraft no. 42-3031.
12. See U.S. Bomber Command Narrative of Operations; and 351st BG's Teletype Field Order No. 172 A, Narrative, U.S. National Archives, RG18, E7, Box 1002, Folder 22.

CHAPTER 14: THE EYE OF THE STORM

1. Clem McCarthy, radio commentator, describing boxer Max Schmeling seconds before the "Brown Bomber," Joe Louis, knocked him out in the famous 1938 world heavy-weight title fight; quoted by David Margolick, *Beyond Glory: Joe Louis vs. Max Schmeling, and a World on the Brink* (London, 2005), p. 298.
2. These are British reconnaissance observations; see Immediate Interpretation Report Nos. S.A. 410 and S.A. 417, UK National Archives, AIR 24/257; and Supplement to Immediate Interpretation Report No. K.1626, UK National Archives, AIR 40/426. American intelligence reports agree, but are slightly less detailed; see U.S. Immediate Interpretation Report Nos. 9 and 10, U.S. National Archives, RG18, E7, Box 1040, Folder 3.
3. Rudolf Schurig, quoted in Rudolph Wolter, *Erinnerung an Gomorrha* (Hamburg, 2003), p. 125.
4. Hiltgunt Zassenhaus, quoted in Volker Hage, *Hamburg 1943* (Frankfurt am Main, 2003), p. 165.
5. See Hamburg damage report, UK National Archives, AIR 40/426; Hans Brunswig, *Feuersturm über Hamburg* (Stuttgart, 2003), pp. 198–99, 202–6; Martin Middlebrook, *The Battle of Hamburg* (London, 1980), pp. 153, 155–59. See also eyewitness reports by, among others, Ilse Grassmann; Mathilde Wolff-Mönckeberg; and Erwin Garvens, Heinrich Reincke, Franz Termer, and Vilma Mönckeberg-Kollmar in Renate Hauschild-Thiessen, *Die Hamburger Katastrophe vom Sommer 1943* (Hamburg, 1993).
6. UK National Archives, AIR 20/7287, Hamburg Police Report, pp. 32–33.
7. Hiltgunt Zassenhaus, quoted in Volker Hage, *Hamburg 1943* (Frankfurt am Main, 2003), p. 162.
8. Ibid., pp. 161–62.
9. Franz Termer quoted in Renate Hauschild-Thiessen, *Die Hamburger Katastrophe vom Sommer 1943* (Hamburg, 1993), pp. 51–52.
10. Unpublished transcript of group conversation, "Klöntreff 'Eimsbüttel im Feuersturm,'" Galerie Morgenland/Geschichtwerkstatt, p. 12, "Sprecherin 2."
11. Indeed, Goebbels himself had insisted that taxes on cinema and theater tickets would not be raised for this very reason. See *Goebbels Diaries*, trans. and ed. Louis P. Lochner (London, 1948), March 20, 1943, p. 241.
12. There are many eyewitness reports from the time attesting to how distressed the loss of these buildings made people. See, for example, the testimonies by Franz Termer and Vilma Mönckeberg-Kollmar in Renate Hauschild-Thiessen, *Die Hamburger Katastrophe vom Sommer 1943*, pp. 50–51, 54.
13. Official report, "Bericht über die Katastrophennacht am 25.7.43 im Tierpark Carl Hagenbeck," sent to the author by Klaus Gille of Hagenbeck Tierpark.

14. Middlebrook claims these animals were killed by American bombs (p. 201), but he misinterprets the account in the Hamburg Police Report: When it says they died in the "second attack," it means the second *large* attack—i.e., the British night raid of July 27/28.

15. For witnesses to the destruction of these churches, see Ilse Grassmann, *Ausgebombt* (Hamburg, 2003), July 25, 1943, p. 22; and Otto Johns and Heinrich Reincke in Renate Hauschild-Thiessen, *Die Hamburger Katastrophe vom Sommer 1943*, pp. 28, 39.

16. Hauptpastor Simon Schöffel quoted in Renate Hauschild-Thiessen, *Die Hamburger Katastrophe vom Sommer 1943*, p. 23.

17. Hiltgunt Zassenhaus, op. cit., p. 166; Erwin Garvens in Renate Hauschild-Thiessen, *Die Hamburger Katastrophe vom Sommer 1943*, p. 37.

18. Erwin Garvens in Renate Hauschild-Thiessen, *Die Hamburger Katastrophe vom Sommer 1943*, p. 37.

19. In the chaos that followed the first night of attacks, all the city's newspapers had been forced to merge into one: the *Hamburger Zeitung*. However, since there was only enough paper to print this on a single sheet, it was really only an emergency organ for getting essential messages to the people about where they could find special rations and water, who could leave the city, and so on.

20. Renate Hauschild-Thiessen, *Unternehmen Gomorrha* (Hamburg, 1993), p. 25.

21. Fredy Borck in Kerstin Hof et al. (eds.), *Rothenburgsort 27/28 Juli 1943*, p. 10.

22. *Hamburger Zeitung*, July 26, 1943, "Die Papierblättchen sind harmlos."

23. *Hamburger Zeitung*, July 27, 1943, "Gegen sinnlose Gerüchte."

24. For this, and the rest of the disaster plan, see the Hamburg Police Report, op. cit., pp. 70–86 and Appendix 7.

25. Wilhelm Küper, quoted in Renate Hauschild-Thiessen, *Die Hamburger Katastrophe vom Sommer 1943* (Hamburg, 1993), p. 30.

26. See Erwin Garvens in Renate Hauschild-Thiessen, *Die Hamburger Katastrophe vom Sommer 1943* (Hamburg, 1993), pp. 36–37.

27. See Hamburg Police Report, op. cit., p. 4; and *Hamburger Zeitung*, July 26.

28. See *Hamburger Zeitung*, July 25, "Sonderzuteilung an die Bevölkerung"; and July 26, "Warmes Essen durch Großküchen."

29. Hamburg Police Report, op. cit., p. 70.

CHAPTER 15: CONCENTRATED BOMBING

1. Giulio Douhet, *The Command of the Air*, trans. Dino Ferrari (London, 1943), p. 22.

2. See 139 Squadron Operational Record Book, UK National Archives, AIR 27/960. Such nuisance raids were extremely effective. Earlier in the year Joseph Goebbels had complained that "ten nuisance planes drove fifteen to eighteen million people out of bed" (*The Goebbels Diaries*, ed. and trans. P. Lochner [London: Hamish Hamilton, 1948], May 16, 1943, p. 301). On this occasion, some German firemen and rescue workers were convinced that the nuisance raid was specifically aimed at preventing them from continuing their work. The fact that so many firefighters were still concentrated in the west of the city on the following night was one of the factors that contributed to the catastrophe.

3. UK National Archives, AIR 24/257, Bomber Command Intelligence Narrative of Operations No. 651.

4. For this night's plan, see D Form July 27, UK National Archives, AIR 24/257.

5. See Martin Middlebrook, *The Battle of Hamburg* (London, 1980), pp. 235, 242. While some bombers might indeed have strayed over this city, it was by no means part of the plan: The actual route took the bomber stream some sixteen miles or so to the

west of Lübeck. See the RAF Operational Summary, UK National Archives, AIR 24/257.

6. On July 24, 724 planes dropped 1,349.6 tons of high explosives and 932 tons of incendiaries on Hamburg. On July 27, 721 planes dropped 1,104.4 tons of high explosives and 1,174 tons of incendiaries. In the second attack, therefore, approximately the same number of planes dropped 245 tons less of high explosives and 242 tons more of incendiaries. See Operational Summaries in UK National Archives, AIR 24/257.

7. See Martin Middlebrook, *The Battle of Hamburg* (London: Allan Lane, 1980), p. 235.

8. UK National Archives, AIR 24/257.

9. Group Captains H. I. Edwards, VC from Binbrook, S. C. Elworthy from Waddington, H. L. Patch from Coningsby, A. D. Ross from Middleton St. George, and A. H. Willets from Oakington.

10. See UK National Archives, AIR 27/687, which mentions General Anderson's trip to Essen, but not his flight to Hamburg. However, Martin Middlebrook, who corresponded with Anderson, is adamant that he did indeed fly to Hamburg on this night's raid; see *The Battle of Hamburg*, p. 236.

11. The rendezvous point tonight was at 54.30N 07.00E.

12. Herrmann himself later implied that it was his disregard for the dangers of flying into their own flak that gave the tactics their name; see Hajo Herrmann, *Bewegtes Leben* (Stuttgart, 1984), p. 256.

13. For the early history of Herrmann's "Wild Boars," including the attack on Hamburg, see Hajo Herrmann, op. cit., Chapters 10 and 11, pp. 247–307.

14. Ibid., p.273.

15. See Middlebrook, op. cit., p. 248, and Musgrove's *Operation Gomorrah* (London, 1981), p. 73. According to the RAF Operational Record Book for the Pathfinder Force, the original plan was for red TIs to be used if and only if crews were 100 percent sure that they had identified the correct aiming point. However, the final report seems to indicate that red TIs were never used. See UK National Archives, AIR 25/156 and AIR 14/3410.

16. Other historians give very different figures for the number of airplanes that bombed Hamburg on this night. Max Hastings says 722, Robin Neillands says 735, Martin Middlebrook says 729; the American historian Earl R. Beck says 722; the German historian Uwe Bahnsen says 739. While this might look to the layman like errors of research, it is actually quite common to find different figures given in different official documents. For example, the U.S. Strategic Bombing Survey gives the number that bombed as 739, citing the RAF Operational Summary as its source. However, the RAF summary (issued just eight days after the attack) actually gives a number of 736. To further complicate matters, the appendixes of the RAF Operations Summary claim that only 721 aircraft bombed the *primary* target—presumably indicating that fifteen aircraft dropped their bombs on targets other than Hamburg (see UK National Archives, AIR 24/257, Bomber Command Intelligence Narrative of Operations No. 651). There are occasionally different figures in other official documents, and it is easy to get bogged down by such minor details. Here, therefore, as elsewhere, I have assumed that the final official intelligence report issued by the force that actually carried out the attack is most likely to be accurate, and have given their figure accordingly—see UK National Archives, AIR 14/3410. All figures quoted in this chapter are from the same source, unless otherwise specified.

17. Interview with the author, December 8, 2004.

18. Interview with the author, December 8, 2004.

19. Interview with the author, November 17, 2004.

20. Telephone interview with the author, November 19, 2004.

21. For a fuller description of this engagement, see Gordon Musgrove, *Operation Gomorrah* (London: Jane's, 1981), p.76.
22. According to Martin Middlebrook, op. cit., p. 245. The general claims, though not the exact time and altitude, are backed up by Peter Hinchliffe, *The Other Battle* (Shrewsbury, 2001), p. 157.
23. Quoted by Middlebrook, op. cit., pp. 246–47.
24. Telephone interview with the author, November 11, 2004.
25. F. H. Quick, private manuscript diary sent to the author.

CHAPTER 16: FIRESTORM

1. John Milton, *Paradise Lost*, ed. Alastair Fowler (London, 1968), Book II, lines 170–76 (pp. 97–98). These are the words spoken by Belial in the depths of hell, as he warns the rebel angels of the possible consequences of embarking upon a new war.
2. See Chapter 10, in particular the passages relating to footnotes 47 and 48 (Liselotte Gerke and Johann Johannsen).
3. For a discussion of the different types of firestorm, see Gordon Musgrove, *Operation Gomorrah* (London, 1981), pp. 102–03.
4. According to Hans Brunswig, who was the senior fire engineer on duty that night, the wind speeds probably reached 75 meters per second and more; see Brunswig's *Feuersturm über Hamburg* (Stuttgart, 2003), p. 266. Charles H. V. Ebert prefers a lower estimate of about 50 m/s; see his "The meteorological factor in the Hamburg Firestorm," in *Weatherwise*, vol. 16, no. 2 (April 1963), p. 73.
5. Charles H. V. Ebert, "The meteorological factor in the Hamburg Firestorm," in *Weatherwise*, vol. 16, no. 2 (April 1963), p. 73. For an eyewitness account, see for example the situation report given by the head of FE-Bereitschaft 3/X ("Fire Service Stand-by Crew 3/X"), quoted by Hans Brunswig, op. cit., p. 232: The whirlwind at the junction of Vogelweide and Volksdorfer Strasse in Eilbek was strong enough to lift large pieces of burning timber from a timber merchant and send them hurtling down the street.
6. Police engineers in Hamburg estimated that general temperatures were more likely around 800°C—see Horatio Bond, *Fire and the Air War* (Boston, 1946), p. 116 (Horatio Bond was a U.S. adviser to the Strategic Bombing Survey in Hamburg after the war).
7. For a much more detailed analysis of how the weather conditions contributed to this firestorm, see Professor Charles H. V. Ebert, "The meteorological factor in the Hamburg Firestorm," in *Weatherwise*, vol. 16, no. 2 (April 1963), pp. 70–75. According to Professor Ebert, this firestorm is "unmatched in the records."
8. See Musgrove, op. cit., p. 109; and Hans Brunswig, *Feuersturm über Hamburg* (Stuttgart, 2003), pp. 271–72.
9. Indeed, the Germans took great pains to keep their findings about the meteorological factor in such firestorms secret. See Brunswig, op. cit., p. 270.
10. For contemporary theories on the relative effectiveness of incendiary bombing over high explosives, see J. Enrique Zanetti, *Fire from the Air: The ABC of Incendiaries* (New York, 1941), particularly pp. 49–50.
11. See the British official history, Professor Sir Solly Zuckerman's *The Strategic Air War Against Germany 1939–45: Report of the British Bombing Survey Unit* (London, 1998), p. 6: "The technical lessons of the German attacks on our cities were beginning to be driven home, and it was becoming more and more recognised that, in order to destroy built-up areas, incendiary bombs, and medium-charge and high-charge H.E. bombs, were preferable to the types of load that we were then employing." For British and

German experiments and development of incendiaries, see also Frederick Taylor, *Dresden* (London, 2004), pp. 113–15.

12. UK National Archives, AIR 20/7287: *Secret Report by the Police President of Hamburg (as local Air Protection Leader) on the heavy air raids on Hamburg in July/August, 1943,* p. 16. The original German is in Erhard Klöss, *Der Luftkrieg über Deutschland 1939–1945: Deutsche Berichte und Pressestimmen des neutralen Auslands* (München, 1963), p. 41.

13. Fredy Borck, quoted in Hof, Kerstin (ed.), *Rothenburgsort 27/28 Juli 1943,* unpublished booklet produced by Stadtteilinitiative Hamm e.V., pp. 13–14.

14. Herbert Wulff, typescript account, Forschungsstelle für Zeitgeschichte in Hamburg, FZH 292–8, T–Z.

15. See Hamburg Police Report, op. cit., pp. 7–12, for a description of the city's fire protection service.

16. Ibid., p. 19.

17. See Zanetti, op. cit., p. 20: "On boards, flooring, beams, and other combustible but not easily ignitable material, phosphorus is not only useless but, as a matter of fact, somewhat fire retardant, since it forms a glassy deposit of phosphoric acid on exposed combustible material, thus protecting them from ignition." Thermite, on the other hand, which is a mixture of metallic aluminum and iron oxide, burns at much higher temperatures, creating "a white hot fluid that flows like water, setting fire to all combustible matter which it comes into contact with" (p. 34).

18. Henni Klank, Internet account, http://www.seniorennet-hamburg.de/zeitzeugen/vergessen/klank1.htm, last viewed September 1, 2005.

19. Ibid.

20. Erich Titschak, in Renate Hauschild-Thiessen, *Die Hamburger Katastrophe vom Sommer 1943* (Hamburg, 1993), p. 77.

21. Ibid.

22. Hans Jedlicka, typescript account, FZH 292–8, G-Kra.

23. In June 1953 a reporter for North German Radio interviewed a man who claimed that he and his colleagues often had to force people out of their cellars "with kicks and slaps"—see Uwe Bahnsen and Kerstin von Stürmer, *Die Stadt, die sterben sollte* (Hamburg, 2003), p. 34. Musgrove also quotes a Herr Bey, who had repeatedly had to stop a woman from running back into the cellar from where he'd just rescued her (p. 97).

24. Wolf Biermann interview, *Der Spiegel,* July 25, 2003.

25. Ibid.

26. Hamburg Police Report, op. cit., p. 66. To be safe in an open space tonight, that space had to be over 300 meters in diameter.

27. Manuscript account by "Albert H.," quoted in Hamburg secondary school project, *Als die Bomben fielen: Hamburg vor 40 Jahren,* Museum für Hamburgische Geschichte, HaIII 68, pp. 134–43.

28. Pastor Jürgen Wehrmann, *Briefe an einen Pastor,* collated and edited by Günther Severin (unpublished), letter 12.

29. Hans Brunswig, op. cit., pp. 233–34. According to the Police Report, op. cit., the spraying of water upon fugitives as a protective "cloak" while they escaped from burning houses was one of the most important lessons learned this night (p. 39).

30. Quoted by Hans Brunswig, op. cit., p. 226.

31. Ludwig Faupel, typescript diary, FZH 292–8, A–F.

32. Ibid.

33. Ibid.

34. Ibid.

35. Wolf Biermann interview, *Der Spiegel,* July 25, 2003.

36. Ernst-Günther Haberland quoted in Kerstin Hof (ed.), *Rothenburgsort 27/28 Juli 1943*, unpublished booklet produced by Stadtteilinitiative Hamm e.V., p. 80.

37. See, for example, Heinrich Johannsen's description of being knocked onto his face by flying timber: Hamburg Police Report, Appendix 10. A German transcript of this account is available in Erhard Klöss (ed.), op. cit., pp. 84–87.

38. Anonymous letter from August 1, 1943, reproduced by Marcus Petersen in "Den Feuersturm in Hamburg überlebt," *Die Heimat*, vol. 94, no. 3/4, March/April 1987.

39. Erika Wilken's account appears in Appendix 10 of the Hamburg Police Report—see Carl F. Miller (ed.), *Appendixes 8 through 19 to the Hamburg Police President's Report on the Large Scale Air Attacks on Hamburg, Germany, in World War II* (Stanford, December 1968), pp. 82–83: This translation differs very slightly from my own. The original German account has been reproduced in Erhard Klöss (ed.), op. cit., pp. 80–84.

40. Italian author Curzio Malaparte propagated a gruesome story in the late 1940s, about hundreds of people swimming in the waterways, unable to extinguish the phosphorus burning on their skin, who had to be put out of their misery by German soldiers. The story has been repeated by later historians, most notably the American author Martin Caidin in his book *The Night Hamburg Died* (New York, 1960), pp. 142–47. For a comprehensive refutation of this urban myth, see Martin Middlebrook, *The Battle of Hamburg* (London, 1980), pp. 328–29 (following Brunswig, op. cit., pp. 244–45). Martin Caidin claimed to have found corroborating evidence for the story, but both Middlebrook and Brunswig find this very difficult to believe. See also Horatio Bond, op. cit., p. 121.

41. Ben Witter interview in *The World at War* (Thames TV program), translated by Ben Shephard: Imperial War Museum Sound Archives 2916/01.

42. Hamburg Police Report, op. cit., p. 22; Klöss, op. cit., p. 55.

43. Heinz Masuch's letter to his parents, August 28, 1943, quoted in Renate Hauschild-Thiessen, op. cit., pp. 98–99.

44. Wolf Biermann interview, *Der Spiegel*, July 25, 2003.

45. Hans Brunswig, op. cit., pp. 214, 216.

46. Ibid., p.266.

47. See the Hamburg Police Report, op. cit., p. 16; see also the Fire Department's chronology of events, reproduced verbatim in Hans Brunswig, *Feuersturm über Hamburg* (Stuttgart, 2003), pp. 214–17.

48. Hans Brunswig, op. cit., map on pp. 218–19.

49. See the Town Plan of Hamburg drawn up by the War Office in 1943, sheet 2.

50. Max Kipke, quoted in Kerstin Rasmußen and Gunnar Wulf (eds.), *Es war ein unterirdischer Bunker* (Hamburg, 1996), p. 22.

51. Ruth Schramm, quoted in Kerstin Rasmußen and Gunnar Wulf (eds.), *Es war ein unterirdischer Bunker* (Hamburg, 1996), p. 32.

52. Else Lohse's letter to Frau Schilske in Kerstin Rasmußen and Gunnar Wulf (eds.), *Juli 1943: Hamburg errinern sich* (Hamburg, 2001).

53. Traute Koch quoted by Martin Middlebrook, *The Battle of Hamburg* (London, 1980), p. 274. The description of the bodies being like tailors' dummies is fairly common: See also, for example, Waltraut Ahrens in Hof, Kerstin (ed.), *Rothenburgsort 27/28 Juli 1943* (unpublished booklet, 2003), p. 43.

54. Erich Titschak in Renate Hauschild-Thiessen, *Die Hamburger Katastrophe vom Sommer 1943*, p. 79.

55. Manuscript account by "Maria K.," quoted in Hamburg secondary school project, *Als die Bomben fielen: Hamburg vor 40 Jahren*, Museum für Hamburgische Geschichte, HaIII 68, p. 163.

56. Hans Jedlicka, typescript account, FZH 292–8, G–Kra.

57. Herbert Wulff, typescript account, FZH, 292–8, T–Z.

58. UK National Archives, AIR 48/19: United States Strategic Bombing Survey, *A Detailed Study of the Effects of Area Bombing on Hamburg, Germany,* tables on pp. 7a and 7e.

59. Hamburg Police Report, op. cit., p. 18.

60. Early estimates put the death toll in Hammerbrook at about 36 percent of the total population. See Hans Rumpf, *The Bombing of Germany,* trans. Edward Fitzgerald (London, 1963), pp. 83–84.

61. The exact figure quoted by the United States Strategic Bombing Survey, Hamburg Field Report (p. 7a), was 37,439. See UK National Archives, AIR 48/19.

62. Hamburg Police Report, op. cit., p. 22; Klöss, op. cit., p. 56.

63. Manuscript account by "Maria K.," quoted in Hamburg secondary school project, *Als die Bomben fielen: Hamburg vor 40 Jahren,* Museum für Hamburgische Geschichte, HaIII 68, p. 163.

64. See Horatio Bond "Fire Casualties of the German Attacks" in Horatio Bond, op. cit., pp. 112–121. See also Professor Siegfried Gräff's *Tod im Luftangriff* (Hamburg, 1955), quoted at length in Erhard Klöss (ed.), *Der Luftkrieg über Deutschland 1939–1945* (München, 1963), particularly the report on the state of the corpses by "W.W.," a fifty-one-year-old air raid warden (Klöss, p. 110).

65. "N.N." quoted by Renate Hauschild-Thiessen, op. cit., p. 92.

66. This was typical of a heavy incendiary attack. See Hans Rumpf, op. cit., p. 157.

67. These bodies became the subject of intensive scrutiny by pathologists during and after the war. The Hamburg Police Report Appendixes contain pathologists' reports on the various causes of death in the firestorm (see Appendix 15, pp. 213–39). See also the exhaustive study made by Professor Siegfried Gräff, quoted in Klöss, op. cit., pp. 122–163, particularly pp. 128–140 on corpses found in the basements.

68. Herbert Wulff, typescript account, FZH, 292–8, T–Z.

69. Erich Titschak in Renate Hauschild-Thiessen, *Die Hamburger Katastrophe vom Sommer 1943,* p. 79; Hans Jedlicka, FZH 292–8 G–Ha; Else Lohse in Kerstin Rasmußen and Gunnar Wulf (eds.), *Juli 1943,* p. 37.

70. Erika Wilken quoted in the Hamburg Police Report, op. cit., Appendix 10. A transcript of her report is available in Klöss, Erhard (ed.), *Der Luftkrieg über Deutschland 1939–1945: Deutsche Berichte und Pressestimmen des neutralen Auslands* (München, 1963), p. 83.

71. Henni Klank, op. cit.

Chapter 17: The "Terror of Hamburg"

1. Adolf Galland, *The First and the Last* (London, 1955), p. 239.

2. Joseph Goebbels, *Die Tagebücher von Joseph Goebbels,* ed. Elke Fröhlich (München, 1993), vol. II, August 6, 1943.

3. Joseph Goebbels, *The Goebbels Diaries,* trans. and ed. Louis P. Lochner (London, 1948), July 29, 1943, pp. 333–34.

4. Albert Speer, *Inside the Third Reich* (London, 1970), p. 389.

5. Milch quoted by David Irving, *The Rise and Fall of the Luftwaffe* (Boston, 1973), p. 232.

6. Ibid.

7. Speer, op. cit., pp. 388–89. From the flurry of meetings that took place around this time it seems that Hitler was far more concerned about the situation in Italy in the wake of Mussolini's resignation. See Goebbels diary, op. cit., July 24–29, 1943.

8. The *Times,* July 29, 1943, pp. 4, 6.

9. *Daily Express,* July 31, 1943, p. 1.

10. Headlines from the *New York Times*, July 31, 1943, p. 6; *New York Herald Tribune*, August 1, 1943, p. 10; *Washington Post*, July 26, 1943, p. 2.

11. Royal Air Force Museum, propaganda leaflet G61.

12. Herr K. St. quoted in Volker Böge and Jutta Deide-Lüchow, *Eimsbüttler Jugend im Krieg* (Hamburg, 1992), p. 28.

13. See, for example, Galerie Morgenland/Geschichtswerkstatt—Klöntreff "Eimsbüttel im Feuersturm," unpublished typescript, p. 13, Sprecher 6: "Das habe ich von Frontsoldaten gehört, die haben mehrmals gesagt, an der Front sei es nicht so schlimm." Contemporary reports agree. Directly after the attacks, for example, a reporter for the *Stockholm Aftonbladet* claimed that "what the German people have been experiencing . . . is an ordeal by fire without example in history, which, in certain respects, is more horrible than the gigantic fight on the Eastern Front"—quoted in the *Daily Express*, August 2, 1943, p. 1.

14. Martha Bührich quoted in Renate Hauschild-Thiessen, *Unternehmen Gomorrha* (Hamburg, 1993), p. 25. Significantly, the soldier was talking about the first British night raid, which was not nearly so devastating as the second. Others also compare Hamburg to Stalingrad: See "N.N." and Adolf Freydag's accounts in Renate Hauschild-Thiessen, *Die Hamburger Katastrophe vom Sommer 1943* (Hamburg, 1993), pp. 189, 215.

15. Giulio Douhet, *The Command of the Air*, trans. Dino Ferrari (London, 1943), p. 159.

16. For the official description of the evacuation that follows, see the Hamburg Police Report, op. cit. pp. 62, 70–72, and Appendixes 7 and 14. See also Martin Middlebrook, *The Battle of Hamburg* (London, 1980), p. 278.

17. These figures are Martin Middlebrook's, but unfortunately he does not give his source for them. Goebbels says in his diary that 300,000 loaves of bread were sent from Berlin (July 29, 1943), and Georg Ahrens claimed that as many as 1,600,000 loaves were handed out (see Renate Hauschild-Thiessen, *Die Hamburger Katastrophe vom Sommer 1943* [Hamburg, 1993], p. 226).

18. See, for example, Ilse Grassmann's description of trying to leave Hamburg, in her diary *Ausgebombt* (Hamburg, 2003), July 28–29, 1943, pp. 43–46; and the story told by a woman who found it almost impossible to hitch a lift out of the city despite being heavily pregnant, quoted by Uwe Bahnsen and Kerstin von Stürmer, *Die Stadt, die sterben sollte* (Hamburg, 2003), p. 35.

19. Heino Merck, in Renate Hauschild-Thiessen, *Die Hamburger Katastrophe vom Sommer 1943* (Hamburg, 1993), pp. 114–16.

20. Ilse Grassmann, op. cit., July 30, 1943, p. 48.

21. Letter to Pastor Jürgen Wehrmann in Günther Severin (ed.), *Briefe an einen Pastor* (unpublished collection).

22. Helmuth Saß, FZH 292–8, Ri–S.

23. Hans J. Massaquoi, "Operation Gomorrha" in Volker Hage (ed.), *Hamburg 1943: Literarische Zeugnisse zum Feuersturm* (Frankfurt am Main, 2003), p. 265.

24. Ibid., p. 262.

25. Lore Bünger, "Operation Gomorrha," in Claus Günther (ed.), *erlebt—erkannt—erinnert: Zeitzeugen schreiben Geschichte(n) 1932–1952* (Hamburg, 2003), p. 134.

26. Hans Erich Nossack, *Der Untergang* (Hamburg, 1981), pp. 63–64.

27. Ibid., p. 64.

28. Adolf Galland, *The First and the Last* (London, 1955), p. 239.

29. Margret Klauß quoted by Uwe Bahnsen and Kerstin von Stürmer, *Die Stadt, die sterben sollte* (Hamburg, 2003), p. 60.

30. Hiltgunt Zassenhaus quoted in Volker Hage, *Hamburg 1943*, p. 160.

31. Imperial War Museum Sound 10380/5, Hannah Hyde (née Voss) interview.

32. Story in the *New York Times,* August 6, 1943, p. 4.
33. Friedrich Reck, *Tagebuch eines Verzweifelten* (Frankfurt am Main, 1994), August 20, 1943, p. 216.
34. Ernst-Günther Haberland, quoted in Hof, Kerstin (ed.), *Rothenburgsort 27/28 Juli 1943* (unpublished booklet produced by Stadtteilinitiative Hamm e.V.), p. 80.
35. See, for example, W. G. Sebald, *On the Natural History of Destruction* (London, 2003), p. 89. Sebald interviewed a woman who had been a volunteer helper at Stralsund railway station when a train full of refugees arrived. Several of the women on this train alone brought their dead children with them.
36. Hans Erich Nossack, op. cit., p. 26.
37. For the difficult relationships that developed between refugees and their hosts see Nossack, op. cit., pp. 26–29. For an example of one of the rare exceptions to the general charity extended to refugees, see FZH 292–8, T–H: When Herbert Wulff and his family knocked on a door in Lauenburg to ask if they could have some water to brew coffee they had the door slammed in their faces with the words "We are not a hotel!"
38. Story recounted by Luise Solmitz in Renate Hauschild-Thiessen, *Die Hamburger Katastrophe vom Sommer 1943* (Hamburg, 1993), p. 62.
39. Erich Titschak, quoted in Renate Hauschild-Thiessen, *Die Hamburger Katastrophe vom Sommer 1943* (Hamburg, 1993), pp. 78–79.
40. Nossack, op. cit., p. 62.
41. "Berlin Given '3 Weeks to Live' by U.S.," *Daily Mail,* August 4, 1943, p. 1. RAF press conference quoted in the *New York Herald Tribune,* August 6, 1943, p. 3.
42. Quoted in the *Daily Express,* August 2, 1943, p. 1. See also the *Daily Mail,* August 2, 1943, pp. 1, 4; the *Times* August 2, 1943, p. 4; *New York Times,* August 2, 1943, pp. 1, 3; *Washington Post,* August 2, 1943, pp. 1, 2.
43. See, for example, "Stampede Out of Berlin Is Reported," *Washington Post,* August 7, 1943, pp. 1, 2; "German Life Is Badly Disrupted by Air War" in *New York Times,* August 8, 1943, p. E3; "Evacuation of Berlin," *Manchester Guardian,* August 7, 1943, p. 5; "Berlin Evacuates: Official," *Daily Express,* August 2, 1943, pp. 1, 4.
44. While Harris firmly believed that the key to winning the war was the destruction of the Reich capital, it seems he thought this would happen by bombing the target in isolation, rather than by destroying it in quick succession with other cities. See his letter to Churchill, November 3, 1943: "We can wreck Berlin from end to end if the USA will come in on it. It will cost us between 400 and 500 aircraft. It will cost Germany the war." Quoted in Sir Charles Webster and Noble Frankland, *The Strategic Air Offensive Against Germany 1939–1945* (London: HMSO, 1961), vol. II, p. 48.
45. See Sir Arthur Harris's own memoirs, *Bomber Offensive* (London, 1947), p. 180.

Chapter 18: Coup de Grace

1. *Macbeth,* III, iv, 136–38.
2. See Hamburg Police Report, p. 34; and Hans Brunswig, *Feuersturm über Hamburg* (Stuttgart, 2003), p. 248.
3. Statistics taken from Roger Freeman, *The Mighty Eighth* (London, 1986), p. 66, and Roger Freeman, *The Mighty Eighth War Diary* (London, 1990), pp. 80–82.
4. While Zero Hour tonight was fifteen minutes earlier than before, at 12:45, the slightly shorter route meant that takeoff and return times did not vary much from previous operations on Hamburg. The first turning point was at 54.30N 0700E, exactly as it had been on July 27. The second turning point was at 54.03N 09.44E, very close to that of July 24 (53.55N 09.45E), which meant that the approach into Hamburg was only slightly more northerly than it had been on that night. After leaving the target,

their next turning point was at 53.23N 09.38E, which was about midway between the turning points used on the two previous attacks (53.15N10.00E on July 24, and 53.20N 09.30E on July 27). Once out at sea again, their final turning point was again identical to that used Tuesday, July 27: 54.20N 07.00E. See the various operational plans of attack in UK National Archives, AIR 24/257.

5. The decoys were dropped at 53.33N 07.33E, about thirty miles along the coast west from Cuxhaven. For the route of these four Mosquitos see Interceptions/Tactics document no. 155/43 for July 29/30, UK National Archives, AIR 24/257.

6. See UK National Archives, AIR 27/796.

7. For a discussion of how the advent of Window changed German night-fighter tactics, see Peter Hinchliffe, *The Other Battle* (Shrewsbury, 2001), pp. 154–61.

8. The Hamburg Police Report mentions a "second strong wave of bombers approaching from the direction of Bremen." Martin Middlebrook also mentions that one of the Mosquitos attracted the attention of a German night fighter—but there is no record of this in the official summary of combats and enemy aircraft encountered (Interceptions/Tactics document no. 155/43 for July 29/30, UK National Archives, AIR 24/257). See Martin Middlebrook, *The Battle of Hamburg* (London, 1980), p. 286.

9. The losses around the route markers are as follows: a 78 Squadron Halifax piloted by Sergeant R. Snape, a 61 Squadron Lancaster (Phillips), a Halifax from 51 Squadron (Fletcher), and a Halifax from 102 Squadron (Gaston) all went down in the sea (the last one a long way from the route markers, as far south as Heligoland); a 7 Squadron Stirling (Forbes) and a 467 Squadron Lancaster (Park) were lost without trace, presumably also at sea; a Halifax from 158 Squadron (MacDonald) was shot down just after crossing the coast.

10. See Interceptions/Tactics document no. 155/43 for July 29/30, UK National Archives, AIR 24/257.

11. UK National Archives, AIR 27/796. Martin Middlebrook also interviewed Pickles's navigator on this operation—see *The Battle of Hamburg* (London, 1980), pp. 285–86.

12. These were probably Sutton's Halifax from 77 Squadron, Macquarie's Halifax from 102 Squadron, and Fraser's Halifax from 78 Squadron. See Chorley, op. cit., pp. 247–51.

13. These were: a 9 Squadron Lancaster piloted by F/L C. W. Fox, a Wellington of 166 Squadron (Birbeck), and a Lancaster of 57 Squadron (Parker), which was one of those that arrived late on the target (see below).

14. Six bombers were shot down by fighters in this area: a 460 Squadron Lancaster piloted by F/S H. L. Fuhrmann, a 428 Squadron Halifax (Bates), a 432 Squadron Wellington (Kerby), a 35 Squadron Halifax (Spooner), a 97 Squadron Lancaster (Schnier), and a 57 Squadron Lancaster piloted by Allwright (who arrived late on target—see below). Those hit by both flak and fighters were: a Stirling of 218 Squadron piloted by Sergeant J. Clark, a Halifax of 35 Squadron (Pexton), and a Stirling of 218 Squadron (Pickard).

15. Quoted by Middlebrook, op. cit., p. 289.

16. According to the 1 Group summary. Fifty-eight of 1 Group's Lancasters were in the final wave of the attack, and so saw the fires when they were approaching their brightest. See UK National Archives, AIR 24/257.

17. Bill McCrea, *A Chequer-Board of Nights* (Preston, 2003), pp. 80–81.

18. All statistics quoted are from the RAF Operations Record Book Appendices, UK National Archives, AIR 24/257. The last four planes to be destroyed were probably from 76 Squadron (Bjercke), 460 Squadron (Johnson), 214 Squadron (Shann), and 97 Squadron (Marks).

19. Generaloberst Weise was originally skeptical of the worth of Herrmann's *Wilde Sau* fighters, but was won over by their successes in this period. For a discussion of this,

and for the text of his order on July 30, 1943, see Peter Hinchliffe, *The Other Battle* (Shrewsbury, 2001), pp. 131, 159–160.

20. See Hamburg Police Report, pp. 17, 35–36; and Erhard Klöss, *Der Luftkrieg über Deutschland 1939–1945* (München, 1963), p. 43. For a picture of which areas were hit, see Plot of Night Photographs No. 172 (taken July 29/30, 1943), UK National Archives, AIR 24/257.

21. Helmuth Saß, FZH 292–8, Ri–S.

22. Ibid.

23. See Carl F. Miller (ed.), *Appendixes 8 through 19 to the Hamburg Police President's Report on the Large Scale Air Attacks on Hamburg, Germany, in World War II* (Stanford, December 1968), Appendix 19, sheet 28 (pp. 405–07). See also Hans Brunswig, *Feuersturm über Hamburg* (Stuttgart, 2003), p. 257.

24. A monument to these 370 people sits today in the central reservation of Hamburger Strasse, close to a huge new shopping center.

25. Adolf Pauly's letter to Pastor Jürgen Wehrmann in Günther Severin (ed.), *Briefe an einen Pastor 1943*, unpublished collection collated by Günther Severin, letter 43.

26. Ibid.

27. Hans J. Massaquoi, "Operation Gomorrha" in Volker Hage (ed.), *Hamburg 1943* (Frankfurt am Main, 2003), p. 261.

28. Horatio Bond, who handled fire damage analysis for the Physical Damage Division of the USBSS, estimated 800 died—see *Fire and the Air War* (Boston, 1946), p. 86. Uwe Bahnsen and Kerstin von Stürmer estimate 1,000–5,000—see *Die Stadt, die sterben sollte: Hamburg im Bombenkrieg, Juli 1943* (Hamburg, 2003), p. 54.

29. Adolf Pauly, op. cit.

CHAPTER 19: THE TEMPEST

1. William Shakespeare, *Julius Caesar,* I, iii, 46–52: Cassius tries to convince Casca that the terrible thunderstorm over Rome is a good omen.

2. Hans Erich Nossack, *Der Untergang* (Hamburg, 1981), p. 69.

3. See Hamburg Police Report, pp. 70–72. The four special hospital trains were destroyed in the night raid of July 29.

4. Interview with Wanda Chantler (née Wanziunia Cieniewska-Radziwill), July 5, 2004.

5. Hamburg Police Report, p. 21. The German text is reproduced in Erhard Klöss, *Der Luftkrieg über Deutschland 1939–1945* (München, 1963), p. 53.

6. Franz Termer, quoted in Renate Hauschild-Thiessen, *Die Hamburger Katastrophe vom Sommer 1943* (Hamburg, 1993), p. 175.

7. On July 30, 1943, Harris split his force into three for raids on Turin and Genoa in northern Italy, and Remscheid in the Ruhr valley. The Italian raids were called off by the Air Ministry at short notice, so only the Remscheid raid went ahead. See UK National Archives, AIR 24/257.

8. See UK National Archives AIR 14/3410, Night Raid Report no. 391.

9. UK National Archives, AIR 29/867, Operations Record Book of 1409 Met. Flight.

10. UK National Archives AIR 27/687, Operations Record Book of 83 Squadron, Pathfinder Force.

11. UK National Archives AIR 27/538.

12. These were a 7 Squadron Stirling piloted by P/O W. E. Stenhouse, whose undercarriage collapsed on landing; and a 300 Squadron Wellington of the Polish Air Force, which burst into flames when F/L J. Spychala was forced to crash-land in a field in Nottinghamshire. See UK National Archives, AIR 27/1657 and AIR 27/100. See also W. R. Chorley, *Bomber Command Losses 1943* (Hersham, 2004), pp. 254, 258.

13. Bill McCrea, *A Chequer-Board of Nights* (Preston, 2003), p. 82.

14. Typescript diary of Major J. K. Christie, August 2–3, 1943, RAF Museum Hendon, MF10016/5.

15. Bill McCrea, op. cit., p. 82.

16. Colin Harrison, 467 Squadron, interview with the author, December 8, 2004. James Sullivan quote: interview with the author, December 9, 2004.

17. Sergeant C. C. Leeming, 620 Squadron, quoted by Martin Middlebrook, op. cit., p. 310.

18. Ted Groom, 460 Squadron, interview with the author, November 11, 2004.

19. Manuscript diary of Sergeant Dennis George Eli Brookes, RAF Museum Hendon, X001–3536/010.

20. UK National Archives, AIR 27/203. See also Gordon Musgrove, *Operation Gomorrah* (London, 1981), p. 153.

21. Sergeant A. Stephen quoted in Martin Middlebrook, *The Battle of Hamburg* (London, 1980), pp. 312–13.

22. These were: a 35 Squadron Halifax piloted by Sergeant E. Solomon (of which Sergeant Stephen was a crew member), a 214 Squadron Stirling (McGarvey), a 300 Squadron Wellington (Smyk), and a 419 Squadron Halifax (Sobin). All these planes had survivors to testify to the fact that it was ice that brought them down. Several others were lost without trace, and it is likely that some of these were also victims of the conditions.

23. This was a Lancaster of 115 Squadron piloted by P/O R. J. Mosen. See Chorley, op. cit., p. 257.

24. That is, 3rd *Gruppe* of 1st *Nachtjagdgeschwader*. There are no accurate equivalents to German units in the RAF or the USAAF; however, this can be loosely translated into British terms as 3 Squadron of No.1 Night Fighter Group, or in American terms as 3rd Group of First Wing. See Appendix D.

25. Wilhelm Johnen, *Duel Under the Stars* (London, 1975), p. 73.

26. There are several instances of this happening tonight. For example, Leonard Cooper's 7 Squadron was attacked five times by a pair of night fighters before his pilot managed to lose them (interview with author, November 19, 2004); F/Lt. C. M. Shannon's 76 Squadron was approached three times by the same Messerschmitt before losing it (see Gordon Musgrove, *Operation Gomorrah* (London, 1981), p. 151.

27. See Chorley, op. cit., p. 256.

28. These four are: a 12 Squadron Lancaster piloted by F/O S. Norris, a 158 Squadron Halifax (Davie), and two 405 Squadron Halifaxes (Phillips and Gregory). See Chorley, op. cit., pp. 255–58.

29. Rudolf Schurig quoted in Rudolf Wolter, *Errinerung an Gomorrha* (Hamburg, 2003), pp. 125, 131–32.

30. For Peter Swan's own description of his ordeal, see Kevin Wilson, *Bomber Boys* (London, 2005), pp. 276–78.

31. Trevor Timperley, interview with the author, November 17, 2004.

32. Colin Harrison, interview with the author, December 8, 2004. Bill McCrea quote from interview on same date.

33. This figure does not include the 57 Squadron Lancaster written off on takeoff, but it does include a Wellington of 166 Sqn (Burton) that was lost while laying mines in the Elbe estuary. See Chorley, op. cit., pp.254–59.

34. UK National Archives, AIR 14/3410.

35. Hamburg Police Report, p. 17; Erhard Klöss, op. cit., pp. 43–44.

36. See, for example, Waldemar Hansen's, Friedrich Sparmann's, Helene Hadenfeldt's, and N.N.'s accounts in Renate Hauschild-Thiessen, *Die Hamburger Katastrophe vom Sommer 1943* (Hamburg, 1993), pp. 169, 182, 183–84, 186–88.

37. Hamburg Police Report, pp. 36–37.

CHAPTER 20: CITY OF THE DEAD

1. Dante Alighieri, *The Divine Comedy of Dante Alighieri,* ed. and trans. Robert M. Durling (New York, 1996), Vol. I: Inferno, Canto 28, lines 1–3. This canto describes the beginning of Dante's final descent through the ninth circle of hell to its frozen core. Dante goes on to say, "It is no task to take in jest, that of describing the bottom of the universe" (Canto 32, lines 7–8), sentiments that I could not help but keep with me as I wrote this chapter.
2. For statistics on damage to the harbor installations, see United States Strategic Bombing Survey, Hamburg Report, p. 12.
3. Hamburg Police Report, p. 37.
4. Interview with Annegret Hennings, in Kerstin Rasmußen and Gunnar Wulf (eds.), *Es war ja Krieg* (Hamburg, 1993), p. 94.
5. Gretl Büttner, Hamburg Police Report Appendixes, Appendix 10, pp. 119–20, although my translation differs very slightly. Erhard Klöss gives the original German, pp. 104–05.
6. Hamburg Police Report, p. 43.
7. Ibid., pp. 72–73, 75.
8. Ludwig Faupel, "Feuersturm 1943," FZH 292–8, A–F, p. 8.
9. See Luise Solmitz's diary, August 17, 1943, in Renate Hauschild-Thiessen, *Die Hamburger Katastrophe vom Sommer 1943* (Hamburg, 1993), p. 343; see also Hans Erich Nossack, op. cit., p. 99.
10. Hamburg Police Report, p. 74.
11. Jan Melsen quoted in Ulrike Jureit and Beate Meyer (eds.) *Verletzungen: Lebensgeschichtliche Verarbeitung von Kriegserfahrungen* (Hamburg, 1994), pp. 149–50.
12. Ibid., p. 150.
13. Hamburg Police Report, p. 22.
14. Article in *Die Zeit,* July 30, 1993.
15. Ben Witter interview for Thames Television's *The World at War,* Imperial War Museum Sound Archive, 2916/01. This quotation has been lightly edited, but only to remove repetition of the same phrases.
16. Jan Melsen, op. cit., p. 151.
17. Ben Witter interview for Thames Television's *The World at War,* IWM Sound Archive, 2916/01.
18. *Hamburger Zeitung*: articles of July 29, August 1, and August 15, 1943. See also Hamburg Police Report, pp. 4, 82–83; and Hamburg Police Report Appendixes, Appendix 17.
19. See Hamburg Police Report, p. 82.
20. Mathilde Wolff-Mönckeberg, op. cit., pp. 76, 80.
21. Nossack, op. cit., pp. 99–100.
22. See, for example, Herman Sieveking in Renate Hauschild-Thiessen, *Die Hamburger Katastrophe vom Sommer 1943* (Hamburg, 1993), p. 299.
23. Gretl Büttner in Carl F. Miller (ed.), *Appendixes 8 through 19 to the Hamburg Police President's Report on the Large Scale Air Attacks on Hamburg, Germany, in World War II* (Stanford, December 1968), Appendix 10, p. 119. The original German account has been reproduced in Erhard Klöss (ed.), *Der Luftkrieg über Deutschland, 1939–1945* (München, 1963), p. 104.
24. Hans Erich Nossack, *Der Untergang* (Hamburg, 1981), p. 68.
25. Ibid., pp. 72–73.
26. Hamburg Police Report, p. 79.
27. Ibid., p. 76.

28. United States Strategic Bombing Survey, Hamburg Field Report, p. 7a.
29. See contemporary photographs of Gothenstrasse.
30. There is perhaps some truth in this rumor—the Hamburg Police Report mentions it, and one woman I interviewed (Liselotte Gerke) says this actually happened to her. She was convinced for months that this was a sort of divine punishment for entering the forbidden area.
31. Hans Erich Nossack, *Der Untergang* (Hamburg, 1981), p. 99. According to police pathologists this was unlikely to be true, at least in the early days (Hamburg Police Report Appendixes, Appendix 15, p. 211), and I have not come across any firsthand accounts describing such scenes.
32. See Martin Caidin, *The Night Hamburg Died* (London, 1966), pp. 142–47, and the refutation of this myth in Martin Middlebrook, *The Battle of Hamburg* (London, 1980), pp. 328–29, and Hans Brunswig, *Feuersturm über Hamburg* (Stuttgart, 2003), pp. 244–45.
33. See Hans Erich Nossack, op. cit., p. 98 for rumors. See United States Strategic Bombing Survey, Hamburg Field Report, p. 7a for probable number of deaths.

CHAPTER 21: SURVIVAL

1. The words of the angels to Lot, as they saved him from the destruction of Sodom and Gomorrah. Lot's wife did look back, and as a consequence was turned into a pillar of salt.
2. Hans Erich Nossack, *Der Untergang* (Hamburg, 1981), p. 136.
3. René Ratouis, *Mémoires de guerre d'un non-combattant* (Paris, 2003), p. 117.
4. According to the Situation Report of the Head Welfare Officer at the end of September 1943, cellars everywhere were overflowing with people, and families were often forced to sleep six to a room. This report is quoted by Monika Sigmund et al. (eds.), *"Man versuchte längs zu kommen, und man lebt ja noch . . .": Frauenalltag in St. Pauli in Kriegs- und Nachkriegszeit* (Hamburg, 1996), p. 25.
5. Mathilde Wolff-Mönckeberg, *On the Other Side* (London, 1979), p. 81.
6. To add to the huge destruction to the transport infrastructure, 600 of Hamburg's 1,600 tram cars were completely destroyed, and half of its underground trains either destroyed or very badly damaged. What few trams, buses, and trains still existed were strictly rationed at rush hours: Even those who were permitted to use them often could not cram their way in and were obliged to walk anyway. See Hamburg Police Report, p. 86; and United States Strategic Bombing Survey, Hamburg Field Report, p. 24.
7. Mathilde Wolff-Mönckeberg, op. cit., p. 81.
8. Johannes Schoene in Renate Hauschild-Thiessen, op. cit., p. 304.
9. Ilse Grassmann, *Ausgebombt* (Hamburg, 2003), July 26, 1943, p. 28.
10. Maria Bartels letter, September 15, 1943, in Renate Hauschild-Thiessen, *Die Hamburger Katastrophe vom Sommer 1943* (Hamburg, 1993), p. 314.
11. Maria Bartels, letter to her husband September 8, 1943, in Renate Hauschild-Thiessen, *Die Hamburger Katastrophe vom Sommer 1943* (Hamburg, 1993), p. 312.
12. Uwe Bahnsen and Kerstin von Stürmer, *Die Stadt die sterben sollte . . .* (Hamburg, 2003), p. 67.
13. United States Strategic Bombing Survey, Hamburg Field Report, p. 22.
14. Hamburg Police Report, p. 84.
15. See United States Strategic Bombing Survey, Hamburg Field Report, pp. 23–24; and Hamburg Police Report, pp. 84, 91; and Hamburg Police Report Appendixes, Appendix 18. For restoration of phone lines, see also Kurt Ahrens's and Friedrich Ruppel's

accounts in Renate Hauschild-Thiessen, *Die Hamburger Katastrophe vom Sommer 1943* (Hamburg, 1993), pp. 308, 318.

16. United States Strategic Bombing Survey, Hamburg Field Report, pp. 44–46 and Charts 15 and 16.

17. Ibid., pp. 44–45 and Chart 15.

18. René Ratouis, *Mémoires de guerre d'un non-combattant* (Paris, 2003), p. 111.

19. Eberhard Rössler, *The U-boat* (London, 1981), p. 266; see also Uwe Bahnsen and Kerstin von Stürmer, *Die Stadt, die sterben sollte . . .* (Hamburg, 2003), p. 71. This U-boat, U-792, was finally commissioned on November 16.

20. Hannah Kelson interview, IWM Sound Archive, 15550/5.

21. Pastor Jürgen Wehrmann, round-robin letter to his parishioners, January 1, 1944, in Günther Severin (ed.), *Briefe an einen Pastor* (unpublished), letter 161.

22. Georg Ahrens quoted in Renate Hauschild-Thiessen, *Die Hamburger Katastrophe vom Sommer 1943* (Hamburg, 1993), pp. 225–28.

23. See, for example, Hans Erich Nossack, op. cit., p. 108; Hans Brunswig, *Feuersturm über Hamburg* (Hamburg, 2003), p. 305; Renate Hauschild-Thiessen, op. cit., p. 285; and Hiltgunt Zassenhaus, *Ein Baum blüht im November* (Hamburg, 1974), the very title of which refers to this event.

24. Gretl Büttner, quoted in Hamburg Police Report Appendixes, Appendix 10, p. 122. The original German is reproduced in Erhard Klöss (ed.), *Der Luftkrieg über Deutschland 1939–1945* (München, 1963), pp. 107–08. There are dozens of other accounts of this happening across the city.

Chapter 22: Famine

1. Heinrich Böll, *The Silent Angel* (London, 1994), p. 75. Food, and its lack, is the central theme of this novel about the aftermath of war in Germany.

2. Figures according to Hans Brunswig, *Feuersturm über Hamburg* (Stuttgart, 2003), p. 454–56.

3. Hermann Holthusen, diary account, August 11, 1943, quoted by Renate Hauschild-Thiessen, *Die Hamburger Katastrophe vom Sommer 1943* (Hamburg, 1993), p. 235.

4. Mathilde Wolff-Mönckeberg, *On the Other Side* (London, 1979), April 29, 1944, p. 88.

5. Adolf Hitler's political testament, April 29, 1945, reproduced in Hans-Adolf Jacobsen, *1939–1945: Der zweite Weltkrieg in Chronik und Dokumenten* (Darmstadt, 1961), p. 531.

6. Tommy Wilmott, Imperial War Museum Sound Archive, 19806, reel 9.

7. Dr. P. J. Horsey, typescript diary, IWM Department of Documents, Con Shelf.

8. Ibid.

9. Philip J. C. Dark, *Look Back This Once: Prisoner of War in Germany in WWII*, typescript account, IWM Department of Documents, 94/7/1. Professor Dark returned to his memories of Hamburg in an exhibition of his paintings at the Honolulu Academy of Arts in 1994.

10. Katherine Morris, *Destination Hamburg*, typescript account, IWM Department of Documents, 91/27/1, p. 3. Ruth Evans, a native of Hamburg, expressed much the same sentiments when she returned there after the war: "Would this town ever be rebuilt? I doubted that"—see Mathilde Wolff-Mönckeberg, op. cit., translator's epilogue, p. 163.

11. Janet Flaner's description for the *New Yorker*, quoted in W. G. Sebald, *On the Natural History of Destruction* (London, 2003), p. 31.

12. Herbert Conert, quoted in Frederick Taylor, *Dresden* (New York, 2004), p. 396. The description of Dresden as a moonscape comes from Kurt Vonnegut, *Slaughterhouse-Five* (London, 1991), pp. 130–31.

13. Victor Klemperer, *To the Bitter End: The Diaries of Victor Klemperer 1942–45* (London, 1999), trans. Martin Chalmers, May 22, 1945, p. 596.

14. Harry Hopkins diary entry, quoted in Hans Rumpf, *The Bombing of Germany* (London, 1963), trans. Edward Fitzgerald, p. 126.

15. This was the figure taken before Congress in 1947. The actual investment was somewhat less. See Gregory A. Fossedal, *Our Finest Hour: Will Clayton, the Marshall Plan, and the Triumph of Democracy* (Stanford, 1993), p. 252.

16. Dr. P. J. Horsey, typescript diary, IWM Department of Documents, Con Shelf.

17. Victor Gollancz, *In Darkest Germany* (London, 1947), pp. 28–29, 53–55, and plate 143.

18. Ibid., pp. 55–56.

19. Ibid., p. 52.

20. Katherine Morris, *Destination Hamburg*, typescript account, IWM Department of Documents, 91/27/1, p. 15.

21. Ibid., p. 31.

22. Quoted by Victor Gollancz, op. cit., p. 93.

23. Katherine Morris, *Destination Hamburg*, typescript account, IWM Department of Documents, 91/27/1, p. 15.

24. According to the Food Committee of UNRRA (United Nations Relief and Rehabilitation Administration), a normal population required 2,650 calories per day to maintain health. Official rations provided only 1,550 calories, but were rarely delivered. In Belsen the rations provided only 800 calories per day. See Victor Gollancz, op. cit., pp. 28–29, 35.

25. Undated newspaper clipping from 1946/47 kept by Katherine Morris: "Death warning to food rioters: U.S. may invoke military law," IWM Department of Documents, 91/27/1.

26. Victor Gollancz, op. cit., p. 29.

27. E. G. W. Ridgers, *The Life of a Sapper in World War Two*, typescript memoir, IWM Docs, 99/16/1, p. 32. For winter temperatures in 1946/47 and their effects, see Eckart Klessmann, *Geschichte der Stadt Hamburg* (Hamburg, 2003), p. 595; and Nora Heather, "Experiences with Control Commission in Germany immediately after World War Two," typescript account, IWM Docs 03/1/1 (Mrs. Heather kept a diary of temperatures, and even includes an official contemporary temperature chart).

28. For power cuts, see Nora Heather, op. cit.; and Eckart Klessmann, op. cit., pp. 594–95. For several stories of children raiding coal trains, see Monika Sigmund et al. (eds.), *"Man versuchte längs zu kommen, und man lebt ja noch . . .": Frauenalltag in St. Pauli in Kriegs- und Nachkriegszeit* (Hamburg, 1996), p. 21.

29. There were only eighty-five deaths from "exposure" entered on official registers, but this is a hopelessly low figure and does not include those who died from other conditions related to the severe cold: See Klessmann, op. cit., p. 595.

30. In February 1962 the city suffered a catastrophic flood that ruined the underground train network, caused hundreds of millions of Deutschmarks in damage, and claimed 315 lives. Smaller floods also occurred in 1976 and 1983.

31. In 2001 there were more than 6,000 companies involved in media based in Hamburg, including 3,200 advertising firms, 1,600 publishers and printers, and 700 film companies. See Anna Brenken, *Hamburg: Metropole an Alster und Elbe* (Hamburg, 2001), p. 45.

32. Hildegard Huza's memorial to the 370 people who died in the shelter at Karstadt shopping center, at the junction of Hamburger Strasse and Oberaltenallee in Barmbek.

33. Alfred Hrdlicka's antiwar memorial at Dammtor comprises one sculpture of the Hamburg Firestorm, and one of the concentration camp prisoners who died when

Allied bombs sank the ship (the *Cap Arcona*) that was transporting them in the last days of the war.

34. Gerhard Marcks's sculpture, *"Fahrt über den Styx,"* is a memorial to the 36,918 bodies that lie in the mass graves.

35. Klaus Müller, *"Sprecher* 3," unpublished transcript of local history group conversation, *"Klöntreff 'Eimsbüttel im Feuersturm,'"* Galerie Morgenland/Geschichtswerkstatt, p. 13.

36. Hans Jedlicka, FZH 292–8, G–Kra.

37. Wanda Chantler, interview with the author, July 5, 2004; and Jan Melsen, quoted by Karin Orth, "Jan Melsen: 'Hamburg beschäftigt mich emotional am meisten.': Errinerungen eines KZ-Überlebenden an den Hamburger Feuersturm," in Ulrike Jureit and Beate Meyer (eds.), *Verletzungen: Lebensgeschichtliche Verarbeitung von Kriegserfahrungen* (Hamburg, 1994), p.153. Wanda Chantler suffered an immediate breakdown as a result of the horrible scenes she witnessed during the first night of bombing (see Chapter 10), and years later she was to suffer psychotic episodes that saw her hospitalized. Jan Melsen, who was one of those concentration camp inmates forced to clear dead bodies from the cellars, also had a breakdown in 1971. This was not the result of the firestorm alone, but of years of abuse in Neuengamme; even so, the events that affected him most deeply were those he experienced in the aftermath of the firestorm: "Hamburg damaged me the most emotionally. The work there saved my life, when I was practically dead before I went there—but on the other hand, after the war it was this that most weighed on my mind, especially the corpses of all the old and young people. The worst came back to me as a syndrome—then you have dreams as if it's happening all over again."

CHAPTER 23: THE RECKONING

1. Though this quotation refers to nuclear warfare, what happened at Hamburg fits better in a nuclear context than it does in the context of conventional bombing; see below. In 2003 Eisenhower's words were quoted during a debate on nuclear weapons in the U.S. House of Representatives; see "Notable Words: S&T Policy Quotations from 2003," in *FYI: The American Institute of Physics Bulletin of Science Policy News,* no. 2, January 8, 2004.

2. All statistics here and in the following paragraphs are taken from the United States Strategic Bombing Survey, Hamburg Report, pp. 7–10. The Hamburg Police Report also contains most of these figures (pp. 17–18), and by and large they agree. Where they do not agree, I have assumed that the compilers of the former document, who based many of their findings on data from the Hamburg Police Report, also had access to later, more accurate sources of information. The report of the British Bombing Survey unit is slightly less reliable, since the unit was run on a shoestring budget.

3. United States Strategic Bombing Survey, Hamburg Report, pp. 9–11. The Hamburg Police Report claims that 2,632 "commercial establishments" and 580 "industrial establishments" were destroyed, but this does not seem to square with the huge amount of damage done to residential property, nor the figure given by the United States Strategic Bombing Survey of around 40,000 industrial buildings lost.

4. Hamburg Police Report, pp. 17–18.

5. The figures for the number of dead, which had not yet been completed by the time the Police Report was finished, are taken from the United States Strategic Bombing Survey, Hamburg Report, pp. 1, 7A. I have assumed that the bulk of those 2,000 reported as "missing" were also dead, since many bodies were completely incinerated, and corpses were still being discovered in rebuilding works as late as 1951. The Ham-

burg Police Report has the number of wounded slightly lower at 37,214 (p. 17), but it is likely that the real figures were much higher than either estimate.

6. This figure does not include the many deaths in months and years to come from radiation poisoning. For a detailed discussion of casualty estimates at Hiroshima and Nagasaki, see Richard B. Frank, *Downfall: The End of the Imperial Japanese Empire* (New York, 2001), pp. 285–87.

7. United States Strategic Bombing Survey, Hamburg Field Report, p. 33A. The percentage of industrial workers who still had not returned is slightly lower: Of the city's 250,000 *industrial* workers, 75,000 (or 30 percent) had still not returned by the end of 1943 (see United States Strategic Bombing Survey Field Report, p. 1).

8. This unrecoverable loss in production is estimated at about 11.6 percent. See United States Strategic Bombing Survey, Hamburg Field Report, p. 42.

9. United States Strategic Bombing Survey, Hamburg Field Report, p. 1.

10. United States Strategic Bombing Survey, Submarine Plant Report no. 2, p. 13. The British Bombing Survey Unit put the estimate higher, at twenty-six or twenty-seven U-boats lost: See Sir Charles Webster and Noble Frankland, *The Strategic Air Offensive Against Germany 1939–1945* (London: HMSO, 1961), p. 287.

11. United States Strategic Bombing Survey, Submarine Plant Report no. 2, p. 13. See also Eberhard Rössler, *The U-boat: The Evolution and Technical History of German Submarines* (London, 1981), p. 250.

12. Hamburg Police Report p. 84.

13. United States Strategic Bombing Survey, Hamburg Field Report, Chart 15. The figures for shipbuilding are slightly odd because production was only reported in the month when a completed ship was delivered (p. 45).

14. UK National Archives, AIR 10/3866 (also published as *The Strategic Air War Against Germany, 1939–45: Report of the British Bombing Survey Unit* (London, 1998)), p. 161. See also United States Strategic Bombing Survey, Hamburg Field Report, p. 2.

15. See, for example, Max Hastings, *Bomber Command* (London, 1979), p. 241.

16. Ibid., p. 241.

17. For a comprehensive analysis of the shortcomings of the Luftwaffe, as told by the Luftwaffe generals themselves, see Harold Faber (ed.), *Luftwaffe: An Analysis by Former Luftwaffe Generals* (London, 1979).

18. Adolf Galland, *The First and the Last* (London, 1955), pp. 241–42.

19. Ibid., p. 243. Cajus Bekker quotes Hitler as having made this same declaration at a situation conference on 25 July, directly after the first Hamburg raid, to his Luftwaffe adjutant, Major Christian—see *The Luftwaffe War Diaries*, trans. Frank Ziegler (London, 1966), p. 312. It is quite possible he said it on both occasions: It was a sentiment that he had been repeating ever since 1940.

20. Galland, op. cit., pp. 252–53. In fact, Göring never took him up on this resignation, and Galland retained his post.

21. Air Force Historical Research Agency, Maxwell, Alabama, film copy A1107, 1654–56: "Cost of destruction of Hamburg 24 July–2 August 1943" according to U.S. Statistical Control Division, Office of Management Control, September 1, 1943. This figure does not take into account the huge amount of time spent in planning, administration, and so on.

22. Original figure taken from United States Strategic Bombing Survey, Hamburg Report. The website http://eh.net, which uses fairly reliable sources, has the historical exchange rate as 1 Reichsmark to $0.40, and projects $1 in 1943 to be worth about $11.29 today. Website last viewed April 19, 2006.

23. This is A. J. P. Taylor's figure, in *The Second World War* (London, 1975), p. 129. While Webster and Frankland's official history claims that only 7 percent of the nation's

manpower was involved in keeping the bomber offensive going, this does not repre-sent the true cost: The bomber offensive monopolized not only the skilled workforce but also the majority of scientific and technological institutions.

24. For reactions to the Butt Report, which showed the bombing war to be a huge drain on national resources for disappointing results, see Max Hastings, *Bomber Command* (London, 1979), pp. 108–15.

25. Quoted by F. H. Hinsey et al., *British Intelligence in the Second World War* (London: HMSO, 1979–1990), Vol. III, Pt. I (1984), p. 44.

Chapter 24: Redemption

1. Agathon, quoted by Aristotle; see *The Nicomacheaen Ethics*, trans. H. Rackman (London, 1926), VI.ii.6. This is a passage where Aristotle defines the concept of "choice," and is particularly apt because he uses the sacking of Troy as his example of something that cannot be undone.

2. *Hamburger Abendblatt*, July 24, 1993.

3. Even in clear conditions their bombing was not as accurate as the Americans liked to believe. All bombardiers were supposed to drop their bombs at the same time as the formation leader, but if they were just a fraction of a second late it could mean that the bombs landed hundreds of yards from where they were supposed to. Cloudy or smoky conditions merely compounded this problem. Toward the end of the year, Hap Arnold finally accepted the reality that precision bombing was rarely possible in the cloudy skies over Germany and gave a general order instructing U.S. bomber crews to use radar to locate their general targets whenever they were obscured—in other words, to employ exactly the same methods of "blind bombing" that the British used. By the end of the following year, around 80 percent of *all* U.S. bomber raids over Germany were conducted by means of blind bombing. See Eric Markusen and David Kopf, *The Holocaust and Strategic Bombing* (Boulder, 1995), pp. 165–66.

4. See Immediate Interpretation Reports S.A. 410 and S.A. 417, UK National Archives, AIR 24/257.

5. See Bombardier's Log, July 26, 1943, 351st BG, U.S. National Archives, RG18, E7, Box 1002, Folder 22.

6. For statistics on total war losses for the RAF and USAAF, see Robin Neillands, *The Bomber War* (London, 2001), p. 379.

7. Statistics from Robin Neillands, op. cit., p. 379. See also Max Hastings, *Bomber Command* (London, 1979), p. 11. The United States Strategic Bombing Survey estimates casualties at the bottom end of this scale, but is probably overly conservative—see its Summary Report, p. 1. Likewise, the British Bombing Survey Unit estimates the total number of deaths at 305,000—see *The Strategic Air War Against Germany, 1939–45: Report of the British Bombing Survey Unit* (London, 1998), p. 69.

8. Quoted in Brian Bond, *Liddell Hart: A Study of His Military Thought* (London, 1977), p. 145. For further voices of dissent, see A. C. Grayling, *Among the Dead Cities* (London, 2006), pp. 179–208.

9. According to Kenneth McDonald of 78 Squadron, quoted in Robin Neillands, op. cit., p. 389.

10. See Robin Neillands, *The Bomber War* (London, 2001), pp. 402–03. For Churchill's attempts to distance himself from Harris, see Frederick Taylor, *Dresden* (New York, 2004), pp. 375–79; and Max Hastings, *Bomber Command* (London, 1979), pp. 343–44.

11. Associated Press report, February 16, 1945, quoted in Robin Neillands, op. cit., p. 368; and Frederick Taylor, op. cit., p. 361. There are slight differences in the wording between these two; I have favored the latter, who cites his source more completely.

12. The huge popularity of antiwar novels like Joseph Heller's *Catch-22* and Kurt Vonnegut's *Slaughterhouse-Five* did a great deal to acquaint America with the arbitrary nature of American bombing in Germany. However, the popularity of such novels was arguably more about the war in Vietnam than about the Second World War. The American burden of shame over Vietnam is the closest equivalent to British shame for the RAF bomber offensive on Germany.

13. Ted Groom, interview with the author, November 11, 2004. Ted Groom's observation is borne out by all the contemporary diaries and log books I have come across.

14. Doug Fry, interview with the author, November 16, 2004. See also Doug Fry's interview for the Imperial War Museum Sound Archive, 27255, Reel 7.

15. Colin Harrison, interview with the author, December 8, 2004.

16. See Martin Middlebrook, *The Battle of Hamburg* (London, 1980), p. 352; see also Mathilde Wolff-Mönckeberg, *On the Other Side* (London, 1979), p. 27.

17. Hans Erich Nossack, *Der Untergang* (Hamburg, 1981), p. 65.

18. Max Brauer, *Nüchternen Sinnes und heißen Herzens . . . : Reden und Ausprachen* (Hamburg, 1952), p. 430.

19. Bürgerschaft der Freien und Hansestadt Hamburg Parlaments-Dokumentation, Elisabeth Kiausch speech, July 23, 1993, p. 3.

20. Frau Bishöfin Maria Jepsen, *"Predigt am 23 Juli 1993 in der St. Michaelis Kirche: 'Gomorrha.'"* Manuscript of the sermon courtesy of the bishop herself. For an excellent analysis of the bishop's speech, see Mirko Hohmann's dissertation for the University of Hamburg, *"so wurde die Zerstörung ihres Lebens für uns alle zu einer furchtbaren Anklage": Die Juliangriffe auf Hamburg in der hamburgischen Errinerungskultur 1943 bis 1993* (University of Hamburg, 2003), pp. 97–99.

21. Jörg Friedrich, *Der Brand: Deutschland im Bombenkrieg 1940–1945* (Berlin, 2002).

22. Ironically, these sentiments were echoed in the speech of the bishop of Hamburg herself, who, unusually, laid the burden of guilt not with the Nazis but with the "people" as a whole. See Jepsen, op. cit., p. 3.

23. See, for example, Rainer Hering, "Operation Gomorrha—Hamburg Remembers the Second World War" in *German History,* Vol. 13 (1995), no. 1, p. 93.

24. The authors of the United States Strategic Bombing Survey attributed the growth of German pacifism to the horrors they had witnessed during the bombing war: "The city area raids have left their mark on the German people as well as on their cities. Far more than any other military action that preceded the occupation of Germany itself, these attacks left the German people with a solid lesson in the disadvantages of war. It is a terrible lesson; conceivably that lesson . . . could be the most lasting single effect of the air war." United States Strategic Bombing Survey, Summary Report (European Theater), p. 4. In 2003, Germany was among the first to criticize Britain and America for their invasion of Iraq.

ARCHIVES CONSULTED

1. Archives in Britain
Imperial War Museum
National Archives
British Library
RAF Museum, Hendon

2. Germany

a. Local history archives (*Geschichtswerkstätten* and *Stadtteilarchiv*)
Altona: Stadtteilarchiv Ottensen
Barmbek: Geschichtswerkstatt Barmbek e.V.
Barmbek Süd: Jarrestadt-Archiv
Bergedorf: Kultur & Geschichtskontor der Initiative historischer Bauten
Dulsberg: Geschichtsgruppe Dulsberg
Eimsbüttel: Galerie Morgenland e.V.
Eppendorf: Stadtteilarchiv Eppendorf
Fuhlsbüttel: Willi-Bredel-Gesellschaft Geschichtswerkstatt e.V.
Hamm: Stadtteilinitiative Hamm e.V.
    Bunker Museum
Harburg: Honigfabrik
St. Georg: Geschichtswekstatt St. Georg
St. Pauli: St. Pauli-Archiv e.V.
Wandsbek: Stadtteilarchiv Bramfeld

b. Other archives
Bürgerschaft der Freien und Hansestadt Hamburg Parlaments-Dokumentation
Förderkreis "Rettet die Nikolaikirche" e.V.: Dokumentenzentrum in the cellar of the
    ruined church
Forschungsstelle für Zeitgeschichte in Hamburg (FZH), especially their oral history
    project "Werkstatt der Erinnerung"
Kirchenkreis Alt-Hamburg (Church Archives)
Museum für Hamburgische Geschichte, particularly their library
Hamburg Staatsarchiv
Carl Hagenback Archiv
Bundesarchiv

3. United States of America

National Archives
Mighty Eighth Air Force Museum, Savannah, Georgia
Rutgers Oral History Archive of World War II
Reichelt Oral History program at Florida State University
National Fire Protection Association
National Technical Information Service
United States Air Force University, Alabama

4. Internet sites

http://www.91stbombgroup.com—official USAAF 91st BG website
http://www.303rdbg.com—official USAAF 303rd BG website
http://www.polebrook.com/history.htm—USAAF 351st BG website
http://freespace.virgin.net/ken.harbour—USAAF 351st BG history
http://www.379thbga.org—official USAAF 379th BG website
http://www.381st.org—official USAAF 381st BG website
http://www.384thbg.iwarp.com—official USAAF 384th BG website
http://fas-history.rutgers.edu/oralhistory—Rutgers University oral history online
http://www.calvin.edu/academic/cas/gpa/ww2era.htm—German propaganda archive
http://www.hamburgmuseum.de—website of the Museum für Hamburgische Geschichte
http://www.lostplaces.de/flakhamburg—website listing flak positions and air raid
    shelters in Hamburg
http://www.seniorennet-hamburg.de/zeitzeugen/vergessen/—website where Hamburg's
    senior citizens record their memories of the city
http://eh.net—website containing historial exchange rates

SELECT BIBLIOGRAPHY

PUBLISHED BOOKS AND BOOKLETS

OFFICIAL HISTORIES

Craven, W. F., and Cate, J. L., *The Army Air Forces in World War II* (Chicago, 1949).
Hinsey, F. H., et al., *British Intelligence in the Second World War* (London, 1979–1990).
Webster, Sir Charles, and Frankland, Noble, *The Strategic Air Offensive against Germany, 1939–1945* (London: HMSO, 1961).
Zuckerman, Solly et al., *The Strategic Air War Against Germany, 1939–45: Report of the British Bombing Survey Unit* (London, 1998).

UNATTRIBUTED BOOKLETS

Gnadenkirche Hamburg 1907–1987 (Hamburg, 1987).

ATTRIBUTED WORKS

Aust, Alfred, *Der Ohlsdorfer Friedhof* (Hamburg, 1964).
Bahnsen, Uwe, and von Stürmer, Kerstin, *Die Stadt, die sterben sollte: Hamburg im Bombenkrieg, Juli 1943* (Hamburg, 2003).
Bajohr, Frank, and Szodrzynski, Joachim (eds.), *Hamburg in der NS-Zeit* (Hamburg, 1995).
Beck, Earl R., *Under the Bombs: The German Home Front 1942–45* (Lexington: University of Kentucky, 1986).
Bekker, Cajus, *The Luftwaffe War Diaries*, trans. Frank Ziegler (London, 1966; reissued, New York, 1994).
Bessel, Richard, *Nazism and War* (London, 2004).
Betz, Frank L., and Cassens, Kenneth H. (eds), *379th BG Anthology* (Paducah, 2000).
Böge, Volker, and Deide-Lüchow, Jutta, *Eimsbüttler Jugend im Krieg* (Hamburg, 2000).
Bond, Horatio, *Fire and the Air War* (Boston, 1946).
Boyle, Andrew, *Trenchard: Man of Vision* (London, 1962).
Brauer, Max, *Nüchternen Sinnes und heißen Herzens . . . : Reden und Ansprachen* (Hamburg, 1952).
Brenken, Anna, *Hamburg: Metropole an Alster und Elbe* (Hamburg, 2001).
Brunswig, Hans, *Feuersturm über Hamburg* (Stuttgart, 1983; reissued Stuttgart, 2003).
Büttner, Ursula, *Gomorrha: Hamburg im Bombenkrieg* (Hamburg, 1993).
Caidin, Martin, *The Night Hamburg Died* (New York, 1960; reissued London, 1966).
Caldwell, Donald L., *The JG26 War Diary* (London, 1998).
Campbell, Sir Malcolm, *The Peril from the Air* (London, 1937).
Chorley, W. R., *Bomber Command Losses, vol. 4 (1943)* (Hersham, 2004).
Clarke, Basil, *The History of Airships* (London, 1961).

.d.), *The Tale of the Next Great War 1871–1914: Fictions of Future Warfare and Still-to-come* (Liverpool University Press, 1995).

Ken, *Memories of the 384th Bomb Group* (New York, 2005).

.s, Herbert, *Friedhof Ohlsdorf auf den Spuren von Naziherschaft und Widerstand* (Hamburg, 1992).

Dissen, Adolf, *75 Jahre Horne Martinskirche* (Hamburg, 1961).

Douhet, Giulio, *The Command of the Air,* trans. Dino Ferrari (London, 1943).

Erdmann, Heinrich (ed.), *Hamburg und Dresden in Dritten Reich: Bombenkrieg und Kriegsende* (Hamburg, 2000).

Faber, Harold (ed.), *Luftwaffe: An Analysis by Former Luftwaffe Generals* (London, 1979).

Fossedal, Gregory A., *Our Finest Hour: Will Clayton, the Marshall Plan and the Triumph of Democracy* (Stanford, 1993).

Freeman, Roger A., *The Mighty Eighth* (London, 1986; reprinted London, 2000).

———, *The Mighty Eighth War Diary* (London, 1990).

Freeman, Roger, and Osborne, David, *The B-17 Flying Fortress Story* (London, 1998).

Friedrich, Jörg, *Der Brand: Deutschland im Bombenkrieg 1940–1945* (Berlin, 2002).

Fulbrook, Mary, *The Divided Nation: A History of Germany 1918–1990* (Oxford, 1992).

Fuller, J. F. C., *The Reformation of War* (London, 1923).

Galland, Adolf, *The First and the Last,* trans. Mervyn Savill (London, 1955).

Goebbels, Joseph, *Die Tagebücher von Joseph Goebbels,* ed. Elke Fröhlich (München, 1993).

———, *The Goebbels Diaries,* trans. and ed. Louis P. Lochner (London, 1948).

Gollancz, Victor, *In Darkest Germany* (London, 1947).

Grassmann, Ilse, *Ausgebombt: Ein Hausfrauen-Kriegstagebuch von Ilse Grassmann Hamburg 1943–1945* (Hamburg, 2003).

Grayling, A. C. *Among the Dead Cities* (London, 2006).

Groehlen, Olaf, *Der Bombenkrieg gegen Deutschland* (Berlin, 1990).

Günther, Claus (ed.), *erlebt—erkannt—erinnert: Zeitzeugen schrieben Geschichte(n) 1932–1952* (Hamburg, 2003).

Hage, Volker (ed.), *Hamburg 1943: Literarische Zeugnisse zum Feuersturm* (Frankfurt am Main, 2003).

Harris, Sir Arthur, *Bomber Offensive* (London, 1947).

Hastings, Max, *Bomber Command* (London, 1979).

Hauschild-Thiessen, Renate, *Unternehmen Gomorrha* (Hamburg, 1993).

———, *Die Hamburger Katastrophe vom Sommer 1943 in Augenzeugenberichten* (Hamburg, 1993).

Herrmann, Hajo, *Bewegtes Leben* (Stuttgart, 1984).

Hinchliffe, Peter, *The Other Battle* (Shrewsbury, 1996; reissued 2001).

Hof, Kerstin (ed.), *Rothenburgsort 27/28 Juli 1943* (Stadtteilinitiative Hamm e.V., no date).

Hoffman, Egbert A., *Als das Feuer vom Himmel fiel* (Hamburg, 1983).

Howard, Michael (ed.), *Restraints on War* (Oxford, 1979).

Irving, David, *The Rise and Fall of the Luftwaffe* (Boston, 1973).

Jacobsen, Hans-Adolf, *1939–1945: Der zweite Weltkrieg in Chronik und Dokumenten* (Darmstadt, 1961).

Johnen, Wilhelm, *Duel Under the Stars* (London, 1957; reissued Manchester, 1994).

Jureit, Ulrike, and Meyer, Beate (eds.), *Verletzungen: Lebensgeschichtliche Verarbeitung von Kriegserfahrungen* (Hamburg, 1994).

Kennett, Lee, *A History of Strategic Bombing* (New York, 1982).

Klemperer, Victor, *I Shall Bear Witness: The Diaries of Victor Klemperer 1933–1941,* trans. Martin Chalmers (London, 1998).

———, *To the Bitter End: The Diaries of Victor Klemperer 1942–1945,* trans. Martin Chalmers (London, 1999).

Klessmann, Eckart, *Geschichte der Stadt Hamburg* (Hamburg, 2002).

Klöss, Erhard (ed.), *Der Luftkrieg über Deutschland 1939–1945: Deutsche Berichte und Pressestimmen des neutralen Auslands* (München, 1963).

Kruse, A., *Aufestehungsgemeinde und Kirchgemeinde Nord-Barmbek* (Hamburg, 1995).

Liddell Hart, B. H., *Paris, or the Future War* (London, 1925).

Lindqvist, Sven, *A History of Bombing*, trans. Linda Haverty Rugg (London, 2001).

Ludendorff, Erich, *Der Totale Krieg*, trans. A. S. Rappoport as *The Nation at War* (London, 1936).

Markusen, Eric, and Kopf, David (eds.), *The Holocaust and Strategic Bombing: Genocide and Total War in the Twentieth Century* (Boulder, 1995).

McCrea, Bill, *A Chequer-Board of Nights* (Preston, 2003).

Middlebrook, Martin, *The Battle of Hamburg* (London, 1980).

Miller, Carl F. (ed.), *Summary of Damage Inflicted by Air Raids on the City of Hamburg in the Period July 25 to August 3, 1943* (Stanford Research Institute, 1968).

———, *Appendixes 1 through 7 to the Hamburg Police President's Report on the Large Scale Air Attacks on Hamburg, Germany, in World War II* (Stanford, 1968).

———, *Appendixes 8 through 19 to the Hamburg Police President's Report on the Large Scale Air Attacks on Hamburg, Germany, in World War II* (Stanford, 1968).

Mitchell, William, *Winged Defense: The Development and Possibilities of Modern Air Power—Economic and Military* (New York, 1925).

Müller, Rolf-Dieter, *Der Bombenkrieg 1939–45* (Berlin, 2004).

Musgrove, Gordon, *Operation Gomorrah* (London, 1981).

Neillands, Robin, *The Bomber War* (London, 2001).

Nossack, Hans Erich, *Der Untergang* (Hamburg, 1981).

Okraß, Hermann, *Hamburg bleibt rot* (Hamburg, 1934).

O'Neill, Brian D., *303rd Bombardment Group* (Oxford, 2003).

Overy, Richard, *War and Economy in the Third Reich* (Oxford, 1994).

———, *Why the Allies Won: Explaining Victory in World War II* (London, 1996).

Paris, Michael, *Winged Warfare: The Literature and Theory of Aerial Warfare in Britain 1859–1917* (Manchester, 1992).

Peukert, Detlev J. K., *Inside Nazi Germany: Conformity, Opposition and Racism in Everyday Life* (London, 1989).

Plagemann, Volker, "*Vaterstadt, Vaterland . . .*": *Denkmäler in Hamburg* (no date).

Rasmußen, Kerstin, *Veränderungen 1894–1994: Hamburg—Hamm im Spiegel erlebter Geschichte(n)* (Hamburg, 1994).

Rasmußen, Kerstin, and Wulf, Gunnar (eds.), *Es war ja Krieg* (Hamburg, 1993).

———, *Es war ein unterirdischer Bunker* (Hamburg, 1996).

———, *Juli 1943: Hamburg errinern sich* (Hamburg, 2001).

———, *Wir zogen in die Hammer Landstraße* (Hamburg, 2001).

Ratouis, René, *Mémoires de guerre d'un non-combattant* (Paris, 2003).

Ray, John, *The Second World War* (London, 1999).

Reichel, Peter, *Politik mit der Errinerung* (Frankfurt, 2001).

———, (ed.), *Das Gedächtnis der Stadt: Hamburg im Umgang mit seiner nationalsozialistischen Vergangenheit* (Hamburg, 1997).

Reiker, Michael, *Hamburg—Hamm 1693–1993* (Kiel, 1993).

Robb, Derwyn D., *Shades of Kimbolton: A Narrative of 379th Bombardment Group* (San Angelo, 1981).

Rumpf, Hans, *The Bombing of Germany*, trans. Edward Fitzgerald (London, 1963).

Schaffer, Ronald, *Wings of Judgement: American Bombing in World War II* (New York, 1985).

Sebald, W. G., *On the Natural History of Destruction*, trans. Anthea Bell (London, 2003).

ɔnika, et al. (eds.), *"Man versuchte längs zu kommen, und man lebt ja noch ..."*: ..alltag in St. Pauli in Kriegs- und Nachkriegszeit (Hamburg, 1996).

, J. M., *Air Power and the Cities* (London, 1930).

, Albert, *Inside the Third Reich*, trans. Richard and Clara Winston (London, 1970).

, lor, A. J. P., *The Second World War* (London, 1975).

..aylor, Frederick, *Dresden* (London, 2004).

Wells, H. G., *The War in the Air, and Particularly How Mr. Bert Smallways Fared While It Lasted* (Leipzig: Bernhard Tauchnitz, 1909).

Wilson, Kevin, *Bomber Boys* (London, 2005).

Wolff-Mönckeberg, Mathilde, *On the Other Side*, trans. and ed. Ruth Evans (London, 1979).

Wolter, Rudolf, *Errinerung an Gomorrha* (Hamburg, 2003).

Zanetti, J. Enrique, *Fire from the Air: The ABC of Incendiaries* (New York, 1941).

Zassenhaus, Hiltgunt, *Ein Baum blüht im November* (Hamburg, 1974).

Zuckerman, Solly, *From Apes to Warlords: The Autobiography (1904–1946) of Solly Zuckerman* (London, 1978).

JOURNALS

Die Heimat, March/April 1987.

German History, Vol. 13, No 1 (1995).

Lutherische Monatshefte, Vol. 32, 1993.

Weatherwise, Vol. 16, No 2 (April 1963).

NEWSPAPERS AND MAGAZINES

Der Alter Hammerbrooker, July–August 1953.

Bild, July 22, 1965.

Hamburger Abendblatt, August 16/17 1952; July 18–August 4, 1953; July 18/19, 1963; July 1–31, 1983; July 17–24, 1993.

Hamburger Anzeiger 1943–44.

Hamburger Echo, July 25–29, 1953.

Hamburger Fremdenblatt, 1943.

Hamburger Morgenpost, August 15–22, 1952.

Hamburger Tageblatt, 1943.

Hamburger Zeitung, July 25–August 14, 1943.

Memo, October 1993 (magazine produced by the Museum für Hamburgische Geschichte).

Der Spiegel, July 25, 2003.

Uhlenhorster Warte, July 7, 1953.

Die Welt, special edition, July 1993 "Unternehmen Gomorrha."

CD-ROMS

The Molesworth Story (2nd edition) produced by 303rd Bomb Group Association.

UNPUBLISHED MATERIAL

OFFICIAL REPORTS

Secret Report by the Police President of Hamburg (as local Air Protection Leader) on the heavy air raids on Hamburg in July/August, 1943 [*Geheim. Bericht des Polizeipräsidenten in Hamburg als Örtlicher Luftschutzleiter über die schweren Grossluftangriffe aug Hamburg im Juli/August 1943*], translated by the British Home Office, Civil Defense Department, Intelligence Branch, January 1946. This document is available in the UK National Archives, AIR 20/7287. Alternatively, it can be bought from U.S. Department of Commerce, Technology Administration, National Technical Information Service under the following title: Carl F. Miller (ed.), *Summary of Damage Inflicted by Air Raids on the City of Hamburg in the Period July 25 to August 3, 1943* (Stanford Research Institute, July 1968). The Hamburg Police Report Appendixes are also available from the National Technical Information Service.

Summary Report of the United States Strategic Bombing Survey (European Theatre), available from the UK National Archives, DSIR 23/15754.

United States Strategic Bombing Survey, *Economic Effects of the Air Offensive against German Cities: A Detailed Study of the Effects of Area Bombing on Hamburg, Germany* (November, 1945), available from the UK National Archives AIR 48/19.

SPEECHES

Brauer, Max, "Gedächtnisstätte für die Hamburger Bombenopfer," delivered August 16, 1952—in Max Brauer, *Nüchternen Sinnes und heißen Herzens . . . Reden und Ansprachen* (Hamburg, 1952).

Ehlers, Hermann, speech on the opening of the memorial at the Ohlsdorfer Friedhof on August 16, 1952 (Staatarchiv, 141–20 Friedhof Ohlsdorf/Bombenopfer).

Giordano, Ralph, *Rede zur 60. Wiederkehr des Luftangriggs auf Hamburg an der Nikolaikirche*—typescript from Förderkreis archive.

Jepsen, Frau Bischöfin Maria, "Predigt am 23 Juli 1993 in der St. Michaeli Kirche: 'Gomorrha'" (provided by bishop's office).

Kiausch, Elisabeth, "Wer es erlebt hat, wird es nie vergessen," delivered at 11.00 A.M. on July 23, 1993 in the Great Hall of the Hamburg Rathaus. From Bürgerschaft der Freien und Hansestadt Hamburg Parlaments-Dokumentation (Press and public relations document 66/91: 17.00 100/23.07.1993/1.03 Kiausch, Elisabeth).

Schönfelder, Adolf, speech given on August 16, 1952, at the Ohlsdorfer Friedhof (Staatarchiv, 141–20 Friedhof Ohlsdorf/Bombenopfer).

Witter, Ben, *Speech 1993*—from Berichte und Dokumente 952 (September 27, 1993), Staatliche Pressestelle, Hamburg.

LETTERS AND DIARIES

Gerke, Liselotte, typescript account.

Schult, letter to Pastor Kreyer.

Severin, Günther (ed.), *Briefe an einen Pastor*—collection of letters written to Pastor Jürgen Wehrmann in Eilbek from his parishioners.

Select Bibliography

...ITY THESES

...ohmann, "*so wurde die Zerstörung ihres Lebens für uns alle zu einer furchtbaren ...nklage*": *Die Juliangriffe auf Hamburg in der hamburgischen Errinerungskultur 1943 bis 1993* (University of Hamburg, 2003).

Unattributed

Hamburg secondary school project, *Als die Bomben fielen: Hamburg vor 40 Jahren*, Museum für Hamburgische Geschichte, HaIII 68.

"Klöntreff 'Eimsbüttel im Feuersturm'"—unpublished transcript of local history group conversation at Galerie Morgenland/Geschichtswerkstatt.

INDEX

ABOUT THE AUTHOR

Keith Lowe was born in London, England, in 1970. He graduated with a master's in English Literature from Manchester University and now works as an editor for a British history publisher. His first novel, *Tunnel Vision*, was shortlisted for the 2002 Author's Club First Novel Award. This is his first work of nonfiction. He lives in London with his wife and son.